MARIKANA

Related James Currey titles on South & Southern Africa

South Africa. The Present as History: From Mrs Ples to Mandela & Marikana, John S. Saul & Patrick Bond

Liberation Movements in Power: Party & State in Southern Africa, Roger Southall

The New Black Middle Class in South Africa, Roger Southall

Mandela's Kinsmen: Nationalist Elites & Apartheid's First Bantustan, Timothy Gibbs

Women, Migration & the Cashew Economy in Southern Mozambique, Jeanne Marie Penvenne

Remaking Mutirikwi: Landscape, Water & Belonging in Southern Zimbabwe, Joost Fontein

Writing Revolt: An Engagement with African Nationalism, 1957–67, Terence Ranger

Colonialism & Violence in Zimbabwe: A History of Suffering, Heike I. Schmidt

The Road to Soweto: Resistance & the Uprising of 16 June 1976, Julian Brown

Markets on the Margins: Mineworkers, Job Creation & Enterprise Development, Kate Philip

The War Within: New Perspectives on the Civil War in Mozambique, 1976–1992, Eric Morier-Genoud, Michel Cahen & Domingos M. do Rosário (eds)

Township Violence & the End of Apartheid: War on the Reef, Gary Kynoch

Limpopo's Legacy: Student Politics & Democracy in South Africa, Anne K. Heffernan

Cyril Ramaphosa: The Road to Presidential Power, Anthony Butler

Archaeology and Oral Tradition in Malawi: Origins and Early History of the Chewa, Yusuf M. Juwayeyi

Manhood, Morality & the Transformation of Angolan Society: MPLA Veterans & Post-war Dynamics, John Spall

Young Women against Apartheid: Gender, Youth and South Africa's Liberation Struggle, Emily Bridger

The Vaal Uprising of 1984 & the Struggle for Freedom in South Africa, Franziska Rueedi

Namib: The Archaeology of an African Desert, John Kinahan

Whites & Democracy in South Africa, Roger Southall

Peacemaking and Peacebuilding in South Africa: The National Peace Accord, 1991–1994, Liz Carmichael

MARIKANA
A People's History

Julian Brown

James Currey
is an imprint of
Boydell & Brewer Ltd
PO Box 9, Woodbridge
Suffolk IP12 3DF (GB)
www.jamescurrey.com
and of
Boydell & Brewer Inc.
668 Mt Hope Avenue
Rochester, NY 14620–2731 (US)
www.boydellandbrewer.com

Published in paperback in Southern Africa in 2022
by Jacana Media (Pty) Ltd
10 Orange Street, Sunnyside
Auckland Park 2092
Johannesburg
South Africa

© Julian Brown, 2022

First published in Rest of World by James Currey in 2022
Paperback edition 2024

The right of Julian Brown to be identified as
the author of this work has been asserted in accordance with
sections 77 and 78 of the Copyright, Designs and Patents Act 1988

All Rights Reserved. Except as permitted under current legislation
no part of this work may be photocopied, stored in a retrieval system,
published, performed in public, adapted, broadcast,
transmitted, recorded or reproduced in any form or by any means,
without the prior permission of the copyright owner

British Library Cataloguing in Publication Data
A catalogue record for this book is available from the British Library

ISBN 978-1-84701-284-5 (James Currey hardback)
ISBN 978-1-84701-373-6 (James Currey paperback)
ISBN 978-1-4314-3151-9 (Jacana paperback)

The publisher has no responsibility for the continued existence or accuracy of URLs
for external or third-party internet websites referred to in this book, and does not
guarantee that any content on such websites is, or will remain, accurate or appropriate

Contents

Acknowledgements	vii
Abbreviations and Acronyms	xi
Introduction	1

PART I: THE LIVES OF WORKERS

1	Migrant Lives	17
2	A Company Town	29
3	Politics Underground	43

PART II: THE STRIKE AND THE MASSACRE

4	The Strike Begins	59
5	Monday, 13 August 2012	77
6	Tightening the Screws	93
7	The Massacre at Scene One	113
8	The Massacre at Scene Two	139

PART III: AFTER THE MASSACRE

9	Burying the Dead	163
10	The Farlam Commission	177
11	Communities of Resistance	191
12	'Let us Not Lose Hope'	207
	Conclusion: The Work of Mourning	225
	Sources and Interpretation	245
	Bibliography	253
	Index	263

Acknowledgements

THIS BOOK was written in Johannesburg, between 2015 and the first months of 2021. In the years of research and writing, I have incurred more debts that I can ever pay.

The first of these debts is to the families of the deceased. Many of them have allowed me to listen to their stories, to see their homes, and understand a small part of their grief. They shared the memories of their loved ones with me, and allowed me to glimpse something of what their lives were like. I have been – and remain – humbled by their generosity and their kindness to me, over these many years.

The second is to the staff of the Socio-Economic Rights Institute of South Africa (SERI). SERI represented both the families of the deceased and the Association of Mineworkers and Construction Union (AMCU) at the Marikana Commission of Inquiry, and continues to represent the families in their ongoing compensation claims. I have worked closely with SERI's staff in the research and preparation of this book, and remain deeply grateful for the support that they have given to me and this project. In particular, I want to thank Nomzamo Zondo, Lauren Royston, Khuselwa Dyanti, Grace Gomba, Naadira Munshi, Nkosinathi Sithole, Tiffany Ebrahim, Maanda Makwarela, Sanele Garane, Mami Molefe, and Princess Nkuna.

From the very first days of this project, Jim Nichol challenged and encouraged me. His care for the families, and his keen sense of ethics and morality, have inspired me throughout. Along with Noor Nieftagodien, he provided a critical eye on the early parts of this project, and helped shape the approach that I have taken in this book.

I am also grateful for the support of my colleagues and students at the University of the Witwatersrand. My colleagues in the Department of Political Studies have had to endure my absorption in this project, and my occasional distractedness when faced with the day-to-day administration during my term as Head of Department. I am particularly grateful for the practical support given to me by Joel Quirk, Thandeka Ndebele, and Lindiwe Lesele. I have also had the pleasure of supervising and working with many wonderful graduate students, several of whom have helped me talk through and understand this project with them. There are more than I can name, but I do want to single out Stanley Malindi, Dineo Skosana, Thato Masiangoako, and Kelebogile Khunou, all of whom have influenced me more than they know.

A large part of this manuscript was completed during a brief fellowship at the Max Planck Institute at Sciences Po, Paris, and I'm grateful for the time they gave me.

The front cover image (*Crowd I*) was painted by Mary Wafer as part of a powerful series of artworks made in response to the strike and the massacre. It has haunted me for years, and I am pleased that she has allowed me to use it on this book.

I must also thank the editorial team at James Currey and Jacana for all their assistance. In particular, Jaqueline Mitchell, Emily Champion, Bridget Impey, Megan Mance, Nicholas Jewitt, and Christopher Merrett have corrected my errors, encouraged me to clarify my thoughts, and generally improved this book in every stage of its production.

Beyond the professional world, the support of my friends and family has been vital. I have been truly lucky in both. My parents, Keith and Carol, and my sister, Gabrielle, are always with me. My friends in and beyond Johannesburg have been a constant source of energy and excitement, sometimes in the face of exhaustion and frustration. In Johannesburg, Irene de Vos, Zweli Makgalamele, Emma Broster, Kathleen Hardy, Prinisha Badassy, Hatim Eltayeb, and others, have shared food and ideas with me, have given me the benefit of their own knowledge and insight, and have kept my spirits high. Beyond Johannesburg, Daniel Russell, Dalia Majumder-Russell, Tim Gibbs, Juliette Genevaz, Miriam Prys, Dara Kell, Michael Leonard, Beena Ahmad, Alejandra Anchieta, and Margaret Renn have opened their homes to me, given me abiding hope, and have kept me engaged with the wider world.

I owe all of these people – and many more, who simply cannot be listed and named in these few pages – deep and abiding debts of gratitude and acknowledgement.

I owe Stuart something more. For more than a decade, we have shared everything – our lives, our work, our politics, our beliefs, our struggles. We share jokes, passions, and enthusiasms. This book is one more thing that we have shared. For seven years, Stuart was the Executive Director of SERI, and co-ordinated the organization's efforts to provide the families of the deceased with legal, personal, and financial support. He fought to ensure that the families were not forgotten in the rush to make political capital out of the miners' deaths, and worked to make sure that their representation at the Commission would continue. He encouraged me to write this book, supported me when I doubted myself, and pushed me to make it better. I have written every word, every sentence, and every paragraph for him to read.

Every morning, I wake excited to share this day and the next and the next with him.

* * *

Many years ago, the Scottish writer Alasdair Gray took some lines from another author's poem and remade them into the instruction: 'Work as if you live in the early days of a better nation'. Although this book is about a gross abuse of the state's power to use force, and about the deaths of forty-four people in the course of a strike, and about the efforts of the South African Police to cover up and obscure their culpability in many of these deaths, it has not been written in despair.

Instead, I have taken Gray's charge to heart and have written this book as if this work – the work done with the families of the deceased, with the staff at SERI, with my colleagues, my friends, my family, and my husband – is being done in the early days of our better nation, one which will never again abuse its power in this way.

It may be naïve, and it may be foolish. But I hope, fervently, that it is not. And if it is not, it will be because of the work that all those named in these pages have been doing, and will continue to do. Because of them, a better world is still possible.

Abbreviations and Acronyms

ANC	African National Congress
AMCU	Association of Mineworkers and Construction Union
CCMA	Commission for Conciliation, Mediation, and Arbitration
COSATU	Congress of South African Trade Unions
CUSA	Council of Unions of South Africa
EFF	Economic Freedom Fighters
FEDUSA	Federation of Unions of South Africa
IPID	Independent Police Investigative Directorate
JOCOM	Joint Operational Command
LRC	Legal Resources Centre
MPWU	Mouthpiece Workers Union
NIU	National Intervention Unit
NMF	National Management Forum
NPA	National Prosecuting Authority
NUM	National Union of Mineworkers
POP	Public Order Policing
RDO	Rock drill operator
SERI	Socio-Economic Rights Institute of South Africa
SAPS	South African Police Services
STF	Special Task Force
TRT	Tactical Response Team

Introduction

ON THE afternoon of 16 August 2012, officers of the South African Police Services shot and killed thirty-four striking mineworkers at a platinum mine in Marikana.

The men were killed in two phases. In the first of these, the police officers took aim at a moving group of workers and – in the course of eight seconds – fired 284 rounds of live ammunition at them. Seventeen men were killed. Most had been at the front of the group, but others were several hundred metres away, far from the police line. Many of these men died quickly. Some, though, bled to death in the dirt over the next hour, while the police denied them access to medical attention.

The police then left the initial site of the shooting and followed a smaller group of workers to a nearby cluster of rocks and boulders. They surrounded these men as they hid, and again opened fire. Some police officers fired indiscriminately in the direction of the rocks. Others climbed onto the larger boulders and aimed downwards, shooting at the men crouching below. Another seventeen men were killed in this, the second phase of the massacre at Marikana. Again, most died quickly. Again, others bled to death in the dirt. Still others died later, in custody.

This was the worst abuse of state power since the end of Apartheid: the bloodiest display of the state's ability to do violence to its citizens in almost twenty years.

* * *

At first, the full extent of this abuse was hidden from the public.

The police sought to hide their culpability. While the men they had killed were still lying on the ground, several senior police commanders on the scene immediately began to falsify evidence. They moved weapons from where they had fallen and put them into the hands of the dead. They took photographs that suggested that unarmed workers had in fact been armed at the time of the shootings.[1] The commanders then concocted a story about the events of the day that freed the police of all responsibility for these deaths. In this story, they portrayed the striking

---

1   This is the conclusion drawn by the Evidence Leaders at the Marikana Commission of Inquiry, in their survey of the photographs taken by the police on the evening of 16 August 2012. I discuss these efforts to falsify evidence in detail in Chapter 8, and discuss their exposure in Chapter 12.

workers as a mob of faceless and violent criminals, jointly responsible for several deaths that had occurred in the week before. They claimed that the workers were acting outside of the constraints and protections of the law. In the moments before the shooting started, the police said, this mob had charged forward with weapons raised – and the officers on the ground had no choice but to fire in self-defence.

There was no real truth to this story. Although ten men had died in the course of the strike, some of these were killed by the police themselves – and while others might have been killed by strikers, there was no evidence that suggested that this was in any way co-ordinated. The account given by the police was a mix of half-truths, mis-directions, and outright lies. It was designed to absolve themselves, and to place the blame for the massacre on the shoulders of the men that they had killed.

It was also limited to the events of the first phase of the massacre. It made no mention of any the workers who were shot afterwards, and gave no indication that officers had continued to hunt down men who could never have posed a threat.

But it was the first story that was told about the massacre – and it was the story that was most widely repeated in the weeks and months that followed. It was embraced by senior figures in the police services: the next day, the National Commissioner of the Police repeated it to a group of assembled journalists, who reported her words without question.[2] It was encouraged by the government: Ministers and Premiers and other officials all echoed the National Commissioner's words.[3] It quickly became conventional wisdom. Every public discussion of the events at Marikana, whether in the mainstream printed media or online, took this story for granted.

And the strategy worked. In the weeks, months, and then years, after the massacre, the prejudices of the police – their disdain for the workers, and their depiction of them as a faceless mob of violent criminals – shaped public ideas of the killings at Marikana. The police's culpability in the deaths of these men was obscured, and the full extent of the abuses committed in the massacre was hidden.

---

2   South African Government. 'General Phiyega Pronounces on Mine Unrest', 17 August 2012. www.gov.za/general-phiyega-pronounces-mine-unrest (Acc. March 2021).

3   For a typical example, see the 'Tribute Delivered by the Premier of Gauteng Ms Nomvula Mokonyane at the Memorial Service for the Marikana Disaster held at the Johannesburg City Hall' on 12 August 2012, in which the Premier emphasized that the 'shootings … happened after a week of violence that led to the killing of 10 people by striking workers', before adding that political opponents had since gathered 'like vultures hovering over the carcasses of the dead animals' to criticise the actions of the government and the police: South African Government, 'Tribute Delivered by the Premier of Gauteng', 23 August 2012. www.gov.za/tribute-delivered-premier-gauteng-ms-nomvula-mokonyane-memorial-service-marikana-disaster-held (Acc. March 2021).

Telling another story

That was then. In the years since, it has become possible to tell another story.

The first cracks in the police's story were revealed by a small group of investigative journalists and critical academics. In the months after the massacre, these writers were able to poke holes in the police's account of the events – in particular, drawing attention to the existence of the second phase of the massacre, the phase that the National Commissioner of Police and her political commanders had not mentioned.[4]

At the same time, the Commission of Inquiry into the events at Marikana was instituted by the South African President, Jacob Zuma. The Commission's formal Terms of Reference limited its focus and its prosecutorial authority. Still, the Commission was given wide powers to subpoena documents, compel testimony, and interrogate witnesses.[5] The Commission's leaders also chose to allow the legal representatives of each of the parties to the Commission – which included those miners who were arrested after the massacre, and the family members of those miners who were killed by the police – to cross-examine all of the witnesses. The effect of this was to create an archive of evidentiary material, much of which was then tested under oath, by the lawyers for the other named parties.

The size of this archive is remarkable.[6] The Commission sat for 300 days, between September 2012 and November 2014. About 1,000 different documents were entered into evidence during this period. The list of numbered exhibits begins at A and continues through to ZZZZ 49 – and includes post-mortem reports, police records, email exchanges, witness statements, press releases, photographs, videos, audio files and transcripts, minutes of meetings, news reports,

---

4   In later chapters of this book, I deal more directly with these initial critiques of the police's story. See: Mandy de Waal, 'Marikana: What Really Happened? We May Never Know', *Daily Maverick*, 23 August 2012, www.dailymaverick.co.za/article/2012-08-23-marikana-what-really-happened-we-may-never-know (Acc. March 2021); Greg Marinovich, 'The Murder Fields of Marikana. The Cold Murder Fields of Marikana', *Daily Maverick*, 8 September 2012. www.dailymaverick.co.za/article/2012-09-08-the-murder-fields-of-marikana-the-cold-murder-fields-of-marikana (Acc. March 2021); and Peter Alexander, Thapelo Lekgowa, Botsang Mmope, Luke Sinwell, and Bongani Xezwi, *Marikana: A View from the Mountain and a Case to Answer* (Johannesburg, Jacana: 2012). Greg Marinovich's later book – *Murder at Small Koppie: The Real Story of the Marikana Massacre* (Cape Town, Penguin SA: 2016) – clearly describes his own investigative practice. See also the note on Sources and Interpretation before the Bibliography for more detail.

5   The Terms of Reference for the Commission were first set out in: South African Government, 'Proclamation by the President of the Republic of South Africa No. 50, 2012', *Government Gazette*, No. 35680 (12 September 2012).

6   For further discussion of this archive, see the note on Sources and Interpretation at the end of this book.

and scholarly commentary. The 300 days of hearings produced almost 40,000 pages of verbatim transcripts of witness testimony and legal argument. This archive contains the vast majority of the documents – of whatever sort – that were produced in the course of the strike and in the run-up to the massacre. It also contains many documents that were created in its aftermath. And, of course, it contains the explanations and justifications given by senior police commanders for their actions – alongside a record of their struggles to defend these explanations under cross-examination.

This large archive provides all the evidence needed to demonstrate the falsity of the police's story, to confirm the initial critiques of some critical journalists and scholars, and to produce a new, more accurate and more honest, account of the massacre.

* * *

But despite the availability of the evidence, there is still no comprehensive or authoritative account of the strike and the massacre at Marikana. Despite the efforts of committed scholars and activists, the lies told by the police have persisted, and influenced the most prominent public and scholarly accounts of the massacre.

This influence can be seen in a musical theatre production that assumes the inevitability of a clash between violent workers and police as its starting point; or in an academic article that restricts itself to the events of the first phase of the shootings – and fails to discuss the police's murderous actions in the second phase.[7] It can also be seen when the massacre is used as a colourful backdrop to the story of a journalist's career; or when it is used as merely another anecdote in a discussion about the costs of labour in the mining industry, and its impact on the national and international economy.[8] In each of these cases, the distortions

---

7   *Marikana: The Musical* was performed at the Grahamstown Festival of Arts in 2014, before being produced at the State Theatre in Pretoria later that year. It has recently been revived in December 2020, despite widespread criticisms of its approach. (See, for a summary, Nduka Mntambo, 'How "Marikana: the Musical" has contributed to cultural amnesia', *The Conversation*, 17 August 2017, https://theconversation.com/how-marikana-the-musical-has-contributed-to-cultural-amnesia-82651 [Acc. March 2021]). There are a great many scholarly articles which fail to mention the second phase of the massacre. A representative example is Raphaël Botiveau, 'The Politics of Marikana and South Africa's Changing Labour Relations', *African Affairs*, 113.450 (2014), which discusses the 'romantic' naivety of approaches that underplay the workers' violence, on the basis of other incidents and other strikes, elsewhere, without itself discussing the specific actions of the police at Marikana on 16 August 2012.

8   See, for an example of the former case, the memoir by Gia Nicholaides, *Reporting from the Frontline: Untold Stories from Marikana* (Johannesburg, Jacana: 2014), in which she discusses the fears she felt in front of faceless groups of miners, while

of the police's story – the depiction of the workers as violent, the concealment of their own actions in the second phase of the massacre – have shaped these later accounts of the events.

Most importantly, the influence of the police's false story about the strike and the massacre can also be seen in the final Report of the Commission of Inquiry itself.

Although the Commission's Report draws upon the large archive of evidence to demonstrate that police commanders and officers were complicit in the falsification of evidence and that they lied under oath, it nonetheless does not draw the obvious conclusion – that the whole of the police's story is tainted by these lies. Instead, the Commission's Report largely accepts and repeats the structure of that story, and treats the falsified documents and false testimony as exceptions to the overall reliability of the police's self-serving account of the strike and the massacre.[9]

Beyond this, the Report also adopts the prejudices of the police in its discussions both of the motives and actions of the striking workers, and of the motives and actions of the officers on the ground. It criticizes the conduct of the workers during the strike, condemning the violence that had taken place in the week before the massacre. It repeats hearsay and second-hand allegations that some of the workers believed themselves to be invulnerable to harm, on the basis of a religious ritual, without ever engaging with the truth or falsity of these allegations. Every worker who was asked about these allegations denied them – but the Commission refrained from considering what the effect of these denials were on the plausibility of the allegations. The Report thus repeatedly stereotypes the workers.

As a consequence, the Report largely accepts that the police officers on the ground during the first phase of the massacre may have been justified in believing that the workers posed a threat to them, and that – therefore – many of the police could be said to have been acting in self-defence. Although the Report does accept that the second phase of the massacre could not be justified in this way, it does not attempt to explain the police's motives in hunting down and shooting at this group of stragglers. Instead, its criticisms of the police's conduct – unlike its strongly worded and moralistic criticism of the miners' conduct – focus on technical aspects of police training, on the misuse of certain types of weapons, and on the failures of the commanders to properly plan for their operation.

Overall, the Report fails to set out a coherent story of the strike and massacre. It dips in and out of specific events and decisions. It puts competing accounts of disagreements beside each other, and then refrains from evaluating them. It delves into the operational technicalities of the police, but does not link them to

---

barely considering the police's massacre.

[9] The factual and narrative shortcomings of the Commission's Report form the subject of Chapter 12 of this book. Unless otherwise noted, notes to the claims made here can be found in this chapter.

the actions taken during the strike. It merely adds another layer of confusion to the public story – and so does nothing to dispel the police's lies.

Indeed, the Report's adoption of many of the institutional prejudices of the police – and its reluctance to acknowledge that the falsehoods told by many of the police's witnesses must taint the evidence of all – means that its effect has been to legitimize the general thrust of the police's story, and to obscure its falsity.[10]

The official history of the strike and massacre at Marikana – the document produced after three years of investigations, cross-examinations, and legal adjudications – is simply not fit for purpose. It inches closer to the truth, before backing away again.

Correcting the record

The chasm between the wealth of evidence produced in the course of the Commission of Inquiry's processes and the poverty of its final Report means that there is still a need for a comprehensive, detailed, and careful account of the strike and the massacre at Marikana – one that draws all the evidence together.

This book sets out to provide that account.

It does so by addressing the fundamental flaws of the popular narrative about the events at Marikana. The first of these flaws lies in the widespread acceptance of the falsehoods originally spread by the police – and often unchallenged in the Commission's Report. It seeks to correct the factual inaccuracies, misleading characterizations, and outright lies of that story. In their place, it provides a detailed, accurate, and careful account of the events that led to the strike and the massacre.

In doing so, it draws extensively upon the archive produced for the Commission of Inquiry. It makes use of the documents placed into evidence, as well as the testimonies recorded and transcribed by the Commission. It uses these sources – alongside other texts produced by journalists and scholars – to recreate the events of the week between the beginning of the strike and the massacre that ended it.

Of course, not all of these sources agree on the sequence of events, or indeed on the explanations for them. Some of these sources are clearly intended to mislead, while others reflect the confusion caused by trauma and the vagueness of memory. But the work of adjudicating distinct factual versions and interpretations of the same sequence of events is the ordinary work of an historian – or,

---

10 A similar conclusion has been drawn in Peter Alexander, 'Marikana Commission of Inquiry: From Narratives Towards History', *Journal of Southern African Studies*, 42.5 (2016). For an immediate response to the release of the Report, published in the South African media see: Stuart Wilson, 'Judge Farlam's Accidental Massacre', *Daily Maverick*, 26 June 2015, www.dailymaverick.co.za/opinionista/2015-06-26-judge-farlams-accidental-massacre (Acc. March 2021).

indeed, of a judge.¹¹ The Commission's failure to do so is not a sign of its impossibility. It is often possible to reconcile many of these factual and interpretive differences – and where it is not, it is still possible to judge which is the more plausible and more convincingly truthful account of the event and its causes. In these difficult cases, the book indicates the presence of these alternatives before drawing its conclusions.

The story that emerges from this is a very different one. In telling this story, this book seeks to correct the historical record and establish an authoritative account of the events of the strike and the massacre – an account grounded in fact. It seeks to move beyond the more limited claims made by other scholars and activists, and to bring together all the information that is currently known about the strike and the massacre. In place of the earlier, incomplete, and partial attempts to challenge the police's story, this book tells a single, detailed, and complete story of the massacre.

This is in itself a modest project: no more or no less than what that official history set out in the Commission's final Report should have provided – and yet did not.

Listening to the dead

This book does not stop there, because is not enough simply to cut through the confusion created by the Commission. There is another flaw in the existing account.

In concocting their false story, and spreading it so widely, the police did not only lie. They did not only absolve themselves of blame for the massacre. They also acted to erase the individuality of the men who were killed at Marikana. They stripped these men of their names, their histories, their thoughts and their motives for joining the strike, and the details of their deaths. They turned these men into mere statistics.

This meant that they erased the stories of men such as Khanare Monesa – who was thirty-six years old, who was expecting the birth of his first child, and who was shot at least six times by the police; or Akhona Jijase – twenty-six years old, and a newcomer to the region, who had only worked on the mines for a month when he died; or Fezile Saphendu – who was just twenty-four, and whose brother remembers him as someone who 'liked to sing and joke ... loved to cook [and] got along with elderly people' before he was killed by the police at Marikana.¹²

---

11   There are many different texts which attest to the adjudicative role of the historian faced with contradictory and incomplete testimony. The one which has given me the most guidance in this project has been Carlo Ginzburg, *The Judge and the Historian: Marginal Notes on a Late-Twentieth Century Miscarriage of Justice*, trans. Anthony Shugaar (London, Verso: 1999).

12   I have taken these details from the presentations made on behalf of the families of the deceased at the Marikana Commission of Inquiry, and entered into evidence

They erased the stories of men such as Mgcineni Noki – who was known as 'Mambush', who became a leader of the strike, and who left behind a wife and five children; or Jackson Lehupa – whose family said that they relied on him for everything, their clothes, their education, and their food; or Mzukisi Sompeta – who was also the only breadwinner in his family, and whose elderly father died within weeks of hearing the news, saying that all his sons were dying before him.[13]

If it is to be complete, any story told about the massacre at Marikana must do more than merely refrain from lying about the actions of the police, or their motives. It must even do more than merely describe the events of the day of the massacre. It must reckon with these lives, and these deaths. They must not be ignored, or glossed over. The lives of these men must not be reduced to a story of faceless criminals and violent strikers; and their deaths must not be reduced to mere statistics. Any story which does so – any story which fails to reckon with the human cost of the death of more than forty men at Marikana – is incomplete.

And it is not only the initial story told by the police that fails this test. The Report of the Commission also neglects to value or even include the voices of the miners – those who had taken part in the strike, and those who were killed in the massacre – in its account of the events of August 2012. Nor does it find the space to include the stories told by the men and women who were still mourning their loved ones.

Instead, the Report – and the official history that it represents – chooses to elevate the voices of police commanders, political leaders, and technical experts. It puts their perspectives at the centre of its account of the events of the strike and massacre, and, in doing so, reduces that account to one of political and economic imperatives, of operational and technical decisions, and of the struggle of commanders, leaders, and experts to balance the competing demands on them.

There is no doubt that some part of the story of Marikana can be told in this way – and perhaps a conventional account of the massacre could correct the official history's evidentiary failures while still maintaining its focus on powerful actors.

But there should also be no doubt that this cannot ever be the full story of Marikana. The full story of Marikana must include the experiences of those who took part in the strike; must tell the stories of those who died in it; and must ensure that the memories and voices of those who still mourn their loved ones are clearly heard.

---

as: Exhibit KKKK 21 – Khanare Elias Monesa; KKKK 40 – Patrick Akhona Jijase; and KKKK 15 – Fezile David Saphendu.

13 Exhibit KKKK 11 – Mgcineni 'Mambush' Noki; KKKK 32 – Jackson Lehupa; and KKKK 9 – Mzukisi Sompeta. See also: Interview with Nomawabo Sompeta, Lusikisiki, 3 December 2015.

And so, this book seeks to put the miners and their families at the centre of the story of Marikana. It describes the events of August 2012 from their perspectives, and highlights their own interpretations of the strike and the massacre. Whenever possible, it seeks to use their own words to describe what happened. It seeks to tell the stories of each of the dead miners' lives – who they were, what they hoped to achieve in the strike, and how they have been remembered by those left to mourn.

Sources of this book

To do this, this book draws upon a wide range of sources, including contemporaneous documents, documents produced for the Commission of Inquiry, sworn affidavits and transcripts of testimony given under oath, and transcripts of interviews with miners and their families. Although some of these sources were available to earlier scholars, no other book draws upon so wide a range of evidence – and thus no other book can claim to present as complete a story as this one.[14]

The contemporaneously produced sources are particularly important to this account. They include 'occurrence registers' compiled by the police and the mine, and maintained throughout the period of the strike – documents in which a wide range of events were recorded.[15] They also include the official minutes and unofficial transcripts of the meetings held between the police commanders in Marikana and the executives representing the mine; emails exchanged between the mine's managers, and between the mine's managers and the police; transcripts of press conferences, including the questions posed by journalists; records of decisions taken; and copies of the documents and plans circulated among police commanders and to their subordinate officers.[16] These documents provide the best insight into the processes followed by the police and the mine – by the representatives of the state and of capital – throughout the strike and the massacre.

These sources were entered into evidence in the Commission of Inquiry that followed. Some documents were submitted willingly, and were intended to bolster and support the stories told by the police and the mine.[17] Others were subpoenaed, however, and their disclosure compelled by the Commission's

---

14 For example: Alexander et al., *Marikana*, was written in the immediate aftermath of the massacre, before the Commission began to gather any evidence. It could not draw upon most of the material that I use in this book. For more on this, and other secondary sources, see the Note on Sources.
15 For example: Exhibit JJJ 128 – Occurrence Register and Notes for 16 August 2012.
16 For example: Exhibit XXX 9 – Minutes of Meeting held on 13 August 2012; Exhibit BBB 4 – Bundle of Emails exchanged among leadership of Lonmin; and Exhibit JJJ 153 – Draft of Document purporting to be Operational Plan.
17 For example: Exhibit L – SAPS Presentation.

Evidence Leaders and other legal teams.[18] When read together, these key documents not only set out the story that the police and the mine wished to have told – they also reveal the limits of that story, its cracks, its contradictions, its flaws, and its outright falsities.

The contents of these documents, and their accuracy as records of the events, were also tested in the course of the testimony and cross-examination of witnesses at the Commission. The transcripts of these interactions reveal the habits of speech of the various witnesses, their rote repetition of certain stories and accounts, and the difficulty – or ease – that some had in addressing contradictions in their testimonies. In addition, and although their testimonies were given years after the fact, and thus suffered from the vagaries of memory, the transcripts of these interactions also provide important details about the events of the strike and the massacre. They flesh out the telegraphic prose of police incident books and hand-written minutes.

This book draws upon all of these documents, subjecting them to a close and sceptical analysis. It uses them to establish a coherent timeline of the strike and the massacre, to detail the failures of planning and policy that marked the police's actions in this period, and to understand the commercial and political pressures that drove the police's decisions to intervene aggressively to break the ongoing strike.

* * *

Of course, the testimonies given at the Commission did not only test the documents submitted in evidence. They also sought to set out new and alternate accounts of the events of the strike and the massacre, to tell the stories of the individual experiences of police commanders and the officers on the ground, of mining executives and security guards, of union leaders and members, of participants in the strike themselves, and of the surviving families of the dead.

These accounts were provided to the Commission in sworn statements and affidavits, often prepared with the assistance of their own legal representatives.[19] They were also provided in person, when witnesses took to the stand under oath and faced aggressive cross-examination from opposing legal representatives.[20]

This book draws on these stories to deepen its account of the period of the strike and the massacre. It uses the stories told by police officers, union members,

---

18 For example: Exhibits JJJ 14, JJJ 15, and JJJ 16 – screenshots and file properties from a SAPS hard-drive, demonstrating the manipulation of digital evidence by the SAPS.
19 For example: Exhibit BBB 8 – Statement of Vusimuzi Mandla Mabuyakhulu.
20 For example: Testimony of Vusimuzi Mandla Mabuyakhulu at the Marikana Commission of Inquiry, Day 48 (14 February 2013), where he gave his evidence in chief, and Day 49 (15 February 2013), where he faced cross-examination by legal representatives of the NUM and Lonmin.

and security guards employed by the mine to show how the strike was perceived from outside; and it uses the stories told by participants in the strike and by the loved ones of the dead to show how the strike was understood by those deep in it.

It also draws upon stories that were not provided to the Commission. In the course of researching and writing this book, I have conducted interviews with widows and relatives of the dead. I have visited their homes, and met their extended families.[21] I have listened to the questions and concerns of their neighbours, and I have sought to draw upon their voices throughout this book – both directly, as quotes from these interviews, and indirectly, in the focus and sympathies of the story it tells.

Their words are at the heart of this book, and of the history of Marikana.

Writing a people's history

In placing the stories of the people at the centre of the narrative, this book follows in the footsteps of a tradition of scholarship that seeks not only to include the perspectives and voices of people like the miners and their families in authoritative accounts of historical events, but also to go further and to place their experiences and their words at the heart of these historical accounts.

This tradition could be labelled as either 'history from below' or 'people's history' – two terms which indicate the shared political project of this tradition. The core of this project can be understood in the words of Howard Zinn, in *A People's History of the United States*: it is the task of writing 'a history disrespectful of government and respectful of peoples' movements of resistance'.[22] Or, as E.P. Thompson put it, in *The Making of the English Working Class*: it is the task of resisting those forms of historical scholarship that 'tend to obscure the agency of working people, the extent to which they contributed, by conscious effort to the making of history'. It is the task of seeking, instead, to 'rescue the poor stockinger, the Luddite cropper, the "utopian" artisan, and even the deluded follower' – alongside all other representatives of their classes – 'from the enormous condescension of posterity'.[23]

Where official histories have traditionally focused on the experiences and stories of the obviously powerful – politicians and businessmen, kings and soldiers – these histories focus on the stories of the relatively powerless: ordinary men and women, the working classes and the poor, those who have been colonized and oppressed.[24]

---

21 For more details on these interviews and engagements, see the note on Sources and Interpretation.
22 Howard Zinn, *A People's History of the United States* [1980] (Expanded Edition: New York, Harper Perennial: 2010), p. 631.
23 E.P. Thompson, *The Making of the English Working Class* [1963] (Harmondsworth, Penguin: 1991), pp. 11–12.
24 This work is associated with History Workshop, and its Journal, in the United

They place the experiences of these people at the heart of history. They tell the stories of how ordinary working class men and women understood their lives at the time of the Industrial Revolution; how the residents of great cities made their living in the cracks of the economic system; and how radicals fought for political change in the face of great opposition. As Zinn suggested, it was in these moments and these contexts that ordinary 'people showed their ability to resist, to join together, occasionally to win' – even if they could only do so in 'brief flashes'.[25]

This does not mean that these histories abandon the study of the powerful, or of power. The interactions between ordinary people and the state are key to their lives. Zinn also accepted that the victories of these communities formed through acts of resistance were rarely successful. Often, the stories of these communities are stories of failure – of the collapse of a rebellion, of the immiseration of a class – or, alternatively, of the quiet struggles of ordinary lives in the shadows of the powerful.

But to study these, and to write about them, and to insist on their importance within history is still a vital act: 'I don't want to invent victories for people's movements', Zinn wrote. 'But to think that history-writing must aim simply to recapitulate the failures that dominate the past is to make historians collaborators in an endless cycle of defeat'. But by focusing our attention on the lives of ordinary people and on their acts of resistance, he argued, we make a political statement about the kind of world that we want to live in: 'I am supposing, or perhaps only hoping, that our future might be found in the past's fugitive moments of compassion'.[26]

* * *

This approach to the writing of history – and its acknowledgement of the political choices that have framed the ways in which historians of the past and present have chosen to direct their attention towards or away from one or another class of actors within society – has been particularly influential in South Africa. During the Apartheid period, scholars sought to write histories that placed the stories of Black South Africans at the centre of their stories. Their histories challenged the racial ideologies of Apartheid, and insisted on the importance of Black experiences.[27]

Kingdom. See, for an overview: Raphael Samuel (ed.), *People's History and Socialist Theory* [1981] (Abingdon, Routledge: 2016), in particular Samuel's Preface, 'People's History', pp. xiv–xxxix; and Anna Davan, 'The Only Problem was Time', *History Workshop Journal*, 50:1 (2000), pp. 239–245.

25 Zinn, *A People's History*, p. 11.
26 Zinn, *A People's History*, p. 11.
27 On the tradition in South Africa, see: Philip Bonner, 'New Nation, New History: The History Workshop in South Africa, 1977–1994', *The Journal of American History*,

Introduction

These books did not shy away from politics. Some scholars made their politics explicit, and linked their scholarship to anti-Apartheid activism. But even when they avoided clear statements of commitment, and framed their works as 'neutral' or 'objective' histories, their argument – that South Africa was a country of all those who lived in it, and not just its colonial rulers; and that its history stretched back before colonization and that would stretch into a future after the fall of the government – was an unavoidably political one.

In effect, these were all histories that were, in Zinn's words, 'disrespectful of governments and respectful of people's movements of resistance'. The failure of the Apartheid state, and the establishment of a new order in South Africa – one which at least theoretically places the experiences of all South Africans at the core of politics – does not erase the political nature of this tradition of history-writing.

This book – *Marikana: A People's History* – is rooted in this tradition. Although it has been written twenty-five years after the end of Apartheid, it tells a story that is fundamentally disrespectful of the claims of government ministers, police commanders, mining company directors, and other powerful voices. It tells a story that seeks instead to respect the experiences and agency of the people who participated in the strike at Marikana, and to hear the voices of those men and women who loved and mourn them. This is an approach that is inevitably political.

The structure of the story

So, this is not a neutral book. Its sympathies are obvious, and explicit. But it is nonetheless a careful book, one that seeks to provide a solid foundation for every claim that it makes, by providing sources for every fact in it. The notes at the foot of each page provide the sources for every claim, and ground every interpretation.

When telling a people's history, it is the people's voices – their words, their stories – that must sound out. As I have said, this is a book built from the voices of those who died in Marikana, those who survived the massacre, those who have to live without their loved ones, those who continue to struggle in the names of dead. While this book does not try to imitate their voices, it is their stories that are its heart.

The first three chapters of the book therefore explore the world within which the miners were living when they made the decision to launch their strike. Chapter 1 discusses the history of migrant labour in South Africa, and how it still shapes the lives of most miners. Chapter 2 turns to the history of the mine at Marikana, and of the town that has grown up around it. It looks at where the miners constructed their homes, and at how they built everyday

---

81.3 (1994), pp. 977–985.

lives. Chapter 3 then considers the history of political organization on these mines: the rise of the union movement, its decline, and the rebirth of new forms of localized organization and spontaneous labour activism outside of the formal union sector.

The second part of the book sets out the events that took place over in August 2012. Chapter 4 starts from the initial conversations between miners, and then sets out the sequence of events that led them to strike. It shows how the strike was bedevilled by violence from its earliest days. Chapter 5 turns to the day of the first major clash between the miners and the police – a clash that left three miners and two police officers dead. Chapter 6 shows how the mining company, the government, and police commanders all came to share in the decision to use armed force to break the strike. Chapter 7 then tell the story of the first phase of the massacre – from the doomed attempts of some sympathisers to negotiate an end to the strike, and the operational manoeuvres of the police, to the first moment of gunfire. Chapter 8 turns to the second part of the massacre, and follows the miners as they fled. It tells the story of how they were surrounded and killed, how the police celebrated their deaths, and how the evidence on the scene was falsified.

In each of these chapters, the book tells the stories of those who died at Marikana – the thirty-four who were killed by the police on the afternoon of 16 August 2012, and then ten who died in the week that preceded it. In each and every case, the details of their lives and their deaths are given the particularity that they deserve.

The rest of the book continues the story into the weeks, months, and years that followed. Chapter 9 tells how the families of the deceased learned that their loved ones had died, and how they struggled to find, identify, and bury the bodies. It also examines the police's story, and how it was disseminated. Chapter 10 looks at the first year of the Commission, setting out its conceptual limits, and considering how it struggled to find a place for the families' concerns. Chapter 11 considers the types of popular support that emerged in these years, and the ways in which communities of resistance formed around the memory of the miners. Chapter 12 returns to the last days of the Commission, weighs up its accomplishments, and engages with its failure to establish an authoritative account of the massacre.

The book could end here. But the story of Marikana is not the story of official attempts to explain and contain it. It is a story of people – of their lives and their loves, as much as of their deaths. The book ends with a snapshot of the lives of the families of the deceased in the years after the Commission, and sets out to answer as best as it can their lingering questions. The book ends – but their stories do not.

It is to these stories that we must now turn.

Part I

The Lives of Workers

1

Migrant Lives

Sixty years before he was killed by the police at Marikana, Thembelakhe Mati was born in Ntabankulu, in South Africa's Eastern Cape. Ntabankulu is a land of mountains, ravines, black soil, heavy skies, and brilliant green grass. Seen from above, from a high point of a mountain road, the earth seems barely occupied, dotted with small homesteads, scratched over by the chicken-tracks of dirt roads and foot-worn paths. The spaces between houses stretch out, a huge emptiness.

Thembelakhe was a teenager, and still in school when he met the woman would become his wife, and share her life with him. Florence remembers him as a mischievous youth, full of nonsense and noise. 'I don't know what made me fall in love with him', she says. 'First he asked me out, and I refused ... I wasn't sure about him ... and he was still in school. He was young and so was I, but he wanted to marry me and take me home.' Thembelakhe overcame her resistance. By the time he was twenty, their first child was due. At the start, life was hard: 'he was unemployed then, and just sitting at home. I had another baby who has passed away now, and he was still unemployed ... He kept looking for work but jobs were scarce ... he kept going back to look for work, and having no luck.'[1]

They were not alone in this. Life was hard for many people. Ntabankulu has never been a wealthy area. Today, the area is home to 114,000 people living in 24,000 households, scattered over 1,400 km². More than half of the population is of working age – between the ages of 15 and 65. (The rest are children, or the elderly.) Of the 65,000 people who could be working, fewer than 7,000 are formally employed. A similar number say that they are unemployed, but looking for work. They are the optimistic ones. Another 7,500 say that they have given up. And almost 44,000 do not work, are not looking for work, and cannot be called – according to the measures used to count these things – 'economically active'.[2]

Without access to jobs, most households have to find alternative means of survival. Almost two-thirds of the households in the district farm the land in one

---

1   Interview with Florence Mati, KuNdile, 3 December 2015.
2   These figures – and those that follow – come from the 2011 Census, as report by Statistics South Africa. www.statssa.gov.za/?page_id=993&id=ntabankulu-municipality (Acc. October 2020).

way or another, and a large minority of these households derive no income at all from their farming – in other words, they farm purely to survive. The others earn a relatively small income. For almost all families in Ntabankulu, though, farming is only part of a complex economic strategy. Many of them also depend on the incomes earned by one or two members of their families, working in some other part of South Africa.

For years, the Matis were one of these families. In 1988, Thembelakhe moved north, to work on platinum mines in Marikana. He would work there for the next twenty-four years. As the years passed, the salary that he earned had to support not only his wife, Florence, but also their six children, his mother and three sisters.[3]

At the start, Thembelakhe had an advantage over some of the other young men moving from the Eastern Cape to the mines: he joined his cousin, Lanford Gcotyelwa, who was already working in a mine near Rustenburg. Lanford helped him settle in, saw him regularly, and maintained their links with home and family.[4]

This was important, because when Lanford and Thembelakhe moved to the Rustenburg area in the last years of the Apartheid period, South Africa's formal laws and informal practices effectively forced miners to live far apart from their families.

For decades, the government had controlled the movement of Africans across the country, putting in place a system of passes and permits that controlled movement and residence. Africans were told to avoid urban areas, unless explicitly permitted. They were restricted to their rural homesteads and their designated places of employment. For much of the year, work and home were kept strictly separate. Families were split. Women and children were discouraged from travelling between their homesteads and their husband's place of work. If they were nonetheless able to overcome the restrictions, they were then prevented from staying nearby.

All of this was symbolized, for miners, by the standard practice of housing workers in single-sex hostels. Lanford remembers his time in these dormitories: 'life in the hostels is not okay ... there would be twenty people living in a small room. The beds, one on top of the other ... All twenty of you would live like that. Hostel life was terrible.'[5] In saying this, he echoes the complaints of miners over many generations. Hostels were cramped, crowded, and uncomfortable. Many of them were places of conflict and violence, of gangs and quick tempers. If you were going to live in hostel, you had to learn to leave part of your life outside – the part that was a husband to your wife, a father to your children, a son to your parents. In the hostel, both Lanford and Thembelakhe faced the reality that you

---

3 See the presentation prepared for the Marikana Commission of Inquiry: Exhibit KKKK 23 – Thembelakhe Mati.
4 Interview with Lanford Gcotyelwa, KuNdile, 3 December 2015.
5 Interview with Lanford Gcotyelwa, KuNdile, 3 December 2015.

had to live in this way. You had to offer a hard face to the world. You had to keep your heart hidden.

For these men, the everyday world was shaped by this system, which told miners where and how they worked, what they earned, how they lived, where and when they could see their families, where and when they would retire. For over a hundred years, men and women like them had moved between home and work, backwards and forwards over the course of the year, without being able to fully live in either.

And even after the end of Apartheid, when the formal systems of forced migration and influx control were abolished, the after-effects of these systems still shaped Thembelakhe and Lanford's lives in Marikana. At the time of the strike, the structures set up over the course of more than a century were only just starting to dissolve.

The migrant labour system

To understand these systems, we need to go back more than a hundred years. The migrant labour system emerged during the nineteenth century in response to efforts by colonial authorities to impose new forms of taxation on African families. These new 'hut taxes' had to be paid in cash – which meant that families' existing wealth in terms of cattle or status meant nothing. Many historians have suggested that this was part of an attempt by colonial governments to break up the existing structures of African societies, and to bring them into a new economic system. Africans were increasingly expected to take up some form of salaried work, and to use their salaries to pay these taxes if they wanted to maintain their lives and livelihoods.[6]

At first, this meant people going to work for short periods on farms or in small towns. Then, in 1867, diamonds were discovered beneath the ground in Kimberley. Over the next decade, vast deposits of gold were found across the Witwatersrand. As the diamond rush was followed by the gold rush, the migrant labour system was taken over by the mining industry. Speculators sought to dig deeper and faster – to take more from the land, to build their fortunes, and to outpace their competitors. The new mining industries needed labour, and needed it quickly. African men were encouraged to work on the mines, to provide the strength to dig below the ground, to sift through soil, and to pull precious stores

---

6   The best overall account of the process is still Francis Wilson, *Migrant Labour in South Africa* (Johannesburg, South African Council of Churches: 1972). For more details on the colonial administration of the hut tax, see: Colin Bundy, *The Rise and Fall of the South African Peasantry* (Cape Town, David Philip: 1979), Shula Marks, *Reluctant Rebellion: The 1906–8 Disturbances in Natal* (Oxford, OUP: 1970), and Narissa Ramdhani, 'Taxation without Representation: The Hut Tax System in Colonial Natal, 1849–1898', *Journal of Natal and Zulu History*, 11 (1986), pp. 12–25.

and ore from the earth. Soon, large numbers of workers began to move away from farms and towards the mines.[7]

At first, these workers were only loosely regulated. It has been estimated that, before the diamond rush, no more than about 5,000 people lived in the area around Kimberley. Four years later, the population had increased more than seven-fold, to 37,000 people. About two-thirds of the new residents were African or Coloured. According to the classic history written by Jack and Ray Simons, none of the colonial authorities were prepared for the population explosion, and no one would take responsibility for it: 'housing, hospitals, water supplies, sanitation, power and transport had to be improvised, usually by private agencies at rising prices. Diggers, some with families, lived in wagons, tents, huts or galvanised iron sheds.'[8]

On the one hand, this lack of regulation enabled the gross exploitation of Coloured and African workers. As the Simons emphasized: 'There were no laws to regulate wages and working conditions, impose safety measures against accident and disease, or enforce the payment of workmen's compensation.' But on the other hand, it allowed some freedom: a handful of Coloured and African men were able to register claims in their own names, and to profit off the rush as speculators and owners, rather than as workers or employees. Many Black workers moved to the area and settled, in the hope of joining them. Some sought to establish homes. Tens of thousands of them lived together, mingling across languages and cultures.

This period of relative freedom did not last. After all, this improvised society threatened the colonial order: if Africans could live where they chose, the colonial authorities would struggle to control them. And so, in 1872, authorities acted to restrict the ability of African and Coloured people to register claims in their own names, restricting new migrants to manual work. They also set out a system within which all working contracts would have to be registered, and written down on a piece of paper that workers would have to carry at all times to prove that they were employed. Any policemen could ask them to show their contract, and – if they could not – would be able to act to control them, to punish them, or to expel them.

This system, according to the Simons, was a forerunner of the later pass system. If African workers could not produce the document proving that they were employed, the penalties were severe: 'any person found wandering in a

---

[7] See, for standard surveys of the diamond rush and the development of a mining industry in this early period, Rob Turrell, *Capital and Labour on the Kimberley Diamond Fields, 1917–1890* (Cambridge, CUP: 1987) and William Worger, *South Africa's City of Diamonds: Mine Workers and Monopoly Capitalism in Kimberley, 1867–1895* (New Haven, CT, Yale University Press: 1987).

[8] H.J. Simons and R.E. Simons, *Class and Colour in South Africa, 1850–1950* (Harmondsworth, Penguin Books: 1969), pp. 35–38.

mining camp without a pass and unable to give a satisfactory account of himself ran the risk of summary arrest, a £5 fine and three months' hard labour or twenty-five lashes'. These contracts became the means through which colonial authorities could regulate the life of Africans: their legal presence in the area was dependent on their continuing employment, and their lives became the subject of endless police harassment.

At the same time, the mining industry was beginning to change. The 'wild west' days of the diamond fields were coming to an end, and larger companies – with more aggressive owners – were beginning to buy up the smaller claims and drive competitors out of business. The most successful of these businessmen was Cecil John Rhodes, who became the founding chairman of De Beers Consolidated Mines in 1888.[9] By the end of the century, De Beers controlled the majority of the Kimberley diamond field. In the next century, Rhodes and De Beers would become major players in the developing gold mining industry, establishing a near monopoly.

The company held enormous power. Legal and political requirements forced African workers to be in possession of labour contracts at all times, and only the mining companies decided who could work. This gave each mining company enormous power over the lives of its employees. African workers could only legally be in town for as long a company employed them, and they became, in effect, illegal residents the moment that company decided to end their work contracts. As Rhodes and others established monopolies, it was harder for workers to move from one to the other. Each mine kept records of its workers, and regulated their working histories. They set up recruitment bureaus across the country, and preferred to hire migrant workers from the Eastern Cape, and elsewhere, over those who lived in the area.[10]

But the mining companies did not stop there. It was not enough to control the movement of workers into the mining areas: the movements of workers within these areas, and within the towns that were springing up around the mines, also had to be controlled. To this end, the companies built gigantic compounds to house African mine workers. For the length of their contracts, these workers would be required to live in accommodation owned by the mine, under a regime

---

9 Rhodes is one of the most controversial figures in South African history, and biographical texts – some hagiographic, some condemnatory – abound. Robert Rotberg's 1988 biography of Rhodes lists 23 earlier biographies, all written in the twentieth century. See: R. Rotberg and Miles F. Shore, *The Founder: Cecil Rhodes and the Pursuit of Power* (Oxford, OUP: 1988). Richard Macfarlane, 'Historiography of Selected Works on Cecil John Rhodes (1953–1902)', *History in Africa*, 34 (2007), lists yet more.

10 Alan Jeeves, *Migrant Labour in South Africa's Mining Economy: The Struggle for the Gold Mines' Labour Supply, 1890–1920* (Kingston, McGill-Queens University Press: 1985).

of rules controlled by the mine – and they would be required to leave this accommodation at the moment that their contracts ended, to return to homesteads on the other side of the country.

At first, these compounds were designed to hold workers without respite during their contract: on the De Beers West End compound, in Kimberley in the 1880s, thousands of workers slept in dormitories, woke, ate in mess-halls, and were then funnelled through wire fences to their work down a company mine shaft. They could not leave the company's property. They were trapped, living in a kind of prison.[11]

Later, the mining compounds relaxed some of these more prison-like features. But even in the so-called open compounds, strong pressures were placed on workers to remain on site. Exits were controlled, and workers were searched as they left and returned to the compounds. The buildings themselves were located at a distance from social spaces, such as bars, or food stalls, or churches, or any other meeting place. Workers were discouraged from leading lives outside the compound.[12]

By the beginning of the twentieth century, the essential elements of the migrant labour system were in place. The colonial authorities had created a legal environment that criminalized African life outside of the mine and its compounds. The mining companies had begun to build a new system of recruitment, spreading their reach further across South Africa, and into its neighbouring territories. The companies controlled the entire process of migration. A company would recruit workers directly from their rural homes, transport them to its own mine, accommodate them in a compound for the duration of their contract and then, at contract's end, return them to their old homesteads. The whole arc of a worker's working life – recruitment, labour, retirement – was managed by these companies.

Influx control

This overall structure of the migrant labour system remained intact for most of the first half of the twentieth century. Then, in 1948, the National Party took control of South Africa's government and instituted a policy of 'Apartheid' – a policy of strict social and political segregation, in which White South Africans ruled and Black South Africans were oppressed. In many ways, Apartheid was an intensification of existing practices of segregation – but now these practices

---

11   Jonathan Crush, 'Scripting the Compound: Power and Space in the South African Mining Industry', *Environment and Planning D: Society and Space*, 12 (1994), pp. 301–324.
12   For a survey of the rich social world of mineworkers on the Witwatersrand at this time, often in opposition to the mining industry's rules, see Charles van Onselen: *New Babylon, New Ninevah: Everyday Life on the Witwatersrand, 1886–1914* (Cape Town, Jonathan Ball: 2001 [1982]).

were formalized, institutionalized, and backed up by the full might of the law. The migrant labour system was one of these practices, and the National Party government worked to formalize the system's key elements and bring it in line with its principles of racial separation.[13]

At the core of the new order was a desire to control the movement of Africans across the country. In the first decades of the century, under the pre-Apartheid segregationist state, early versions of the pass laws had been enacted. In this system, Africans were assigned to official 'homes' in the rural area, and laws were passed requiring African people to carry documents identifying them, and proving that they had a right to be in the city – or in any place other than their 'home'.[14]

Although the pass system was largely complete before the Apartheid period began, the new government was eager to strengthen and expand it. In 1950, the government passed the Group Areas Act.[15] This Act officially divided the country into White, African, Coloured, and Indian areas, and declared that only members of these officially described 'races' could live in those areas. It became illegal for an African man to live in a White area, or a White woman to live in an Indian area. In 1952, the Natives Laws Amendment Act was introduced. This law required all African men and women over the age of sixteen to carry a pass at all times. No African was permitted to be in an urban area without a pass – and even then, he was only permitted to remain for 72 hours without explicit permission from an employer or from the state. The only exceptions were those few Africans who the government recognized as having been born in an urban area, and who had never lived outside – in other words, someone for whom no rural 'home' could be identified.

In the 1960s and 1970s, the Apartheid government set out to create designated 'homelands'. In theory, all Africans in South Africa would be placed in a 'homeland' according to the language they spoke and the part of the country where they or their parents had been born. They would then become 'citizens' of this homeland rather than of South Africa – they would no longer be South Africans, but would instead become Transkeians or Bophuthatswanans. When-

---

13   The best one-volume survey of South Africa's political history in the past century is William Beinart, *Twentieth Century South Africa* (2nd edition, Oxford: OUP: 2001).

14   For the history and politics of the pass laws: Michael Savage, 'The Imposition of Pass Laws on the African Population in South Africa, 1916–1984', *African Affairs*, 85.339 (1986), pp. 181–205; Philip Frankel, 'The Politics of Passes: Control and Change in South Africa', *The Journal of Modern African Studies*, 17.2 (1979), pp. 199–217.

15   Alan Mabin, 'Comprehensive Segregation: The Origins of the Group Areas Act and its Planning Apparatuses', *Journal of Southern African Studies*, 18.2 (1992), pp. 405–429.

ever they travelled, then, they would be doing so as foreigners in the country of their birth.[16]

The effect of these policies was that Apartheid had now extended the pass system far beyond its origins in the migrant labour system, and used it to lay the foundations for its grand vision of 'influx control' – a system that would govern the movements of all African people in the country. During the Apartheid years, these laws would be used to justify the mass removal of people from their homes – and their relocation to official 'homeland' areas scattered across the country. They would be used to undermine ordinary family life, making criminals of women living with their husbands near workplaces and cities without state permission.

And these laws also supported the efforts of employers to control their workers. Mining companies could continue to pack their workers into single-sex hostels, separated from their families and from life outside. They could continue to pay cheap wages, because workers could not move from company to company – workers were bound by distance and by the practices of labour recruitment to one company, one mine. And the mine could continue to control their own workers, dismissing troublemakers and keeping only the more cautious and quiet employees.

Resisting the system

Many miners lived their entire lives within the cracks of this system. Even some of the men at Marikana, still working in 2012, had spent decades within it. Tokoti Mangcotywa, for example, started working in 1975, at the height of Apartheid's power. He had been born near Sterkspruit, on the border between the Eastern Cape and Lesotho. As the possibility of work dried up in the area around his family home, he began to travel. For decades, he worked under the Apartheid system's labour rules, signing up for a six-month contract, then returning home to his family, and then moving back to the mines for another six-month contract. When he was at home, he would fix up the homestead, enlarge the rooms, and build new facilities for his wife and children. He would bring home small luxuries, new pieces of furniture, and treats for the children. He would stay for three months, live his life with his family, and then leave. The law shaped this routine for twenty years.[17]

---

16 For the link between the homelands and the mining industry, see Harold Wolpe, 'Capitalism and Cheap Labour-Power in South Africa: From Segregation to Apartheid', *Economy and Society*, 1.4 (1972), pp. 425–456, and Bernard Magubane, 'The "Native Reserves" (Bantustans) and the Role of the Migrant Labour System in the Political Economy of South Africa', in Helen I. Safa (ed.), *Migration and Development* (The Hague, Mouton: 1975), pp. 225–268.

17 Group interview with family members of Tokoti Mangcotywa, Sterkspruit, 6

But despite their undeniable effects, these laws were far too ambitious to ever fully succeed. They were meant to apply to millions of people, across South Africa. The police were required to suspect every African person that they saw. They would have needed to inspect every document, multiple times every day, for the law to catch everyone. This was simply impossible for them to do. And so, instead, the laws were enforced unevenly – meaning that people could sometimes find ways to avoid them, or could sometimes manipulate them, or could sometimes resist them.

From the earliest days of the migrant labour system – when the first passes were being created, but before the Apartheid government sought to strengthen the system – resistance was public, and often effective. Women were often at the forefront of the struggle against the system. In 1913, African women marched through Bloemfontein against a recent attempt to extend the permit system to women, meaning that women would have to prove that they had official employment – and could not continue to earn a living through beer-brewing and other informal work. They tore their passes into rough shreds, and shouted at watching policemen. Eighty women were arrested. Their actions sparked a new wave of political organization in the Free State, and across South Africa. The women were successful – the new law was abandoned, nothing new introduced, and for many years African women were able to avoid the worst of the pass system.[18]

The state returned to the fight in the 1950s. African women once again took to the streets – this time to protest against efforts by the Apartheid government to incorporate passes for women into its influx control system. On 9 August 1956, more than 10,000 women marched to the Union Buildings in Pretoria, chanting a slogan that shines bright in South African history: *'Wathint' Abafazi, Wathint' Imbokodo!'* – 'You strike a woman, you strike a rock!' These women showed that resistance to Apartheid was alive and well. But this time, the state did not flinch before them. The pass system was extended and entrenched over the next years.[19]

But even though the state continued to insist on these laws, many people continued to defy them. In the 1950s and the first years of 1960s, several million African people were arrested for violations of the pass laws – roughly 300,000 each year, or more than 800 people every day. After 1962, the rate of arrests more than doubled.[20]

December 2015.

18 Julia C. Wells, *We Now Demand! The History of Women's Resistance to Pass Laws in South Africa* (Johannesburg, Wits University Press: 1993).

19 Cherryl Walker, *Women and Resistance in South Africa* (2nd edition, Cape Town, David Phillip: 1991).

20 This is a conservative estimate. For the figures for 1955–1960, see Muriel Horrell, *A Survey of Race Relations in South Africa: 1962* (Johannesburg, SAIRR: 1963), p. 109, which shows between 337,604 and 565,911 arrests per annum. By the end of the decade, 632,077 arrests were made in one year – 'an average of 1,732 a day'. See: Muriel Horrell, *Legislation and Race Relations: A Summary of the Main South African*

And yet, despite putting vast numbers of people in jail, this crackdown did not stop African men and women from moving across the country, or even from settling in South Africa's urban areas. At best, the government's efforts succeeded only in slowing the rate at which people moved from place to place.

Before long, the whole system of influx control was beginning to fall apart. By the late 1970s, the rural 'homelands' had developed large urban sprawls – unplanned, unhealthy, and uncomfortable settlements spreading out from small town centres.[21] The rise of popular protest in urban South Africa before and after the Soweto Uprising was changing African politics.[22] In the cities, workers were organizing themselves, launching trade unions and challenging management. As 'troublemakers' were fired, they were forced to return to their 'homelands' – where they could spread the news of the new politics far and wide. Even though employers sought to recruit workers from far-flung rural areas in the hope that they would not have been affected by the new politics, their hopes were rapidly frustrated. No part of South Africa was untouched by resurgent resistance.

The death-knell for influx control came in the 1980s. In the early years of the decade, anti-Apartheid lawyers launched legal challenges to the ways in which the pass laws worked.[23] In one case, they argued that the wife of an African man with a job in an urban area should be permitted to live with him, even if she did not have a job and a permit of her own.[24] In 1983, another legal challenge set out to establish that workers who moved between urban jobs and rural homesteads were in fact continually employed – even if a mining company, or another employer, officially ended the contract at the end of one year before offering the same worker a new contract for the next year.[25] The purpose of this challenge was to establish that these workers had the right to live near their jobs throughout the year, and not just during the eight or nine months of their official contract. Both of these legal challenges were successful, and both eroded the legal basis for 'influx control'.

Laws which affect Race Relations (Johannesburg, SAIRR, 1971), p. 46.

21 Colin Murray, *Black Mountain: Land, Class, and Power in the Eastern Orange Free State, 1880s to 1980s* (Edinburgh, Edinburgh University Press, 1992) gives an account of how this process led to the explosion of a peri-urban settlement in Thaba 'Nchu, in the Free State.

22 Baruch Hirson, *Year of Fire, Year of Ash: The Soweto Revolt – Roots of a Revolution?* (London, Zed: 1984) and Julian Brown, *The Road to Soweto: Resistance and the Uprising of 16 June 1976* (Woodbridge, James Currey: 2016).

23 Richard L. Abel, *Politics by Other Means: Law in the Struggle against Apartheid, 1980–1994* (London, Routledge: 1995).

24 *Komani NO v Bantu Affairs Administration Board, Peninsula Area* 1980 (4) SA 448 (A).

25 *Rikhoto v East Rand Administration Board and Another* 1983 (4) SA. 278 (W).

In 1986, the Apartheid government accepted the inevitable. On 1 July, the formal pass laws were repealed – although a large number of secondary laws and policies remained in effect. Almost immediately, African men and women began taking advantage of the relaxation of these restrictions. They moved away from the impoverished and over-crowded rural 'homelands' to Johannesburg, to Durban, and elsewhere. They also moved to the small towns and new settlements that were growing around the mines. In a few years, the population of these areas exploded.

After the end of influx control

When the Apartheid system began to unravel, the lives of men and women like Thembelakhe and Florence Mati began to change. Florence was able to travel to Marikana and the Rustenburg region. She would bring her children to visit Thembelakhe, and they would spend time together – not just the time allowed to them once a year, back at home, but time that they had chosen for themselves. Sometimes, she would go to Marikana and spend up to four months at a stretch.[26]

As the possibilities of travel increased, the ability of the hostel system to maintain a strict segregation between male mineworkers and their families, as well as between them and the surrounding local communities, began to crumble. Florence was only one of thousands of women travelling from the Eastern Cape. The Matis were only one of thousands of families who found ways to maintain a family life across the hundreds of kilometres that separated them, moving back and forth through the year. As the new political order emerged, so too did a new social order.[27]

African men and women moved across the country in ever larger numbers. Men moved to find work for themselves, outside of the systems of labour recruitment controlled by the mines. Women also moved to find work. Some moved to join their spouses – moving so that they could live as a family in urban areas near work. Others moved back and forth, never settling finally in the city – but always being able to visit their husbands and brothers, their sisters and their wives. People built shacks in yards behind existing houses. Informal settlements sprung up on vacant land, as people sought to live in a place of their own choosing, a place near to work and to economic opportunity, a place where their children could grow up in a different world, and could have opportunities that they themselves had never had.

In Marikana, and elsewhere, informal settlements began to grow. In the areas around the mines, miners set up new homes, places outside of their hostels where they could meet their families, or where – for those who did not have families visiting – they could live without the constant supervision of the mine's managers.

---

26   Interview with Florence Mati, KuNdile, 3 December 2015.
27   Dorrit Posel, 'Have Migration Patterns in Post-Apartheid South Africa Changed?', *Journal of Interdisciplinary Economics*, 15.3–4 (2004), pp. 277–292.

The Matis were not the only family to be affected by this change. In the 1990s, Tokoti Mangcotywa stopped working short contracts. He also began to work a steady shift at Marikana, and set up a shack in the informal settlement near the mine. This became a second home, where his wives and children could now visit him. This changed the way in which the family lived, and their relationships. As one of his nephews remembers, thinking back to this time in their lives, when he also lived and worked in the neighbouring region:

> Each time Auntie came ... I think she would miss him and decide to go and see the place that Uncle was living in ... She would take her family with her, her children, and they would go and stay with him. He would always let us know when she was around and we would go visit.[28]

By the late 2000s, miners no longer had to live alone in the region. An extended network of cousins, nephews, and nieces worked on the mines and in the new industries that had sprung up to support the expanding settlements around them. Instead of living alone on the mines, with a family at the other end of the country, miners like Tokoti Mangcotywa and Thembelakhe Mati could maintain a life that spread across the country: with family living in both Marikana and the Eastern Cape, with regular travel between the two now possible, and with a new kind of closeness.

* * *

But the past is not easily forgotten. The long history of state controls over African movement continues to cast a shadow over miners' lives – even several decades after these controls were officially ended. Although the end of legal segregation has brought about a significant relaxation in the restrictions that had shaped family lives, the mines are still far away from the most populous areas of the country. Travel still costs money, and employers are still slow to raise wages. Not everyone can afford to take advantage of the new freedoms. Most miners still live migrant lives: split between rural life and urban work, between family homes and monastic months spent on the mines. The dynamics of migrancy, established over more than a century, still shape everything: from the ways in which people arrange their lives, to their hopes and ambitions, to their dreams of retirement. These dynamics even shape the land on which these miners live – as we will see in the next chapter.

---

28 Group interview with family members of Tokoti Mangcotywa, Sterkspruit, 6 December 2015.

2

A Company Town

THE PLATINUM that lies below Marikana is unimaginably ancient. Two thousand million years ago, half-way through the earth's life to date, blazing magma pulsed up from the depths. As the millennia passed, the volcanic heat subsided, the earth cooled, and a complex of minerals and metals formed. Gold and platinum mingled.[1]

For millions of years, the metal lay hidden underground. Then, in the mid-1920s, a farmer in the Waterberg region of South Africa found what he suspected to be grains of platinum on his land. He sent the metal for assessment, and was soon proved correct – not only was platinum running through the waters on his land, but his farm and the farms of all of his neighbours sat on top of the largest deposit of platinum in the world. These metals are found in deep reefs, scattered beneath the soil in varying quantities and depths. The Merensky Reef was the first one to be discovered, beneath this farmer's land, and is the richest deposit: it stretches over at least 150 km of land, and it is mined more than a kilometre below the surface.[2]

The discovery of the Merensky Reef came at the right time. Despite its ancient age, platinum is part of the modern world. Unlike other valuable metals – gold, copper, bronze – there is no long history of platinum mining, or of its use. In fact, it was only recognized as a unique element in the mid-1700s. Before then, it was thought to be an impure version of silver, something to be removed in refining. After it had been identified, though, platinum was recognized only as a precious metal, a form of 'white gold' that could be used decoratively in jewellery and porcelain, as well as in the manufacture of specialized instruments. For many decades, platinum was little more than another meaningless luxury – a cold sparkle of expensive beauty.

It is only in the last hundred years that platinum has had real commercial value. In the beginning of the twentieth century, platinum came into its own as part of

---

1   C.A. Cousins, 'The Bushveld Igneous Complex: The Geology of South Africa's Platinum Resources', *Platinum Metals Review*, 3:3 (1959), pp. 94–99.
2   R. Grant Cawthorn, 'Seventy-fifth Anniversary of the Discovery of the Plantiniferous Merensky Reef: The Largest Platinum Deposits in the World', *Platinum Metals Review*, 43.4 (1999), pp. 146–148.

sophisticated electrical equipment, telephone systems, and now computers. As the globe was electrified, and contemporary information technology swarmed and spread, the demand for platinum grew.[3] Platinum is now one of the core elements of our modern world, woven through its systems. And mining it is a big business.

It is that business which defines life in the company town of Marikana.

The business of platinum

At present, five countries produce more than ninety per cent of the world's platinum: Russia, Canada, the United States of America, Zimbabwe, and South Africa. Of these, South Africa produces by far the greatest amount: in 2012, the country produced three-quarters of the world's mined platinum – 133 metric tons of the metal. By comparison, Russia – the second largest producer of platinum in the world – produced just less than 25 metric tons of mined platinum in that same year.[4]

A century ago, the size of this business was unimaginable. After the discovery of the Merensky Reef, the first attempts to mine platinum in South Africa were small in scale and haphazard in development. Although mines were established at the start of the 1920s, the Great Depression threw these first efforts into disarray. In the 1940s, the Second World War increased demand, and made platinum mines profitable. It was only after the War, in 1948 – the same year that the National Party took power and began to implement its racist policy of Apartheid – that a new company bought up several smaller mines in the area around Marikana, and established a large-scale presence on the Reef. Annual production began to skyrocket, increasing three-fold between 1948 and 1955, and then five-fold again by 1973. Soon, the area was producing two-thirds of the world's platinum.[5]

In the 1970s, as the business of platinum was increasingly important and profitable, many of the smaller platinum mines around Marikana were bought up by a company called Lonrho – originally known as the 'London and Rhodesian Mining Company' when it was founded in the early 1900s. Although Lonrho had existed in Southern Africa since it was established, a period during the 1960s had seen key changes in its approach to business in Southern Africa, leading to its sudden growth-spurt.[6]

3   L.A. Cramer, 'Presidential Address: Platinum Perspectives', *Journal of the South African Institute of Mining and Metallurgy*, 100.5 (2000); Donald McDonald and Leslie B. Hunt, *A History of Platinum and its Applied Metals* (London, Johnson Matthey: 1982).

4   www.statista.com/statistics/273645/global-mine-production-of-platinum (Acc. October 2020).

5   Gavin Capps, 'Victim of its Own Success? The Platinum Mining Industry and the Apartheid Mineral Property System in South Africa's Political Transition', *Review of African Political Economy*, 39.131 (2012), pp. 63–84.

6   For background on the company, and its work in Africa, see: Andrew Cohen,

The spark for these changes occurred when Lonrho was taken over by a particularly flamboyant businessman, Roland Rowland – better known by his nickname, 'Tiny'.[7] Under his leadership, the company would develop a mixed reputation in Africa. On the one hand, Rowland's willingness to trade with newly independent African countries won him many allies on the continent. He was a prominent supporter of the African National Congress in exile, lending his personal plane to Oliver Tambo and other exiled leaders. On the other hand, though, he was happy to ignore sanctions placed on Rhodesia and South Africa, and to continue to trade there even when the world was turning against these oppressive regimes. Indeed, Lonrho's practices of taking every advantage offered to an international company to avoid paying tax would lead the British Prime Minister at the time to describe the company as 'the unacceptable face of capitalism'.[8] The company's political and ethical malleability was fully on display in its South African platinum mines.

At the time, Marikana was part of the Bophuthatswana homeland, which had been created as part of the Apartheid state's population control strategy. Bophuthatswana was granted a form of limited self-rule in 1971, and formally declared independence in 1977.[9] The homeland was entirely dependent on Apartheid South Africa, but it pretended to have the ability to control its own political system. As part of this political system, Bophuthatswana recognized some forms of communal land tenure – meaning that communities could own land collectively, rather than as individuals. The land around Marikana was one of these places, and the land on which Lonrho's mines would have to be built was owned communally by the Bapo ba Mogale, a Tswana-speaking community.[10] Under Bophuthatswana's system, the chief and his council had the sole authority to negotiate for the community – and to profit off of the community's land.

Rowland's reputation as a cut-throat dealmaker is backed up by the agreements that Lonrho concluded with the Bapo ba Mogale in the 1970s and the 1980s. The

---

'Lonrho and the Limits of Corporate Power in Africa, c. 1961–1973', *South African Historical Journal*, 68.1 (2016), pp. 31–49; Andrew Cohen, 'Lonrho and Oil Sanctions against Rhodesia in the 1960s', *Journal of Southern African Studies*, 37.4 (2011), pp. 715–730.

7   Tom Bower, *Tiny Rowland: A Rebel Tycoon* (London, Vintage: 1993).
8   Edward Heath was the Prime Minister, and the year was 1973. The statement was widely reported, and repeated in the years since.
9   There is no good one-volume introduction to Bophuthatswana's history, but the articles in the following collection provide some context: Shireen Ally and Arianna Lissoni (eds), *New Histories of South Africa's Apartheid-Era Bantustans* (Abingdon, Routledge: 2017).
10 See, for a survey of the history and the contemporary politics of the community: Stanley Malindi, 'Continuity or Rupture? The Shaping of the Rural Political Order through Contestations of Land, Community, and Mining in the Bapo ba Mogale Traditional Authority Area', MA Thesis, University of the Witwatersrand (2016).

agreements that gave Lonrho the ability to mine beneath Marikana were obviously structured to the company's benefit. In 1977, for example, a mining lease was agreed that saw the mining company pay the Bapo traditional authority R2,000 in cash and 9,000 litres of water for its cattle each year. In exchange, the company received the right to mine, and to profit off the platinum that it pulled from the ground. Even when these agreements were re-negotiated, a decade later, the company continued to benefit. It would pay the traditional authority R200,000 each year in 'royalties' in exchange for the right to mine – regardless of the profits earned from its operations.[11] With minor alterations over time, this would continue to be the arrangement under which the company operated in Marikana.

For decades, Lonrho ran these mines, and earned massive profits. In the 1990s, though, the internal politics of the company changed as the winds of change swept across South Africa. In 1993 – thirty years after he had first taken control of the company – Tiny Rowland was ejected from his position. Almost immediately, Lonrho restructured its operations and split its Southern African mining operations from its other global interests. One part of the company, Lonrho Africa, kept control of Lonrho's non-mining businesses across the continent. A second company was then created to control its mining operations, including those on the African continent. This company went through a number of different names, but finally settled on 'Lonmin' – the name under which it continues to trade in platinum in South Africa.

In the decades since then, Lonmin has continued to be a major player in the platinum industry. It is traded internationally, with a base in the United Kingdom. It has faced off attempts by competitors to leverage a hostile takeover, and has continued to turn significant profits – even in the face of shifting labour costs, strike disruptions, and the fluctuations of international currency markets. After more than forty years of operations in the region, Lonmin remains a power in the business of platinum – a force that still shapes all aspects of life in the areas around its mines.

The growth of Marikana

That Lonmin remains a power in the platinum business matters because, since the 1970s, men have come from across the country to Marikana to work on its mines. The business of platinum has brought them here, and it keeps them here. Without platinum, and the mines, Marikana would not exist. It would still be a rough patchwork of highveld farms, grazing areas, and traditional homesteads. Without the mines, there would be no town – and most of its population would not be living here. The town is the product of the company.

---

11   Gavin Capps and Stanley Malindi, 'Dealing with the Tribe: The Politics of the Bapo/Lonmin Royalty-to-Equity Conversion', *SWOP/MARTISA Working Paper*, No. 8 (2017).

In the first period of Lonmin's mining operations in Marikana, during the height of the Apartheid years, the workers lived in hostels and compounds operated by the mining company itself. As we saw in the previous chapter, for much of the twentieth century, these hostels and compounds were the standard means of housing miners.

By the 1970s and 1980s, though, hostels had developed in the many decades since their creation a century earlier. Most mining hostels had assumed a similar form: miners would live together in single-sex institutions, sleeping alongside each other in large dormitories. Hostels were male spaces, forbidden to women. Ordinarily, miners would form friendships and other bonds with their colleagues in the hostel – and, as a means of encouraging this, workers would often be housed on the basis of shared languages and shared 'homelands'. Local rivalries were common, with sports teams facing off against each other in public – and gangs of young men often using violence and petty criminality to establish a shared identity within the hostel.[12]

Few enjoyed the experience. As Lanford Gcotyelwa put it, remembering the 1980s: 'At the hostels, there would be twenty people living in a small place like this. The beds, one on top of the other like this. All twenty of you would live like that. So hostel life was terrible.'[13] But there was no option – this was where you had to live.

Although the majority of the migrant labourers were living in hostels in this period, the construction of Lonmin's mines also had immediate effects on the resident Bapo ba Mogale community. In the early 1970s, three villages had been forcibly removed from their land – which would now be mined by Lonmin – and relocated to a newly created site, called Segwaelane, about ten kilometres from the centre of Marikana. This caused a great deal of social upheaval within the region, destabilizing the community. From the first moments of its construction in 1973, the soon-to-be residents of Segwaelane fought their removal, and have never been content with their lot. They have challenged the authority of the traditional council, and continue to demand restitution for the homes that they lost when they were moved to this new place.[14]

At the same time as existing communities were being relocated to provide the sites for Lonmin's mines, some men and women were beginning to move themselves. In the early 1970s, the first shacks of an informal settlement were

---

12 See, for recent attempts to consider the intertwined social histories of hostels and violence in late-Apartheid South Africa: Noor Nieftagodien, 'Life in South Africa's Hostels: Carceral Spaces and Places of Refuge', *Comparative Studies of South Asia, Africa, and the Middle East*, 37.3 (2017), pp. 427–436; and Franziska Rueedi, 'The Hostel Wars in Apartheid South Africa: Rumour, Violence and the Discourse of Victimhood', *Social Identities*, 26.6 (2020), pp. 756–773.
13 Interview with Lanford Gcotyelwa, KuNdile, 4 December 2015.
14 Malindi, 'Continuity or Rupture?' Chapter 2.

built on the traditional grazing areas between Marikana town and Segwaelane village. This brought further changes to the social fabric of the area, and of the Bapo ba Mogale.

For many years, the tensions brought on by these changes merely simmered. The residents of Segwaelane village fought with the traditional council. A handful of people lived outside the town, and outside the community. Most of the mineworkers still lived in Lonmin's hostels, only coming out into the community to relax and escape from the suffocating closeness of life under the company's eyes.

In the 1990s, though, these tensions finally exploded. At the end of Apartheid, hundreds of thousands of men and women left their rural homesteads, and moved to towns and mining areas in search of jobs. They were not always employed by the mines when they arrived – and many would never be hired to work below ground. Instead, they would queue up to find daily piecework at the mine, or would end up employed in shops and shebeens, doing odd jobs while they waited for more reliable work. They established homes in new informal settlements, renting back-yard rooms or putting up shacks on empty land.[15] These new settlements did not only give homes to these newcomers – they also provided a place for those who, like Lanford or like Tokoti Mangcotywa, no longer wanted to live in the mine's hostels, sleeping in dormitories run by their bosses.

At the same time, the entire country was undergoing a change in government and in governing structures. South Africa's first democratic elections were held in April 1994, and were won by the African National Congress (ANC). In government, the ANC sought to dismantle the workings of the Apartheid state, bringing the homelands back into the country and changing the ways in which both urban and rural areas were run. Local government was restructured into a set of district and local municipalities, each of which would have responsibility for providing services – like electricity, water, and sewerage, as well as street-lighting and tarred roads – to communities that fell into their areas. In parts of the country, this meant that a whole new system of government was to be implemented – and some areas struggled to keep up with the changes. Many parts of the country were unevenly developed.[16]

Marikana was one of these areas. It falls on the boundary between two large municipalities. The town of Marikana falls within the Rustenburg local municipality, while the village of Segwaelane falls into the Madibeng municipality. The

---

15 Anthony Lemon (ed.), *Homes Apart: South Africa's Segregated Cities* (Cape Town, David Philip: 1991); David M. Smith (ed.), *The Apartheid City and Beyond: Urbanization and Social Change in South Africa* (Abingdon, Routledge: 1992).

16 Susan Parnell, Edgar Pieterse, Mark Swilling, and Dominique Wooldridge (eds), *Democraticising Local Government: the South African Experiment* (Cape Town, UCT Press: 2002); Christopher Pycroft, 'Integrated Development Planning and Rural Local Government in South Africa', *Third World Planning Review*, 22:1 (2000).

informal settlements between them spread over the boundary – and have, at times, fallen into the bureaucratic cracks. This has meant that responsibility for the development and maintenance of the social and economic infrastructure of the region has been passed from office to office. The promised development has been slow to come.

The consequences of this can be seen throughout the region.

Everyday life in Marikana

The road from Rustenburg to Marikana moves through a landscape of grass and dust. Rocks and hills bubble up from the earth, breaking the horizon. The stacked concrete towers of mining operations rise up, signalling the start of the town. There's a railway line, and then the town itself: a police station, the offices of the mining company and the mineworkers' union, some houses, and then a mass of small shops – shops selling airtime and phone-chargers; shops selling fast food, vegetables and newly slaughtered meat; shops selling cement, timber, metal sheeting, nails and all the tools needed to pull together a cheap shack.

After the shops comes the mine. Its buildings stretch across the town. It is a construct of heavy concrete walls, metal fences, and – at night – brilliant, blinding lights. At the foot of this complex, the first shacks start – the beginning of a series of settlements that spread across the landscape near Marikana, along the side-roads, reaching out towards Segwaelane, sucking in people as far as their eyes can see.

By the start of this century, according to the Bapo ba Mogale authority, there were up to twenty times as many outsiders living around Marikana and Segwaelane than there were people who had been born there.[17] According to the national Census, statistically, the average resident of the area is a single man in his twenties, thirties, or forties. He lives alone, or with one or two other people. If he has a family, they live far away – in the Eastern Cape, perhaps, like the Matis, or the Mangcotywas. In some ways, his life resembles that his father might have once lived – the life of a migrant worker, separated from his family for most of the year. But in other ways, his life is different. He is unlikely to live in a hostel. Instead, he sleeps in a shack that he owns or rents in one of the area's sprawling informal settlements. His time is his own – and maybe he spends it in a Bible study group, or in a shebeen, drinking and socialising with his friends, or maybe playing football on the weekends.[18]

---

17 Bapo ba Mogale, Heads of Argument in the Marikana Commission, p. 17. These Heads of Argument draw extensively on the preliminary report of Phase 2 of the Commission (which was never completed, or finalised): Exhibit NNNN 2 – Phase 2 Marikana Commission: Preliminary Report, 15 August 2014.

18 These averages come from a reading of the Census 2011 data for the area. Statistics South Africa, Madibeng Local Municipality – Wonderkoppies: www.statssa.

This is the average resident, but of course not everyone lives like this. About thirteen per cent of the households in Marikana are headed by women, and an increasing number of families live in the settlement. For example, Jackson Lehupa – who, like many others, would be killed in 2012 – lived in Marikana with his wife, Zameka Nungu, and their six children. Jackson and Zameka had first met in the 1990s, when Zameka's parents were working in Rustenburg, and moved in together in 1997. In 2006, they built a shack of their own in an informal settlement near Lonmin's mine. They made a home for themselves, before Zameka moved to the Eastern Cape to set up a household where they might one day retire. Even after she moved, she was still able to return regularly to Marikana, to visit friends, and to spend time with Jackson. Their lives were at least in part rooted here.[19]

Other men also lived with their families, or used their shacks to host their loved ones. One miner, Thobile Mpumza lived with his sister, Phelakazi, and other family members who worked in and around Marikana.[20] As we know, Lanford Gcotyelwa kept a shack that he could retreat to, whenever he and his cousin, Thembelakhe, wanted to be alone – or whenever Florence or other family needed to visit them.

But families like these are the exception, and most households in Marikana consist of single men. Unsurprisingly, no one is particularly happy about this situation.

In the eyes of the Bapo chiefly council, the influx of male mineworkers over the previous decades has degraded 'the moral fabric and standards' of their society. The council suggests that the miners' presence in the region has led to an increase in crime, in alcohol abuse, and in 'abuse against women and children' – by which they mean an increase in prostitution and relationships between young women and migrant men.[21]

The mineworkers themselves do not share the authority's interpretation of their presence as the cause of all these problems – but do agree that crime, alcoholism, and casual violence are all too common in the area, spoiling their lives. In a report put together by the Benchmarks Foundation in 2011, the residents of Marikana – including both locals and mine workers – identified a series of shared concerns.[22] They were worried by overcrowding in the settlements, and

---

gov.za/?page_id=4286&id=10597 and Segwaelane: www.statssa.gov.za/?page_id=4286&id=10596 (Acc. March 2021).

19 Interview with Zameka Nungu, Matatiele, 4 December 2015. See also Exhibit KKKK 32 – Jackson Lehupa.
20 Interview with Xolelwa and Phelokazi Mpmuza, Matatiele, 4 December 2015. See also Exhibit KKKK 13 – Thobile Mpmuza.
21 Bapo ba Mogale, Heads of Argument in the Marikana Commission, p. 17.
22 See the sub-section, 'Marikana Community Report' in Benchmarks Foundation, 'Rustenburg Community Report: 2011' (Benchmarks Foundation, 2011), pp 38–49.

by a lack of formal housing. The roads were crumbling. There were not enough schools for the children in the district; many adults were unemployed – sometimes because they were from the area, and couldn't get jobs at the mine, sometimes because they were migrants who had been laid off.

Unemployment, everyone insisted, leads to crime. Young men with nothing else to do became violent and aggressive. Crime matters, because the local police force is corrupt and weak – incapable or unwilling to take the steps needed to resolve crime.

The mine loomed behind every testimony. The sounds of blasting and of demolition shook their houses. The light from Lonmin's mining compound kept them awake at night, dazzling them. Many of the residents of Segwaelane still remembered their relocation in the 1970s, and continued to list it as a concern. Others were still moving from scattered farms into the settlements around Marikana, driven both by the collapse of the farming economy and the jobs offered on the mines.

Residents complained that pollution flows from the mines, tainting the air that they breathe. There aren't enough sewerage pipes, and filth spills out into the open. The water is infected with bilharzia, a parasitic worm that lives in stagnant streams. It is hard to avoid the sense that the mine has turned the air and water against them.

As one of the residents put it, in an interview published in another report on living conditions in the area: 'How can we be happy living in these conditions? Normally we would want better houses, to have electricity, to live in healthy conditions'.[23]

This resident added:

> Many of us do not come from this area, some are coming from other areas. We are not happy leaving where we were staying, where we lived before, but we did not want to come here to stay here, to stay in these conditions … this is no way to live.

To live in Marikana is to live in a state of crisis.

Lonmin's town

This crisis has not gone unnoticed by the state. The post-Apartheid government has recognized the unique position of the new settlements that have emerged around the mines, and has adopted a set of policies that place a great deal of responsibility on mining companies to provide social services, housing, and other forms of support to their workers – and, by extension, to the communi-

---

[23] Khulumani Support Group, '"We Have to Talk, We Need Changes": Voices from Platinum Belt Mine Workers and Worker Communities', (Khulumani Support Group, 2016).

ties in which they live. These policies all recognize the central role of mining companies in the creation of these settlements, and require the companies to contribute to their maintenance.

The key pieces of legislation were passed in 2002. These are the Mineral and Petroleum Resources Development Act and the Broad-Based Socio-Economic Empowerment Charter for the South African Mining and Minerals Industry. Their titles are long-winded, and so is the language in which they were written – but their meaning is plain. The Act requires that companies draw up a 'Social and Labour Plan' for the areas around their mines. The meaning of this requirement is fleshed out in the Charter, where it states that companies must 'co-operate in the formulation of integrated development plans for communities where mining takes place', and plan to 'establish measures for improving the standard of housing, including the upgrading of hostels, the conversion of hostels to family units and the promotion of home ownership options for mine employees'.[24]

This makes mining companies responsible for the environment in which their employees live. In this case, Lonmin is responsible for the living conditions of its employees living near its mines – and that means those who live in Marikana itself. Where the state has been unable to establish services, the mine must step in.

In 2006, Lonmin set out a Social and Labour Plan for its operations in the Marikana area. In it, Lonmin made a number of commitments to provide housing and other services for its employees. It promised to phase out all of its single-sex hostels in the area, and to convert these buildings into bachelor flats and family units. It promised to build 5,500 new houses in the area around its mines, houses which would be available for Lonmin's workers to buy or rent. At the time, 8,000 workers were living in hostels – and the new accommodation would permit these workers to move from single-sex dormitories into private and family accommodation.

In the same document, Lonmin also promised to provide electricity, water, and sewerage connections to 4,800 existing stands where workers had already built their own homes. These actions would relieve the pressure on the local authorities, help mineworkers integrate with the communities around the mines, and ensure the steady development of a local economy, sponsored and supported by Lonmin.[25]

---

24   Mineral and Petroleum Resources Development Act (28 of 2002); Department of Minerals Rources 'Broad-Based Socio-Economic Empowerment Charter for the South African Mining and Minerals Industry' (2004). See also: Lochner Marais, 'Housing Policy in Mining Towns: Issues of Race and Risk in South Africa', *International Journal of Housing Policy*, 18.2 (2018), pp. 335–345.

25   See the analysis of this SLP provided to the Marikana Commission by the Centre for Applied Legal Studies: Louis Snyman and Robert Krause, 'Qualitative and Quantitative Assessment of Lonmin's Social and Labour Plan' (Johannesburg:

These promises were to be completed by 2011. In its Social and Labour Plan, Lonmin presented a budget, setting out the costs of each of the phases of these developments. The impression that this document gives is one of confidence that Lonmin had a plan, a budget and timeline, and every intention of fulfilling it.

Lonmin's promises held the potential to completely change the nature of housing in the region. If Lonmin was able to complete its own plan, on budget and on time, the fabric of Marikana would have changed. It would house a few thousand workers and their families in new apartments created out of the converted hostels. Another 5,500 workers and families would live in houses – some of which they rented, some of which they owned – in the area around the mine, creating a new suburb. And even those workers who were currently living in the informal settlements around the mine would have access to homes with water, and electricity connections.

These efforts would have had a large impact on the lives of many of Lonmin's workers. Jackson Lehupa and Zameka Nungu, for example, would have been clear candidates for Lonmin's proposed housing: they had lived with their family in the area for decades, had established a household, and were trying to put down roots for their old age. The company's plan would create a place where they could settle.

But Lonmin's promises were not to be fulfilled. By 2011 – the official completion date given in its Social and Labour Plan document – Lonmin had barely begun the work of implementing it. One figure tells the whole sorry story: instead of the 5,500 new houses that it had promised to build, Lonmin had only managed to construct three. As for the rest of its promises: it had converted some of its hostel accommodation from dormitories to apartments, but not all. By the year before the massacre, it had not made any appreciable effort to service existing stands in the area.[26]

In fact, the effect of Lonmin's actions, such as they were, was to reduce the number of workers it housed – and thus worsen the housing crisis. In 2006, 8,000 workers lived in the unconverted hostels. In 2011, after some were converted, only 2,500 workers lived in them. Without any of the new houses having been built, everyone else was driven into the private market – which meant, in and around Marikana, into unserviced shacks hand-built and jerry-rigged in informal settlements, like Nkaneng.

Instead of the houses which it had promised, Lonmin rather chose to provide its workers with what it calls a 'living out allowance' – an amount of money paid to them on top of their official salaries, intended to cover the costs of either living outside of company-owned accommodation in the area, or of renting accommodation from Lonmin. In 2012, this allowance was set

---

2013). See also the Phase 2 Marikana Commission: Preliminary Report, pp. 52–61.

26 Amnesty International, *Smoke and Mirrors: Lonmin's Failure to Address Housing Conditions at Marikana South Africa* (Amnesty International, 2016), p. 23.

at R1,800 per month – which, according to Lonmin's estimates, would cover the expense of renting a shack in an informal settlement, probably including 'water, lights and transport'.[27]

In its own reports, Lonmin recognizes that the living out allowance is an imperfect tool for fulfilling its social obligations. In fact, the company admits that it might lead to people living in substandard or dangerous homes – and that 'better regulation is required to ensure that the allowance is indeed spent on adequate accommodation that is in line with the minimum living standards we are trying to achieve for our employees'. The company suggests that something is needed to prevent beneficiaries of the living out allowance from spending it on things other than homes. In the short term, it might 'train employees on personal financial management ... to improve employee understanding about this allowance'.

* * *

Lonmin's excuses cannot be accepted. They are too simple and too self-serving.

The company's actions have actively shaped the social and physical fabric of Marikana, Segwaelane, and the informal settlements that surround them. Its failure to build new housing for its employees has driven workers into the private housing market. Its decision to offer its employees a 'living out allowance' as a cash supplement to their salaries has created a perverse incentive – when salaries are too low, and bills are tight, workers are obviously tempted to take the cheapest accommodation possible and to use the remainder of the allowance to help make ends meet. When there is no decent accommodation – in large part because none has been built, despite being promised – and salaries are low, it is ridiculous to suggest that 'personal financial management' will somehow solve these problems. The responsibility for the dire state of Marikana cannot simply lie with the residents.

In another context, perhaps the principal responsibility would lie with the state. But Marikana is Lonmin's creation. This is true at every level. Lonmin's mines have changed the physical structures of the earth itself, looming large over the informal settlements and towns that surround it. Without the mines, the platinum would still sit below the earth. The ground is now riddled with mine shafts, and shaken by explosive demolitions. The air above is stained by pollution, the water is sour with unidentified run-off. The world below and the world above been tainted by mining.

Without Lonmin, the town itself would not exist. The overwhelming majority of its residents have moved here to serve the mine – whether as workers underground, or as their wives, and sisters, and children. The informal settlements that have spread across the landscape – and that so many of the residents

---

27 Lonmin plc, 'Annual Report and Accounts for the Year Ended 30 September 2012' (2012), pp. 28–29.

see as a blight – have emerged to serve the needs of the mine's workers and their families. They exist because the mine does not provide enough accommodation to house its own workers; they have grown because Lonmin's living out allowance creates an incentive for workers to invest as little as possible in their own living conditions.

In this light, the company must take some responsibility for the ways in which people live in and around Marikana – a responsibility encoded in the state's requirements for a Social and Labour Plan. But the company has not taken its responsibilities seriously. It has not helped its workers, or the other residents of Marikana. Instead, it has washed its hands of the residents of Marikana.

In a company town, every part of life revolves around the company – and so too do all forms of political struggle. In Marikana, the workers themselves have long since realized this and – as we will see in the next chapter – have spent decades seeking to organize, and to use their bargaining power as workers to better their own lives, and the lives of their families. This struggle shapes their experience of life in this region.

3

Politics Underground

AT THE start of their day, miners descend into the dark. They pick up drills, pumps, and other heavy machinery. Their work is hard, straining both muscle and attention. As Siphethe Phatsha, a rock drill operator and one of the miners who survived the massacre told the Farlam Commission: 'We work with machines there, we push the machines inside and we'll pull it out and we also have … ropes, which we put inside, into the Milford [machine]. There are pipes … to remove the dust, to blow the dust out, and also ropes, pipes that contain water.'[1]

It is exhausting work. It takes everything. Phatsha continued:

> Firstly, the machine that we use for tracking, for burrowing into the rock, it's a heavy machine. One has got to pick that machine up. One puts the jumper inside this machine and then pick it up. It is heavy. In using this kind of machine, one has got nobody to assist him. You do this all by yourself.

The pain of injury was everywhere: 'you switch this machine off and you hit against the rock, one can easily cut off his fingers … Many workers have died … holding this machine, grinding against the rock'.

In one way or another, every miner underground faces dangers – the threat of exhaustion, of injury, of death. The air chokes you, your hands sweat in your gloves, and your eyes burn. The machines shake. Any mistake could bring about disaster.

Underground, you need to know that you can speak out, and report a problem as soon as it emerges, before it becomes a disaster. But when the first workers came to dig in the shafts beneath Marikana, they were given no official voice – and no way to speak about their work. African trade unions had been banned within the country and, although recent disputes had begun to change the pattern in large cities like Johannesburg and Durban, few African workers had a recognized voice. There was no one to complain about the dangers underground, about questions of safety, of fair wages and just compensation for the risks they took. Instead, workers had to rely on the good will of their employers – and this was never enough.

---

1   Testimony of Siphethe Phatsha at the Marikana Commission of Inquiry, Day 50 (20 February 2013), p. 5,426.

And so, for as long as there have been miners at Marikana, there have been struggles for recognition – for the right to speak and be heard, the right to defend oneself. The struggles that led to the strike in August 2012 were rooted in the long history of politics on the mines, in that of the efforts to organize miners into trade unions and that of the successes and failures of those unions in the new century.

This chapter tells that story.

The rise of the NUM

The story of unions in Marikana begins in the in the early 1970s, when a series of labour disputes and mass strikes shook South Africa's segregated cities. Although the Apartheid government had long tried to suppress any attempt to organize African labour, it now decided that it would be better to provide some limited role for workers committees and, ultimately, formal trade unions. Towards the end of the 1970s, then, the first African trade unions began to emerge, driven by automobile workers, food and canning workers, textile workers, the drivers of municipal buses, and others. These new unions began to reshape the urban working environment.[2]

But unions were slow to come to the mines. At the time, migrant mineworkers were believed to be almost impossible to organize. They came from all parts of the country, and were divided by language and culture. They lived in company-controlled hostels, and had little opportunity to meet outside of the company's sight. The nature of migrant labour, too, meant that almost all mineworkers were on short-term contracts – and their employment was thus highly vulnerable.

In July 1982, however, an outbreak of strikes at several mines raised the possibility that mineworkers might be able to organize themselves. During this period, between 30,000 and 40,000 workers went on strike – and the state responded violently. Ten miners were killed. This led to the widespread recognition of the importance of organizing the sector, and so, in August, the newly formed Council of Unions of South Africa (CUSA) decided that it should organize the apparently un-organizable mines, and delegated a young lawyer, Cyril Ramaphosa, to do so.[3]

---

2   These events have been the subject of a number of excellent scholarly studies. The classic starting point is Steven Friedman, *Building Tomorrow Today: African Workers in Trade Unions, 1970–1984* (Johannesburg, Ravan: 1987). A notable recent effort to bring some of these disputes into a comparative framework is Peter Cole, *Dockworker Power: Race and Activism in Durban and the San Francisco Bay Area* (Urbana, University of Illinois Press: 2018).

3   The story of the launch of the NUM and CUSA is told in Friedman, *Building Tomorrow Today*. Also: Tom Lodge, *Black Politics in South Africa* (Johannesburg, Ravan: 1983). For Ramaphosa's role, see Anthony Butler, *Cyril Ramaphosa* (Johannesburg, Jacana: 2007; revised edition, 2019).

Against all expectations, the union that he created – the National Union of Mineworkers (NUM) – was immediately successful. At its first conference, held only a few months after its launch, it was able to claim 14,000 members – 1,500 of whom were able to attend the conference. By June 1983, the NUM claimed to have 25,000 members across South Africa's mines. By January 1985, 75,000 workers had joined the union. By the end of the year, it would represent 200,000 miners.[4]

In this early period, the NUM offered the best hope for miners – including those who worked in the platinum mines in and around Marikana. For a migrant mineworker like Lanford Gcotyelwa, joining the NUM was just something you did when you moved to the mines. He remembers that when he and his cousin, Thembelakhe, moved to the platinum belt in the late 1980s they joined the union as a matter of course.[5] Siphethe Phatsha tells a similar story, saying that he joined the union shortly after its foundation and remained a paid-up member for thirty years. At the start, he says, the union earned his loyalty and his trust. In fact, as he puts it, in those years: 'I loved the NUM'.[6]

This loyalty was earned. The NUM fought hard for its members. It insisted on the development of better safety standards on the mines, arguing that the precautions accompanying underground blasting be improved, and that the mines consider the way in which exposure to asbestos was harming workers. It changed the ways in which hostels operated, converting dormitories into power bases that opposed the company's oversight. It fought for better wages, and for health care for injured workers. It organized huge strikes, and, in 1987, resisted efforts to destroy it.[7]

It also began to represent the political interests of its members beyond their workplaces. In 1985, the NUM – by now the largest union in the country – left CUSA and helped set up the Congress of South African Trade Unions (COSATU), a grouping that linked the struggles of African workers in the workplace to the struggle against Apartheid, electing the still-imprisoned Nelson Mandela as its Honorary Life President and adopting the 1955 Freedom Charter of the anti-Apartheid Congress Movement. As the struggle against Apartheid spread across the country in the late 1980s, COSATU – and its most important members, including the now-dominant NUM – was at the front of the wave.[8]

When the Apartheid state failed, COSATU and the NUM played a significant part in the transition to democracy. In particular, Cyril Ramaphosa – who had been the NUM's General Secretary throughout the past decade – became

4 Jonathan Crush, 'Migrancy and Militance: The Case of the National Union of Mineworkers of South Africa', *African Affairs*, 88.350 (1989), pp. 5–23.
5 Interview with Lanford Gcotyelwa, KuNdile, 3 December 2015.
6 Phatsha, Day 54 (26 February 2013), p. 5,780.
7 T. Dunbar Moodie, 'Becoming a Social Movement Union: Cyril Ramaphosa and the National Union of Mineworkers', *Transformation*, 72/73 (2015), pp. 152–180.
8 Jeremy Baskin, *Striking Back, a History of COSATU* (London, Verso: 1991).

the Secretary General of the now-unbanned ANC, and took a leading role in the negotiations to produce a new South African Constitution.[9] At the same time, COSATU entered into a formal alliance with the ANC and the South African Communist Party, and its leaders and members took part in the first democratic election of 1994 as a part of this alliance.

After the elections, many unionists were appointed to President Mandela's new cabinet. Ramaphosa chose to stay outside of the government, though, instead remaining in his position as the ANC's Secretary General. At the time, many commentators speculated that he intended to become the country's second president, when Mandela stepped down. If so, Ramaphosa's ambitions were frustrated. Before the next elections, Ramaphosa was replaced as the ANC's Secretary General, and left national office to become a private businessman.[10]

Throughout, the unions remained powerful. COSATU was part of the governing alliance – and the NUM was the largest union in that alliance. In the 1990s and early 2000s, the NUM still boasted a membership of around 250,000 workers across all mining industries – including gold, coal, and platinum.[11] Its members – in Marikana and elsewhere – could believe that their voices were heard in the corridors of state. Its officials held high office in government, and their statements on the economy, on politics, and even on social and cultural issues always made it to the evening news.

The NUM spoke for the workers, and when the NUM spoke, the country listened.

* * *

There were consequences to the new context, however. As the new order came into being, the relationship between the NUM and South Africa's mining companies changed. When it was first launched, in the 1980s, the NUM was an outsider – an insurgent trade union that challenged the powers of the mining companies. It organized strikes, disrupted cosy workplace arrangements, and forced the companies to the negotiating table, insisting on better deals for its members. It did so in the face of opposition from both the companies and the national state itself.

By the early 2000s, though, the NUM was no longer outside the system. It

---

9 Butler, *Cyril Ramaphosa*. For a popular history, see also: Lauren Segal and Sharon Court, *One Law, One Nation: The Making of the South African Constitution* (Johannesburg, Jacana: 2011).

10 A useful survey of this period of post-Apartheid politics can be found in Tom Lodge, *Politics in South Africa: From Mandela to Mbeki* (Oxford, James Currey: 2003).

11 See the figures in National Union of Mineworkers, '30 Years of Unbroken Revolutionary Trade Unionism Struggle: Secretariat Report to the 14th National Congress' (Johannesburg: 2012).

was, instead, a political insider – part of the government, an influential broker of national deals, and a training ground for future leaders. It was no longer an insurgent force, but rather a part of the establishment. It still brought companies to the negotiating table, and it still organized strikes, but it now did so with the backing of the state.

One sign of its new status was the adoption of what has become a standard practice in the mining industry: whenever one union within a mining company could demonstrate that it had the membership of more than half of the company's employees, that union could become the sole official bargaining partner in labour negotiations.[12] This 'fifty per cent plus one' rule gives significant power to the largest union on a mine, cutting out any smaller unions – even a union that represented more than forty per cent of the mine's employees. This policy helped the NUM to maintain its dominant position within the mining sector, frustrating the emergence of new unions while continuing to get the best deals for its members.

Unsurprisingly, given this, many mining companies began to abandon their earlier confrontational stances, and sought to cultivate good relations with the NUM.

Lonmin was one of these companies. In the early 2000s, the NUM was the sole recognized union at its platinum mines in Marikana – it represented a majority of Lonmin's employees, and so occupied the only available seat at the negotiating table. As these two parties – the union and the company – repeatedly engaged with other, relations between negotiators became familiar. The processes of negotiation became comfortable, predictable, and reliable. The union and the company found it easy to strike deals, and to maintain a non-confrontational public relationship.

Meanwhile, Lonmin sought to obtain any advantage it could within the system. One of the ways it did this was by appointing Cyril Ramaphosa – in 2010, at the time of his appointment, a successful businessman, officially out-

---

12   The Labour Relations Act (66 of 1995), as amended, grants a specific status to a 'representative trade union' which is a union that has 'as members the majority of the employees employed by an employer in a workplace'. Among the factors of this status is that the majority union may agree with the employer that no other unions will be recognized in the workplace (in a 'closed shop' agreement) or – if other unions are nonetheless permitted in the workplace – what rights will be given to these minority unions to participate in collective bargaining. In effect, an agreement between a majority union and an employer can restrict the powers of minority unions to bargain – an agreement which is common practice in the mining industry. See, for discussions of the extent and the use of this power, J. Theron, S. Godfrey, and E. Fergus, 'Organizational and Collective Bargaining Rights through the Lens of Marikana', *Industrial Law Journal*, 36 (2015), pp.846–864; Temogo Geoffrey Esitang and Stefan van Eck, 'Minority Trade Unions and the Amendments to the LRA: Reflections on Thresholds, Democracy, and ILO Conventions', *Industrial Law Journal*, 37 (2016), pp. 763–778.

side of politics – to its Board of Directors. Of course, there were many reasons to appoint Ramaphosa. He brought with him a wealth of experience. He ran his own companies. He sat on dozens of boards. But, as Lonmin's 2011 Annual Report made clear, he also brought other qualities to the table. He had been the General Secretary of the NUM, and the Secretary General of the ANC. Even without a formal office, he had enormous political influence – both within the government and with the union itself.[13]

In the world of multinational companies, influence matters. In addition to his experience in business, it was likely understood that Ramaphosa would use his contacts on behalf of Lonmin. He would have been expected to be able to speak to government ministers as a colleague and a friend, to move behind the scenes, and to present the most favourable version of the company's efforts to the relevant regulatory authorities. His presence would help smooth all sorts of things over.

Ramaphosa's appointment to Lonmin's Board was a sign of the new political reality. Mining companies and large unions no longer needed to be in political competition with each other: they both had official places in the post-Apartheid system, and could find ways to work together to achieve a mutually satisfying balance between the needs of their particular constituencies. On the one hand, shareholders sought to see Lonmin and other companies turn profits; on the other hand, workers sought to reap the benefits of South Africa's political and economic liberalization.[14] When high profile unionists could be persuaded to lend their influence to the cause of maximizing profits, in the apparent interests of workers, then everyone might win.

But this was something of an illusion. As the NUM and its leaders became used to wielding this influence, their connections with miners underground began to weaken. As these connections weakened, miners began to wonder whether their concerns were in truth being heard – and whether their union still spoke for them.

Once their faith in the union was shaken, the union's authority had to decline.

The NUM stumbles

The first signs of discontent came early in the post-Apartheid period, when the NUM was at its height. In the mid-1990s, a dispute over pensions at one of the largest companies in the region – Anglo Platinum, known as 'Amplats' –

---

13   Lonmin, 'Annual Report and Accounts for the Year ended 30 September 2011', 'Board of Directors', www.lonmin.com/reports/2011/online_annual_report_2011/business_review/board_of_directors.html (Acc. 2015; no longer available online).

14   Among several useful surveys of these dynamics, see: Patrick Bond, *Elite Transition: From Apartheid to Neoliberalism in South Africa* (London, Pluto: 2nd edition, 2014) and Hein Marais, *South Africa Pushed to the Limit: The Political Economy of Change* (London, Zed: 2011).

demonstrated the fragility of the NUM's authority in the sector. This dispute began near Rustenburg, on mines which had operated across the borders of South Africa and the Bophuthatswana homeland. As the majority union on Amplats's Rustenburg mines, the NUM administered a provident fund for workers employed in the South African parts of the mines – but not those employed in Bophuthatswana.[15]

Throughout the 1980s and into the early 1990s, the mines in Bophuthatswana itself operated under a parallel legal and political system, and so the NUM-run provident fund existed alongside a second, Bophuthatswanan state-managed fund. Workers employed in the homeland were required to pay their pensions into this state fund.

If nothing had changed, this might have been an uncontroversial difference. But then, in 1994, the homeland collapsed. The state-managed fund closed down, and workers were paid out their pension savings. The union-administered fund, though, continued to operate as usual – leaving the NUM's members wondering why other miners belonging to the same union had received an apparent cash windfall.

The workers at Amplats's Rustenburg mines who belonged the NUM's provident fund decided that they also wanted to access their pension monies. When the NUM refused, some workers decided to strike outside of the official system. In February 1996, they elected a committee of five men to represent them. Their committee demanded that the provident fund administered by the NUM pay out its monies. Unexpectedly, the company management agreed to bypass the official union negotiating system, and to sit down directly with the strikers and their committee. In this meeting, the company then agreed to overrule the NUM, to access the provident fund themselves, and to pay out pensions in cash to the workers.

There is a strong case to be made that this was highly improper behaviour – as T. Dunbar Moodie, the pre-eminent historian of labour in South Africa's mines, has suggested. The legal situation should have favoured the NUM's decision to protect the workers' pensions – and should have made it difficult for the company's managers to interfere with the fund. And yet, nonetheless, it happened. Moodie speculates that the managers may have 'wanted to discredit the NUM'. He suggests that:

> If so, they certainly succeeded. The union was hamstrung. If events have consequences, Amplats local managers' decision in 1996 to pay out the provident

15 These events are described and explained in T. Dunbar Moodie, 'Making Mincemeat out of Mutton: Social Origins of the NUM Decline on Platinum', *Journal of Southern African Studies*, 42.5 (2016), pp. 841–856. See also, Moodie, '"Igneous" Means Fire from Below: The Tumultuous History of the National Union of Mine workers on the South African Platinum Mines', *Review of African Political Economy*, 42.1 (2015), pp. 561–576. The following account draws on both.

funds on its mines was a crucial early nail in the coffin of the NUM – and one over which it had ... no control.[16]

At the time, only a handful of workers would have known these details. For the majority a simple story sufficed: while the NUM had refused to liquidate the provident fund, the five-man committee, known as the Five Madoda, or the Five Old Men, had been able to persuade the company to distribute cash to the workers. In this story, the union was weak – and the Five Madoda seemed to be very strong.

This strength was tested in June, when the Five Madoda decided to call the workers out on another strike. They now demanded additional payments from the provident fund, as well as other forms of payments. Riding high on their successes in February, the Five Madoda were able to convince the workers on Amplats's mines to down tools – and for three weeks, work on the mines was brought to a stop by their strike.

During the strike, the NUM was forced to play a difficult role. The strike was as much as rejection of the union's authority over its members as it was a demand directed at management. The NUM tried to get government ministers to intervene – drawing upon its national profile to bring political leaders to talk to the Five Madoda and their supporters. This seems to have backfired. According to a report written at the time, and found by Moodie, 'workers ... closed in on NUM and accused them of being management spies. The delegations from NUM, provincial government and mine management were forced to flee after a whistle was blown.'[17] The NUM's intervention fizzled out, and the strike continued without the union's involvement.

And then, at the end of three weeks, Amplats fired all its striking workers.

In the chaos afterwards, the NUM tried to stay in the background – letting the Five Madoda and their independent committee attempt to negotiate with the government and the company. This didn't help the union, though. The deal that was eventually agreed was unquestionably bad for workers. Although they were re-employed, they would now be treated as new employees – losing all their seniority, promotions, and pension entitlements. They also had to reapply to join the union.

Lanford Gcotyelwa, who was working at Amplats's Rustenburg mines at the times, remembers this period with clarity.

> I remember in '96, we went on strike and we got fired in June. We were NUM members, and yet we got fired for a month. When we went back they said that they were going to hire us anew, and that killed our service for us. We had to start afresh ... That's why I decided that I'd rather break away.

---

16 Moodie, 'Making Mincemeat', p. 846.
17 Network of Independent Monitors' report, as quoted in Moodie, 'Making Mincemeat', p. 857.

He summed up his attitude:

> [W]e began to realize that the NUM was dishonourable and that it no longer stood for the people ... As a result, when I returned I was no longer part of a union. Even when I had a case, I would represent myself. I had decided that it would be better to be fired than to let NUM get me fired.[18]

The bungled 1996 strike at Amplats dealt a blow to the NUM's authority on the mines. Even though the union had not organized the strike, it bore the brunt of workers' blame for the terrible bargain that ended it. In the years immediately afterwards, the membership of the union dropped sharply, as men like Lanford either chose not to return to the union or joined other, smaller and newer, unions on the mine. Even though the NUM would recover its membership figures – and its majority status – in the following years, its public status was irrevocably damaged.[19]

After this strike, it was hard for workers to see the NUM as the crusading union it had once been. Instead, they saw the union as yet another tool of control – a second level of bureaucracy inserted between workers and management, serving its own interests while pretending to help workers. It was tied up in government, and more concerned with national politics than with shaft-level issues. For many, membership in the union was a necessary evil – one that no longer held a sense of belonging.

New unions appear

This changed workers' struggles in the region. In the absence of a strong sense of belonging to the NUM, workers began to look for other organizations to represent them. In the fifteen years after the Amplats strike, many groups tried to form new unions on the mines. Several of these had some success, convincing disenchanted mineworkers to leave the NUM and take the risk of joining a new minority union.

One of the earliest of these new unions was the Mouthpiece Workers Union (MPWU), which was formed on Amplats's mines after the Five Madoda strike.[20] This union had sporadic support on the mine in the late 1990s and early 2000s. In 2004, for example, it represented half of the machine operators at an Amplats shaft studied by Paul Stewart – significantly more than the 30 per cent repre-

---

18   Interview with Lanford Gcotyelwa, KuNdile, 3 December 2015.

19   A more sympathetic article on the NUM in the period is Raphaël Botiveau, 'The Politics of Marikana and South Africa's Changing Labour Relations', *African Affairs*, 113.450 (2014), pp. 128–137.

20   Paul Stewart, '"Kings of the Mine": Rock Drill Operators and the 2012 Strike Wave on South African Mines', *South African Review of Sociology*, 44.3 (2013), pp. 42–63, gives the background to the MPWU, and provides the membership figures I quote here.

sented by the NUM. The MPWU sought to gain broader recognition, and joined the Federation of Unions of South Africa (FEDUSA), a post-Apartheid alternative to COSATU. It remained, however, a minority union in the industry – and it was never capable of displacing the NUM from its dominant 'fifty plus one' position in any mine.

A number of small groups then split from the MPWU, forming the Building Motor Engineering Allied Workers Union and the Commercial Workers Union of South Africa. Neither of these attracted large followings – and it seemed as though the fragmentation of the new unions would leave the NUM in its dominant position.

This may have been true of the new unions that arose in the wake of the Five Madoda strike in the platinum mines. But another union emerged in a different part of the country at about the same time, also rising out of a strike and a dispute about the NUM's relationship to a mining company. This union would prove far more effective.

In September 1999, coal-miners at the Douglas Colliery in Mpumulanga Province embarked upon a two-week-long wildcat strike. One of the reasons they gave for striking was that they were protesting against the company's firing of the local NUM branch chairperson, Joseph Mathunjwa. They believed he had been singled out by the company's management, and unfairly dismissed. They sought his reinstatement, and occupied underground shafts for a full ten days before ending the strike.[21]

Mathunjwa was reinstated in his job, but this did not end the problems at the Colliery. The protests to defend him had taken place without the consent of the NUM. The union therefore decided to investigate whether Mathunjwa himself had been involved in stirring up the strike. The leadership sent two officials to investigate. Both found that there was no reason to hold him responsible. Nonetheless, the union's General Secretary summoned Mathunjwa to face a disciplinary hearing – and to answer the charges that he had brought the NUM into disrepute by backing an unlicensed strike, and thus undermining its authority.

Mathunjwa refused to participate in this hearing. The NUM then expelled him.

In response, all 3,000 workers at the Douglas Colliery resigned from the NUM. They set up a new organization, under Mathunjwa's leadership – the Association of Mineworkers and Construction Union (AMCU). It was formally registered as a union in 2001, with Mathunjwa as its most prominent face.

---

21   The history of AMCU's early years still awaits a dedicated treatment. I draw this summary from Naadirah Munshi, 'Platinum Politics: The Rise, and Rise, of the Association of Mineworkers and Construction Union (AMCU)', MA Thesis (Sociology), University of the Witwatersrand (2017), particularly pp. 36–46; and the interview with Joseph Mathunjwa by Thapelo Lekgowa and Peter Alexander, reproduced in Peter Alexander et al., *Marikana: A View from the Mountain and a Case to Answer* (Johannesburg, Jacana: 2012), pp. 43–56.

Over the next decade, AMCU sought to expand its presence from this one mine into other parts of the industry. It developed networks in other coal, chrome, and platinum mines in Mpumulanga, northern KwaZulu-Natal, and Limpopo. Progress was slow. Although AMCU became the majority union at a handful of its mines, it was still clearly a marginal player. It was the second or third largest union on several mines, and only very rarely invited to take part in general salary negotiations with the management of the big mining companies.

There were reasons for AMCU's organizers to be optimistic, however. As they were growing, the membership profile of all these unions was changing. The NUM was professionalising – drawing more of its membership from a growing class of clerical and office workers on the mines, including secretaries, accountants, and managers. The MPWU, AMCU, and the other smaller new unions attracted members from among the ranks of manual and underground workers – machine operators, rock drill operators (RDOs), and other men who worked with their hands.[22] Although the NUM could still count on its majority status on the mines to convince most workers to stay within its embrace, the steady rise of these new unions suggested that many of the workers at the rock face were unhappy with the NUM and looking for alternatives.

This encouraged AMCU to keep trying to expand into the platinum sector. In 2010, the union began to gain members in Lonmin's Karee shaft – one of the main parts of the company's Marikana operations. In 2011, AMCU tried to get Lonmin to recognize the union's right to organize. This was not a straightforward process, and illustrated the difficulties smaller unions faced. At first, Lonmin's management would not meet with the union – at least not until after the union had officially complained to the Commission for Conciliation, Mediation and Arbitration (CCMA), a body tasked with resolving labour disputes. Only then would Lonmin speak to AMCU.[23]

In December 2011, AMCU gained limited rights to organize on the Karee shaft – but not on any of Lonmin's other shafts in Marikana. At first, AMCU was merely given access to the workplace and the ability to collect dues from its members. In May 2012, after further negotiations, AMCU was permitted to elect shop-stewards on the shaft and in the hostels, to hold meetings on Lonmin's property, and to sit on some of the company's consultative committees. It was not granted bargaining rights, and its presence was limited to the one shaft in

---

22 Andries Bezuidenhout and Sakhela Buhlungu, 'Old Victories, New Struggles: The State of the National Union of Mineworkers', in Sakhela Buhlungu et al. (eds), *State of the Nation: South Africa 2007* (Cape Town, HSRC: 2007), pp. 245–264. For a more recent analysis of the changing class basis of the NUM and other unions, see: Alexander Beresford, 'Organised Labour and the Politics of Class Formation in Post-Apartheid South Africa', *Review of African Political Economy*, 39.134 (2012), pp. 569–589.

23 Exhibit NN – Witness Statement of Joseph Mathunjwa, p. 3.

Lonmin's mines.[24] Nonetheless, it was now positioned as the second union on the mine – and thus as a rival to the NUM.

A precursor strike

The expansion of AMCU into Lonmin's mines attracted relatively little attention, though, because a major eruption was taking place in a neighbouring district.

At the beginning of 2012, tensions ran high at the Impala Platinum ('Implats') mine near Rustenburg – about forty kilometres from Lonmin's mines in Marikana.[25] These tensions had developed over the previous few years: in 2010, some underground miners set up an independent committee to organize meetings outside of the NUM's official framework, and convinced the Implats management to speak to them as well as to the union. In 2011, the NUM concluded a three-year deal with Implats – an agreement that controlled wage increases, and linked end-of-year bonuses to performance targets. When many of the miners failed to meet these targets, and thus did not receive end-of-year bonuses, they turned to the existing independent committees to complain about the union, and to air their frustration with its deal.

On 12 January 2012, a committee of rock drill operators – a class of workers who had been particularly affected by the wage deal – decided to embark upon an unlicensed and unprotected strike. This strike lasted three days. Then, on 17 January, another group of rock drill operators presented a petition to management – before downing tools. Because the strike was not licensed by the NUM, and thus not protected by labour law, Implats management was able to get a court order permitting it to fire about 3,000 workers and to evict them from its hostels.

This action backfired. Within days, 17,200 workers had joined the strike. Tensions and tempers ran high in the region. The strike was not peaceful, and conflicts arose between strikers and other mineworkers. The police watched from the sidelines.

Implats's management responded by dismissing all of the striking workers, and evicting them all from the company's hostels – leaving them without any accommodation in the region. This did not end the disturbances on the mines, nor did it end the conflicts between the striking workers and those who were continuing to work underground. According to Crispen Chinguno – who was studying labour practices on the mine at the time of the strike – on 16 February 2012, 'a worker employed by a subcontractor at Impala Platinum was attacked …

---

24 Exhibit XXX 2 – Da Costa Supplementary Affidavit.
25 The primary source for these stories – and the source of the direct quotes below – is Crispen Chinguno, 'The Shifting Dynamics of the Relations between Institutionalisation and Strike Violence: A Case Study of Impala Platinum, Rustenburg (1982–2012)', PhD Thesis (Sociology), University of the Witwatersrand (2015). See also: Stewart, 'Kings of the Mine'.

He was stripped naked and assaulted in the early morning hours by fellow workers who were hunting down strike breakers. He died in an ambulance on the way to the hospital'.[26] On 20 February, the police intervened violently – opening fire on striking workers at a hostel, killing another worker and seriously injuring seven more.

While this was happening, management was negotiating with workers to resolve the strike – largely by offering to re-employ them on new terms. These terms were familiar from the Five Madoda days. The workers would lose their seniority and privileges, and return under a cloud. On top of this, the company was determined to retain the right to decide who would be offered a deal, and who would not.

In the course of these discussions, the company's management was also attempting to bring NUM officials into the negotiating process – often, in place of the unofficial miners' committees. Again, this was reminiscent of the earlier strike at Amplats, fifteen years before. For many workers, the company's attempts demonstrated the union's complicity in the structures of power – the NUM had negotiated the original deal, which the workers were now rejecting, and yet still claimed to be able to represent them.[27] And, of course, it was clearly the company's preferred partner.

Workers told Chinguno that they had lost all faith in the NUM's independence. According to one miner:

> Our biggest enemy is the union. The union can be corrupted. We have left it … We have all resigned from the NUM but the employer is insisting that he can only talk the NUM. How can this be when the NUM does not have the support of the majority of the workers?

Another worker went further in his disenchantment: 'NUM was never for us even in 1994 … It has never served the ordinary workers. All the guys in the office are just there for their individual benefit not for us … They just want to move up and that's it … nothing is for us'.[28]

* * *

In this context, not even the end of the strike could bring about the resurrection of the NUM's authority on Implats's mines. Other unions – including AMCU – were rapidly able to expand their presence in the platinum mines around

---

26 Chinguno, 'Shifting Dynamics', p. 218.
27 Greg Nicolson, 'Impala Strike: Welcome to the Age of Retail Unionism', *Daily Maverick*, 22 February 2012, www.dailymaverick.co.za/article/2012-02-22-impala-strike-welcome-to-the-age-of-retail-unionism (Acc. March 2021); Gavin Hartford, 'The Mining Industry Strike Wave: What Are the Causes and What Are the Solutions?' *GroundUp*, 10 September 2012, www.groundup.org.za/article/mining-industry-strike-wave-what-are-causes-and-what-are-solutions (Acc. March 2021).
28 Chinguno, 'Shifting Dynamics', p. 199.

Rustenburg. Workers around Rustenburg were aware of AMCU's presence at Lonmin's Karee shaft, and were beginning to talk about the new union. While researching at the Implats's mine, Chinguno noticed AMCU organizers at meetings during the strike, convincing workers to join the union. At least some officials in the NUM were certain that AMCU was playing a role in the strike, suggesting to Chinguno that they believed AMCU to be 'assisting in formulating strategies and advising workers and committees not to listen to management and NUM'. One of these officials suggested that AMCU's influence was behind the unexpected 'level of arrogance and belligerence exhibited by our members [towards the NUM]'.[29]

Although the Implats strike seems to have been organized by shaft-level committees – often, explicitly invoking the example of the Five Madoda movement at Amplats in 1996 – many NUM officials came to see AMCU as the real threat. Perhaps this was because AMCU looked more like a direct competitor – unlike workers' committees, AMCU aimed to replace the NUM as the representative of workers on the mines. The new union had the same kind of membership structures, the same kinds of offices and officials, and the same kinds of ambitions. It was possible for workers to be both a member of temporary strike committee and retain the membership of the NUM. It was not possible for them to be members of both unions at the same time – and so AMCU posed a greater threat to the dominance of the NUM than any number of committees. The company shared this approach.[30]

However, the workers themselves were slow to draw this conclusion. Their disenchantment with the NUM did not convince them to become members of AMCU. Most workers at the Implats's mines in Rustenburg and even at Lonmin's Karee shaft remained members of the NUM in these months. At Marikana, AMCU increased in size – but remained a smaller union than the NUM. In the weeks leading up to August 2012, few workers saw their salvation in moving from one union to the other – instead, strike committees and shaft-level organizing seemed to be the way forward, to be the most effective means of building their own struggles.[31]

They knew that would soon have to take their struggles to improve their lives, their homes, their environment, and their working conditions into their own hands. The history of labour politics in the region made it inevitable: the rise and fall of the NUM's authority had eroded their trust in the union system, and the successes of some wildcat strikes – based on the willingness of some mining companies to go outside of the union system, when it suited them – meant that they were always more likely to choose to act themselves than to wait for others to represent them.

It was not a question of whether it would happen. It was just a question of when.

---

29 Chinguno, 'Shifting Dynamics', p. 216.
30 Exhibit XXX 2 – Da Costa Supplementary Affidavit.
31 See the analysis of the situation in Luke Sinwell with Siphiwe Mbatha, *The Spirit of Marikana: The Rise of Insurgent Trade Unionism in South Africa* (London, Pluto: 2016).

Part II

The Strike and the Massacre

4
—
The Strike Begins

IN SOUTH Africa, 9 August is a public holiday – Women's Day. In 2012, this holiday fell on a Thursday – and, for some workers across the country, it heralded the start of a long weekend. For workers at Lonmin's mine in Marikana, though, it signified the start of a process that would radically change their lives, and their world.

On this morning, a group of between 350 and 500 workers gathered on a patch of dry land beside the road at the Wonderkop Stadium in Marikana.[1] A low outcrop of rocks rises to one side of this land, cutting the wind and casting a morning shadow. The workers were dressed in ordinary everyday clothes, some wearing jackets and soft caps against the morning chill, while others went bareheaded. Most of the workers were rock drill operators, and had come to discuss their dissatisfaction with their salaries, and with the ways in which the NUM was failing to put their perspectives forward.

According to Vusi Mabuyakhulu, who worked at Karee shaft as a rock drill operator, the workers were disappointed by the union's previous agreements – and felt that their work had been neglected in the broad salary agreements that the NUM had negotiated with Lonmin. On top of this, the rock drill operators belonged to several different unions – and so they made a decision to exclude not only the NUM, but all other unions, from their discussions on 9 August. They would talk alone.[2]

By about 10:30, their discussion was underway. Lonmin security officers filmed the meeting from the other side of the road, and commented that it was clearly peaceful and calm.[3] Their videos show workers standing in clusters, or

---

1   This is the estimate of P.W. Botha, a Lonmin security officer, recorded on the video of this group put into evidence at the Commission as Exhibit V1 – Video of 9 August 2012. My descriptions of this meeting come from what can be seen in this and another video, also filmed by Botha, and put into evidence as Exhibit V2 – Video of 9 August 2012.
2   See Exhibit BBB8 – Witness Statement of Vusimuzi Mandla Mabuyakhulu, and his evidence in chief in the Commission Testimony of Vusimuzi Mabuyakhulu at the Marikana Commission of Inquiry, Day 48 (14 February 2013).
3   Exhibits V1 and V2, as described above, are these videos. Notably, Botha comments –

sitting on thick pipes at the edge of the road, talking to each other. According to Mabuyakhulu, they spoke about their demands and their tactics, seeking to come to a shared approach. They decided that they would take the next day – Friday 10 August 2012 – to go and speak to Lonmin's managers:

> after a lengthy discussion it was decided that we're not going to go on a strike, but that we're going to clock for the one day ... this was not meant to be a strike, it was not intended as a strike. The decision was that we would go and talk to the employer and after meeting the employer, the people working at Karee ... they would go back to work.[4]

At about 11:40, with this approach agreed, the crowd began to disperse. Men moved off in small groups of two or three, talking quietly to each other. Another group danced together, toyi-toying in formation, singing quietly. Most, though, just walked away. Cars drove past, the sun shone, and the ordinary routines of a day off work – a day to spend at leisure, with friends or alone – resumed.

There was nothing in this meeting to suggest the events that would follow: no signs and symbols, no auguries of what was to come. There was nothing to suggest that the workers imagined that their discussion would lead to a week-long strike, during which ten people – including miners, security guards, and police officers – would die. Nor was there anything to suggest that the strike would end in a brutal massacre, in blood, and in the death of another thirty-four miners at the hands of the police.

Instead, the sun shone on a quiet road, and the miners went home. For many of them, this was a last moment of peace, a moment of reflection, before the storm.

The rock drill operators' complaints

As they walked home, the workers may have been thinking back to their discussion, rehearsing what they had said, and what better arguments they could have made, what better words they could have used, how they could have been more persuasive.

Almost everyone who had gathered that morning worked as a rock drill operator in one of Lonmin's shafts at Marikana, and almost all had complaints about their wages.[5] Their wages were assigned in a complex way, and although Lonmin claimed that the 'cost to company' wage that an average rock drill operator earned was close to R10,000 a month,[6] in practice many workers were living on

---

on the audio track of V2 – that the meeting dispersed 'peacefully – no incidents at this stage – no illegal activity' and clearly acknowledges the calmness of the gathering.

4 Mabuyakhulu, Day 48, p. 5,263.
5 For an account of the role of rock drill operators in this strike, and others at the time, see Stewart, 'Kings of the Mine'.
6 'In response to a separate query from *Politicsweb*, Lonmin's Mark Munroe, Exec-

much less. A payslip from the time disclosed by one worker shows how their salaries were calculated, and gives a sense of their complaints. On this slip, a 'basic pay' of R4,365.90 is supplemented by a 'living out allowance' of R1,850 (as discussed in Chapter 2). To this is added a special allowance for rock drill operators, which Lonmin set at R750, and a small 'holiday leave' allowance. A pension contribution and a medical aid contribution are added to these figures. Then there are union fees, and tax. The workers themselves do not see the cash that goes into these contributions, fees, and taxes – even though the sums are printed on the pay slip. At the end of the month, this worker – representative of most rock drill operators – took home about R5,000.[7]

Even then, workers at Marikana only lived off a part of this sum. According to this same worker, every month he would send about R2,000 of this R5,000 to his extended family in the Eastern Cape. This was not in any way uncommon – most workers would support their families in this way. In addition, other workers would be servicing large debts, run up by local predatory short-term loan companies.[8]

The rock drill operators were adamant that this wage was not enough to compensate them for the dangers of their work. At the meeting, they agreed to demand a wage of R12,500 a month – not a paper wage, calculated as 'cost to company', but an actual and comprehensible cash salary.

This figure – of R12,500 a month – seems to have bubbled up from discussions held by workers' committees at the Karee shaft in July 2012, a few months

---

utive Vice President of Mining, basically confirmed these amounts. He stated: 'Lonmin's Rock Drill Operators earn in the region of R10,000 per month without bonuses and over R11,000 including bonuses. These levels are in line with those of our competitors and are before the wage hike of some 9% which will come into effect on 1 October 2012' – The Ratcatcher, 'How much do Rock Drillers at Lonmin really earn?', *PoliticsWeb* (20 August 2012), https://www.politicsweb.co.za/news-and-analysis/how-much-do-rock-drillers-at-lonmin-really-earn (Acc: November 2020).

7 This payslip is described in detail in two articles: Sipho Hlongwane and Greg Marinovich, 'Lonmin: Malema Fans the Flames, but the Victims are Still Out in the Cold', *Daily Maverick* (18 August 2012), www.dailymaverick.co.za/article/2012-08-18-lonmin-malema-fans-the-flames-but-the-victims-are-still-out-in-the-cold (Acc. November 2020); and Sipho Hlongwane, 'Lonmin Strike: Why the R4,000 Figure is No Trivial Matter', *Daily Maverick* (27 August 2012), www.dailymaverick.co.za/opinionista/2012-08-27-lonmin-strike-why-the-r4000-figure-is-no-trivial-matter (Acc: November 2020).

8 There is a growing scholarship on short-term loan companies, and the predatory economy that surrounds them, in South Africa. See, in particular: Deborah James and Dinah Rajak, 'Credit Apartheid, Migrants, Mines and Money', *African Studies*, 73.3 (2014), pp. 455–476, and Deborah James, 'Deeper Into a Hole? Borrowing and Lending in South Africa', *Current Anthropology*, 55:S9 (August 2014), S17–S29.

after the Implats strike earlier in the year. Karee shaft was also the site of the first AMCU branch in Lonmin's Marikana operations, and the site of much worker activism. At the time, Lonmin management indicated that it would be willing to meet with the workers' committee to listen to their demands, and to engage them – but this indication went nowhere.[9] No one came, and the workers were not willing to wait.

The workers were complaining about more than Lonmin's management, though. They also felt that their struggles had been ignored by the National Union of Mineworkers (NUM). Some miners argued that rock drill operators needed to have a voice of their own – and that their wages should be negotiated separately, not as part of a package-deal covering the wages of all types of workers in Lonmin's mines. Others remembered that the rock drill operators had tried to persuade the union to negotiate on their behalf in 2006 or 2007, and that nothing had come of that.[10] They were no better off for having tried to go through official channels then, these miners said. They shouldn't try again now, not if they wanted things to change.

And so, it was agreed: if they wanted better wages, they needed fight for themselves.

The workers walked away from the meeting, and went back to their families in the informal settlement, or back to their one-room shacks, or even back to their hostel beds. Some of them would have eaten a meal, and moved to a local bar to watch a football game on the television. Some would have spent the afternoon quietly. Others picked up their cell-phones and spoke to their families, half-way across the country. They spoke about their hopes and their fears. Their hopes: that their struggles would succeed, and that a pay increase would make their lives easier. And their fears: that this would be yet another failure, that nothing would come of it, that the mining company would retaliate and they would all be fired, losing their seniority and their benefits, just as had happened to other workers in the past.[11]

Later, after they'd spoken, the workers would have switched their phones off, or turned back to the game, or settled down to bed. They closed their eyes, and dreamed again about what might happen on Friday – what might

---

9   This is according to the account of negotiations that took place in July 2012, given by Miguel Gomes da Costa, a vice president of Lonmin responsible for the Karee mine's operation. Testimony of Michael [sic] Gomes da Costa at the Marikana Commission of Inquiry, Day 239 (3 June 2014). The relevant sections, covering this meeting in July, run across pp. 30,022–30,030. See also: Exhibit OO 17 – Witness Statement of Michael Gomes da Costa and Exhibit XXX 2 – Da Costa Supplementary.

10   Mabuyakhulu, Day 48, pp. 5,261–5,262.

11   The contents of some of these conversations can be found in the final section of this chapter.

be won, what might be lost. They slept, and the concerns of the day ebbed away for a while.

'This is where the problem started'

The day dawned, and workers began to leave their beds.

According to Lonmin's records, between twenty and fifty rock drill operators gathered again outside the Wonderkop Stadium, on the empty land between it, the road, and the rocky outcrop on one side of the informal settlement, at about 06:00. Over the next two hours, the crowd grew substantially, coming to number between 1,500 and 2,000 people. At about 08:00, they began to move away from the Stadium, along the main road, and towards the Lonmin offices in Marikana.[12]

It takes a while for a large crowd to move a relatively short distance. Over the next two hours, hundreds of men shuffled along the road towards the town. Lonmin security watched them through closed-circuit cameras, and in person. Officers from the South African Police Services (SAPS) came out from their barracks, and followed the crowd in heavy vehicles, known as 'Nyalas', as well as in ordinary police-cars.

By 10:00, the crowd had moved to a four-way crossing about six hundred metres away from the Lonmin office. At this point, Henry Blou, a member of Lonmin's security team, stepped onto the road with Graeme Sinclair, his boss, and a group of uniformed police officers.[13] They stopped the crowd while Blou and his colleagues tried to identify a leader, someone who could speak for the whole crowd. They could not isolate anyone, so called out to the whole group, demanding to know what they wanted to achieve. At this, a half dozen men came forward – apparently spontaneously – and began to lay out what they understood the group's demands to be.[14] First and foremost, they said, the group wanted to speak to Lonmin's managers – not its security officers.

For a while, nothing happened. Blou, Sinclair, and the police stood in one part of the road, the six spokesmen stood before them, and the crowd waited behind. As the men in the front spoke, the crowd shuffled. Many of them sat on the tarmac of the road. Others wandered off into the bushes on the side, to stretch and relax. They stood in clusters of four or five men, some talking quietly

---

12   Exhibit RRRR 1.1 – Witness statement of HM Blou, paras 8–9.
13   Henry Blou was the Manager of Mining Security at Lonmin's Western Platinum Division. His witness statements – including several amendments and supplementary statements – are marked as Exhibits RRRR 1.1 to RRRR 1.5. See also: Testimony of Mntunaye Henry Blou at the Marikana Commission of Inquiry, Day 281–283 (29 August, 1 September, and 2 September 2014). Graeme Sinclair was the Group Mining Emergency and Security Manager. His witness statement is FFFF 1 – Statement of Graeme Sinclair. See also: Testimony of Graeme Miller Sinclair at the Marikana Commission of Inquiry, Day 266–268 (30 July – 1 August 2014), and Day 283 (2 September 2014).
14   Mabuyakhulu, Day 48, p. 5,264.

to each other, others sitting silently. The crowd was waiting, hoping for Lonmin's managers to arrive.[15]

Meanwhile, Sinclair tried to convince the workers to disperse. He asked for their demands to be put into writing – which the workers refused to do, explaining that many of them were illiterate and all struggled to write in English. Blou and Sinclair then asked the workers to tell them their demands, and allow them to relay the workers' messages to the management. Again, the workers refused. They repeated their request to speak directly to Lonmin's managers, and only to them.

The security officers stepped back, and moved quickly to Lonmin's main office. They spoke to the Executive Manager for Human Capital, Abram Kgotle, and told him that the crowd was demanding to speak directly to management. According to Blou and Sinclair, Kgotle refused to come out. He said that he would not speak to a 'faceless crowd', or a 'crowd of people without identifiable leadership' – and insisted that he would only engage with demands sent through the NUM.[16]

As Blou, Sinclair and Kgotle were talking behind the walls of Lonmin's office, the crowd was growing restive. They had now been waiting in the sun and on the road for hours, without anything to show for it. It was becoming obvious that no one from Lonmin's management was going to come out from their offices and walk the short way down the road to talk to them. Instead of sitting on the ground, they began to stand and shuffle forward – squeezing slowly past the policemen and their vehicles, and beginning to inch forward in the direction of the offices.

A little later, Sinclair returned to the crowd to tell them that the managers would not come out – and that they should instead go to the majority union, the NUM, and have it speak on their behalf. The crowd did not accept this, and over the next hour slowly crossed the six hundred metres to the office. Between 13:00 and 14:00, they gathered outside the office. They were singing, and making noise. Some were toyi-toying, dancing to keep their spirits up. There was no way to miss their presence.

And still, neither Kgotle nor any other representative of Lonmin's management would come out.

* * *

Vusi Mabuyakhulu saw the crowd's spokesmen trying to intervene, moving to speak to Sinclair and the other Lonmin staff outside the offices: 'The five that were selected went in and after some time returned back to us and made the

---

15 This is captured in the videos recorded by Lonmin security officers and the police on 10 August 2014, and put into evidence at the Marikana Commission. See, in particular, Exhibit W 4 – Video of 10 August 2012.
16 Exhibit FFFF 1 – Statement of Graeme Sinclair, para. 25. Also, Exhibit RRRR 1.1 – Statement of GM Blou, para. 19.

following report, that the employer had said to them that the NUM had said they should, the employer should not talk to us'. The crowd were confused by this, and asked them to put pressure on Lonmin: 'We asked them to return back to the employer to go and ask what should be done next. They came back to us and reported that the employer says we can do what we want... This is where the problem started'.[17]

The workers were at an impasse. The mine's management would not listen to their demands. It ignored their reluctance to approach the NUM, or any union. And – if what their representatives was telling them was true – it was now dismissing them outright.

At this point, the crowd chose to leave the offices. According to Blou, the crowd was unhappy, muttering threats. According to Sinclair, the crowd was 'showing displeasure and displaying aggressive behaviour'.[18] Video footage only shows the crowd dispersing, trudging up the road. They walked back the way that they had come, and ended up at the stretch of dry land outside the Wonderkop Stadium – where they had met yesterday, and where they had left from left early that morning.

The workers turned over the events of the day – the excitement of the march, the tension of its interruption, and the disappointment they faced at its end. They thought about what to do next: whether they should accept the management's insistence that they approach the NUM first, and, if so, how they should do so, and what kind of relationship they should adopt with the union. They talked through these ideas, going backwards and forth sharing their thoughts, but did not manage to reach any conclusions. Instead, they decided to meet again the next day.[19]

And so, at the end of the afternoon, the men scattered. Most, now tired out, went back to their beds, spoke to their families, and slept – preparing for the next day.

Some, though, wandered over to the entrances of the mines, and approached small groups of miners who were coming off work – miners, that is, who had not joined the rock drill operators' march. They were spoiling for some kind of fight. At least some of these miners confronted their colleagues, either asking or demanding that they support the rock drill operators' action. They challenged them outside the mine gates, and at the entrances of the mine's buses. They fought. Two workers were said to have been assaulted by the rock drill operators after night fell.[20]

---

17 Mabuyakhulu, Day 48, pp. 5,265–5,266.
18 Exhibit FFFF 1, Sinclair, para. 28.
19 Mabuyakhulu, Day 49, p. 5,266.
20 Exhibit YY 1 – Statement of Malesela William Setelele, paras 10–14. This statement sets out some of the complaints received by the NUM about assaults on its members, and the actions of the union in response. See also Exhibit EEEE 19.2 – Hard Copy of Lonmin Karee RDO OB, which is a document that provides a contemporary record

However, these were not the only groups moving in the dark. At the same time, NUM members were driving around in a Toyota Quantum van, loaned to the union by Lonmin, picking up workers from the shafts and dropping them off at their hostels and homes.[21] Security guards clashed violently with workers – driving past in cars, firing rubber bullets seemingly at random, at anyone they suspected of being involved in the strike, or of intimidating other workers.[22] Walking home was dangerous that evening – and the whole town was on edge. But the only two men shot and wounded by these security guards were themselves returning from work.

Although these events happened in the dark, several hours after the end of the march, they gave rise to fast-spreading rumours – and in the morning the stories that emerged around these clashes began to shape the rock drill operators' actions.

'Why don't we go to the NUM?'

'We met again the following day at about 9 o'clock', Vusi Mabuyakhulu remembered afterwards.

> We discussed, people came with different views, seeing things differently about what transpired on the 10th. As a result of these discussions some people came out with ideas that why don't we go to the NUM and ask them why is it that they don't want the employer to talk to us?

As they considered the events of the previous day, and the frustrations they had felt, they were also discussing the events of the night that had just past – particularly the clashes between security officers and workers. The rumours that surrounded these events conflated the NUM's actions with Lonmin's: 'A report was also received by others … that some people had been shot by members of the NUM who were driving around in a Quantum [vehicle] that is owned by the mine'. These were supplemented by fresh rumours, that the company and union wanted to break the work stoppage: 'There were also reports … that some of the people that had gathered there with us later went to the buses to go and find out what is happening, and when they arrived at the buses … guns were pointed at them and they were told to get to work.'[23]

---

of 'occurrences' at the Karee mine. This confirms the general testimony of Setelele.
21   Testimony of Mabuyakhulu, Day 48, p. 5,267. According to Setelele (Exhibit YY1), this van was used to ferry workers away from sites of potential conflict.
22   Or, from the perspective of the guards: 'We approached this group in our vehicle (a Nissan Livina). Kellerman and I fired rubber bullets in the direction of the group, aimed at their legs'. Exhibit ZZZZ 32 – Witness Statement of Pieter Willem (PW) Botha, para. 14. Mabuyakhulu's testimony seems to suggest that some of the striking workers may have conflated the Toyota Quantum van – used by the union – with the Nissan Livina used by Lonmin's security officers, and assigned responsibility for the shootings to the union by mistake.
23   Mabuyakhulu, Day 48, pp. 5,266–5,267.

All of this was circulating in the rock drill operators' minds when they decided to march from the area outside the Stadium to the NUM's office in Marikana. They had heard that the company would only engage with the NUM – and many of them may have believed that this was at the NUM's insistence. They had heard rumours that members of the NUM were trying to force them back to work, and confused the union's actions with those of Lonmin's security guards during the night. By now, there was no doubt that they had embarked upon a strike – an action that went beyond their plan to speak to the managers, but that now incorporated a challenge to the union system.

About three hundred miners left the strip of land outside the Stadium, at about 11:00, and began to move towards the NUM offices. They moved off in smaller groups, a few dozen at a time. Several men were carrying tall, thin sticks – some with carved, rounded ends, others painted white or black. A small number were carrying long knives, and sharpened tools, which they banged together to create a beat. At least one man was carrying a musical instrument, a thin metal string stretched along a gourd-shaped body. [24] The workers sang as they marched forwards.

Confusion about their intentions reigned. Lonmin's security officers had heard rumours that the crowd planned to burn the offices of the NUM, and to assault any union officials that they found there. They drove to the NUM offices, ahead of the crowd, and told the union officials of these rumours. At this point, according to the chairperson of the NUM's Western Platinum branch office at Marikana, Malesela Setelele, the union started to prepare itself for the crowd's arrival by arming its members:

> There were at the time a number of weapons such as knobkerries, sticks and spears at the NUM office. That was not usually the case. Ordinarily there would be none. Some of the weapons that were there that morning had been taken away from strikers in the course of the night before. Others had been brought in by members who had gone home to fetch them in response to their experience of threats and intimidatory conduct by strikers.

The union officials decided to parcel out these weapons to 'those who decided to defend the NUM office against the approaching strikers'.[25]

Another NUM official, Saziso Gegeleza, was on site at the NUM branch office that morning. He joined a group of shop-stewards at the NUM offices, and was given a knobkerrie and a spear by the Branch Secretary.

---

24 These sticks can be seen in the videos filmed by Lonmin security, and put into evidence at the Commission: Exhibits X1–X6 – Video of 11 August 2012. See, for example X3, which shows a group of men walking slowly down the road, singing, while being followed by the videographer in a moving vehicle. The sticks are clearly visible. The knives, tools, and musical instrument can also be seen.
25 Exhibit YY 1 – Statement of Malesela William Setelele.

> We then all moved out of the office and onto the road ... There was a good deal of anxious discussion about what we should do. Although many people spoke in favour of remaining and trying to protect the office, it was clear that most of us, if not all, were very afraid of the strikers given the information that we had received.

Gegeleza and about twenty of his colleagues decided to stay near the office, waiting fearfully for the strikers.[26]

In this atmosphere of tension, mistrust and misunderstanding – in which the marching workers believed the NUM sought to undercut their strike, and to keep them from speaking to Lonmin's managers, and in which shop-stewards and NUM officials believed that the workers were marching to destroy their offices and assault them – there could have been little hope on either side for a simple resolution.

What came, though, was beyond what either could have reasonably expected.

Mabuyakulu was moving with his fellow strikers when he saw 'members of the NUM who were singing a song ... The first thing I heard was AMCU Karee'.[27] Gegeleza, on the other side of the clash, saw a crowd of strikers moving towards him. He believed that they were throwing stones.

Then – from Gegeleza's view, just 'when we were just about then to meet these strikers so that it would be clear as to whether a fight would start or whatever would happen' – a gunshot rang out. The NUM members ran out, chasing the striking workers – 'we never wanted them to plan a second attack'.[28] They chased the workers towards a fence, and at least one more shot was fired.

Mabuyakulu turned and ran.

> As we were running away, I saw one person dropping, I thought he had been hit ... as we were running round there, I felt some cold substance on my back as I was running. I told some other people with whom I was running because I'd become aware of the fact that I'd been shot, I drew their attention to the fact that I was shot but I tried to run away.

He stumbled onwards, trying to escape the shooting.

> I tried to run away, turning towards the buses, the bus rank, and as I was going up, when I entered the main road my right hand side just became dizzy and I collapsed. It was difficult for me to come up after I'd fallen. The NUM members were following me from behind. They found me lying there.

---

26   Exhibit ZZ 2 – Statement of Saziso Albert Gegeleza. See also, Testimony of Saziso Albert Gegeleza at the Marikana Commission of Inquiry, Day 39 (29 January 2013).
27   Mabuyakulu, Day 48, pp. 5,268–5,271. The following quotes come from his description on these pages.
28   Gegeleza, Day 39, pp. 4,245–4,259.

Mabuyakulu tried to pretend that he hadn't been part of the strike, but the union members saw through his evasions. They insisted that he had been marching.

> One of them that I could see was standing on my left hand side … had a spear but he hit me on the back with the handle of the spear until it broke. There was one who was standing right in front of me wearing white overalls and with an NUM T-shirt. He had a butcher's knife. I felt a blow to the back of my head … from there I lost consciousness.

* * *

He survived. Mabuyakulu was one of two men injured by bullets fired from in or around the NUM offices.[29] He woke up in hospital, dazed and wounded, having been beaten up as well as shot. He spent the next several days there, missing the conflicts and clashes that would follow. In fact, no one died on this day.

But in the hospital, he could not communicate with his fellow workers – and rumours once again began to spread. Dozens of men had heard the gunfire from the NUM offices. Many had seen some men fall, bleeding, before their bodies were lost to sight: to confusion, to clouds of dust, and to their worst imaginings. Before long, the two men were thought to have been killed – and the striking workers believed they were in danger, their strike was threatened, and that they must defend themselves.[30]

The first deaths

On the morning of 12 August, the striking workers gathered together once more – this time, though, they were almost all clearly armed. Most of the workers carried weapons similar to those that Siphethe Phatsha, one of Lonmin's workers who stood on the edge of the strike in its first days, remembered carrying: a long knife, sometimes described as a 'bush knife' or a 'butcher knife' or a panga, and a sharpened iron rod. These were weapons and tools that were easily available: a long knife

---

29 The other was Bongani Ngema, another striking mineworker. Both were admitted to the local hospital, and police dockets were opened into their injuries – but these dockets seem never to have been seriously investigated, and no prosecutions have followed.

30 The rumour was widespread, and repeated at several points in the days to come. Exhibit Z 1 – Video of 13 August 2012 and its transcription as Exhibit QQ 2 – Transcript of Video Clip record at least two striking workers stating that the NUM had killed two of their fellow strikers. This belief was confirmed in Exhibit HHH 14 – Statement of Lt-Col Stephen James McIntosh, where he indicates that he was told by a prominent striking worker that members of the NUM had killed striking workers. Although this was not true, there is no indication that this belief was insincerely held – the disappearance of Mabuyakhulu and Ngema after the incident was never explained, and their presence in the hospital was not known.

would be used for all sorts of household tasks, to carve meat, trim rope, cut small chunks of wood. The sharpened rod – also described as an *incula* – was commonly used in cultural rituals, as well as in self-defence in the dark of the nights.[31]

According to Phatsha, at least some workers were carrying weapons because they believed that two men had been killed in the clash outside the NUM's offices the previous day – and they feared that more violence would follow. The workers believed that their weapons would help them defend themselves. Phatsha argued strongly that there was no co-ordination of this decision – and that there was no need for any. In his words – 'each person made his own decision, or decided on himself that he will carry his own weapon'. Once this decision had been made – whether by a majority of the striking workers or, perhaps, by a minority – the rest soon armed themselves.

An armed crowd thus gathered and, having been frustrated in their attempts first to approach Lonmin's managers on Friday and then to approach NUM officials on Saturday, now had to decide where to go.

In the early hours, they milled around without a clear destination. Phatsha saw between ten and twenty people gather in the morning, before he left the group. A Lonmin employee reported that a crowd of thirty people had gathered by about 08:00. An hour and a half later, other Lonmin employees reported a 'mob' moving in the direction of Nkaneng and one of the mine's hostels. Near the hostel, a group of Lonmin security officers confronted two groups of strikers – a small group of about fifty men, and a larger group of around a thousand. One of the strikers threw a stone. In response, two of Lonmin's security officers opened fire – with rubber bullets – while trying to retreat. These officers were caught by the crowd, beaten and cut, before they were able to climb into a waiting car and drive rapidly away.[32]

Meanwhile, one of the security officers called for backup. The radio control room passed this call on to a nearby security team. This team included Frans Mabelane and Hassan Fundi, two of the senior security officers on duty that day. Both were in their late forties.[33] Mabelane was a member of the Bapo ba Mogale, and had been born near Segwaelane. Fundi was a migrant, born in Malawi, who had moved with his family to the Rustenberg area. They had worked for Lonmin

---

31 Testimony of Siphethe Phatsha at the Marikana Commission of Inquiry, Day 50 (20 February 2013), pp. 5,457–5,460. See also the discussion of the appropriate translation of '*incula*' between Captain Mohlaki and the Commission's Evidence Leaders during the Testimony of Captain Mohlaki, Day 7 (31 October 2012), pp. 702–204.

32 Exhibit EEEE 19.2 – Hard Copy of Lonmin RDO OB. See the entries for the morning of 12 August 2012. ZZZZ 32 – Statement of Botha; Exhibit FFFF 1 – Statement of Sinclair; RRRR 1.1 – Statement of Blou.

33 See the presentations made by their families at the Marikana Commission: Exhibit KKKK 36 – Mabelane, and KKKK 1 – Statement prepared by Mrs Fundi.

for years, marrying and bringing up children in the area. That morning, they had reported for duty no doubt knowing that tensions were flaring – but not knowing what it would bring.

The security team moved to respond to the call. According to Mogomotsi Masibi, another Lonmin security guard who was on duty that morning, about six security vehicles and a dozen security guards met on the road. There, Mabelane told them that a group of striking workers was heading towards the NUM offices again, with the aim of burning them. He told the guards that they would line up and fire rubber bullets at the workers, forcing them to scatter. At the time, the guards did not know about the attack on their colleagues – and although not all agreed with Mabelane's instruction, they seemed to believe that rubber bullets would be sufficient to disperse the crowd, protect the mine's property, and restore a degree of order to a very volatile situation.[34]

As these instructions were given, the crowd was approaching the guards' position.

The guards were nervous. Some shouted, trying to warn the crowd off, to stop the strikers from moving forward. Others panicked. Without an order being given, one of the guards started shooting rubber bullets from his shotgun. Within seconds, others joined in – Masibi remembers firing off seven rounds, without seeing any effect. The crowd did not disperse. They did not scatter. Instead, they continued to move quickly and forcefully towards the gathered guards.

Out of the corner of his eye, Masibi saw the other guards pulling back, letting their useless weapons dangle at their sides, and retreating. As the crowd grew closer, they began to run. Masibi ran past a car, and climbed into a security van. He fired another seven shots, trying to break the crowd in front of the van. The crowd thinned enough for them to drive hurriedly away.

In the chaos, and the panic, he did not think to check who was with them. It was only afterwards, when they reached the local hospital, and regrouped, that he realized that neither Frans Mabelane nor Hassan Fundi were with them. The last time Masibi had seen them, he had been running and had passed a small car. They had been trapped in that car, surrounded by a crowd. They had been left behind.

The guards now looked back at the site of confrontation, and saw a plume of filthy smoke rising up. None of the guards could see either of their missing colleagues.

In this crush, someone had set the car on fire – with both Frans Mabelane and Hassan Fundi inside. In the next violent moments, Fundi was pulled out of the car, and stabbed and slashed with sharp weapons – with knives, with sharpened rods. He was killed on the ground. Mabelane was left, and burned to death in the car.

They were the first people to die during the strike at Marikana.

---

34   Exhibit AAAA 37 – Statement of Joseph Masibi. Exhibit DDDD 7 – Statement of Masibi.

* * *

The afternoon that followed was chaotic: the crowd scattered from the site of the deaths, a police helicopter flew overhead, security officers returned to rescue the bodies of their colleagues. Uncertainty ruled. Some workers gathered at the small hill – the koppie just to one side of the Wonderkop Stadium and the main road through Marikana and the settlement – that had begun to serve as a meeting place for the strike. Others retreated to their homes in the informal settlement. And yet others continued to mill around the area, moving alone or in small groups.

As night fell, groups of striking workers began to spread out again. They moved towards the mine, once again confronting their still-working colleagues at bus ranks, challenging them for their decision to continue working while the strike was underway. Some strikers threw stones at passing cars. By about 20:00 – twelve hours since the first group had gathered in the morning – the air was thick with tension, this time as striking workers gathered at Lonmin's K4 Shaft in Marikana.

Between 20:00 and 21:00, a crowd reached the shaft and clambered over the wire fencing. Hermanus Andries Janse Van Vuuren, a diesel mechanic working the night shift, saw strikers throw blankets over the razor-wire, and push the barrier down. He shouted at the crowd, telling them to 'stop now with your nonsense!'[35] When this failed to slow them, he ran – pelted with stones, and threatened by the sight of sharp blades and heavy sticks. He hid behind a rock wall, and listened to the sounds of the crowd. He heard them move through the parking lot. He saw the glow of flames, as cars were set on fire. He would have felt the warmth of the fire in the air.

> After a while it was quiet and so I stood up. I saw that the lights in the car park were no longer on. The only light that there was came from the cars that I saw were on fire. I then walked towards the front of the car park. I saw that somebody was lying on the ground next to a Toyota Avante motor vehicle, which was also on fire … I saw that he had been hit with what I assumed was a panga over his eyes and chin. He was bleeding heavily … I grabbed hold of this man's feet and dragged him away from the burning motor vehicle. He was still able to speak and complained about being in a lot of pain. I told him not to worry because the ambulance was coming soon.[36]

This man was Thapelo Mabebe. At the time, he was thirty-seven years old, and working as a crane operator at Lonmin's Marikana mine. He had three children, the oldest of whom was twenty and the youngest, two. He supported them, as well as his five siblings.[37] He had reported for duty that day, and was

---

35   Exhibit EEEE 27 – Statement of Janse Van Vuuren.
36   EEEE 27 – Janse Van Vuuren, para. 7.
37   The presentation made by his family at the Commission provides some informa-

caught up in the violence of the striking workers' invasion of the K4 complex. No one saw exactly what happened, but he must have been rushed by a group of armed strikers. There must have been a clash. And he must have been hit with a heavy blade.

After a while, he and the others – including Janse Van Vuuren – were taken to the hospital for treatment. Janse Van Vuuren saw him stretched out on a bed, with a mask over his face. He leaned over: 'I felt the man's feet and they were very cold'. At the moment, Janse Van Vuuren knew that this man was dead. A little later, a doctor confirmed it. 'I am informed that this man's name is Thapelo Eric Mabebe'.[38]

And so, Thapelo Mabebe became the third person to die during the strike.

Conversations in the night

Meanwhile, during the nights between the march on 10 August and the first deaths on 12 August, miners were calling their families. They shared their experiences, their hopes, and their fears with their wives, cousins, and parents. Jackson Lehupa told his wife, Zameka, that they had gone on strike for a greater wage. Afterwards, she tried to remember the conversations: 'He would just generalize about the strike. But I gathered from what he said that he had hope that there could be a possible solution, and that the employer would come down and speak to them'.[39]

Semi Jokanisi and his father, Lunga, worked on the same shaft in Marikana. Both had been in Marikana during July, and during the initial attempts of workers' committees to negotiate with management. Lunga took leave at the end of July and returned to the family in Lusikisiki, in the Eastern Cape. Semi remained at work. He was a winch-operator, and he kept a close eye on the events at Marikana as they were unfolding. He called home every day. 'Even on the day that the strike began, he called me and told me that the strike was on … on Friday, he said to me that they were downing tools on Saturday. The RDOs had blocked the way to work'.[40]

Lunga Jokanisi had experiences of strikes in the past: 'I know how people can get hurt in a strike. I realized that at a previous company that I worked for where a similar strike to this one had taken place. A lot of people got hurt there, too.' He needed Semi to understand the danger: 'I said to him, hey man, try to watch your back now because strikes are dangerous. You have to watch your back when you're on strike and not be in the frontlines. You have to be in the mix of the people.'

---

    tion about his life: KKKK 33 – Eric Thapelo Mabebe.
38 EEEE 2 – Janse Van Vuuren, para. 10.
39 Interview with Zameka Nungu, Matatiele, 4 December 2015.
40 Interview with Lunga Jokanisi, Lusikisiki, 2 December 2015.

Still, Semi was eager to take part in the strike. He was part of the marches on Saturday and Sunday, and spoke to his father each evening. He went to the meetings on the koppie beside the Wonderkop Stadium, and kept himself involved. He was 29 years old, and deeply excited by the possibility of these events.

Both Jackson Lehupa and Semi Jokanisi had been in the strike from the beginning. Other workers, though, found themselves being drawn to it during these days – despite the growing dangers.

Early in the strike, Thembelakhe Mati told his wife, Florence, that he was watching the strike and thinking of joining. He told her not to call him back, because he would not be able to keep his phone on him during the day. He said that he would call, and keep her up to date. Florence tried to warn Thembelakhe, but he would have none of it. He was confident, and joked with her: 'he mocked me for being chicken, and said that on second thought, he should not have told me'.[41]

Thembelakhe also spoke to his cousin, back in the Eastern Cape. He sketched the progress of the strike for Lanford, and shared his expectations with him:

> He even went so far as saying that he wanted to take some time off but that he [also] wanted to stick around and see how far this thing would go … He never told me in detail about the strike because he was never at the helm of it. He joined later because at first it was a matter between the machine operators. He joined it later.

They spoke on the evening of 12 August, and Thembelakhe said that he had 'decided to join the meeting and started walking with them … I think he wanted to sit in and to ascertain what was going on. So he said to himself, let me go and find out for myself'.[42]

It was possible for men like Thembelakhe Mati, or Semi Jokanisi, to see the strike as part of a broader struggle: not simply as a fight for an increase in the salaries of rock drill operators alone, but rather as part of wide struggle for better working conditions, wages, and recognition from both the mining company and the official union. Although the size of the protesting group shifted from day to day – up to two thousand on Friday, down to a few hundred on Saturday, and over a thousand on Sunday – it increasingly drew men other than the rock drill operators.[43] Mati, Jokanisi, and others joined the strike and helped it swell beyond its original core.

Perhaps, on the first days, it may have seemed like an ordinary strike. On Friday, the marching workers had faced recalcitrant managers and befuddled

---

41   Interview with Florence Mati, KuNdile, 3 December 2015.
42   Interview with Lanford Gcotyelwa, KuNdile, 3 December 2015.
43   See, for example, the Testimony of Mzoxolo Magidiwana, Day 54 (26 February 2013), pp. 5,863–5,864, where he indicates that he – and others who were not rock drill operators – began to join the strike.

security officers. On Saturday, they had planned to confront the NUM – but had, instead, fled from gunshots and an armed group of union supporters. No one had died. As serious as the injuries to Vusi Mabuyakhulu and others were, the other workers could not have been certain of what was happening. The rumours of death, though, were enough to inflame the situation – and perhaps even drive some to thoughts of revenge.

But on Sunday, the situation exploded. By midnight, three men were dead. More would follow. Everything that happened now would take place in the shadow of these deaths. There was no easy way to turn back – and no doubting the stakes.

5

Monday, 13 August 2012

On 1 February 1993, Julius Langa and Mary Segwegwe Funzama married each other in a traditional ceremony. For almost twenty years, Mary lived in their family home near Nelspruit, in Mpumulanga Province, while her husband and her brother worked four hundred kilometres away, in Marikana, where Julius was employed by Lonmin as a production team leader at the Saffy Shaft.

On Friday, 10 August 2012, Julius phoned Mary and asked her to take the long bus journey to Marikana, and to spend the weekend. She arrived on Saturday, as the shadows stretched in the afternoon.

They spent that afternoon and evening together, and then the whole of the next day. 'I spent Sunday with him, we slept and then we woke up'. At about 03:00 in the morning of 13 August, long before the sun was beginning to rise, Julius began to get ready for work. Mary rose with him.

> I woke up, I prepared food for him, and then he went away. Ja, he put his one foot outside the house, and then he asked me to lock the door, which I did. That's the moment when he was leaving ... it was at 3 o'clock when he left.

After locking the door, she prepared for her day.[1]

Julius Langa's fears for his wife's safety at home were well founded. After three days of conflict, the atmosphere in Marikana was now poisoned: by the mysterious shooting at the NUM's office on Saturday, which had put two men in hospital, and which had inflamed fears among the strikers; by the murders of two security officers and a working miner at K4 Shaft by groups of striking workers on Sunday; and by the inability of the police to identify or arrest anyone involved in either explosion of malice and violence. By the early hours of Monday morning, Marikana – the town, the mine, and the settlement – was a dry tinder box, ready to burn.

But it was not Mary who was at risk that morning. When Julius Langa left his home, and walked along the railway line through Marikana, towards where he would catch a bus to take him to the mine, he walked towards his death. At some point along this route, he was confronted by a group of unknown men.

---

[1] Statement of Mary Langa at the Marikana Commission of Inquiry, Day 290 (12 September 2014), pp. 37,806–37,811. See also: Exhibit KKKK 34 – Julius Langa.

They must have been armed with knives and spears. They attacked him. He fell to the ground, curled up around his stomach, desperately trying to protect himself, to offer as small a target as possible. It was in vain. Julius Langa was stabbed fourteen times in the back, and bled to death in the dark, on the ground beside the railway tracks.[2]

In the hours before sunrise, he became the fourth man to die at Marikana.

Dawn broke, and the men who had killed Julius Langa slipped away. We don't know who they were, or what they did next. Some may have run home, shaken, horrified, suddenly recognizing what they had done. Others may have swallowed their doubts and regrets, wiped their knives clean of his blood, and chosen to forget that they were now and for always murderers. Others may have celebrated. All of them melted into the gathering crowd, safely anonymous among their unknowing colleagues.

Julius's body lay in the dirt for several hours. At about 09:30, a police officer arrived to inspect the murder site. He recorded the brutal injuries that Langa had suffered, and tried to collect information from the people that were milling around the site. No one, though, could or would tell him anything, and he was forced to conclude that 'more than one person' had been involved in the murder – but that there were no witnesses, and no evidence to identify anyone in particular.[3]

When Mary was told, later that day, she was at once certain that he had been killed by strikers. Her mourning was mingled with fear:

> his colleagues, I am very scared of them. I didn't expect that my husband would die in that way … I put my hands on top of my head because of the loss of my husband because I've seen previously some other people did the same after they lost their husbands.[4]

Every day from now, she would have to live with the knowledge that her husband had been killed by men who might have known him – and that no one could identify them. She was haunted by the knowledge that she might even know her husband's killers.

* * *

In the first phase of the strike, acts of violence had taken place in the early hours and in the dark, committed by unidentifiable men, and committed for unknown reasons. Individuals had been murdered, and others had been assaulted, but there had been no large scale confrontation – no clash between armed groups.

On Monday, that changed. The morning began with Julius Langa's murder, and continued on into a confrontation between striking workers and the

---

2   Exhibit AAAA 23 – Affidavit of Simon Henry Kgopana.
3   AAAA 23, Kgopana, p. 2.
4   Mary Langa, Day 290 (12 September 2014), p. 37,810.

police – a confrontation that started with harsh words and ended in the deaths of five more men. This clash took place in the light of day, was partially filmed by police cameras, and involved the use of force not only by rogue strikers but by the police.

After this, the strike was no longer just a labour dispute – a fight between workers and the mine. Instead, it was now a three-way struggle between the workers, the mine, and the police. This day that had begun with Julius Langa's death would now end with the deaths of another five men – two police officers and three strikers.

The men on the 'mountain'

Of course, no one yet knew that the strike was moving into a new phase. Their thoughts were elsewhere. As the sun rose above Marikana on Monday morning, the strikers faced a dilemma: four men had been killed in Marikana in less than twenty-four hours. All had died at the hands of anonymous groups of men. The murderers were almost certainly participating in the strike. How could the strike continue after this? Did the protest have any moral foundation? What should happen next?

The murderers may have even have believed themselves to acting in the strike's best interests: by forcing workers to join them, by assaulting those who resisted, and by taking revenge for the rumoured deaths of their friends outside the NUM offices on Saturday, they may have believed that they were strengthening the strike. Their actions, though, threatened it – they undermined the conviction and courage of the striking workers, drove a wedge between the strike and the communities of Marikana, and brought the force of the police to bear upon the other miners.[5]

In this context, something had to change. The striking workers had to be brought back together, disciplined, and refocused to ensure the longevity of their action. Someone had to assume some kind of leadership role – if only to prevent the violent hotheads from taking control by default. As had happened on Friday, when a half dozen men had stepped forward to speak to Lonmin's security officers and police, so too now did other leaders step forward and assume responsibility.

---

[5] A sense of the police response can be gleaned from the reports and comments in Exhibit JJJ 128.1 – Occurrence Register Timeline 13 to 18 August 2012, and in Exhibit FFF 25 – Occurrence Register: Marikana JOC. These documents suggest a wide disruption in the daily life of the region over these days, and suggest further that the police were regularly intervening in relatively minor public clashes.

One of these new leaders was Mgcineni Noki, also known as 'Mambush'.[6] Like many miners, Noki had been born in the Eastern Cape and had moved to the mines for work. In 2009, he joined his cousin at Lonmin's mine in Marikana where he began to work as a rock drill operator. His decision to step forward as a leader was not inevitable, and his role in the strike took time to develop. He had been part of the discussion on Thursday, and present on Friday morning – but had to leave Marikana that day. His uncle had just died of tuberculosis, and so Noki and his cousin had to leave Marikana to claim the body for the family. They spent Friday at Impala Platinum's mines, where their uncle had worked – and so missed the march to the Lonmin offices. They only returned to Marikana hours later, as the strike escalated and security guards shot rubber bullets into the night.

His wife spoke to him over the phone that night. He told her that he believed that the workers needed to strike – it was the only way to force either the NUM or the mining company to act. He mistrusted the NUM's shop-stewards, and was attracted by the insurgent energies of the new union on Lonmin's mines, AMCU. Even before the strike, he had already become one of AMCU's first members at Lonmin – but he was not participating as a member of AMCU. Like all the other rock drill operators, he had agreed that union loyalties should be put to one side for the length of the protest. It was more important that the workers stood together, united in their call.

On Saturday, as rumours spread about the events of the night before, Noki joined his colleagues and friends in the march to the NUM office. Xolani Nzuza – a colleague on the mines, a friend, and the manager of the amateur football team that Noki belonged to – was there with him.[7] They were both caught up in the

---

6 Noki – 'the man in the green blanket' – has become a symbol of the protests, both in journalists' written accounts and in the photographs taken of the strike. His distinctive green blanket – worn around his shoulders – set him apart from the other striking workers. Noki was killed in the massacre, and left no first-person record of these events. The background on his life, and his wife's engagement with him in these days, is drawn from Exhibit KKKK 11 – Mgcineni 'Mambush' Noki. The account of his actions in these days come from the in-depth reporting of Nick Davies in 'Marikana Massacre: The Untold Story of The Strike Leader Who Died For Workers' Rights', *The Guardian* (UK), 19 May 2015, www.theguardian.com/world/2015/may/19/marikana-massacre-untold-story-strike-leader-died-workers-rights (Acc. November 2020).

7 Nzuza was described as the second in command of the strike – although he contested this description, arguing that it assumed a greater co-ordination among the workers than actually existed. Exhibit HHH 21 – Statement of Xolani Nzuza and Exhibit PPPP 1 – Supplementary statement of Xolani Nzuza. The initial statement (HHH 21) makes no mention of the earlier events, but does identify events on 13 August onwards. The supplementary statement (PPPP 1) describes events on 11 and 12 August 2012. See also Nzuza's oral account of the events of the strike: Testimony of

scramble that followed the shooting from the NUM office, and the rush of NUM members towards the strikers. In the panic of the moment, they fled with the crowd and made their way – running and stumbling – back to the Wonderkop Stadium.

But the stretch of dry land between the Wonderkop Stadium and the road no longer seemed a safe haven. They were now obviously exposed. Traffic moved past. Lonmin's security team could watch from across the road. The NUM's offices were close by. And the police could easily drive down the road to get to them.

The striking workers moved away from the road, and towards an area of rocky outcrops further back. They gathered on a large rocky mound, known locally as the small hill, or 'koppie', or – sometimes – as 'the mountain'. Here Noki and Nzuza stepped forward, and began to take on the responsibilities of leading the striking workers – of strengthening their courage and determination, of instilling a communal discipline, and of figuring out a workable plan of action.

That afternoon, they sought to calm the panicking workers and to re-direct their energies. Nzuza joined a group of four men, and went into the settlement to find a local *inyanga* – a traditional healer who could reassure some of the workers.[8] They brought him to the mountain, where several workers spoke to him. On the land in front of the rocks, the *inyanga* led these workers through a ritual in which they washed themselves clean, inhaled burning herbs, and focused their minds through prayer and concentration. While these men went through their rituals, the other workers remained on the mountain – some watching with interest, others bored.[9]

Xolani Nzuza at the Marikana Commission of Inquiry, Days 277, 279, and 280 (14, 27 and 28 August 2014).

8   The presence of this *inyanga*, and the implications of his actions, were passionately debated at the Commission. Mr X – who will be discussed in Chapter 13 – argued that the *inyanga* appeared multiple times during the strike, and used ritual as a tool to inflame the striking workers. One Lonmin security officer claimed to have infiltrated the group, and to have observed part of the ritual. He claimed that this ritual was intended to convince the workers that they would be shielded from future harm. This statement, though, was never tested by the Commission, and can only be found in a police docket quoted by the Commission's Evidence Leaders in their Heads of Argument (pp. 140–142). Nzuza and all other workers denied both of these interpretations. This particular engagement is the only one that can be confidently identified and confirmed, and Nzuza testified that it was a cleansing ritual. The only photograph of this – presented to Siphethe Phatsha in cross-examinastion – shows men washing themselves in the veld. See Testimony of Phatsha, Day 51 (21 February 2013), 5,570–5,572.

9   For a critical analysis of later discussions of these events – and of the ambiguities of the significance of 'tradition' and 'modernity'– see Nokuthula Hlabangane, 'Of Witch Doctors, Traditional Weapons, and Traditional Medicine: Decolonial Medi-

The ritual ended, the sun set, and the panic of the afternoon was forestalled.

Over this evening and the next days, the mountain became a site of discipline for the strike. Noki, Nzuza, and other workers assumed the responsibility of keeping the workers on the mountain, preventing ill-disciplined adventures, and keeping the peace of the strike. They did this by telling workers that different rules applied on the mountain, and in the strike – that it was a place to set aside their daily lives, and their working differences, and come together as part of a community.

A blackout on communications from the mountain was one of these rules. The miners were told to either leave their cell-phones at home during the day, or to switch them off. Almost everyone involved in the strike followed this rule religiously, warning their families not to try to talk to them during the day – but rather to wait until the evening, when they left the mountain, to hear from them. Phumzile Sokanyile, for example, told his sister that the family 'mustn't be worried if his phone is switched off because he'll be on the mountain, and when he comes back he will switch it on and update us'.[10] Sokanyile was one of the hundreds of miners who had joined the strike over the weekend. The discipline of controlling communication – of not using his phone at the mountain – was perhaps one of the ways in which he could feel a part of the strike, one with his colleagues.

These rules helped set the mountain apart from the rest of Marikana – from the mine, where everyone worked at different shafts and in different positions, where they belonged to different unions, and earned different salaries; from the town and the informal settlements, where some lived with their families and others lived alone, where some lived in hostels and others in shacks. On the mountain, none of that mattered. For the men who waited there, the strike was everything.

At the Joint Operational Centre

They were not the only actors in Marikana, though. The police and the mining company were also considering what to do about the strike – and about the violence that had erupted on Sunday.

At first, the police did not know whether to get involved in controlling the strike. On Friday, they merely followed the crowd, and stood between them and Lonmin's office. That night, they stood aside while security officers fired rubber bullets at groups of workers. On Saturday, they stood aside once again as

---

tations on the Role of the Media after the Marikana Massacre, South Africa', *African Identities*, 16:3 (2018), pp. 234–259.

10   Exhibit KKKK 35 – Phumzile Sokhanyile. (The family name is given as 'Sokhanyile' in the Commission's records of evidence and in the title of this Exhibit. It is given as 'Sokanyile' in the text itself, and where members of his family are quoted. I have therefore preferred to keep this spelling.)

armed NUM members chased the crowd of striking workers from their offices. Meanwhile, Lonmin was pressuring the police to increase their presence. On Saturday, before the clash at the NUM offices, Lonmin had telephoned the Provincial Commissioner of the police, Lieutenant-General Mirriam Mbombo, to request that more police be sent to Marikana. Mbombo agreed, and instructed her subordinates to do so.[11]

As part of this process, the police and Lonmin agreed to set up a 'Joint Operational Centre' (JOCOM) – an office and a committee that would co-ordinate the police forces and the security officers to ensure that they would not be working at cross-purposes while they sought to contain or end the strike. This Centre would act as the clearing-house for all information about violence and disruption in the course of the strike.[12]

The establishment of the Centre did not make an immediate difference. On Sunday, as the workers struggled to maintain discipline, and as anonymous crowds moved violently through the area, the police seemed at a loss. They arrived too late to prevent the deaths of Frans Mabelane and Hassan Fundi. They were not at the shaft when Thapelo Mabebe was killed. They were not there when Julius Langa died.

By Monday morning, however, the inaction – or ineffectiveness – of the police at Marikana had been noticed by more senior provincial commanders. The provincial director of crime intelligence was receiving reports of further planned attacks, and trying to convince the responsible commanders to take these threats seriously.[13] Lt-Gen. Mbombo was now concerned, and decided to come to Marikana for a meeting with Lonmin's management. With her was the Deputy Provincial Commissioner of Police, Maj.-Gen. William Mpembe – who had been on leave over the weekend, but who would now assume command over the police operations at Marikana.[14]

As these commanders moved towards Marikana, so too did ordinary police officers. They came from across the North West Province, Mpumulanga, and Gauteng. Warrant Officer Ronnie Lepaaku, for example, was stationed at the Klipgat police station on the border of the North West and Gauteng. On Sunday night, he told his family that he was being deployed to Marikana the next day. He told them that he would be late home on Monday, because he would have to travel back at night.[15] Others came from further afield. Tsietsi Monene was

---

11 Exhibit GGG 5 – Statement of Gen. Mbombo.
12 The establishment and scope of the JOCOM can be gleaned from the contents of JJJ 128.1 – Occurrence Register Timeline, and FFF 25 – Occurrence Register: Marikana JOC.
13 Exhibit JJJ 167 – Statement of Brigadier Engelbrecht, paras 3–4.
14 Exhibit GGG 12 – Statement of Gen. Mpembe.
15 Exhibit KKKK 3 – Statement regarding the death of W/O Ronnie Lephaku [Lepaaku]. See also the expanded statement as read into evidence on Day 273 of the

stationed in Mpumulanga about 150 kilometres from Marikana, and lived with his wife in Gauteng. He had less warning than Lepaaku – it was only on Monday morning that he told his wife and sister about his deployment.[16] These men were among the 121 police officers deployed from across the region to support the force at Marikana on Monday.[17]

As they were moving from their homes to the area, their commanders were meeting the company's managers. The meeting was itself fraught with tensions and dissension, at least according to Mbombo's account of it.[18] The police accused Lonmin of encouraging the strike by attempting to negotiate outside of the union bargaining structures. Lonmin placed the responsibility for the strike on union rivalry – and, in particular, on the resurgence of AMCU. Lonmin pushed the police to be more visible, and to take an active role in controlling the strike. All that they could agree on was that the murders were to be placed at the feet of the strikers.

By mid-morning, Mbombo, Mpembe, and the other police commanders had left this meeting and moved to the Joint Operational Centre – where they received news that more than a thousand workers had gathered once more on the mountain near the Wonderkop Stadium. With that morning's killing of Julius Langa in mind, the police commanders decided that some form of action – perhaps the disarming of the striking workers – would have to be taken by the day's end.

A clash begins

Meanwhile – at the same time as the police and the company were meeting – Noki, Nzuza, and the other leaders of the strike sought to hold the workers together. The group discussed what they should do next – whether they should wait on the mountain for the company's managers, or whether they should begin to march again, perhaps to the union's offices, or to the mine's offices, or the mine's shafts.

In the late morning, they came to a set of decisions. The majority of the workers would remain on the mountain, protecting each other, while a group of several dozen workers would leave and march towards Lonmin's K3 Shaft and hostel. Their motives for doing so were ambiguous, and conflicted. According to Nzuza, they either wanted to find out if anyone was working at the mine – and perhaps to find out if they could convince these workers to join the strike,

---

Commission (14 August 2014), pp. 34,862–34,867.
16 Exhibit KKKK 2 – Statement regarding the death of W/O Monene. See also the expanded statement, and comments by Mrs Monene, as read into evidence on Day 273 of the Commission (14 August 2014), pp. 34,858–34,861.
17 GGG 12, Mpembe, para. 9.
18 Testimony of General Mirriam Mbombo at the Marikana Commission of Inquiry, Day 177 (29 January 2014), pp. 21,289–21,295.

one way or another – or, alternatively, they wanted to speak to the mine's management to convince them to shut down the shaft for the day, and to allow the workers to consider the strike.[19]

Both Noki and Nzuza accompanied this group as they left the mountain, and began to walk away. Several of the men in this group were armed with heavy sticks, knives, and *incula*, as all the workers had been after Saturday.

As they moved, news spread to the police at the Joint Operational Command. Mbombo and Mpembe were both there, having just completed their meeting with the mine's management. Both believed that it was now vital that the police be seen to be operating in Marikana, and that they engage with the striking workers to 'disperse the gathering ... to conduct searches and confiscate all dangerous weapons [and to] ensure that peace prevails'.[20] The police were also instructed to try to arrest anyone that they thought had been involved in the murders.

Mpembe left the centre, and led a team of police officers to intercept the workers before they reached K3 Shaft. This team consisted of about seventy police officers, including those specially trained in Public Order Policing, five of the armoured vehicles known as Nyalas, and a helicopter flying overhead. The officers were armed, carrying stun grenades, tear-gas canisters, and their usual guns.[21]

Meanwhile, the group of striking workers had been met by a contingent of Lonmin's security guards. According to Nzuza, the guards engaged the workers in conversation and – in response to their questions – told them that all the workers at the shaft were already underground, and would thus not be able to receive the group. The guards also agreed to pass along the strikers' demands for a wage increase to the mine's management. In return, the strikers would turn back from the shaft and return to the mountain, avoiding any possible violent confrontation.[22]

The group agreed, and turned back.

They were on their way back to the mountain when the police intercepted them, and brought them to a halt near a bridge beside the railway line that ran through Marikana. The strikers stood in place for a while. Some of the men squatted down on their haunches. Others sat on the dirt. The police stood by, weapons held loosely by their sides. Meanwhile, the helicopter buzzed above all their heads.[23]

---

19 Exhibit HHH 21 – Statement of Xolani Nzuza and Exhibit PPPP 1 – Supplementary statement of Xolani Nzuza. See also Testimony of Xolani Nzuza at the Marikana Commission of Inquiry, Days 277, 279, and 280 (14, 27 and 28 August 2014).
20 Quoted from JJJ 128.1 – Occurrence Register Timeline. A note dated 12:45 on 13 August records the agreement of the JOC, and is signed by Mbombo.
21 GGG 12, Mpembe, para. 9.
22 Exhibit HHH 52 – Statement of Geon Kellerman, records the encounter. HHH 21 – Nzuza describes this meeting at para. 7. Exhibit IIIII 61 – Video of 13 August 2012, shows the workers turning back from their path after this meeting.
23 Some part of this scene is captured in a video taken from the helicopter: Exhibit

At about 14:00, shortly after the police had stropped the march, Mpembe reached the site. He approached the workers. Noki and his colleagues spoke to him. The discussion was tense, but respectful. The workers addressed Mpembe as their elder, speaking quietly and calling him *'tata'* – 'father'.[24] Mpembe asked them to surrender their weapons. They workers refused. They said they were carrying weapons to defend themselves after they had been assaulted by Lonmin's security guards and by the NUM members – not because they sought to attack anyone.

A video recorded the conversation between the workers and the General. 'We are not fighting with anybody', a worker said, 'there was just something we wanted to fix in Lonmin. We came out and found the security that guards the mine … The security tried to shoot at us … We were not fighting … We were just delivering our response … We are not fighting with the government'.

They suggested that they would be willing to give up their weapons if they believed themselves to be safe from attack. They asked the police to escort them to the mountain:

> We did not come here to fight but if you think we came here with malicious intentions … Then it is better that you should go with us, our weaponry in hand … All the way to where we have settled … And we will show you that we are not fighting.

Once there, they would give up the weapons.

> And if you still want to take these weapons then you can take all of them there … We request that you come with us to the workers that we have left behind … At the time we take a decision that we are handing over these weapons … The only person we are disputing with is the one who is attacking us.

They asked that the police bring Lonmin's managers to the mountain, to talk to the miners. 'After you will bring the boss from the mine … The one that we want money from … To give us a response on our money … Then we will give you our weapons … We will do so graciously'.

For a while, the conversation seemed fruitful. Mpembe listened to the workers, and seemed willing to consider their requests. He asked questions, and debated them.

But this engagement did not last. Mpembe stepped away, so as to confer with his colleagues on the site and at the Joint Operational Command centre. According to his account, he explained the situation to Lt-Gen. Mbombo and

---

HHH 61 – Video of 13 August 2012, protestors on the way to Karee mine. See also footage used in an Al Jazeerah news report: Exhibit PPPP 4 – Video footage of 13 August 2012 incident.

24 This and the following direct quotes come from Exhibit Z 1 – SAPS Video (13 August 2012) and QQ 2 – Transcript of Exhibit Z1. The video and its transcription are edited and translated, but provide clear evidence of the exchanges between the strikers and police.

the others. He told them that he wanted to disarm the miners, 'but in the case that they don't disarm, or in the case where they don't voluntarily disarm, we are going to escort them'. He said that he believed that they agreed with him about this approach, and that they left him with the authority to act as he felt best in the situation.[25]

If this is true, then Mpembe's immediate action after ending this telephone call is inexplicable. He abandoned the discussions that he had been having with the workers, and discarded the approach that he has said that he laid out on the telephone. Instead of continuing to engage the striking workers, he turned back to them and shouted out a command – yelling at the workers to drop their weapons.

'I am going to take these spears', Mpembe barked. 'I am counting now! I am counting!'

In response, a miner calls out, shocked at the sudden change: 'I am begging of you sir … Please listen to me … let us return to the place we have settled on'.

And then the recording cuts off.

* * *

Mpembe did not yield. The miners' cries did not stop him. He continued to call his count – one, two, three… And so, the miners picked themselves up off of the ground, unbent their knees, and began to back away from the gathered police. They moved quietly, slowly, and steadily – seeking their return to the mountain.

For a few minutes, little changed. The miners moved. The police kept their distance – following, watching, but not doing anything that could spark a violent confrontation.

This hushed peace was soon degraded, though. Mpembe saw a nearby branch of the informal settlement alongside the workers' path. He instructed his officers to stop the workers – to prevent them from approaching the shacks, to stop the march, and to act to forcibly disarm the workers. According to a police officer on the ground, Mpembe ordered them to prepare to use one tear-gas canister and two rounds of rubber bullets for each person that they saw in the moving crowd.[26]

And then, without warning, a police officer fired his tear-gas canisters.[27]

---

25   Testimony of Mzondase William Mpembe at the Marikana Commission of Inquiry, Day 145 (8 November 2013), p. 16,034.
26   Exhibit HHH 31 – Statement of Const. Benjamin Mahume, para. 6.
27   There is a controversy over whether or not Mpembe ordered the police to fire. There is, however, absolute consensus that after the first, possibly accidental, discharge the police opened fire with tear gas and stun grenades indiscriminately. See the statements of several police officers on the site: Exhibit WWW 5 – Statement from Const. Mabe, Exhibit QQQ – Consolidated statement of Lt-Col Merafe, Exhibit GGG 16 – Statement of Lt S.S. Baloyi, Exhibit HHH 15.1 – Statement of

The canisters hit the ground by the workers, and exploded – pouring bitter white clouds of gas into the afternoon air. For one confused moment, the workers struggled to hold their disciplined calm. They kept moving forward, trying to ignore the noise and the smoke, their stinging eyes and their burning throats, the threat and their fear. They held themselves still, kept themselves calm.

And then, a stun grenade was fired by a police officer. It flashed twice: blinding and deafening. The miners broke. They began to run. They scattered, fleeing the billowing clouds of gas and noise. The wind caught the gas, spreading the white cloud. No one could see through burning eyes. Some workers ran forward, some to escape from the sides, and others – disorientated – ran towards the police line.[28]

Chaos broke out. The police were primed to attack the workers, and now did so. They fired more stun grenades and more tear-gas canisters. They fired the rubber bullets that they had been preparing. From above, the police officers in the helicopter dropped yet more grenades and canisters. The noise shattered the air. The clouds covered the ground. Workers and the police ran, stumbled, and fell.

In the confusion that followed, in the clouds of tear gas and smoke, in the noise and terror, five men died – two officers of the police, and three of the striking workers.

The clash turns deadly

Warrant Officer Tsietsi Monene was forty-seven years old when he left his home and his family in Mpumalanga on Monday morning, and came to Marikana. He was part of the police operation under Maj.-Gen. Mpembe's command, and had watched over the workers as they waited by the railway line. He would have listened to Mpembe arguing with the workers, and he would have shouldered his weapon, loosened his stun grenades, and prepared himself for a confrontation.

In the chaos that followed the explosions of tear gas and stun grenades thrown into the crowd of workers, Monene was almost lost to sight – his fellow officers could barely see through the clouds, and struggled to identify one man among the moving figures. Maj.-Gen. Mpembe thought he saw him in the crowd, about fifteen metres away from him. In the noise and confusion, no one could hear, no one could tell who was screaming in fear, or in pain, or in desolation, or in anger.[29]

Samuel K. Thupe. See also: Exhibit OOO 20 – CALS Analysis of Exhibits Z2 and Z3 (use of tear gas and stun grenades on 13 August).

28   OOO 20 – CALS Analysis, provides an account of the movement seen on video footage that has been redacted by the Commission because it may depict individual violent deaths.

29   See the statements by officers at the site, referenced above: WWW 5 – Mabe; QQQ 1 – Merafe; GGG 16 – Baloyi' HHH 15.1 – Thupe.

In these moments, Monene was confronted by a group of panicking workers. He was lost in the tear gas that he and his colleagues had fired, dazed by his own stun grenades. The world would have been spinning around him. And when he faced a group of men who believed that the police were attacking them, he was not able to defend himself against their sudden violence. Monene was assaulted with a series of sharp weapons – knives, spears – and slashed and stabbed in a hurried assault. Mpembe believed that there were five assailants, and that they killed Monene, although he could not identify any of them with any certainty. It didn't matter. Monene collapsed. By the time any officer could reach him, he was beyond help.[30]

He was one of two police officers killed that morning. Warrant Officer Ronnie Lepaaku also found himself caught apart from his colleagues. A devout member of the Zion Christian Church, and the secretary of his local parish organization, Lepaaku might have offered up a brief prayer as he turned and ran from the scattering workers. Another officer saw him trip, and fall. Armed workers followed him, and leapt on him. He was stabbed and killed as bullets cut through the air, as stinging smoke blinded him, and as his colleagues watched, unable to reach him.[31]

* * *

If there had been any hope that further violence could be avoided, that the police would regain control over themselves, and exercise restraint, then the deaths of Warrant Officers Monene and Lepaaku brought that to an end. In the moments that followed, the violence of the afternoon increased – and left three more men dead.

At twenty-nine years old, Semi Jokanisi was the youngest of these men. He was shot by the police, about a hundred metres from the first clash. The bullets that killed him entered his shoulder, hip and back, slicing into his spine and crippling him. He stumbled to the ground, bleeding, as the police caught up with him. He was handcuffed, and restrained, his body pushed into the dust and dirt.[32]

It was only a day earlier that Semi's father had spoken to him about the dangers of protesting, warning him of the risks that he was taking by being on the frontline of the strike. Semi, though, believed in the struggle – in his desperate need for a living wage, an income capable of supporting his five children, and his extended family. And so he continued to struggle, to join the frontline of the

---

30 Monene's death is described by Mpembe in his testimony, in greatest detail on Day 119 (13 August 2013), pp. 12,263–12,271.
31 The fullest description of Lepaaku's death is that given by Merafe in QQQ 1 – Merafe, at paras 5.20–5.23.
32 Exhibit KKK 4 – Statement prepared on behalf of the late Jokanisi. For details of his injuries, see Exhibit ZZZZ 33 – Dr Naidoo report in respect of Mr Jokanisi.

strike, and to stake his body and his life on the outcome of the ongoing fight – whatever might happen.[33]

Now, the worst had happed. He lay on the ground, bound and handcuffed. Heavy blood poured out of his wounds, spilling onto the hungry dirt. The life left his body. Semi Jokanisi died on the ground, unable to move, while nearby police holstered their weapons, counted their own losses, and paid no attention to him or his pain.

Meanwhile, other police officers were chasing after groups of fleeing workers. About half a kilometre away from the initial clash, police and workers met again. The workers were running, the police following. The police fired their weapons, sending bullets into the backs of the retreating workers. Phumzile Sokanyile was in this group, running from the police along with his colleagues, when he fell behind.

The police saw him separate from the crowd. At least three policemen fired in the direction of Sokanyile, leaving dozens of cartridge shells on the ground around him.

Phumzile Sokanyile was shot once in the face. He must have been looking at the men who shot him. He may have turned to see them coming up behind him. The bullet passed through his cheek, sliced through his neck, and cut his spine. He staggered, and fell. He hit the ground face-forward. He was forty-eight years old.[34]

Thembelakhe Mati was fifty. He had last spoken to his wife, Florence, and his cousin, Lanford, over the weekend. He had shared his hopes for the strike, and dismissed Florence's fears for his safety.[35] On Monday, he had joined his colleagues at the mountain – and as the day passed, he had followed Noki, Nzuza and the other leaders on their march towards the K3 Shaft. As the leaders spoke to Maj.-Gen. Mpembe, he crouched on the edge of the crowd, listening. As the discussion collapsed, he too stood and began the slow, shuffling retreat towards the mountain.

When the police fired stun grenades and tear-gas canisters into the crowd, Thembelakhe ran. He split from the crowd, and moved towards some nearby shacks – homes where he might have hoped to evade the police, or where he might have found shelter from the stinging clouds of gas and the shattering explosions.

The shacks provided no shelter, no safety. The police fired bullets in the direction he was running, towards the shacks. They did not discriminate between protestors and bystanders, between those who might have taken part in the attacks on their colleagues, and those who were innocent. They fired without care or caution.

33 Interview with Lunga Jokanisi, Lusikisiki, 2 December 2015.
34 See Exhibit ZZZZ 34 – Dr Naidoo report in respect of Mr Sokhanyile [sic].
35 For Mati's life, see my Interview with Florence Mati, KuNdile, 3 December 2015.

Thembelakhe almost made it to safety. But as he ran, he was hit by the police bullets and began to bleed. His body weakened, and his legs gave way. He collapsed near the shacks, about two hundred metres away from the main clash. His body was marked by these vicious wounds: bullet holes in his thigh and buttocks, scars across his face, and scratches on his elbow where he fell to the ground. He died there.

When the noise and chaos lessened, and the family hiding within the fragile shack pushed opened their door, they found Thembelakhe's body lying on their doorstep.[36]

Claiming the dead

At 16:00 that afternoon, Warrant Officer Monene's wife received a telephone call from a police chaplain. He told her that her husband had been 'severely injured' and that she should come immediately to the hospital near Marikana where he was lying unconscious, approaching death.[37]

No one seems to have been able to contact Warrant Officer Lepaaku's wife, Shuna Lepaaku. The first she knew of the day's events, she was watching the 19:30 news broadcast on her television at home: 'it was reported that two police officers had been hacked to death by armed striking miners near the railway line. I saw my wounded husband on TV being carried away from the scene to the hospital by his colleagues. I tried to call him, but his cell phone rang unanswered.'[38]

The families of the police officers knew on the same day that their loved ones had died. The families of Semi Jokanisi, Phumzile Sokanyile, and Thembelakhe Mati had to wait much longer to find out what had happened. Semi's father kept trying to reach him: 'I called him again on Monday but I couldn't reach him. On Tuesday, I couldn't get through. On Wednesday, still nothing'. He called another friend in Marikana, and asked him to find Semi.

> He said to me that he'd seen [Semi] at one of the meetings on the mountain but now he had no idea where he was. Later on, he called me and told me that there was a group of people that had gotten injured and he wasn't sure if Semi hadn't been one of them.

The family waited in suspense, worried wondering what was happening. Semi's father remembered that their friend 'searched and ... searched' for days and then

---

36 Exhibit RRRR 5 – Amended Post-Mortem report for Mr Mati. See also the statement of Xolani Nzuza, who describes an injured man who is likely to have been Mati – Exhibit HHHH 21, at para. 10. See also Exhibit RRRR 4 – Security Case Book 55/08/2012.
37 KKKK 2 – Statement regarding the death of W/O Monene.
38 KKKK 3 – Statement regarding the death of W/O Sello Ronnie Lephaku [sic]. See also the expanded account read out to the Marikana Commission of Inquiry on Day 273 (13 August 2014), pp. 34,863–35,867.

'one day he called me and said to me that he had found him in a mortuary. He's at the mortuary. He has died'.[39]

Phumzile Sokanyile's family were equally lost. The last they had heard from him, he was telling them not to worry if he couldn't speak in the day. His phone would be switched off while he was on the mountain. But he also said that 'when he comes back he will switch it on and update us'. His sister remembered: 'That was the last time I heard from my brother'. The family asked a friend – another man from the same village in the Eastern Cape – to try to find Phumzile, and to tell them that he was okay. At first, there was no news. Then on 17 August – four days after Phumzile's death – he called the family to say that he had finally found the body.

Phumzile's mother collapsed when she heard the news. She died on the way to the hospital, unable to recover from the shock of learning of her son's death.[40]

The Matis, too, had to cope with the horror of not knowing whether Thembelakhe was alive or dead. For days, they endured silence. They heard nothing from Marikana. Nothing from his friends. It was only on 16 August that Lanford first realized that his cousin might have been killed, and only the next day that his body was found in the mortuary. Florence found out on 18 August – five days after her husband's death. Even then, they did not know how or when he died. It was only later that they learned that he had died on Monday – and more than a year would pass before the police admitted that he had been killed by their own actions.[41]

---

39 Interview with Lunga Jokanisi, Lusikisiki, 2 December 2015.
40 KKKK 35 – Phumzile Sokhanyile.
41 KKKK 23 – Thembelakhe Mati. See also interviews with Florence Mati and Lanford Gcotyelwa, KuNdile, 3 December 2015.

6

Tightening the Screws

After the clash on Monday afternoon, the police and the miners separated. Xolani Nzuza remembered escaping from the battlefield, trying to assist the injured workers, and running back to the mountain. In a statement, he said: 'Some of us assisted the injured back to the koppie and they were rushed to the hospital. I personally tried to assist another injured worker, but we were forced to leave him next to a shack and continue running'. In the confusion he did not notice what else might have been happening on the way. 'When I eventually arrived at the koppie', he continued, 'I found Mambush busy giving a report back to the crowd. He told them about our encounters with the security guards and the police. On that day, we remained at the koppie until the evening and thereafter went home to sleep'.[1]

As the next day dawned, Nzuza and others came back to the koppie. He, Noki, and other prominent figures in the strike spent the day speaking to the workers and each other, discussing what was happening and would should happen next. On Tuesday, one more man was killed in the shadow of the koppie – but no one left it. No groups separated themselves from the collective. No one approached any of the nearby mine shafts or hostels. Instead, the workers congregated on the koppie and remained there – talking to each other, watching the police as they moved around Marikana, and waiting for Lonmin's management to finally speak with them.[2]

The mood on the ground seemed to ease, and some of the tensions appeared to relax a little. Over the course of these two days, police negotiators, union officials, and journalists visited the mountain. Some stopped at its base, and spoke to and photographed miners from there. Others climbed up and walked among them.

The strike may have seemed to the miners to be entering into a new phase: the mines were closed, and they had gathered in one place. The roaming conflicts

---

1   Exhibit HHH 21 – Witness statement of Xolani Nzuza, paras 9 and 10.
2   Exhibit JJJ 127 – Occurrence Register and Info Notes, 12–15 August 2012 repeatedly suggests that on Tuesday 14 August, the situation in Marikana was calm. Police officers reported 'all in order no serious crime reported' (entries 92–97). About '2500 people' were gathered (108), without any incident.

of the weekend had ceased. At least some must told themselves that surely now – now that the violence had largely stopped – the company was about to negotiate.

If so, they were wrong.

As the miners waited on the mountain, Lonmin's senior managers were meeting in offices, exchanging emails, and making telephone calls. They spoke to each other, and decided on a plan of action that would isolate the striking workers, and put pressure on the state and the police to bring their strike to a quick end. These conversations would shape the next days – and took place without any workers.

This chapter considers these exchanges, and traces the ways in which they shaped the approach that the police took at Marikana. When the conversations began, nothing was certain. When they ended, another confrontation between the police and the workers was inevitable – and the police knew that it could end in blood.

'We need help'

Even before Monday's first clash between the striking workers and the police, Lonmin had been working to produce an official story about the protest. Over the weekend, as the strike intensified and violence began to erupt in Marikana, the directors and senior managers of the company exchanged emails in which they sought to come to a shared understanding of the fraught events.[3] They also sought to come to a shared answer to the question: what did Lonmin want to happen next? Moving from initial uncertainty, they developed a clear approach: one which cast the striking workers as criminals, and one which called upon the state and the police to intervene directly.

The first exchanges between Lonmin's executives contained only the seeds of this approach. On Saturday, Thandeka Ncube – a representative of Shanduka Investment[4] on Lonmin's Executive Management Committee – emailed her boss, Cyril Ramaphosa, to alert him to the 'illegal strike'. She suggested that AMCU could have been involved, and that a shooting had already taken place. She explained that Lonmin was preparing an ultimatum – they would try to bring the workers back by threatening them with dismissal. The threat was needed because, 'the strike is illegal and ... other workers in the business are

---

3 Several of these emails have been compiled into a bundle: Exhibit BBB 4 (1–7) – Bundle of emails exchanged among leadership of Lonmin (Ramaphosa emails). Others are referenced individually.

4 The Shanduka Group was founded by Cyril Ramaphosa in 2001 as an investment holding company with majority Black ownership. In 2004, it was also the vehicle for the launch of the Cyril Ramaphosa Foundation (then called the 'Shanduka Foundation'). In 2014, Ramaphosa announced that he would disinvest from the Group. It has been taken over by the Phembani Group.

watching the situation and if the RDOs are successful to bargain outside the engagement structures it will set a very bad precedent'.[5]

Ramaphosa's response suggests how the conversation could have developed differently. Instead of sharing Ncube's criticism of the 'illegal strike', he wrote that he understood why the workers had embarked on their action: 'This is a grave situation. The problem with this situation is that we know the cause of it. The real cause is the huge differential between the wages paid to the RDO in other companies and what we pay them. I really did not know the differential was so huge'. He noted that 'the solution they have come up with is clearly not workable. I am not surprised that the RDOs have rejected it'. He counselled patience: 'Let us see what happens'.[6]

If this initial approach had lasted, events might have played out quite differently.

On Sunday, though, two security guards were killed. Any possibility of sympathy evaporated – and both the substance and the tone of Lonmin's emails became more critical. Albert Jamieson – one of Lonmin's most senior executives – wrote an email to officials in the national Department of Mineral Resources to advise them of the 'terrible and distressing situation' at Marikana. He asked to 'keep the Minister updated' and continued: 'at this stage it is clear that probably only a massive police and possibly army presence will stop us having a repeat of past experiences ... We simply do not have the capability to protect life and limb'. He then came to the real point: a request for the Minister and her officials to involve themselves in the events at Marikana. 'I ask you to use your influence to bring this over to the necessary officials who have the resources at their disposal. We need help'.[7]

This email was then forwarded to senior executives in Lonmin, including Ncube and Ramaphosa. Jamieson added a covering note especially for them: 'Absolutely tragic events. I know you are trying to help. Thank you.' In the context of the email's appeal to the Ministry, Jamieson's reference to Ramaphosa's 'help' no doubt struck a chord. The implication was clearly be that everyone involved in the management of Lonmin needed to come together and support the company's actions to bring the strike to an end, and to restore the previous order in and across Marikana.

The same day, the company took its approach to the public. It released a statement describing the strike as 'illegal' and suggesting that all the striking workers had become involved in 'criminal actions' as soon as some had acted violently. Lonmin claimed that the strike was not related to any real labour dispute, but was rather caused by rivalry between the majority union, the NUM, and its competitor, AMCU. It also called for the police to take a more active role on the

5 Exhibit JJJ 1 – Email from Mr Ramaphosa dated 11 August 2012. This is in reply to Ncube, and her original email is included in this document.
6 JJJ 1 – Email.
7 Exhibit JJJ 2 – Email from Albert Jamieson dated 12 August 2012.

ground in Marikana. At the end of the statement, Barnard Mokwena – Lonmin's executive Vice President for Human Capital and External Affairs – was quoted saying: 'We condemn these attacks and the intimidation ... We call for calm from all parties involved, and we expect SAPS to continue to take control of the area and prevent further loss of life.'[8]

On Monday, Lonmin continued its appeal to the media. Mokwena invited journalists to the company's offices to hear him read out another statement. In a well-lit conference room, sitting in front of a cluster of microphones, Mokwena told the journalists that a third man had been killed during the night.[9] He did not know who the deceased was, but believed that he had been killed 'either going to work or coming from work'. He deplored the violence, saying that 'if there is any issue, then we can resolve them in a civilized manner and avoid all these unnecessary killings'. But – and he emphasized this – Lonmin did not believe that there was a real labour issue to be resolved, and was certain that while the strike was violent there was nothing it would do: 'Until we know why 3,000 people are under this influence to kill ... it's hard for us to believe this is a genuine complaint about the rights of workers.'[10]

In both public and private, then, Lonmin's executives were coming to a shared way of understanding and speaking about the events. The strike was illegal, and unconnected to labour issues. Union rivalry was playing a suspicious role. The strike, and the striking workers themselves, were now violent. They were no longer – in Mokwena's phrase – 'civilized'. The deaths of security guards and non-participating workers had tainted everyone, staining all their hands with blood. In other words: this was not really a strike, or a labour dispute. This was an act of criminality.

And the police now had to be made to step in.

'Dastardly criminal'

Ramaphosa and Jamieson were at the forefront of the company's effort to lobby the government to instruct the police to act. On Monday, Tuesday, and Wednesday they made overtures to government ministers, union leaders, and senior figures within the African National Congress. They impressed on their interlocuters the need to see the strike not as a labour dispute but instead as criminal action. They argued that the company could not be expected to engage with violent workers – only the police could do so, and so only police action could end the strike.

---

8   Exhibit JJJJ 5 – Lonmin Media Release dated 12 August 2012.
9   This was a reference to the death of Julius Langa, although Mokwena did not know his identity.
10 As reported in, for example, Poloko Tau, 'Mayhem at Mine' *The Star* (14 August 2012) and Associated Press, 'Violent S. African mine protest leads to fatalities', *Yahoo News* (14 August 2012).

On Sunday evening, Ramaphosa received a telephone call from Nathi Mthethwa, the national Minister of Police, about the situation at Marikana. He repeated Jamieson's concerns, highlighted the illegal actions of the strikers, and emphasized the need for police action. Remembering the conversation afterwards, Ramaphosa said that he told Mthethwa that 'the situation was actually worse and more and more violence was occurring and this raised the level of concern even higher'. Ramaphosa advised that the police 'should take immediate steps to ensure that they protect life and property and also take steps to bring those responsible for these acts to book'.[11]

Ramaphosa's interactions with political figures did not end with his conversation with Mthethwa. By the end of Tuesday, he had spoken to – or had arranged to speak to – Senzeni Zokwana, the President of the NUM, Gwede Mantashe, the Secretary General of the ANC, and Mike Temeke, the Deputy Chairman of the Chamber of Mines. He had also spoken to Susan Shabangu, the Minister of Mineral Resources. As he explained to Jamieson: 'I called her and told her that her silence and inaction about what is happening at Lonmin was bad for her and the Government'. He told Jamieson that 'she was going to issue a statement'.[12]

The next morning, Jamieson wrote back to thank Ramaphosa 'for your help so far'. He wanted to emphasize, though, that it was really important to shape how Shabangu was speaking about the strike. 'The Minister was on radio today saying she'd been briefed that this was a wage dispute and management and union should sit down and sort it out? Not sure who's briefed her ... and although it's not too damaging it's also not too helpful'. The implication was that if Lonmin's approach was to work, then they could not afford to have the Minister thinking in these terms. She needed to describe the strike as a criminal act – in the way that the company was doing. Jamieson was pressing this on other officials: 'I've had two conversations with DG [the Director General] and in each case have characterized this as NOT an industrial relations issue but a civil unrest/destabilisation/criminal issue that could not be resolved without political intervention and needs the situation stabilized by the police/army'.

He pushed Ramaphosa on his attempts to use his personal contacts to influence the Minister to adopt their approach. They had to continue to impress upon Shabangu the need for police action: 'We are grateful that the police now have c.800 [officers] on our site. Our next challenge is sustaining this and ensuring they remain and take appropriate action so that we can get people back to work ... If you talk to the Minister', he added, 'please could you influence these things with her...?'[13]

---

11 Testimony of Matamela Cyril Ramaphosa at the Marikana Commission of Inquiry, Day 271 (11 August 2014), p. 34,423.
12 BBB 4 – Bundle of Emails, at the page marked 289a.
13 BBB 4 – Bundle of Emails, at the page marked 289b.

Ramaphosa replied that afternoon, agreeing wholeheartedly with Jamieson's suggestions. 'I thank you for the consistent manner in which you are characterising the current difficulties we are going through. The terrible events that have unfolded cannot be characterized as a labour dispute. They are plainly dastardly criminal and must be characterized as such.' He added: 'In line with this characterization there needs to be concomitant action to address this situation'. He did not spell out what this action might be – but did note that he had not only spoken to Shabangu about this, but also to Mthethwa: 'all government officials need to understand that we are essentially dealing with a criminal act. I have said as much to the Minister of safety and security'.[14]

These emails capture the substance of Lonmin's approach to the striking workers – and demonstrate how this approach led them to seek to influence political figures to reject the legitimacy of the workers' demands. And although the idea of characterizing the strike as illegal and the workers as criminals was probably developed by many of Lonmin's senior executives working together, Ramaphosa's ready adoption of this language remains astonishing. The vividness of his phrase, 'dastardly criminal', makes it stick in the mind – and undoubtedly helped make Lonmin's case more convincing to its audience. The vagueness of the phrase, 'concomitant action', then left the choice of action to the hearer – leaving the company able to disclaim any responsibility for whatever acts might then follow.

The ministers and other officials seemed willing to entertain Ramaphosa's overtures. According to Ramaphosa's recollection of his meeting with Shabangu on Wednesday: 'when she got to hear and understand precisely what is happening, she did say, now she understands ... she also conceded that it is no longer just a labour dispute but now there was criminal activity involved, because why would people just be targeted like this and be killed'.[15] And when Shabangu was asked by the media to comment on Marikana, shortly after having spoken to Ramaphosa, she echoed him: 'It's quite clear it's rivalry between the two unions. If the matter continues we are going to be involved in the process of making sure we find peace'.[16]

After three days, Lonmin's message had clearly been adopted by the government.

'Then it's blood'

But, at first, the police at Marikana did not act according to the company's expectations. In the immediate aftermath of Monday's clash, the police strengthened their presence in the area. According to the police's account, 209 officers were

---

14   BBB 4 – Bundle of Emails, at the pages marked 289c and 289d.
15   Testimony of Ramaphosa, Day 271, p. 34,432.
16   As quoted in SAPA, Reuters, 'Lonmin Mine's Union Crisis Calms', *Mail and Guardian* (15 August 2012), https://mg.co.za/article/2012-08-15-lonmin-mines-union-crisis-calms (Acc. March 2021).

deployed in Marikana on Monday. This number more than doubled on Tuesday, to 552 officers present. The number crept up on Wednesday – to 689 officers – and again on Thursday – to 718 officers.[17] And yet, for more than two days, the police avoided doing anything that might lead to a further confrontation.

Instead, their commanders debated. On Monday afternoon, senior officials in the police – including the National Commissioner, Riah Phiyega, and the Provincial Commissioner, Mirriam Mbombo – met with managers in Lonmin.[18] That evening, the police instructed a group of mid-ranking officers to develop a plan that would allow them to disarm the workers, arrest those suspected of being responsible for the murders, and to restore order to the region.[19] Lt-Col Scott of the police's Special Task Force was deputed to develop this plan, and received input from police officers and Lonmin managers about the situation as it had been unfolding.

According to Col Scott, he drew up a version of this plan overnight – with the idea that it would be put into action early on Tuesday morning.[20] This plan called for the police to arrive at the mountain before dawn, surround it, intercept the workers returning from a night sleeping in the informal settlement, and then disarm the separated groups of workers. However, according to Scott, this did not happen – because none of the senior commanders were present in Marikana early enough in the morning to authorize the operation. By the time they were able to do so, the opportunity had passed and the workers had once again gathered on the koppie.

Later that day, Scott's initial plan was extended and adapted in further discussions with police commanders.[21] They agreed that an initial phase of negotia-

---

17 These figures were calculated by the South African Police Service's legal representatives: Heads of Argument on behalf of SAPS at the Marikana Commission of Inquiry, p. 39.
18 Exhibit LLL 1 – Amplified Statement of General Mbombo, paras 25–30.
19 LLL 1 – Amplified Statement of Mbombo, para. 38.
20 In Scott's first statement to the Commission (dated 18 October 2012), he describes his contribution on Monday evening merely as suggesting a 'hostage negotiation concept'. In this statement he suggests that he first worked on a broader 'operational strategy' from about 05:30 on Tuesday morning. In his second statement (19 November 2012), he suggests that he had 'proposed' a disarmament strategy at about 06:00 on Tuesday. In his third, and most comprehensive statement (10 July 2013), he provides the account relied on here – stating that he was contacted on Monday to develop a plan, that he did so overnight, and that he presented it on Tuesday. The shifting narrative demonstrates the police witnesses' unwillingness to tell a consistent and clear story about the planning of their actions. Nonetheless, in the context of this particular event, nothing serious turns on Scott's evasiveness. Exhibit FFF 18 – Statement of Lt-Col Scott; Exhibit GGG 39 – Additional (Supplementary) Statement of Lt-Col Scott; and Exhibit HHH 20 – Consolidated Statement of Lt-Col Scott.
21 HHH 20 – Consolidated Statement of Scott, paras 7.25–7.29.

tions should precede any direct engagement. If the workers would not surrender weapons peacefully, then the police would be obliged to put into practice a modified plan: they would encircle the mountain, isolate the group of workers, and then move in, using full force, and disarm the workers themselves. Once this was done – they suggested – they would identify and arrest individual suspects. This would end the disorder in Marikana, and restore peace – and mining would resume. Everyone but the workers would be happy.

It is worth noting that this was not a good plan: Scott's initial idea of surrounding the mountain presumed that only a small portion of the several thousand striking workers would be present early in the morning. It required the workers to be split into several groups, and for the police to be able to outnumber or match the size of each separate group. After Tuesday morning, though, this was never again the case. More miners came to the mountain, and more slept there.[22] The moment in which the plan was hatched – and in which it might have worked – had already passed by the time the local commanders of the police had formally agreed to adopt it.

The only element of it that might have worked was the first – the idea that the police would try to negotiate with the striking workers in good faith, and persuade them to surrender their weapons. But this part was already being undermined from within.

On the same Tuesday afternoon, Lt-Gen. Mbombo – the Provincial Commissioner – met with senior managers of Lonmin, including Barnard Mokwena. The purpose of the meeting was supposed to be to exchange information about their respective operations at Marikana. Instead, it rapidly turned into a discussion of their shared disdain for the protesting workers, and their shared desire to bring the strike to a rapid conclusion. By the end of it, Mbombo was promising that – within the next two days – the police would intervene directly, and effectively, to 'kill this thing'.[23]

The meeting started unremarkably. Mokwena explained that, at far as Lonmin was concerned, '[o]ur priority is, we want people arrested, okay'. He went on to add that it 'is very clear the AMCU is behind it ... we want to see someone arrested so that the message gets across ... so that we avoiding legitimising illegal behaviour. That's our position'. On the transcript, it is clear that Mbombo murmured agreement.

22 There are no accurate or undisputed accounts of the numbers gathered at the koppie. The JOC occurrence book (Exhibit JJJ 127) gives estimates ranging from a few hundred people early in the morning to several thousand by midday. These estimates rise on Tuesday and Wednesday – but cannot be taken as anything other than indicative guesses by the police officers on site.

23 This meeting was recorded, and a transcript submitted to the Commission. All quotes that follow are from this transcript. Exhibit JJJ 192 – Transcript of meeting between Provincial Commissioner (Gen. Mbombo) and representatives of Lonmin on afternoon of Tuesday, 14 August 2012.

The conversation then swerved. After she had listened to him for several minutes, Mbombo took the floor and asserted an even stronger position. She felt that the hands-off approach that both Lonmin and the police had adopted was 'creating a situation where these people feel that [they] are in control'. She argued that the police must intervene more directly: first they must go to the mountain and insist that the strikers lay down their arms and surrender. When they did not surrender, though, then 'tomorrow when we go there for the second time ... then it's blood.'[24]

Mbombo was prepared for police officers to shoot at the strikers – even if they were ordered not to do so. She reminded Mokwena that 'we are now tied up by the new amendments in our law that says we should not shoot ... and all that'. But the officers on the ground were unlikely to respect these 'new amendments'. Mbombo said: 'What happened yesterday, it was annoying to the cops ... The emotions are very high. Whatever you, whatever instruction you will have given, but because of the emotions ... they would have forgotten about the instruction and they will act.' She did not want to see 'twenty people ... dead' – but thought it possible.[25]

This was a far stronger statement than anything the police had yet said – whether on the record, within their own conversations, or in public. It suggested that the police were treating negotiations only as a prelude to an aggressive intervention – one which would assert the police's control over Marikana, which would allow police officers to let off steam, and which would allow the company to resume work as quickly as possible. Unsurprisingly, Lonmin embraced these suggestions – and Mokwena and Mbombo agreed to co-ordinate their action and send a 'message'.[26]

'These new amendments in our law'

This discussion was taking place in a fraught historical as well as political context.

When Mbombo said that the police were 'tied up by these new amendments in our law that says we should not shoot, we shouldn't do this' she went on to add: 'You know, you know these things, you know, from Tatane's incident, and all that'.[27] Her words should have horrified her listeners. They referred to a specific and recent incident: almost eighteen months earlier, in April 2011, Andries Tatane had been beaten, shot, and killed by police officers during a protest in the Free State. His death was captured on television, and sparked a national scandal about the use of force by the police.[28] In the course of this, it became clear that

---

24 JJJ 192 – Transcript, p. 6.
25 JJJ 192 – Transcript, p. 7.
26 JJJ 192 – Transcript, p. 9.
27 JJJ 192, p. 6.
28 Sean Tait and Monique Marks, 'You Strike a Gathering, You Strike A Rock', *SA*

the police were regularly using violence in the performance of their duties – the Independent Complaints Directorate (ICD), for example, revealed that in 2010/2011 it had investigated over a thousand cases of deaths in police custody and as a result of police action.[29]

For many people, the death of Andries Tatane at the hands of the police signalled the return of the SAPS to an earlier and bloodier period of its history. In the past, the colonial and Apartheid governments had used the police the enforce policies of racial exclusion and political oppression.[30] During Apartheid, the South African Police (SAP) were closely associated with some of the most violent moments of oppression: the killing of more than sixty peaceful protestors during the Sharpeville Massacre of 1960, for example, or the killings of several hundred men and women during and after the Soweto Uprising of 1976.[31] In the last decades of Apartheid, and in the period of transition to the new democratic order, the police were also intimately involved in the so-called 'third force' – a set of covert operations to kidnap and assassinate leading opposition figures, sow discord and distrust between political groups, and to spread terror throughout the country.[32]

Given this, it is unsurprising that the post-Apartheid state sought to reform and recreate the police force, so that it could shed this violent history and take up a new mantle as the guarantor of the country's Constitutional order. It did so by changing the police's operational structure – replacing the military-style titles given to police commanders with more neutral ones, imposing civilian oversight, and creating an Independent Complaints Directive to investigate complaints against the police. The old South African Police 'force' was renamed the South African Police 'Services' – a change that pointed towards the new ethos that the SAPS was meant to embody.[33]

It is not at all clear that these reforms were ever fully embraced by the new SAPS. Although the titles of the senior commanders were changed, they soon

---

Crime Quarterly, 38 (2011), pp. 15–22.

29 Independent Complaints Directorate, *Annual Report 2010/2011* (ICD: 2011), especially the tables on pp. 30–31. www.ipid.gov.za/sites/default/files/documents/ICD%20Annual%20Report%202010-11.pdf (Acc. March 2021).

30 John D. Brewer, *Black and Blue: Policing in South Africa* (Oxford, Clarendon Press: 1994).

31 Philip Frankel, *An Ordinary Atrocity: Sharpeville and its Massacre* (Johannesburg, Wits University Press: 2001); Tom Lodge, *Sharpeville: An Apartheid Massacre and its Consequences* (Oxford, OUP: 2011); Julian Brown, *The Road to Soweto: Resistance and the Uprising of 16 June 1976* (Woodbridge, James Currey: 2016).

32 Stephen Ellis, 'The Historical Significance of South Africa's Third Force', *Journal of Southern African Studies*, 24.2 (1998), pp. 261–299.

33 Monique Marks, *Transforming the Robocops: Changing Police in South Africa* (Pietermaritzburg, UKZN Press: 2005).

returned to using military-style titles – General, Major-General, etc. Civilian oversight of the police – including the position of the National Commissioner, occupied in this period by Bheki Cele and then Riah Phiyega was weak, often seeming to defer to the police's permanent officer corps in their assessment of the police's actions. So, too, did the political leadership – often speaking in support of the police against public criticism, and emphasizing the need for them to use violent tactics in the 'war against crime' that was gripping the country's political discourse at the time.[34]

By 2010 – the year before Andries Tatane's death, and two years before the strike at Marikana – the SAPS had largely abandoned most of the reform measures instituted in the 1990s. This was fully backed by the political leadership. During a budget speech in May 2020, Nathi Mthethwa, as Minister of Police, announced that the SAPS would resume using military ranks and insignia, 'to ensure clear lines of command and control while instilling a sense of discipline amongst the members'.[35] On the same day, the Deputy Minister of Police, Fikile Mbalula, repeatedly referred to the SAPS as the 'police force' – undoing even the symbolic work of renaming.[36]

And so, the invocation of Tatane's name by a senior police commander at Marikana – not as a symbol of what should be avoided, but as an 'annoying' constraint on the police – suggested strongly that the SAPS, less than twenty years after the end of Apartheid, had drifted away from the ethos of the mid-1990s and had begun to embrace, again, the militarized and violent practices of the past. Mbombo's clear disdain for laws and regulations that might constrain the police was matched by her cavalier acceptance of the fact that the police officers themselves – when their 'emotions are high' – would easily 'forget' to obey these laws. She saw police retaliation as inevitable, and the unlawful use of state violence as unremarkable.

So, too, it seems did everyone involved in this meeting.

* * *

34 Julia Hornberger, *Policing and Human Rights: The Meaning of Violence and Justice in the Everyday Policing of Johannesburg* (Abingdon, Routledge: 2011); and Guy Lamb, 'Police Militarization and the "War on Crime" in South Africa', *Journal of Southern African Studies*, 44.5 (2018), pp. 933–949 both provide useful overviews of this process, from institutional and street levels.

35 South African Government, 'Speech by the Minister of Police, EN Mthethwa, MP on the occasion of the budget vote no 24 and 22', www.gov.za/speech-minister-police-en-mthethwa-mp-occasion-budget-vote-no-24-and-22-parliament-cape-town (Acc. March 2021).

36 South African Government, 'Speech Delivered by the Deputy Minister of Police, Honourable Fikile Mbalula, on the Occasion of the 2010/11 Safety and Security Budget Vote', www.gov.za/speech-delivered-deputy-minister-police-honourable-fikile-mbalula-occasion-201011-safety-and (Acc. March 2021).

This would be concerning on its own, but in the rest of the conversation it also became clear that the police's embrace of this aggressive strategy was taking place in a charged political context – one that Lonmin was exploiting. Mbombo mentioned that she had received a call from the Minister of Police, and 'when I was speaking to Minister Mthethwa he mentioned a name that is also calling him, that it pressurising him, unfortunately it's political high [it's] Cyril Ramaphosa, yes'.[37]

Mbombo linked Ramaphosa not only to Lonmin, as a shareholder in the company, but also to the governing party. He had been – she remembered – part of the ANC disciplinary committee that had taken the decision to expel the leader of the party's Youth League, Julius Malema, from the party. Since his expulsion, Malema had promised to start a new party, and was becoming notorious for attempting to organize in the platinum belt. He had been at the strike at Impala Platinum earlier in the year, and had made the police, the company, and the government look bad. No one wanted to have this repeated, she suggested – and so things at Marikana also needed to be resolved quickly, before the strike could become a political issue.[38]

The police would be best placed, she intimated, to achieve this – and government ministers and other high political officials were happy to let the force now act.

The meeting ended with Mbombo saying that she would communicate their decisions to the National Commissioner for her approval. Mokwena agreed that Lonmin would support the plan, as Mbombo had set it out, and see the strike end. They would look forward to when they could, in Mbombo's words, 'kill this thing'.

'Don't say you know me'

Meanwhile, as Lonmin's managers were meeting with the police, and its directors were reaching out to the government, the strike was still continuing. The workers did not know what was happening behind closed doors – and did not know whether to trust the apparent calm on the ground. Mistrust and suspicion was still in the air.

Isaiah Twala would suffer from this mistrust. He was fifty-two years old when he went to the mountain on Tuesday morning. His son lived and worked

---

37 JJJ 192 – Transcript, p. 10.
38 For a sense of the impact of Malema's presence in the region earlier in the year, see Nickolaus Bauer, '"Because He Cares": Malema Sticks His Oar in at Implats', *Mail and Guardian* (29 February 2012), https://mg.co.za/article/2012-02-29-because-he-cares-malema-sticks-his-ore-in (Acc. March 2021). See also the comments by Crispen Chinguno in 'The Shifting Dynamics of the Relations between Institutionalisation and Strike Violence: A Case Study of Impala Platinum, Rustenburg (1982–2012)', PhD Thesis, University of the Witwatersrand (2015), pp. 242–244.

in Marikana, but the rest of his family – his second wife and his three younger children – lived far away, in KwaZulu-Natal. He had worked on the mines for decades, was a member of the NUM, and was elected as a 'safety steward' at Fourbelt Shaft, on Karee mine.[39]

According to his son, Isaiah Twala had not joined the strike on the weekend. On Tuesday, though, the mine was shut and, rather than sit at home, he went to the mountain. There is no record of what he meant to do, but he was seen speaking to other miners. He may have been arguing with the striking workers, or he may have been there out of curiosity and singled out as a stranger. He may have been seen holding a forbidden cell-phone, and confronted by striking workers because of it.

Certainly, Xolani Nzuza saw him, sometime late in the morning. According to his account, he was sitting nearby when Twala pointed and called out to him. Twala was telling a group of workers that Nzuza knew him. Nzuza remembers him saying, 'The person who knows me is this one, this boy sitting here. He knows where I work and so on.' Nzuza didn't know his name, but did recognize him – Twala was someone he had met at Fourbelt once, and argued with. He said: 'No, old man, don't say you know me. I only met you once, one morning when I came off duty and you wanted goggles from me … I only met you that day. I did not know you.'[40]

He walked away, leaving Twala to his fate.

There are questions about exactly what happened next – but no question that, shortly afterwards, Isaiah Twala was taken to a spot in the shadow of the mountain and killed. He was stabbed, and shot. He died, killed by a group of striking miners.

In the late afternoon, the police received reports that Isaiah Twala's body was lying behind the mountain. They sent a helicopter to photograph the body – and then, once the miners had indicated that they would not interfere, landed the helicopter to collect the body. The police noticed a sun-bleached cow's skull on the body, and suspected that this was a sign that he had been killed as part of some kind of ritual. No evidence other than this suspicion exists to corroborate the claim.[41]

Isaiah Twala was the last man killed by any of the striking workers. His death was followed a period of tense peace – the striking workers were isolated, armed but avoiding confrontation. The police were close enough to watch and to intervene – but did not do so. The mines were shut, and no one tried the break the strike.

---

39   Exhibit KKKK 37.1 – Isaiah Twala; Exhibit KKKK 37.2 – Statement of Wellington Bongani Twala.
40   Testimony of Xolani Nzuza to the Marikana Commission of Inquiry, Day 277 (14 August 2014), pp. 35,513–35,515.
41   Exhibit HHH 14 – Statement of Lt-Col McIntosh.

For forty eight hours – between the afternoons of Tuesday and Thursday – no one would die in the strike at Marikana. But outside, wheels still relentlessly turned.

The unions intervene

This strange peace was in place as the sun rose over Marikana on the morning of Wednesday, 15 August 2012. If any of the miners were listening to their radio that morning, they would have heard that the strike at Marikana was to be the subject of a debate between Barnard Mokwena, representing Lonmin, Senzeni Zokwana, representing the NUM, and AMCU's Joseph Mathunjwa. The debate was to be moderated by Xolani Gwala, the presenter of the Forum at Eight talk show.

This was not the first time that the unions had spoken about the strike – Zokwana had visited the NUM branch on Sunday, Mathunjwa had spoken to his AMCU branch chairperson and to some of the miners on the mountain on Monday, and both unions had released extensive press statements – but it was the first time that they were addressing each other, and the first time that each of their different explanations for the strike would be tested against the other's.[42] The debate between them would bring the unions into a direct engagement with each other, and with the dispute at Marikana.

Shortly after 08:00, the radio show began. Gwala introduced the subject, and invited Mokwena to begin. Mokwena immediately launched into Lonmin's official account, insisting that the strike was 'of course illegal' and that the strikers had 'literally broken all laws' in striking without permission and in committing acts of violence during the strike. Mokwena's combative words set the tone for the rest of the discussion – which was aggressive, irritable, and testy. Both Zokwana and Mathunjwa soon joined in, attacking each other. Hot words were exchanged.[43]

After Mathunjwa had denied that the strike had been organized by AMCU, and had asserted that the striking miners included members of AMCU, of the NUM, and of no union, Zokwana reacted in fury. He accused Mathunjwa of lying, and of treating the dead at Marikana as pawns – expendable pieces in some game that he was playing. He said that it was AMCU members that had killed the 'poor security guards' on Sunday, and AMCU members that were responsible for the violence. Mathunjwa snapped back. He insisted that the strike was not organized by any union, that NUM members were part of the crowd – and then challenged Zokwana directly: how did he know that the murders were committed

---

42   See Exhibit BBB 1 – Statement of Senzeni Zokwana and Exhibit NN – Statement of Joseph Vusi Mathunjwa for their accounts of their separate accounts of the strike in the days before this.
43   This programme was recorded and transcribed. The transcription was entered into evidence in the Commission as Exhibit LL – SAFM Forum at 8 transcript. All quotes are from this transcript.

by AMCU members? Surely it was at least as likely that they were committed by NUM members? Wasn't the NUM at least as much to blame?

Zokwana responded by suggesting that any NUM members that might be on the koppie were there under compulsion – they had been forced to stop work under threat of violence – and were playing no role in the strike. He pressed his attack, referring to Mathunjwa's visit to Marikana on Monday, saying: 'The fact that AMCU was the one union up to now who was able to address these workers shows beyond doubt that AMCU was behind this plan.' There was one conclusion: 'AMCU have chosen out of their own volition to use violence and to use intimidation ... I can assure you that NUM was not part of that ... NUM would never go so low'.

As Zokwana and Mathunjwa turned on each other, Mokwena stayed in the background. He kept to Lonmin's line: the workers were criminals, police action was necessary, and no negotiations could start until the miners had been disarmed, one way or another.

In the call-in session that interrupted the debate, all three faced criticism. One caller – identified as Tsepo Kgladi – summed up the public disgust. He described Lonmin as a 'reckless dealing company' and suggested that Mokwena was 'standing up to lie to the nation'. He spoke directly to Zokwana, saying, 'I'm sorry that you are playing politics with ten people dead, you can't even take ownership that when people were just passing by an office you shot at them'. Mathunjwa was not spared: 'Mr Mathunjwa, I'm sorry, you are an opportunist, when you saw an opportunity you went in'. He ended by addressing all of them: 'The three of you, you should be standing up in the community, in the society, nationally, saying we are sorry and we are going to stop this nonsense today ... Guys, take responsibility and stop this nonsense, okay?'

In the aftermath of these interventions, the talk show began to move towards an end. Gwala – echoing his caller's suggestion – challenged the union leaders to take responsibility for events in Marikana: 'if the leaders of the unions come together, go there publicly together and say, okay, for now let's go back to work and afterwards we'll discuss the little issues amongst ourselves, is that too difficult?'

This challenge galvanized Mathunjwa. 'We are ready', he said, shouting enthusiastically, 'is the car outside ready to take us there? ... We are ready as AMCU! ... We are ready!' Zokwana was less eager – but soon found himself backed into a corner. Between Mathunjwa's triumphant hectoring, and Gwala's insistent follow-ups, he found himself agreeing to the challenge. As the show ended, both he and Mathunjwa were committed to driving immediately to Marikana, to address the striking workers, and to intercede to persuade them to lay down their weapons.

This marked a shift in the both union's relations to the strike. Up until now, they had both kept some distance from the events. Now, they had to get their hands dirty.

* * *

Zokwana and Mathunjwa travelled to Marikana separately. When they arrived, each went to the local police headquarters to meet with Maj.-Gen. Mpembe – who was in charge of the operation on the ground at Marikana. The police had set up a cordon around the mountain, and any attempt to approach the workers would have to be approved of by them, and take place under the conditions that they established. Mpembe insisted that both union leaders join him in a meeting to discuss these conditions – even though the rancour of the morning's debate lingered.[44]

Mpembe chaired the meeting with the aid of a facilitator. Zokwana and Mathunjwa refused to talk to each other, and the facilitator had to ensure that one person spoke at a time. Mpembe was the first up, and he focused on convincing the two union leaders to follow through on their promises. It was vital, he argued, that the miners be persuaded to disarm. If they did not do so – and could not be persuaded to do so – then the police would have to act, and the outcome could be violent. Mpembe told them: 'We are policing in a democracy where negotiation is its weapon, not bloodshed ... The operation has reached a sensitive stage that we might be, we might go and lose more lives'. He begged them to think about the consequences of their not acting: 'We do not want to be seen as a country that is killing its own people.'

However, neither Zokwana nor Mathunjwa could put aside their mutual dislike. Zokwana again said that AMCU bore sole responsibility for inciting the strike, and that 'our members are being grabbed to that mountain and being killed'.[45] So long as the strikers were violent, there was no prospect of negotiation – and so, no matter what Mpembe said, his position remained the same: no negotiations. 'There's a need to make sure that this country is not seen globally as a country that murders its own citizens, I agree with you. But I want to put it that people have to obey the law. Nobody has the right to kill whoever he likes'.[46]

Mathunjwa responded by saying that Zokwana's 'blaming game to say who-killed-what' was nothing but a distraction. They must go to the mountain and show leadership: 'We are not a leader when we are driving a fancy car. We are not a leader when we are in a studio, protected ... You are a leader when the challenge arises, and that is when you show your leadership'. He could not resist, though, gilding his own mythic image of himself as he did so: 'hence I had said to the SABC get me a car and I will go there', he said to Mpembe. 'If they kill me they kill me'.[47]

---

44 This meeting was recorded and transcribed. See Exhibit OO 4 – Transcript of meeting held at Lonmin Offices on 15 August 2012.
45 OO 4 – Transcript, p. 9.
46 OO 4 – Transcript, p. 6.
47 OO 4 – Transcript, 22–23.

It took some time to persuade these two strong-willed men to set aside their argument and to agree to address the crowd. Mpembe insisted that they travel separately to a site adjacent to the police cordon, where they would then climb into police Nyalas – heavily armoured security vehicles. These Nyalas would then drive up to the foot of the mountain. Once there, the union leaders and their chosen companions would be given access to the loudspeaker mounted on top of the vehicle. They would address the crowd from behind the Nyala's armoured walls, where the police could keep them safe.

Once at the mountain, Zokwana and the NUM spoke first. The crowd was not welcoming. As Zokwana remembered, 'the larger group promptly began to sing a derogatory song about NUM and me. They were at the same time beating their weapons together. The song can be translated as "How will we kill NUM? We hate NUM. How will we kill Zokwana? We hate Zokwana".[48] Zokwana tried to get his message across, but had to stop speaking when it became clear that no one on the mountain was willing to listen to him, or to the union that he represented.

Mathunjwa meanwhile tried to persuade the police to allow him out of the Nyala: 'It was getting dark when we arrived … We were about forty metres away from the workers. I wanted to get out of the vehicle to speak to the workers face-to-face'. It was not permitted, though, and Mathunjwa had to follow Zokwana's example of speaking through the loudhailer. He remembered saying that 'we had been to management and that management was asking all the workers to renounce violence and leave the koppie. I told the workers that management said the workers should return to work peacefully … it would then engage the workers on their grievances'.

The workers seemed willing to listen to him – but there were difficulties in communicating. The Nyala was sealed, and although some of the workers – including Mambush – came forward to speak, neither Mathunjwa nor the police officers inside the vehicle could hear them. 'Thereafter one of the workers came up … and spoke through the small window in the Nyala and then he took the loudhailer'. It was dark, and Mathunjwa could not see who spoke, but he was clear that they were interested:

> The worker thanked me for coming to the koppie. He said that the workers did not want to listen to Mr Zokwana because NUM leaders had shot at them … [He] said that they understood the message from management but it was now getting dark. They said I should come back the next day.[49]

---

48 BBB 1 – Zokwana, para. 21.
49 NN – Mathunjwa, paras 48–50.

While the workers slept

It was fully dark by the time that the union leaders and the police commanders left the mountain on Wednesday evening. Mathunjwa was exhilarated: he was certain that he had brokered a breakthrough, and that the workers would continue negotiations in the morning. According to him, the police shared this belief: 'Major-General Mpembe gave us a salute and said that he was very optimistic and impressed and had no doubt that the strike would be over the next day'.[50]

But even if this encounter between the union leaders and the striking workers was the breakthrough that Mathunjwa believed it to be, it had come too late. While Zokwana, Mathunjwa, and Mpembe were at the mountain, Riah Phiyega, the National Commissioner of the Police was speaking to her most senior commanders from across the country – including the Provincial Commissioner of the North West – in an extraordinary meeting of the Service's National Management Forum (NMF).[51]

The details of this meeting are few and far between. The police have attempted to conceal it, hiding evidence of the meeting from the Commission of Inquiry that met after the massacre, claiming to have lost the recordings of the discussions, and then only – after much pressure – releasing a single-page record of the minutes.[52] There can be little doubt that this was a sensitive meeting, and that the National Commissioner spoke to her commanders about a range of issues raised by the strike at Marikana. But it is only possible to speculate about what these issues were. Could the police have discussed Cyril Ramaphosa's interventions – as Mbombo had discussed them with Lonmin's management? Could they have spoken about the political consequences of allowing the strike to continue? Could they have discussed the economic cost to Lonmin, and the

---

50   NN – Mathunjwa, para. 54.
51   The documentary traces of this meeting are few and far between. A very abbreviated note that acknowledges that this meeting was held is Exhibit JJJ 177 – Extract: Minutes of National Management Forum of the Police of 15 August 2012. Exhibit HHHH 11.1 – SA Police Services minutes of NMF Extraordinary Session 15 August 2012, provides marginally more detail. A survey of the SAPS computer records conducted by the Commission's Evidence Leaders uncovered a series of deleted audio files, apparently relating to this meeting. The police submitted affidavits by officers claiming to have mistakenly deleted the only records of this meeting's actual discussions – see, for example, Exhibit HHHH 1 – Statement of Maj. Lethoko. Several other files appeared to have been altered before being submitted to the Commission: see Exhibit HHHH 11.2 – Properties of HHHH 11.1. In all, there is clear evidence that the meeting took place, that a decision was taken there – but no evidence at all of the nature of the discussions that took place.
52   This is the conclusion of the Commission's Evidence Leaders: 'It appears that SAPS deliberately attempted to withhold from the Commission information about this meeting'. Evidence Leaders' Heads of Argument, para. 593.

mining industry, of the strike? Could they have discussed a desire for revenge? Any of these conversations could have taken place – but there is no evidence one way or another. We cannot know.

It is certain, though, that it was at this meeting that the National Commissioner took the decision to order the police to disarm the striking workers on Thursday – regardless of any possible successes in the negotiations that were happening. This decision was endorsed by the senior leadership of the police services, and communicated to both Lonmin's management and the police commanders on the ground by Lt-Gen. Mbombo, the Provincial Commissioner.[53] This was the 'concomitant action' that Ramaphosa had asked for, and that Lonmin wanted.

And so, while the workers slept on the night of Wednesday, 15 August 2012, their fate was decided in a secret meeting of senior police officers gathered in a beige conference room about a hundred kilometres away from Marikana and its mine.

53 LLL 1 – Amplified Statement, Mbombo, para. 45.

7

The Massacre at Scene One

IN THE quiet hours before dawn on Thursday 16 August 2012, Mcgineni Noki called his wife, Noluvuyo. She was scared: the strike had become violent in the week since it had begun, and his role as a leader put him in direct danger. She asked him to step back, to leave the koppie, and to return home, where he would be safe. He said that he could not. He told her – as she later remembered it – 'that he had no choice but to go because he was a leader appointed to represent the workers'. He would stay, despite the danger, because he had a duty to do so.[1]

It is hard to believe that Noluvuyo was in any way reassured when the phone call ended – but she was far away, and all she could do was trust in her husband's judgement. She was not alone in her fears. This conversation was echoed in many others held during Wednesday night and Thursday morning. Across the country, migrant men and women were holding their families together through telephone calls, telling stories about ordinary and unusual days, about home and work, about their hopes and their fears. In these hours, the men and women of Marikana spoke to their families about the strike, and shared their private worries.

Some of the families already knew about the strike. They had been following the events in Marikana over the radio, or in the news. They sought reassurances from their loved ones, promises that they would be safe, that they would avoid danger.

Motlalepula Ntsenyeho's brother and family, for example, spoke to him on both Wednesday and Thursday mornings because they were 'very concerned for his safety because of what we would see on the news'. They remembered that: 'we asked him to come home, but he would always assure us that he was fine and that he would come home when the strike was over'. They lived several hours away, in the Free State, and had to accept his assurances.[2] So too did Anele Mdizeni's wife, who spoke to him daily during the strike: 'He told me that people were shot and killed during the strike ... I was constantly worried for his life ... I was not happy with his involvement in the strike'. Still, he insisted that he was worried about his wages and must return to the koppie and continue fighting for fair

---

1 Exhibit KKKK 11 – Mgcineni 'Mambush' Noki.
2 Exhibit KKKK 44 – Andries Ntsenyeho.

treatment – no matter how much she might worry.[3] Makhosandile Mkhonjwa's wife was more supportive, when she spoke to him from the Eastern Cape every afternoon. On Wednesday he told her that he was worried because 'there was a heavy police presence at the strike'. She told him that she shared his concern, but said that she also 'understood that it was for a good cause'. She knew that he would go to the koppie again, where he would wait for 'a deal in respect of the wage demand [to] be made'.[4]

Other families, though, knew very little about the events in Marikana – and when the miners phoned their wives and mothers, they tried to paint as reassuring a picture as possible. When Jackson Lehupa spoke to his wife, Zameka, he knew that she was at home with their children in the Eastern Cape. She remembered that he had a routine during the strike: he 'used to phone everyday … at about 04:00 am when he would return to the informal settlement to sleep. He would return to the koppie each day at around 08:00 a.m.' He made this seem normal:

> He never mentioned why the workers were gathering at the koppie, nor did he say anything about the police. He would just call me to say that he was now going to the mountain, and they were waiting for Lonmin management to come and talk to them regarding the wage increase.

She added that she thought 'he sounded tired'.[5]

Mzukisi Sompeta also avoided talking about the strike. His mother remembers their conversations as proof of his care for his family: 'even during the strike, my son found the time to phone us'. He didn't tell them much, though:

> He told us that there was a strike at Lonmin. I told him to come back, but he said he could not leave his fellow workers. He did not ask much about the strike itself, but said that they were sitting on a koppie [and] that he would switch his phone off during the day.

At the time, she says, 'I knew nothing'. Even if other members of the family suspected something, they kept it from her: 'I was never told because they were concerned about my high blood pressure'. She just wanted her son home.[6]

Of course, not everyone spoke about the strike at all. For many of the miners and their families, the strike was only one part of their ongoing lives – and perhaps not even the most important part. When Michael Osiel Nosoele spoke to his family on Wednesday, for example, he didn't discuss the strike. Instead, he and his son spoke about their home in Lesotho, about whether they should hire someone to come and plaster the outside walls, and about the

---

3   Exhibit KKKK 6 – Anele Mdizeni.
4   Exhibit KKKK 7 – Makhosandile Mkhonjwa.
5   Exhibit KKKK 32 – Jackson Lehupa.
6   Exhibit KKKK 9 – Mzukisi Sompeta.

heavy snowfall up in the mountain. Ordinary life shaped their conversation – not the events in Marikana.[7]

For others, family emergencies brushed aside any worries about the strike. Mafolisi Mabiya's wife, Phumeza, was visiting Marikana with their young child, Buhle, at the time of the strike. On Wednesday, Buhle fell suddenly and seriously ill. When Mafolisi came back from the koppie that evening, he called an ambulance to take Buhle to the hospital. Phumeza went with them, while Mafolisi waited at home. Phumeza and Buhle spent the night and all of the next day in the hospital. Mafolisi – unable to help – returned to the koppie.[8]

The spread of cellular telephones into all parts of South Africa – no matter how remote – meant that no one was unreachable, and no one was truly alone.[9] The networks of conversation that these phones enabled have changed the lives of all migrants. Their everyday lives are now lived in more than one place, and home is never further away or closer than the sound of a loved voice. This was true throughout the strike: at no point were the workers truly alone, at no point were they fighting in isolation. At every moment, someone was speaking to someone else – on the koppie, at home at night, and over the invisible phone networks.

These workers were all at different points in their lives – some were young, without children or with very new families, others were in their thirties and forties, with established lives and homes, and yet others were beginning to contemplate retirement – and yet, for this week, they were all brought together by the strike. Almost all of them spoke about it to their families, whether they were justifying their choices to remain in the strike or trying to reassure their loved ones of their own safety. They spent their days at the koppie. They spoke to each other, breathed the same air, took part in the same fight. And in their different ways, scattered across the country and separated from each other, so too did their families: although they may have spoken about it differently, the miners' wives and parents and children in the Eastern Cape, the Free State, and Lesotho all heard about the events at the koppie, all knew about the strike, all knew about the miners' struggles.[10]

As they spoke, the miners and their families told stories of their days and shared their hopes: the hope that the strike would succeed, that they would speak to the mine's management, that their lives and their work would become

---

7   Exhibit KKKK 20 – Molefi Osiel Ntsoele.
8   Exhibit KKKK 29 – Mafolisi Mabiya.
9   Michael Bratton, 'Briefing: Citizens and Cell Phones in Africa', *African Affairs*, 112.447 (2013), pp. 304–319 suggests that 94 per cent of South Africans had used a cell phone by 2011/2012.
10 See interviews with Zameka Nungu, Matatiele, 4 December 2015, with Xolelwa and Phelokazi Mpmuza, Matatiele, 4 December 2015, and Group interview with family members of Tokoti Mangcotywa, Sterkspruit, 6 December 2015.

a little more dignified. And they also shared their fears: the fear that the strike would not succeed, and that they were losing pay for no reason, or the fear that the police would become violent again, and that they or someone they knew would be hurt.

On the morning of 16 August 2012, there was no way that the miners or their families could know that their worst fears were about to come true. They did not have the information. They did not know what the police had already decided.

'It's only God that knows'

Centrally, the miners did not know that, on Wednesday evening, the National Commissioner of Police had convened a meeting of her senior commanders, and had issued a clear instruction: on Thursday, the strike must be brought to an end. The police must act to disarm and disperse the workers. No further excuses and no further hesitations would be tolerated – no matter what the consequences.

And so, at 06:00 on Thursday morning, the Joint Operation Command (JOCOM) met once again in Marikana to plan out the coming day's operation. The hand-written notes of this meeting begin by labelling Thursday 'D Day' and suggest that this would mark a new 'Phase 2' in the police action. The police and Lonmin's representatives believed that the attempts they had made at negotiating – through loudhailers and from armoured vehicles – had failed, and that the union's attempts to persuade the workers to lay down their weapons were bound to be fruitless. They did not consider that they had any option now, other than to use police force.[11]

The ways in which they spoke about the police action are chilling. They seem to have discussed putting 'boundaries' on the workers' 'cons[titutional] rights' – suggesting that these had been limited as a consequence of the deaths of ten men, including and especially the two police officers, at the start of the week. They agreed that this new phase of the police operation would involve 'further deployments whilst unions talk' – suggesting that they saw any continuing efforts to negotiate a peaceful resolution as no more than a smokescreen. They would set up an 'intensified' and expanded 'cordon' around the striking workers on the koppie. Within this cordon, 'any person with weapons will be appr[ehended] and arrested'.

An increased police presence in and around Marikana was key to these plans. When the strike had begun, on Friday 10 August, only twenty-nine members of the police services had been present. By Monday, after the weekend's violence, these numbers had been bolstered and 209 members of the police services were in the region. Over the next days this number increased again: on Thurs-

---

11   Exhibit JJJ 168 – JOC Hand Written Notes: 16 August 2012 (06:00). See also: Exhibit TT 4 – Minute of JOCCOM (JOC) meeting of 16 August 2012 at 06:00.

day morning there were 718 members of the police in Marikana, waiting to be deployed.¹² These officers and ordinary members came from across the country: from the North West, from Gauteng, and from the Free State. They included members of different branches of the police: not just the ordinary constables from the local station, but also members drawn from the Public Order Policing (POP) services, the canine (K9) dog units, the National Intervention Unit (NIU), the national Tactical Response Team (TRT), and the elite Special Task Force (STF). These branches of the police services had very different training and experiences: while POP members were trained in policing large crowds, for example, TRT members were often deployed to intervene in cash-in-transit robberies, regularly entering into deadly gunfights with armed criminals. The STF is ordinarily called in to police hostage situations, terror threats, and international crimes.¹³ Not all of these skills were obviously relevant to the management of a large, uncertain, crowd.

Nonetheless, the commanders of the police agreed to make use of all of these different groups of police officers on the frontlines of the protest. At the JOCOM meeting, they proposed that the force would be spit up into ten operational groups – each of which would include a mix of officers from different units. These included frontline 'Monitoring' and 'Defensive Measures' teams, which mostly consisted of members of the POP services, as well as the dedicated Tactical Response Team to back them up, and to protect the many journalists present that day. Other teams would roam the area, incorporating members of the STF, NIU, and K9 services.¹⁴

The first three groups – tasked with Monitoring, Defensive Measures, and Tactical Response – would be the principal points of contact between the police and the striking workers. They would roll out barbed-wire barriers, would drive and support the large Nyala armoured vehicles, and would man the invisible line between the koppie and the informal settlement. The other groups would be positioned further back, would provide information and support, and would only be called upon in the case of any unexpected crisis. At least, that was the arrangement first set out.

---

12 These figures were calculated by the South African Police Service's legal representatives: Heads of Argument on behalf of SAPS at the Marikana Commission of Inquiry, p. 39. See notes of the JOCOM meeting on that morning, as well as the minutes of that meeting.
13 Exhibit GGG 21 – National Instruction on Mobilization of STF and Exhibit GGG 22 – Draft National Instruction on Crowd Regulation and Management both provide an overview of the formal structures that should govern the deployment of these and other specialized units. See also, David Bruce, *Commissioners and Commanders: Police Leadership and Marikana massacre* (Pretoria, ISS Monograph 194: 2017) for a detailed account of the different police participants in the exercise.
14 See Exhibit JJJ 168 – JOC Hand Written Notes: 16 August 2012 (06:00).

By about 08:00, then, the outlines of this plan would have been clear to everyone in the room at the JOCOM meeting. The details, though, still needed to be worked out and communicated to the officers in the field. A set of more junior officers were therefore deputized to develop the practical instructions. Lt-Col Scott – the officer of the STF who had drawn up the first operations plan that had not been put into effect on Tuesday – was tasked with developing his earlier plan, and creating a version that reflected the decisions taken by the JOCOM members.[15]

While Scott was working on this plan, other officers were instructed to put other preparations into place. One of these preparations stands out from all the others. At 08:30, an officer – Lt-Col Claasens – was instructed to telephone the Phokeng mortuary, located just outside of Rustenberg. He was to ask them to send four mortuary vehicles – each equipped to carry several dead bodies, kept cool in their air-conditioned interiors. These vehicles should be sent to Marikana, where they would wait behind the police line. They would then be available during and after the police action planned for that afternoon. Claasens could not say why so many vehicles would be needed – but the request strongly suggests that the police were still expecting significant bloodshed that day. (The mortuary did not have four vehicles available, and so the request had to be altered. As it turned out, only one such vehicle was available and so it was the only one sent to Marikana itself.)[16]

At the same time, the Provincial Commissioner, Lt-Gen. Mirriam Mbombo, held a press briefing in the Lonmin offices at Marikana.[17] She met an audience of journalists in a large room, and told them 'whilst we appreciate that there is laws in this country that allows people to voice out their grievances', nonetheless she did not regard these laws as sufficient to protect the striking workers. In her opinion, they had contravened contrasting laws: those 'that are giving people of this country an opportunity to raise those grievances in proper ways and processes'. Because the striking workers had not followed these processes, 'it leaves us with no option … We are ending the strike today … We will ask them to leave, but I wouldn't want to explain to you if they don't, what then…'

She broke off – but the threat was clear. Resistance would lead to the use of force.

She took a limited selection of questions from the press, and then informed them that they would be required to remain in 'a designated area' during any

---

15   As noted in Exhibit TT 4 – Minute of JOCCOM (JOC) meeting of 16 August 201 at 06:00 and in Exhibit EE – JOCCOM (JOC) Minute of 16 August 2012 (13h30).
16   Exhibit HHH 67 – Affidavit of Lt-Col PWJA Claasens dated 29 October 2013, and Exhibit HHH 66 – Statement of Col Madoda dated 6 November 2013. See also, Exhibit JJJ 180 – Phokeng Mortuary Occurrence Book for a contemporaneous record of the call.
17   Exhibit HHH 40 – Transcript of interview of Lt-Gen. Mbombo on 16 August 2012. All quotes are from this transcript of the briefing.

actions, presumably to guarantee their own safety. After all, as Mbombo herself had said, essentially summing up the approach of the police commanders to the strike: while there was a possibility that the strike might end without blood, she couldn't predict the future. 'What will happen', she said, 'it's only God that knows'.[18]

'The life of a Black person in Africa is so cheap'

Joseph Mathunjwa arrived in Marikana while Mbombo's press briefing was still continuing.[19] While she was speaking, he planned to meet with representatives of Lonmin to plot out a way forward. He was buoyed by the reception that he received the previous evening – both from the workers themselves, and from the police commanders on the site. He now hoped to persuade Lonmin's managers to come with him to the mountain, and to join their voices to his. He also, no doubt, hoped to demonstrate to the company his potential influence over their workers – and to persuade them to offer him an official seat at the table in any future negotiations.

This meeting took place in the room next door to the press briefing.[20] Sounds and half-heard words passed through the thin walls – at one point, Mathunjwa and his colleagues were asked to lower their voices because they could be heard by the journalists sitting in the briefing room next door. Despite this, the two rooms seemed to exist in parallel worlds: as the Provincial Commissioner was telling journalists that she had instructed the police to begin an operation to end the strike, Mathunjwa was talking to Lonmin's representatives in the belief that they still might compromise.

Only one of these worlds was real, however, and Mathunjwa's soon collapsed. The transcripts of this meeting suggest that much of the discussion avoided the question of how to end the strike. Instead, they revolved around the importance of the existing relationship between the NUM and Lonmin, and the company's unwillingness to allow AMCU or other unions to disturb that relationship. Mathunjwa reacted with disbelief: AMCU and other unions were already active in the mines, and the workers were demonstrating their own reluctance to accept the existing relationship between the company and the NUM. Lonmin's representatives refused to listen, and insisted that the company was bound by existing policies – implying, at least, that AMCU would never have a seat at the negotiating table. This conversation spun in circles for well over an hour, until it was obvious that it was a waste of everyone's time. Lonmin was not interested

---

18 HHH 40 – Transcript, p. 6.
19 In general, see Exhibit NN – Statement of Joseph Muzi Mathunjwa, and the Testimony Joseph Muzi Mathunjwa at the Marikana Commission of Inquiry, Day 22 (8 November 2012).
20 For the details of this meeting, see Exhibit OO 13 – Transcript of meeting between AMCU and Lonmin of 16 August 2012.

in negotiating with the workers through Mathunjwa – and had no interest in supporting AMCU.

Mathunjwa realized that he would have to go to the workers empty-handed, without any assurances from the company, without anything to offer them.[21] He would have to ask them to listen to him, surrender their weapons, and to leave the koppie – and all he would have to offer them was his own word, unsupported by any evidence that it was good. This can only have been a bitter experience, a rapid fall from the buoyant confidence of the previous evening, when he had accepted the praise of the police and been able to believe that he – and he alone – was entrusted with the task of saving the day. Still, he nonetheless believed that he had a duty to the workers. Mathunjwa finally left the meeting, determined to go to the koppie.

* * *

At the same time, on the koppie's rocky sides, the gathered workers were experiencing similar disappointment. Many of them had understood Mathunjwa's Wednesday evening speech to mean that Lonmin's managers would finally come to meet them. Rumours had spread, and firmed up: many believed that a meeting had now been promised for 09:00, and that this would allow them to finally leave the koppie and resolve their disputes.[22] As the morning went on, though, and the hours passed, the meeting came to seem less and less likely – and their enthusiasm began to fade away. They waited, without much hope, for something to change.

Some of them may have believed that change would come from the increasing pressure being put on the mine by their families and colleagues. Although only male mineworkers were present on the koppie, they knew that their female colleagues, their wives, and the women of Marikana were organizing their own protest in the town. They would gather and add their voices to the voices of those on the koppie. Perhaps that would help tip the balance of popular opinion, perhaps the women would put new pressure on the company, and force some change.[23]

They may have been hoping for this to happen – but none of them could have been hoping for what happened next. At about 10:30, the workers saw several police Nyalas begin to move towards their encampment on the koppie.[24] Long

---

21 Exhibit NN – Statement of Mathunjwa – paras 63–72.
22 See the claim made by Mzoxolo Magidiwana in his statement: Exhibit EEE 1 – Witness Statement of Mzoxolo Magidiwana, para. 6.
23 The police's occurrence book for the day records up to 100 women moving around the informal settlement, and that 'a group of women wrote on their placards that their husbands in the house must go and join the ones on the koppie'. Exhibit FFF 25 – SAPS JOC OB, entry 986 and others. See Chapter 11 for an overview of women's activism in Marikana.
24 This is the time stamp as reconciled by the Commission's Evidence Leaders on

lines of barbed wire spooled out of the backs of these vehicles, cutting bright lines across the land. They set up a bristling barricade between the workers and their homes in the informal settlement. The wire caught the sunlight, and glinted in the air between the yellow grass below and the brilliant blue sky above. The workers can only have watched this happening with dry mouths – this was a change, to be sure, but it was not a change that suggested that anything good might follow the Nyalas' path.

Shortly afterwards, Mcgineni Noki led a small group of miners off the koppie and approached the nearest Nyala. They intended to ask the police to move their vehicles further away from the koppie, and to persuade them to stop unspooling the barbed wire – to open a path that the workers could follow to leave the mountain and return home.[25] The conversation did not go well. According to a police officer: 'The person with the green blanket was one of the two that came to us. He then informed us that they do not want the police there and he was very aggressive towards us. We could not negotiate with them as they were very angry and aggressive.'[26]

The 'person in the green blanket' was Noki – throughout this strike he wore this distinctive blanket over his shoulders, and so could always be identified from a distance. The police officers knew that he was one of the leaders of the strike, and regularly noted his presence in their brief written notes. They also – despite their official position – paid attention to his words when he spoke. Although the police testimony and notes all suggest that they refused to negotiate with him, nonetheless – about half an hour later – one of the Nyalas moved to a different position, further away from the koppie, just south of a small kraal on the way to the informal settlement.[27] The move effectively opened up a gap in the lines of barbed wire, a channel through which workers could move from the koppie to their homes.

This did little to reassure the workers. They were still waiting for someone to come to address them – if the mine's managers wouldn't come, then at least

---

the images taken by Col Salmon Vermaak, and entered into evidence at the Commission as Exhibit JJJ 11 – Vermaak's Photos, Blackberry Camera. (For the reconciliation see: Exhibit ZZZZ 10 – Evidence Leaders' detailed timeline). For their positioning, see Exhibit JJJ 91 – Evidence Leaders' plotting of Nyala positions.

25 This is recorded in the police's occurrence book, at entry 998 for 16 August 2012. Exhibit FFF 25 – SAPS JOC OB (Occurrence Book) (12 August – 18 August).

26 This comes from an after-the-fact account compiled by several officers: Exhibit JJJ 120.2 – Lonmin Mine HNT Narrative (Brig Calitz/Lt-Col McIntosh/Lt-Col Mere). See also: HHH 13 – Statement of Lt-Col McIntosh, para. 3–7.

27 This was 'Nyala 6' on the police's record. A discussion of its movement, and the strategic consequence of this movement, was held between Scott and the Evidence Leaders during the Testimony of Duncan George Scott at the Marikana Commission of Inquiry, on Day 135 (26 September 2013). See, especially, pp. 14,329–14,337.

Mathunjwa could explain. They waited until – at about midday – Mathunjwa finally joined them.

There is a very detailed record of Mathunjwa's speech to the miners. It was filmed by a group of journalists, and also by plainclothes police officers circulating through the crowd on the koppie. Before Mathunjwa had said a word, his presence was noted. The miners formed up in front of him, and sat down, still holding their placards, sticks, and spears. Mathunjwa stood tall, and spoke in a red microphone – connected to a handheld speaker that broadcast his words across the crowd.[28]

'Let me start by apologising for coming late', he said, before rousing the crowd with a call-and-response chant: 'Amandla! Ngawethu!' 'Power! It is ours!' He continued: 'I bow down before you as just a human being. I am the slave of God', he said, 'come to you to negotiate about this matter that we are facing, the one of capitalism'. And again, he called out: 'Amandla! Ngawethu!'

After a discussion of the broader political economy of South Africa – in which capital is concentrated in a few hands, and the majority are denied access to wealth, or to power – Mathunjwa turned to the situation on the ground at Marikana. 'Comrade', he said, 'we arrived in the morning here because we said we want to talk with the employer again at eight o'clock. We arrived, as AMCU, but we [only] met with the employer around to eleven'. After delaying them, Lonmin would not take any responsibility for anything that was happening to their workers on the koppie: 'They told us that, according to the National Security Act, government saw this place as a security zone … It is no longer a place that the employer has any control over'. This – Mathunjwa emphasized – was a real problem for the workers. It meant that, in his words, 'whatever the government feels like doing, it can do it'. Without restraint on the part of the police, this meant that the possibility of 'bloodshed' was in the air – and that workers should do everything to avoid it. They should be alert to the dangers facing them. They should have noticed that the police had not escorted him to the koppie, as they had the day before; AMCU – and the miners – were now seen as beyond the police's protection, he said, and the miners should beware.

At the end of his speech, Mathunjwa lowered himself to the ground. He pressed his knee into the dirt, and begged the workers to think seriously about the risks they were taking, about the very real danger that they would die; AMCU, he said,

---

28 The principal source for these quotes is the transcript of his speech, prepared for the Commission. There are also a number of partial video clips, also entered into evidence, which provide more of a sense of the atmosphere of the encounter. The transcript is Exhibit OO 9 – Translation of Mr Mathunjwa's address on 16 August 2012. The video clips are Exhibit CC 5 – Video of arrival of Mathunjwa at scene 1 at midday; Exhibit CC 11 and Exhibit CC 12 – Shot of reaction of crowd during Mathunjwa's speech; and CC 19 – Clip of crowd taken by W/O Masinga.

came on our own because we were coming to the nation of God to try and avoid this blood that they want to see flow. Comrade, the life of a Black person in Africa is so cheap. The life of a Black person in Africa is so cheap. They will kill and finish us and get others to put them and pay them these salaries that do not do anything in the Black person's life.

He begged again, pressing them to decide to leave the koppie right away: 'We are requesting you brothers, sisters, men, I am kneeling down, coming to you, as nothing'.[29]

At the end of his speech, Mathunjwa dragged himself back to his feet and stepped aside to allow members of the crowd to respond. Six men rose, one at a time. They each took up the microphone and loudhailer and, facing the crowd, spoke their minds. Their voices captured the shifting tides of emotion – exhaustion, fatalism, and anger – that swept through the workers.

Motlalepula Ntsenyeho was the first to speak. He had a history in the strike. He had been one of the workers who had approached the police on Monday, before the sudden eruption of violence. Then, he had tried to calm everybody down – to persuade both the police and the strikers to avoid violence, and to keep the peace.[30] He had failed then. Nonetheless, when he had spoken to his brother that morning he had refused to come home, believing that his place was with the strike.[31] Now, as he spoke on the mountain, he seemed resigned, exhausted and fatalistic: 'We said that we would leave here after getting the money we want ... Otherwise, we will die on this mountain ... It must be finished ... if it [Lonmin] is finished with us'. He added: 'I am finished'.[32]

Many of the men who followed Ntsenyeho shared his fatalism. They stated – again and again – that they believed that Lonmin was preparing to fire and replace them all. This had happened in other strikes in the past, and was likely to happen here, now. They believed that the police were there to ensure that they were powerless in the face of the company's efforts to dispossess them.

Other men gave vent to their frustrations, and their anger. They thought that another clash was now inevitable, and that – rather than simply await their deaths – they should be ready to fight, to shed blood themselves, and to die on their feet.

---

29   OO 9 – unpaginated.
30   The identification of Mr Ntsenyeho was confirmed by the Evidence Leaders in the Marikana Commission of Inquiry, who explain that he is identifiable by his distinctive outfit of a 'yellow string backpack he wore throughout the week and the brown jersey he wore on the 16th with a light diamond pattern', Heads of Argument (Evidence Leaders), para. 727. See also para. 724.
31   Exhibit KKKK 44 – Andries Ntsenyeho.
32   The responses by Ntsenyeho and others to Mathunjwa's speech were transcribed and translated as ZZZZ 19 – Translation of responses of strikers to Mr Mathunjwa's first address at the koppie on 16 August 2012. Video clips of these responses are filed as Exhibits CC 13 – CC 18, Protestor Speech.

These are among the last recorded words of any of the miners on the koppie – and one of the few sources that provide the voices of any of the ordinary miners at the time. The mix of despair, resignation, stubbornness, and anger that marked these speeches must also have shaped the atmosphere on the koppie that day. The miners had arrived in the early hours of the morning in the hope that today, this day, would be the last day that they had to spend on the koppie. They told their wives and their families that they had heard that the company was coming to speak to him – and no matter how unfounded those rumours may have been, they undoubtedly gave the workers hope and something to look forward to. These hopes were then dashed. The long wait through the morning had sapped their energies, and then Mathunjwa's sober and desperate words shook them. They had to grapple with the real possibility that their sacrifices to date – the deaths of their colleagues, the injuries they had suffered, the stain of the deaths that some of them may have committed, their loss of salary, their insecurity – would be for nothing.

In this light, the presence of Mathunjwa and – shortly afterwards – Johannes Seoka, the Anglican Bishop of Pretoria, offered them a last moment of support. Seoka had heard media reports of the deaths at Marikana, and had come to intercede in the hopes of preventing any further violence.[33] He came directly to the workers, to speak to them, to understand their position, and to persuade them to avoid violence. For a brief period, both men sought to assure the workers that their concerns were being listened to – even if the company was not present to listen to them directly. Noki, representing the workers, told the bishop and the unionist that they needed Lonmin's management to come to the koppie and to address the workers – then, maybe, they could leave.

This was the last cast of the die for the workers. Both Mathunjwa and Seoka agreed to leave the koppie, return to Marikana, and to attempt to convince the company's managers to speak to the workers. Neither man was certain that they would succeed, but there was no other option available: the dispute was deadlocked, and while the miners seemed to be ready to accept a symbolic visit by the management as the price for dispersing, even that now seemed unlikely. Mathunjwa left first, promising to return later that afternoon. Seoka remained for a few minutes longer, talking to the workers, then followed. They left, believing that they took the last chance for a peaceful resolution to the strike and the current standoff with them.

The final pieces

It was already too late, though. The final pieces of the police operation were falling into place. At about 13:30, shortly after Mathunjwa and Seoka had departed, Captain Dennis Adriao – the police spokesperson – instructed all of

---

33   Exhibit M – Statement of Bishop Seoka.

the plainclothes officers to withdraw from the koppie.³⁴ These officers believed that they had been identified by the striking workers, and were now in danger. Most of the journalists left the koppie at the same time, and set up shop behind the police line, in the secure area that the Provincial Commissioner had directed them towards, earlier in the day. The effect of these actions was to remove all film cameras from the koppie – meaning that there is no objective documentary record of the workers' conversations or actions over the next two hours.

At the same time – about 13:30 – a second meeting of the JOCOM began.³⁵ There is almost no record of this meeting, other than a PowerPoint presentation that was apparently shown in this room.³⁶ The presentation set out a plan for an operation that afternoon: it suggested that the police would encircle the koppie, separate the miners from the settlement, move in, and disarm and arrest the striking miners. Although there is no record of any discussions that may have followed, this plan – as set out in this presentation – was adopted by the JOCOM at this meeting.³⁷

It was immediately put into action. By 14:30, Lt-Col Scott was in the field, sitting in an ordinary police car as the operational commanders of the ten units on the ground gathered around him. Scott's job was to explain the plan to them. His task was complicated by the fact that he had nothing other than the PowerPoint presentation to show them: there was no printed plan, no printed map, and no notes. Instead, Scott had to load up the presentation on a laptop, and run through it on screen. Because the sun was harsh, and the laptop's screen not

---

34   Exhibit HHH 8 – Statement of W/O Masinya. Exhibit GGG 31 – Warning Statement: W/O Ndlovu. Masinya and Ndlovu were the two police officers operating cameras on the koppie. Their recordings have been used to produce the transcripts of the speeches and engagements around midday. There are no further police recordings, following their removal from the koppie.

35   A brief document – Exhibit EE – JOCCOM (JOC) minute of 16 August (13h30) – records the existence of this meeting. It is an edited version of the minute produced earlier, for the 06:00 meeting.

36   The presentation that Scott prepared that morning is Exhibit JJJ 48 – Operation Platinum: Lonmin Mine Environment. It is a strikingly thin document, presenting a series of Google Maps images of the area and providing an 'Operational Concept' for a 'Cordon and Search' Operation.

37   A further plan – Exhibit JJJ 163.4 – Plan Dated 16 August – provides more information, and suggests how these earlier plans were developed into a more aggressive operation. The mismatch between the earlier images and the later plans has never been properly explained, and the Evidence Leaders, in their summary of the evidence, suggest that the police attempted – after the massacre – to manufacture a paper trail that made their plans appear more developed and less haphazard than they in fact were. (See Evidence Leaders' Heads of Argument, at para. 606).

bright enough, he had to remain in the shade of the car – and so about twenty commanders were forced to huddle around the open door of the car and squint at the laptop screen.[38]

This scene perhaps should have alerted everyone involved that there were still some kinks in the plan. Scott pointed out key sites on a Google Earth diagram, identifying the positions of police groups and directing them to their assigned sites. However, the map was not accurate: it still reflected the position of the vehicles as they had been at the start of the day, and did not show the movement of the Nyala that had changed its position after Noki's intervention at about 11:30.[39] This meant that there was a hole in the police line, opening up a channel between the koppie and the informal settlement. No police officer seems to have noticed this, or mentioned it.

There were thus two immediate problems with the plan: it did not match the situation on the ground, and Scott's briefing was obviously compromised – too quick, too general, and too uncertain. Nonetheless, at about 15:00, the commanders returned to the groups and spent no more than twenty minutes explaining the details of the plan to their officers. They moved into a state of fraught readiness, expecting the formal operation to begin at any moment.

As the engines of the Nyalas spluttered into life, and the vehicles began to shudder, the police made their final preparations. At the main offices, where the JOCOM was headquartered, one officer, Lt-Col Merafe, received an instruction from his commander to order another 4,000 rounds of live ammunition to be delivered to the site – seemingly because his commander believed that there was a chance that this ammunition would be needed during or soon after the operation.[40]

By 15:30, the police were ready – all of the pieces of their operation were in place, at least as far as they knew. At 15:40, Captain Adriao addressed the media again, and informed them that the operation was about to begin. He told them that they were required to remain behind the police lines, where they could be protected. They would observe from there. All of the journalists complied, warned of the dangers they would face among the workers. Every camera and every recording device, therefore, was now embedded behind the police lines – and everything that they captured that afternoon would reflect the view from the police's eyes.

* * *

38   Testimony of Colonel Scott at the Marikana Commission of Inquiry, Day 135 (26 September 2013), pp. 14,337–14,340.
39   Scott, Day 135, pp. 14,333–14,336.
40   Exhibit HHH 26 – Extracts of diary of Col Merafe. See also Exhibit QQQ 1 – Consolidated Statement of Col Merafe. (This order was not mentioned in Merafe's original statement – Exhibit GG 15 – Statement of Lt-Col Merafe – in which he claimed to have withdrawn from the 'Marikana operation' on 16 August 2012.)

As these final pieces were falling into place, both Mathunjwa and Seoka were making last ditch efforts to engage with Lonmin and the police. While the JOCOM meeting was continuing, Mathunjwa called Lonmin's senior manager in charge of Employee Relations, Jomo Kwadi. He sought to persuade Kwadi that the strikers had actually moderated their position, that they were willing to negotiate, and that there was no need for the police to act, not now, not yet. The company should intercede, he said – and if they did so, then the strike could be resolved quickly.[41]

This conversation went nowhere. Kwadi evaded the issue, and once again insisted on the formal structures of the bargaining agreement – in other words, that only the NUM could represent the workers. Mathunjwa represented AMCU, which was only a minority union, and so could not speak. Neither could the workers themselves: to speak to them would be to undermine the official union. There was nothing to say.

Mathunjwa then made one more effort, calling Lonmin's former Chief Operating Officer and non-executive board member, Mahomed Seedat. He begged Seedat to intercede with management, and to get them to overlook the bargaining agreement in the interests of avoiding bloodshed. But this was no more successful: Seedat would make no commitments, and the phone call ended.[42]

Meanwhile, Bishop Seoka had secured a meeting with Lonmin's public spokesperson, Barnard Mokwena and his deputy, Abram Kgotle. He also met with Lt-Gen. Mbombo, the Provincial Commissioner of Police. He found both of the meetings highly unsatisfactory. Mokwena and Kgotle were evasive, described the striking workers as 'murderers', and suggested that dialogue was impossible. Seoka described Mbombo as 'particularly unfriendly, anxious, and uncooperative'. He received the strong impression that their minds were already set, and that his entreaties had fallen on deaf ears. He was dismissed – empty-handed and angry.[43]

* * *

While Seoka was with the Provincial Commissioner, Mathunjwa returned to the koppie one last time. He begged the miners to leave. He told them that if they did not leave, they would be killed. He told them that there was no one willing to listen to him, or to them. No one would come and save them. They had to leave the koppie, they had to end this strike, and they had to 'go back to the table and negotiate' – because this was the only way to avoid their own deaths.[44]

---

41 Exhibit NN – Statement of Joseph Vuzi Mathunjwa, paras 79–82. See also Exhibit KK – Statement of Peter Fanyana Kwadi.
42 NN – Mathunjwa, para. 82.
43 Exhibit M – Statement of Bishop Seoka, paras 10 and 12 in particular.
44 Portions of this address were captured on film by the media, shortly before they left the koppie at Adriao's instruction. See Exhibit KKK 55 – ETV footage. A transcript of a brief portion of Mathunjwa's address was transcribed as Exhibit KK 56 – Tran-

At this late hour, the miners listened soberly to Mathunjwa's appeal. They were subdued, they heard him out, and then asked him to leave the koppie while they considered what to do now. Mathunjwa left at about 15:30, looking back behind him as the miners spoke to each other.

At about this time, Seoka tried to go to the koppie to report his own failures. The police would not let him past their cordon, though. They held him and his car at a distance from the koppie.

The miners did not debate for long. As the Nyalas shuddered to life, and as more barbed wire began to be stretched out across the plan, they came to a decision.[45] They must have remembered the scramble on Saturday, when members of the NUM had fired at the crowd; they must have remembered the clash on Monday, when three workers and two police officers were killed; they must have heard the desperation in Mathunjwa's voice as he begged them to save themselves.

At about 15:45 – five minutes after Captain Adriao had addressed the media, and told them that the operation was about to start – groups of miners started to leave the koppie, walking slowly down the rocky slopes and towards the flat plain below, heading towards the informal settlement.

Their movement was the final trigger. As they walked, the police operation began.

The massacre at Scene One

Mcgineni Noki led the first group of miners off the koppie. They moved slowly and carefully, hunched over, crouching beneath blankets, trying to make themselves seem small. Noki's green blanket was gathered on his shoulders, and draped over the back of his head. He could be seen from a distance, both by the police and the workers that followed him. In this first group, he was joined by many of the workers who had been active in the strike over the past week, including Siphethe Phatsha, Mzoxolo Magidiwana, Mongezeleli Ntenetya, and Motlalepula Ntsenyeho.

According to Phatsha, 'the idea was to get out there and proceed to the shack settlement'.[46] The workers were not necessarily ready to surrender their weapons in one go, but they were certainly intending to leave the koppie and break up their gathering. They hoped to avoid a violent clash with the police, and must have hoped to buy time to decide whether to continue their long strike.

Their movement, though, did not stop the police operation. The Nyalas began to move towards the crouching workers: long lines of barbed wire spooled from the backs of the police vehicles, carving up the space at the foot of the koppie. The miners hesitated: their usual paths were cut off, and they had to guess at the

---

script of Joseph Mathunjwa's second address.

45 Exhibit ZZZZ 10 – Evidence Leaders' Timeline places the movement of the first Nyala at 15:42, contemporaneous with the end of Adriao's press briefing.

46 Testimony of Siphethe Phatsha at the Marikana Commission of Inquiry, Day 50 (20 February 2013), p. 5,434.

best way to avoid the police and the lines of barbed wire. Their hesitation made them vulnerable. According to Magidiwana: 'Within a few minutes ... I noticed that the police were moving rapidly and then that they were fencing us in from the direction of the residential area.'[47] The front group – including Magidiwana and Noki – turned and moved sideways.

They headed towards one of the only obvious landmarks on the plain, a small cattle kraal near the police line. There was a gap in the police line, here, opened up earlier in the day, as noted above, when a Nyala had moved back from the koppie. The workers hoped to skirt around the back of the thorn-lined kraal, avoiding the police. They would then make their way back home along a worn dirt path.

The police were not anticipating the workers' move. The gap in the police line beside the kraal was not reflected on the plans drawn up and distributed earlier in the day.[48] For the officers on the ground, the movement of this first group of workers caused confusion – and a scramble to act.

At about this time, the Tactical Response Team formed a line on one side of the kraal, a few metres behind the Public Order Policing group and the Defensive Measures team.[49] The TRT was supposed to support these teams and to protect the journalists, clustered slightly behind them. They were not supposed to be in a position to confront the workers. On the map used by Scott, and in the plan he had set out earlier, the area around the kraal was supposed to be separated from the cordon set out by the POP and Defensive Measures team – set back, and out of danger. Of course, all of this was decided before the gap in the police line became visible to the workers.

The police action continued, regardless. According to Magidiwana, the first group of workers was trying to head towards their homes in the settlement when the police vehicles turned to block their route: 'When we got closer to one of the Nyalas, it started moving alongside, dragging barbed wire. The Nyala outpaced us.'[50] They believed that they were being herded away from their homes, their routes cut off by the police vehicles.

Caught between the police, the barbed wire, and the thorn-edged kraal, the workers sought to slip through the net: 'We turned around the kraal in order to get a way towards Nkaneng'. They moved very slowly: the situation was fraught, the plain increasingly crowded, and the available space very narrow. Any sudden move, any action, could now be dangerous.

This was the last gasp of breath before the storm. The workers moved towards two groups of police. The Defensive Measures team was lined up on the same side of the kraal, in sight. The TRT was on the other side – just out of sight of the workers as they moved.

---

47   Exhibit EEE 1 – Witness Statement of Mzoxolo Magidiwana, paras 13–16.
48   Scott, Day 135, pp. 14,333–14,336.
49   Exhibit ZZZZ 10 – Evidence Leaders' Timeline (15:52:38).
50   Exhibit EEE 1 – Magidiwana, para. 13

At 15:53:30[51], members of Defensive Measures team suddenly – and without warning – fired tear-gas canisters and stun grenades at the workers. As these exploded – smoke and loud noise – two high-pressure water cannons began to spray at the workers, hitting the group on their exposed backs.

This front group of workers panicked. Their discipline collapsed. The workers scattered. They ran to avoid the tear gas, to escape the booming noise of the stun grenades, to evade the staggering pressure of the water cannons. They turned around, and around again, and ran in the one direction that seemed to them be clear – away from the Defensive Measures team, around the kraal, and towards the as-yet-unseen line of the TRT and the journalists.

At 15:53:50 – twenty seconds after the first tear-gas canister exploded – about twelve workers came running around the kraal, stumbling with their blankets draped over their heads, rushing towards the TRT line. Instantly, several officers in this line opened fire with live ammunition.

* * *

Over the next eight seconds, the police fired two hundred and eighty-four rounds of live ammunition at the panicking workers.[52] In addition, an unknown number of shotgun pellets also were fired at the workers – unlawfully, as they police were not meant to carry these weapons or use this ammunition.[53] These bullets devastated the front group.[54]

---

51   These timings – and those that follow – come from the Evidence Leaders' reconciliation of the various video, photo, and audio evidence produced. See Exhibit ZZZZ 10 – Evidence Leaders' Timeline. It is worth noting that, in their initial presentation, the police alleged that two confrontational incidents took place in the minute before. No evidence was ever put before the Commission to substantiate the police's claims, though, and the Evidence Leaders concluded that no such incidents had happened. There was no incitement, and no earlier warning given to the striking workers. (See the Evidence Leaders' Heads of Argument, paras 684–689).

52   I derive this figure from the Heads of Argument offered on behalf of the Ledingoane Family by the Legal Resources Centre ('LRC Heads of Argument'), where it reports a selection of figures taken from Exhibit FFF 35 (List of Shooters at Scene One). This Exhibit remains redacted by the Commission. The relevant figures can be found at para. 181–182 of the LRC Heads of Argument.

53   The police denied using shotgun pellets, but according to the Testimony of Maj.-Gen. Ganasen Naidoo at the Marikana Commission of Inquiry on Days 199 and 204 (11 March 2014 and 18 March 2014), while shotgun pellets are not supposed to be used by the police in crowd situations, they remain accessible in many police stations. It is highly likely, therefore, that the police made use of these shotgun pellets (including birdshot, buckshot, and other similar forms of pellets) despite the fact that the use of these pellets was not permitted in crowd situations.

54   A brief explanatory note is in order. In describing the deaths of the men who were

Mcgineni Noki was turning away from the police when he was hit in the back of his head by a high-velocity bullet fired from one of the police's R5 rifles. As he fell, he was hit at least fifteen more times: in his legs, in his arms, in his buttocks, and in his face. His body was scarred by bullets. They cut channels into his flesh. His left leg was fractured. In the cold language of post-mortem reports, he suffered a 'massive brain laceration' – and so although his body was tumbled over by the impact of so many bullets, twisting him as he fell, he must have died almost instantly. He fell in the first seconds, and bullets were still flying around him as he hit the ground.[55]

Mongezeleli Ntenetya's death was caught on camera. He was wearing an orange and black striped jersey, and can be clearly seen on the footage captured by the journalists standing behind the TRT line. He was shot in the chest, wounded in the face, and hit by at least four bullets. He fell. Dust rose up around him, stirred by the bullets and the falling men. He tried to sit up, struggled to breathe, and then fell back again. He bled. Bullets still flew above his head. He died where he fell.[56]

Khanare Monesa was shot in his legs, his left shoulder and arm, and in his buttocks. These were not the wounds that killed him. He was killed by a ruinous gunshot wound to his chest. He was 26 years old, and left a pregnant widow to live without him. His death could not have been caused by anything other than a direct shot fired at chest height – and that shot could have had no intention other than to cause his death. It could not have been a warning shot. It could not have been an accident. The tracery of wounds across his body shows that he was first hit by one bullet, then turned away, before he was struck at least six more times as his body fell dying to the earth.[57]

Thobisile Zibambele was hit in the chest. According to a post-mortem report, the bullet hit him in his upper left-hand side and travelled through his body. The bullet punctured his lungs. They filled with blood, choking him, killing him.

killed by the police at Marikana, I draw upon the post-mortem reports produced for the Commission, filed as Exhibit A – Post-Mortem Reports. I have had access to these, and have drawn upon them wherever possible. These reports are not always entirely consistent, and include material both drawn up by the State Pathologist's office and by independent pathologists. I also draw upon from Exhibit ZZZZ 48 – Post-Mortem Analysis, which is publicly accessible, and which provides a key to the formal identification of the bodies (as Body A, etc). I have read these documents alongside Exhibit FFF 20 – LRC medico-legal report on deceased, which provides a further analysis of the post-mortems. It is worth noting that the Commission's Report – addressed in more detail in Chapter 13 – does not provide this level of detail for each individual death, and cannot be relied on to describe the deaths. In the following notes I will provide page references for the Post-Mortem Reports, and then any further notes or directions that are appropriate.

55 Exhibit A – Post-Mortems, pp. 568–583.
56 Exhibit A – Post-Mortems, pp. 472–495.
57 Exhibit A – Post-Mortems, pp. 584–599.

His body was scarred by two other gunshot wounds, as well as by multiple cuts etched into him by flying shrapnel. On Tuesday, two days earlier, he had called his wife to give her his bank account number, PIN code, and other financial details. She said: 'it was as if he knew that he would be killed'. He told her that he was unable to leave the strike because 'he was fighting for his rights…' He said his meagre salary prevented him from giving his children a decent life. He spoke of this all the time. '[After Tuesday] he did not phone me again'.[58]

Cebisile Yawa was struck by bird-shot pellets on the left-hand side of his face, and across his arm. No explanation has ever been given for these wounds: the police were not permitted to have or use bird-shot ammunition. If they fired the pellets that scarred him, they did so unlawfully. These were not the wounds that killed him, though. He was killed by a bullet that struck him in his lower back, and then travelled through his chest to burst his heart. This bullet was fired from a 9mm handgun, rather than from the high-velocity R5 rifles used by most of the TRT officers. It was enough to kill him, though. He died immediately. He was twenty-four years old, and had lived and worked in Marikana since 2007, when he had taken over his father's job, and his father's responsibility for supporting their whole family. In a matter of seconds, his life was gone.[59]

By 15:53:54 – four seconds since the first shots had been fired from the TRT line – almost everyone who had been in the front group of workers had fallen. They had been struck by bullets from automatic rifles, by bird-shot pellets, or by sizzling shrapnel. They fell, but the police did not stop.

Mphangeli Tukuza's body was riddled with shrapnel. He was a man used to pain – as a rock drill operator, he had been seriously injured during his work, grinding his feet in the guts of a machine underground. He had been transferred from the rock face after that, and was working as a driver at the time of the strike. But in these moments, he was not called upon to endure anything more. He was hit by a bullet in the head, just over the eye. It entered his brain, and killed him instantly.[60]

Jackson Lehupa was struck by bullets in his chest, his stomach, his groin, his back, and even in his feet. The bullets in his chest and stomach were most likely the direct cause of his death, but his body was so broken that he must have collapsed, and bled to death within minutes.[61] 'Before the strike', his wife, Zameka, remembered, many months later,

> Jackson used to tell me that they worked very hard yet earned very little. I always thought that this strike would end like they normally do. I never

---

58 Exhibit A – Post-Mortems, pp. 521–543. See also: Exhibit KKKK 10 – Thobisile Zibambele.
59 Exhibit A – Post-Mortems, pp. 541–567. See also: Exhibit KKKK 25 – Cebisile Yawa.
60 Exhibit A – Post-Mortems, pp. 496–520.
61 Exhibit A – Post-Mortems, pp. 450–471.

thought it would end with the death of so many people ... When I last saw my husband, it was at the bus stop where he said that he would see me when he comes home from work. Little did I know that the next time I would see him was when I had to bury him in a box.[62]

Mzukisi Sompeta fell to the ground bleeding. He had been struck three times, including once in his chest, just above his heart, and once in his stomach. One of the bullets had entered his lower spinal cord, paralysing him – cutting his feet out from underneath his body – but leaving him still able to breathe. He did not die at once. Instead, he lay on the ground and bled into the dust and the dirt. If he had been treated quickly – if his wounds had been bandaged, his head lifted off the ground, his lungs kept clear – he may have survived even these severe injuries. But he was not treated. And so he died where he fell, unable to move, as his fellow workers fell beside him.[63]

* * *

About a dozen men had walked in that first group. Eight of them died, either in these initial seconds, or in the hours that followed. But still, the bullets continued to fly – and men still fell.

Another group of strikers had turned from the tear gas and stun grenades and water cannons, and had ran into the kraal itself, squeezing through the biting thorns. Perhaps they were seeking safety, some sort of shelter – but instead, they found themselves caught up in the police barrage.

Michael Ngweyi was hit by rubber bullets on his upper arm and thigh as he ran into the kraal. He must have stumbled, unbalanced by the force of their impact. He was shot two more times: live ammunition struck him in his chest and his stomach. He fell to the ground, bleeding. He did not die immediately. Like Mzukisi Sompeta, he lay in the dust and dirt. He lived for at least another half an hour. He must have heard the air fall silent around him, and seen his colleagues on the ground. He must have heard the police come into the kraal, and move around him. He must have heard the sounds of their footsteps. He was not treated, he was not bandaged, he was not helped. There is no way to know what he was thinking as he lay there, dying. Perhaps he prayed, perhaps he thought of his wife, of his sons, waiting for him to call them. Perhaps he thought of nothing. As the dust settled around him, as the smoke dispersed, and the sky cleared, he died.[64]

Bonginkosi Yona was also hit by rubber bullets as he stumbled into the kraal. Bird-shot pellets sprayed across his body, stinging his flesh. These did not kill him. Instead, he was killed by two wounds. The first was inflicted by a rifle, and struck him in his upper chest. The second came from a handgun, and hit him

62 Interview with Zameka Nungu, Matatiele, 4 December 2015.
63 Exhibit A – Post-Mortems, pp. 425–449.
64 Exhibit A – Post-Mortems, pp. 323–346.

in the right-hand side of his back – a shot that clearly took place after he had turned away from the police, and could have posed no immediate threat. He was thirty-two years old. His youngest son had just been born, seven days earlier. The infant was waiting with his siblings and his mother in Nkaneng, within hearing of the kraal – waiting for him to come home.[65]

Patrick Akhona Jijase died quickly. He was shot in the head, and in his upper arms. His whole body was scraped raw when he fell to the ground: from the shrapnel flying through the air, from the sharp thorns, from the hard earth. He was twenty-six years old. His parents were waiting in Ntabankulu, in the Eastern Cape. They had called him that morning, but he hadn't answered. They waiting beside the phone: he had always called them back, and they didn't want to miss him. They would spend the night waiting, increasingly worried, not yet knowing that he was dead.[66]

Motlalepula Ntsenyeho had helped lead the strikers down from the koppie. He had been at the forefront of the groups moving off of the koppie – visible, unarmed, and careful. He was generally recognized by his colleagues for his willingness to speak up during the strike. At noon, in response to Mathunjwa's speech, he had spoken of his belief that the company had abandoned them, and that their strike might end with their deaths. Now, his fears were coming true around him. As he and his colleagues fled the water cannons, tear gas, and stun grenades, he too pushed his way through the thorns and into the cattle kraal. It did not protect him. He was struck by a bullet in the neck, slashing through his throat. He was struck twice more in both left and right legs. He fell to the ground, choking. He died quickly.[67]

* * *

At 15:53:58 – about eight seconds after the start of the shooting – the police guns finally fell silent.

The twelve men who had been fatally shot by the police in this area – eight outside the kraal, four inside – lay on the ground, dead or dying. Around them, several dozen others lay in the dust: injured, wounded, scarred, and turning their bodies on the dirt and stone, in agony, but still alive.

Bongani Mdze lay among this group of injured men. He had been hit by a barrage of shotgun pellets, with at least eight of them burrowing deep into his skin. He had also been hit by three bullets: two in his upper left arm, and one in his leg. None of these wounds should have been fatal. He was bleeding heavily from his upper arm – but if he had been able to tie a piece of fabric round it,

---

65 Exhibit A – Post-Mortems, pp. 371–399. See also: Exhibit KKKK 26 –Bonginkosi Yona.
66 Exhibit A – Post-Mortems, pp. 347–370. See also: Interview with Jijase family, 5 December 2015.
67 Exhibit A – Post-Mortems, pp. 400–424.

forming a tourniquet, the bleeding would have been slowed. If a police officer – coming onto the scene after the end of the shooting – had thought to do so, the wound would have been staunched, and Bongani Mdze would have lived. But although the police soon found him, and although the actions needed to save his life were simple, nothing was done. A police photograph shows him, half an hour after the shooting: he is still on the ground, bleeding, uncared for. The police were moving around the kraal, photographing the corpses and injured bodies around him. They ignored him. Help only came once it was far too late. Paramedics – who had been kept from the scene for almost an hour – bandaged him, transported him from the kraal, and took him to the nearest hospital – where he finally died that evening, killed as much by neglect as by his wounds.[68]

It is impossible to know what he saw, or thought, for the long hour he spent lying on the earth. But he was not alone, and some of these who lay nearby survived to tell their stories.

Mzoxolo Magidiwana was one of these survivors. He had been injured in the hail of bullets, hit in his thigh, and had fallen to the ground beside Noki, just outside of the cattle kraal. He watched as the rest of the front group fell beside him. Pale blue smoke poured across the ground. The rifles fell silent. He was in pain, but couldn't move. He heard the heavy footsteps of the police officers, the sounds of single gunshots at close quarters, and the sounds of voices – raised in shouts, in conversation, in the nervous release after the first barrage. He was convinced that the police were still shooting workers – not in the rapid burn of rifle fire, but in single explosive gun shots, aimed at killing the last of the injured miners where they lay on the ground. He believed that they were going to kill him. And so when they came up to him, he believed that this was his moment to die.

'I heard that there were footsteps, or strikes of someone approaching', he remembered. 'They were talking while they were [still] shooting'. After they approached him, they assaulted him:

> It was then that I was hit by a second one on my left side ... And after that, they passed [on, leaving him] and hit the others. When they came back they realized I was still alive. The other one asked the question, 'Why are you still alive?' It was then that the other one then hit me with the other two on my right thigh, and then he hit me again on the right side on the rib cage.

As they assaulted him, they asked him questions.

'He asked, "Where are those firearms that were taken on the 13th?" "Where is the *inyanga*?" I said I knew nothing about these things'. The officers did not accept this:

---

68 Exhibit A – Post-Mortems, pp 433–567. The medical situation that applied to Bongani Mdze was further canvassed in several documents placed in evidence in the Commission. The most important is Exhibit MMM 10 – Medico-legal report by Prof. Boffard, which presents a case that Mdze had a greater than 90 per cent chance of survival if he had been treated in 'a timeous fashion'.

[The one] was saying, 'You are lying. You are going to tell the truth.' He was saying that, hitting me on my lower part, and the other one hit me then on my testicles. It was then that I said, 'It is better than you finish me off and just kill me…' but the other one … stopped him.[69]

Magidiwana then fell into a coma. When the paramedics finally arrived on site, they loaded him into an ambulance and took him to a hospital – where he remained unconscious until October. He knew nothing else of what happened on that day.

* * *

He knew nothing, for example, of those who had died far beyond the kraal and the police line. For although the police had aimed their shots at the first groups of striking workers, they had fired wildly. Their bullets sped through the air, whistling, burning, and hit men a hundred metres away.[70]

Bongani Nqongophele was more than a hundred metres away from the TRT line and the kraal, and was walking quickly towards his home in the informal settlement when he was struck by a single bullet in the head. It entered his skull just over his right eyebrow, and pierced his brain. He fell immediately, dead before he even hit the dirt. He had been a supporter of the strike, telling his wife that he 'could not leave the strike because it was about getting improved salaries'. She remembered that 'he was determined to fight for his rights as a worker'. In the moment that he died, he was not part of any group. He must have left the mountain in advance of the group led by Noki, perhaps slipping away with one or two other colleagues. He was much closer to the informal settlement, and nowhere near the group that encountered the police. It did not save him.[71]

Babalo Mtshazi was close by, at least a hundred metres away from the TRT line, the kraal, and the front groups of the workers. He was struck by a bullet fired from that line, though. It entered his face, broke his neck, and killed him instantly. He was twenty-six years old, and far from the frontline: there was no way in which he could have been seen to present a threat to any police officer, to any journalist, or anyone else. And yet, nonetheless, he was killed.[72]

---

69 Testimony of Mzoxolo Magidiwana at the Marikana Commission of Inquiry, Day 54 (26 February 2013), at pp. 5,874–5,877.
70 In addition to the sources above, see the records of the cross-examination of Lt-Col Classen, where the officer is asked locate these bodies on a map of the area contained in Exhibit B – Crime Scene Pack. Testimony of Classen at the Marikana Commission of Inquiry, Days 238 and 239 (2 and 3 June 2014).
71 Exhibit A – Post-Mortems, pp. 599(a)–599(t). See also: Exhibit KKKK 12 – Bongani Nqongophele.
72 Exhibit A – Post-Mortems, pp. 616–630.

John Ledingoane was heading back to his car. That morning, he had driven his girlfriend, Bertha, to work and had parked his car outside the Wonderkop hostel in Marikana, before walking over to the mountain. He had followed this routine every day of the strike. He spent this day on the mountain, where he would have heard Joseph Mathunjwa speak, and would have taken part in the discussions that followed his warnings. John Ledingoane left the mountain, most likely on his own, following his own path, to one side of the main group. He was at least eighty-five metres away from the kraal and the TRT line when he was shot. The bullet entered his chest, pressed against his spine, and thrust him to the ground. He was probably knocked unconscious – but even if he was not, the impact of the bullet on his spine meant that he could not move. He bled heavily, but he did not die at once. Although his wounds were severe, and would have required major surgery, there is a chance that he might have survived if he had been treated rapidly on the scene, and then rushed to the hospital. But neither of these things happened. Instead, he was left where he fell, ignored, untreated and, unattended, and died there – alone.[73]

Thembinkosi Gwelani was even further away from the kraal and the TRT line when he was shot. He was a relative newcomer to the area. Every morning he would join the long queue of people waiting outside Lonmin's gates, hoping to be given a day's piecework, or to be considered for a longer-term job underground. He had not been part of the strike – he had no salary to argue over, and no job to defend. Instead, he went to the koppie each day to deliver food to his cousin, Musa, who was one of the striking workers.[74] He shared the food before returning home to wait for the evening and to be told the day's news. On Thursday, though, he lingered later than usual. Perhaps he hoped to listen to the speeches, or perhaps he hoped that the police cordon would loosen later in the day, and that he would be able to head home without interruption or harassment. When, after Mathunjwa's second speech, it became clear that everyone was about to leave the koppie, Thembinkosi and Musa decided to leave together. They slipped away from the main crowd, and made their way off of the koppie. They were more than two hundred metres away from the kraal when the shooting began. A bullet sped across the distance, shot high and wild, and struck Thembinkosi in the back of his head. He fell. Musa crouched down and tried to lift his cousin, but Thembinkosi could not move. He was heavy, unconscious, and dying. Musa cradled him in his arms. But then the shooting stopped, and he could see police officers beginning to move from their line, towards the bodies on the ground around

---

73 Mr Ledingoane's Post-Mortem was not available to me. I have taken this information from Exhibit KKK 10 – SAPS Summary of forensic experts' reports, p. 27 and Exhibit FFF 20 – LRC Medico-Legal Report, Annexure C, p. 7.

74 For Musa Gwelani's account of the day, see Exhibit KKKK 17 – Thembinkosi Gwelani.

the kraal, and towards where he was sitting on the ground. He was terrified. He believed that the police would come to finish him off – and so he ran, leaving Thembinkosi's body to be found.[75]

Not one of these four men were part of main groups heading out from the koppie. They each had slipped away alone, or with friends. They were more than a hundred metres away from the TRT line and the kraal. They posed no threat to anyone. They were trying to escape the threat of violence. One of them was not even part of the strike, or employed by Lonmin. It did not matter. They were gunned down by the first wave of bullets fired wildly by the police line.

Last words

When the miners decided to leave the koppie, after hearing Mathunjwa's final pleas, they were not seeking confrontation. Some may have been angry, and others may have been scared – but their immediate aim was clear. They could not allow themselves to be trapped on the koppie.[76] John Ledingoane was planning to pick his wife up from her work that evening. Bonginkosi Yona must have been thinking of his seven-day-old son, and the memories that they would share. Khanare Monesa needed to return to his pregnant wife, to tell her about the long day. They were planning to head back to their homes in the informal settlement and in the hostels. They were planning to return to their wives and their girlfriends, their children and their families. There was too much in their lives to live for, too much to risk.

These men were not interested in rushing at the police, risking their lives and their own deaths. They wanted to live. Their last recorded words – captured in the memories of their wives and mothers, brothers and fathers, their children – were of the future, of their hopes for a pay increase and changes in their working lives, the need for a new coat of plaster on the family house, the opportunity to present a newborn child to its grandparents, concern for another child in hospital, love for parents, for spouses, for all those left in the home – in Marikana and across the country.

Their last known words were of life – and the lives that they looked forward to living – and not of death.

---

75   Exhibit A – Post-Mortems, pp. 631–646. See also: Exhibit KKKK 17 –Thembinkosi Gwelani.
76   It is clear that the fear of being trapped drove the miners from the koppie. Exhibit HHH 21 – Nzuza, para. 24–25. See also: EEE 1 – Magidiwana, para. 11–12; Exhibit DDD 1 – Phatsha, para. 9–10.

8

The Massacre at Scene Two

It took eight seconds for the police to shoot and kill seventeen men at Scene One. Up to a hundred more were wounded in the storm of bullets.[1] And several hundred more – perhaps over a thousand men – were provoked into a panic. Many could not see what had happened. Everyone who could run, did. No one thought about where to go. They simply wanted to flee the shooting. And so, without knowing why the shooting had begun, or where the next threat was going to come from, the workers scattered.

Siphethe Phatsha had been part of the second group near the kraal at the time of the shooting.[2] He remembered the blast of water cannons, the boom of stun grenades, and the sting of tear gas. He stumbled forward and then, as he came up to the kraal, 'the bullets started [the police] fired live ammunition, and people were falling down'. He pushed through the kraal's thorn barrier, and kept going, away from the police: 'I went through the enclosure which is made of some sharp-edged sticks, over them, over the thorns, and jumped on the other side'. He scrambled to get away from the police. In the rush of adrenaline and panic, it took him several moments before he even noticed that he had been shot. His foot had been struck by a ricocheting bullet, and his left toe was bleeding: 'What I noticed on my toe', he said later,

> is that it was burst open and only a piece of flesh was remaining ... [B]ecause that remained, it then gave me some difficulty running, because this was a piece of flesh which was still sticking, so the whole, the bone of in fact of my toe was completely gone, and only a piece of flesh was remaining.

---

[1] The exact numbers of those injured in the shooting is difficult to ascertain. In a press statement released after the massacre (FFF 5 – Media Statement, 17 August) it is said that 'more than 78' protestors were injured. The medical records of the injured are incomplete, but the survey of these records (compiled in the LRC's Heads of Argument at para. 177) suggests that 61 people were treated for injuries sustained during the shooting. The police would detain and arrest over 270 people on the site – and many of these may have had relatively minor injuries that did not require hospitalization.

[2] Testimony of Siphethe Phatsha at the Marikana Commission of Inquiry, Day 50 (20 February 2013), pp. 5,436–5,440. See also: Exhibit DDD1 – Statement of Siphethe Phatsha.

He stumbled. Fell.

The eight seconds ended, and the firing stopped. In the silence that followed, Phatsha took stock of his situation. He could still hear isolated gunshots, and could see the police moving between the bodies of his comrades. He believed that he would be killed if he remained where he had fallen. And so, in that moment, he took an unthinkable decision: 'I decided to cut off the loose toe in order to be in a better position to run', he said. 'I used a bush knife which I was carrying to cut off my ruptured and loose toe'. He sliced off his toe, and let it fall to the dirt.

He limped towards the slim shelter of a second koppie, a few hundred metres away from the first. He crawled between its boulders, and hid from the police. He took advantage of the momentary respite to deal urgently with his own injuries. 'There I found a piece of cloth, which looked like a piece of a pinafore, and I used it to grip and tighten my foot so as to lessen the bleeding'.

Phatsha had not been the only man to flee from the area around the kraal. Several dozen other men fled in all directions – some moving past his hiding place among the rocks. They kept running, leaving him behind. Phatsha watched as groups of the police moved past his position, following the fleeing workers. He waited as the afternoon shadows stretched across the earth, watched as the other workers made their way into a third outcropping of rocks, boulders, bushes, and dry trees. He watched as the police surrounded them – and as the police shot and killed them. He kept silent throughout. Eventually, he was found and – the shooting over – gathered up to be arrested.[3]

He survived – but many of those who ran past him to the next outcropping did not.

Scene Two

This third outcropping of rock and boulder, shaded by dry branches and filled with dead leaves, was the site of the second part of the massacre at Marikana. In the aftermath it was known by two names: first, 'the third koppie' and then, and finally, 'Scene Two'.[4] This outcropping was in sight of the main koppie, and had been used by some of the miners as a toilet, a place to go for a few moments of privacy, to respect the dignity of the koppie and the gathering. It was somewhere familiar – and in the panic that followed the first round of shootings, it seemed to offer sanctuary.

---

3   Phatsha, Day 50, p. 5,442.

4   It is also sometimes referred to as the 'small koppie'. These terms are interchangeable in the early documents produced by the Commission, but have been generally standardized in this account. (It is important to distinguish these from the 'second koppie' – which refers to the outcrop where Phatsha took cover. No killings took place here, although several of the miners were arrested.)

Shadrack Mtshamba was one of the workers who ran from the initial barrage of police fire towards this site. He had turned from the kraal, and was trying to find his way back home. But the movement of people around him disorientated him, and as he struggled to get his bearings he realized that the police vehicles were moving to cut off all obvious routes back to Nkaneng: 'And as the Nyalas were coming behind us', he said, 'sort of chasing towards us, I decided to go and hide in the third mountain [koppie] that is in the vicinity there'. He believed that the koppie might offer him some small protection: 'there are rocks over there, so I hid between the rocks'.[5]

He was not alone. He saw at least fifty other workers around him. There were more, he knew, that he did not see – enough that they were all struggling to fit between the narrow crevasses between the large boulders. They were crouched

> behind the bushes, some between the bushes ... there was a big rock [to one side of the crevasse], we were seated there, and from the other side of the rock they could not see us. And on the one side [the other side] there was another big rock which was – which served as an enclosure.

In this position, he hoped, the police 'could not see us'.

In this, he was wrong. The police knew that at least a hundred workers had gathered at this third koppie, and they were already making plans to surround and contain these workers where they hid.[6] Immediately after the shooting at the kraal, the police groups had started to diverge from their official trajectories. As Mzoxolo Magidiwana had observed, members of the TRT group moved among the dead and injured in the area around the kraal.[7] They saw the wounds that scarred the living, but took no action to staunch them: instead, the police refused to provide even the most basic first aid to bleeding, stunned, and helpless workers as they writhed on the ground.[8]

---

5   Testimony of Shadrack Mtshamba to the Marikana Commission of Inquiry, Day 275 (18 August 2014), especially pp. 35,135–35,141. See also Exhibit MMM 50 – Witness Statement of Shadrack Mtshamba.

6   See Exhibit FFF 25 – SAPS JOB OB (Occurrence Book) for a contemporaneous account of the police's internal reports. Entry 1018, covering the time of the massacre, reports the movement of workers from Scene One to Scene Two, and clearly indicates that the police were aware that large numbers of workers were taking shelter at Scene Two. The Evidence Leaders also refer, in their Heads of Argument, to several statements by police officers collated at Exhibit ZZZZ 3 – Statements of Police Officers – to support the contention that this knowledge was widespread at the time.

7   Exhibit EEE 1 – Witness Statement of Mzoxolo Magidiwana, para. 18–21.

8   See the Testimony of Paul Bismarck Loest at the Marikana Commission of Inquiry, Day 230 (15 May 2014) – where he testifies that the paramedics did not arrive until approximately an hour had passed, and that all references in his initial statement

Meanwhile, as the TRT group secured the area around Scene One, other groups of police officers were reacting to events as they happened. Several teams – including those made up of Special Task Force members, National Intervention Unit members, and K9 Unit members – began to follow the fleeing workers as they retreated towards the third koppie – towards 'Scene Two'.

At the same time, the police's armoured vehicles wheeled to restrict movement across the area. Eight Nyalas were driven into position, and held a line between the workers and the informal settlement. Water cannons, too, were put into place – and at about 16:04, ten or eleven minutes after the first shooting, began to fire hard rushes of water at the workers, drenching them, pushing them to the ground, and forcing them to find shelter.[9] These workers, too, ran towards Scene Two.

The police followed in the wake of the water cannon. A minute later – at about 16:05 – they arrived at Scene Two. They aimed the water cannon in the direction of the boulders, clearly intending to flush the workers out from between the boulders. This, though, was not sufficient – and although a few workers stumbled out, shaken by the water, the police action continued without any hesitation.

At 16:08 – a handful of minutes after the police had arrived at the scene, and mere moments after the water cannon had been aimed at the boulders – the first live bullets were fired by the police at workers hiding between the rocks, lying beneath bushes and dry trees, or moving to surrender.

Over the next eleven minutes, at least two hundred and ninety-five rounds of ammunition were fired in and around Scene Two.[10] Another seventeen miners were shot, and killed – either quickly, from wounds inflicted to the back of their heads, or slowly, bleeding as the police ignored them.

The massacre at Scene Two

There is no comprehensive video footage of these shootings. Nor is there any neutral account of what happened. Some of the police officers have attempted to justify the killings – but in ways that are compatible neither with the stories

---

(Exhibit SSS1 – Statement of Capt. Loest dated 25 September 2012) to medical treatment related only to that provided by the paramedics. No police officer offered first aid in the hour preceding their arrival.

9 The timing comes from the Evidence Leaders' reconciliation of the various video and photographic evidence: Exhibit ZZZZ 10 – Evidence Leaders' Timeline. This first firing of water cannons took place near the 'second koppie' – the site where Phatsha and others hid – and drove strikers in the direction of the 'third koppie', i.e., Scene Two. The cannons pursued, and continued to fire at the workers hiding at this site over the next several minutes.

10 The calculation of ammunition was presented by the Evidence Leaders in their Heads of Argument, and adopted by the Commission's final Report. It is derived from Exhibit FFF 8 – Analysis of shots fired etc. at Scene 2 (list of shooters Scene 2).

told by other members of the police nor with the forensic evidence. Other police officers have – many years after the massacre – begun to tell stories of cold-blooded murder, and the execution of surrendering workers.[11] Some of the survivors have also told their stories of the violence – and although no one saw everything that happened, their stories back up the idea that at least some of police were acting murderously. These stories are all partial and represent only highly contested versions of the massacre.

There is some other, more reliable, information available, however. After the killings, a series of post-mortem analyses of the wounds inflicted upon the dead have allowed for some claims to be made about the specific circumstances in which each individual workers was killed.[12] There have also been forensic analyses of the site, considering the angles at which the police bullets struck the rocks and the ground, as well as where their spent cartridges fell.[13] These analyses have provided an overall picture of the shooting – where the police were most likely to have been standing in relation to the workers, and the distance and angles from which the police shot their weapons.[14] These analyses cannot give a precise timeline, but they do give a clear overview of the events at Scene Two – and pro-

---

11   In 2018, Const. Itumeleng Ntsileng and other colleagues told a reporter from the *City Press* that they had participated in the killing of workers at Scene Two. These workers were surrendering: 'he was shot at close range with an R5 rifle while cowering behind the rock, begging for his life. There was no need for that guy to die like that'. He said that he had been instructed to shoot injured men: 'There were people who were still alive. We were instructed to finish them off'. He said that he had yet to be interviewed by the Independent Police Investigative Directorate (IPID), that their weapons had not been taken for ballistic testing, and that they had been warned not to talk to the Commission or any investigator: Vicky Abraham, 'Marikana Massacre: Witnesses to Slaughter at Scene 2', *City Press*, 11 February 2018, www.news24.com/news24/SouthAfrica/News/marikana-massacre-witnesses-to-slaughter-at-scene-2-20180211-2 (Acc. March 2021). Although this account has obviously not been tested under cross-examination, it resonates with material given to the Commission and used in this book; it also chimes with the account of the police action at Scene Two given by David Bruce in 'The Sound of Gunfire: The Police Shootings at Marikana Scene 2, 16 August 2012' (Pretoria, ISS Research Report: 2018).
12   In this chapter, as before, I draw upon Exhibit A – Post-Mortem Reports, as well as Exhibit FFF 20 – LRC medico-legal report on the deceased and Exhibit ZZZZ 48 – Post-Mortem Analysis.
13   In particular, I draw upon Exhibit ZZZ 5 – Naidoo/Steyl report, which is an independent report by ballistics and forensics experts commissioned by the Evidence Leaders' team to analyse the evidence produced at Scene Two.
14   Bruce, 'The Sound of Gunfire', is also extremely useful in describing the site and the physical properties of the scene. Although I mainly cite the Commission's primary documents, I have used his report to confirm and clarify my understanding of the spatial nature of the action at Scene Two.

vide a picture that largely corroborates testimonies that tell of police violence, brutality, and murder at the second scene of the massacre.

By reading these different sources of information together, it is possible to describe what happened to each person at Scene Two – how they were shot, and how they were killed. The following pages tell these stories, and give the best version of what we can know of these deaths.

* * *

Makhosandile Mkhonjwa was the first person to be killed at Scene Two. He was shot as he emerged from among the rocks and bushes, probably alongside a few other workers. They were bent down, hunched over, and trying to escape the tight corridors between the rocks and move back into the open air. As they emerged, though, they came face to face with a group of police officers. The police say that they believed that Mkhonjwa and his companions were going to attack them – and so, they say, they opened fire with handguns and rifles. At least two of the group of workers were hit – but one managed to scramble away. Mkhonjwa was not so lucky.[15]

He was struck in the upper chest by a bullet fired from somewhere on his left-hand side. It slammed into him, passing through his chest and lung, and – shoved by the force of its impact – he stumbled and fell to the ground. The police claim that he was charging at them when they shot – but the trajectory of the bullet contradicts this. For the bullet to enter his body from one side, he must have been running right past the police officer who shot at him – and could not have been running straight at him.[16]

Mkhonjwa did not die at once. He was alive at least half an hour after he had been shot. After the massacre had ended, the police photographed parts of the scene – and in one of the photographs he can be seen lying on the ground, clearly still alive.[17] He was coughing blood. As he lay there, he must have heard the continuing pop of gunfire from just behind his head. He must have heard the

15 Mr Mkhonjwa's body was recorded in Exhibit CC 42 – Video of Sgt Mohlatsi (Scene 2). The Evidence Leaders' Timeline places this footage at 16:11:36 in the afternoon. The next evidence of further shooting takes place at least a minute later, making it almost certain that Mkhonjwa was killed before anyone else. The official police account of his death is given in Exhibit UUU 2 – Consolidated statement of Capt. Kidd. The evidence given in support of this account (in Exhibit UUU 11 – Statement of W/O Batsi and Exhibit UUU 13 – Additional Statement of Sergeant Mahlatsi) reveals a number of inconsistencies. The police account is too inconsistent to be believed, and is incompatible with his wounds.
16 Exhibit A – Post-Mortems, pp. 91–102. See also: ZZZ 5 – Naidoo/Steyl Report, p. 22.
17 In addition to providing ballistic analysis, the Naidoo/Steyl Report (ZZZ 5) concludes from an analysis of the police photographs that Mr Mkhonjwa was still alive when the photographs were taken (p. 22).

police shout at each other – first in panic, and then in celebration. He must have felt the gathering chill of the evening. He must have slowly lost his strength, as he bled on the dirt, waiting to die. He was twenty-eight years old. His father had died four months earlier, and his family was still mourning. They were waiting for him in the Eastern Cape, waiting for him to call again, to tell them what had happened at the koppie, to tell them he was fine.[18]

They would not hear from him again.

He had been shot at about 16:08. A police officer reported his body on the ground a moment later. In a series of frenzied communications, orders were given to the members of the National Intelligence Unit group to leave their vehicles, and to prepare themselves to confront the workers hiding in and around the rocks.[19] At about 16:12 – four minutes after Mkhonjwa had been shot – police officers again began to fire live ammunition. On the recordings produced by the police, it is possible to hear one officer shouting that there was firing in 'the direction of the dogs' – possibly at the other side of the rocks, where the police's K9 Unit was advancing on the miners.[20]

Johannes Thelejane was shot at around this time. At fifty-five years old, he was not a young man, and had only joined the strike when he had heard that the company's managers would be addressing the crowd at the koppie. He had come down the koppie, seen the shooting at the kraal, and had fled with a crowd of other men.[21] He hid himself on the eastern side of the rocks at Scene Two – but when he saw the police approaching, he tried to slip away. He was just on the outskirts of the rocks when the police opened fire, and shot him from behind. He was struck by bullets in the back of his head, and in his buttocks. The rocks around him were pitted with bullet scars, suggesting that he was subject to a hail of rapid fire. The only conclusion that can be drawn from the evidence of his wounds is that he was facing away from the police at the time he was shot and killed by them.[22] He could not have offered any immediate threat. Instead, he was most likely to have been trying escape the police, and make his way back home, where his wife was waiting for him. He did not escape, though, and died where he had fallen, struck down to the earth.

Anele Mdizeni was only twenty metres away from Johannes Thelejane when he too was shot. The bullet struck his right hip, moved through his pelvis, and

---

18   Exhibit KKKK 7 – Makhosandile Mkhonjwa.
19   Exhibit OOO 11 – Transcript of Exhibit CC22 (Lonmin chopper transcript) – from 16:08:16.
20   See Exhibit CC 42, in addition to recordings captured by the police watching in the mining company's helicopter, hovering above the scene. The video recording is Exhibit CC 22 – Aerial video (Coin Security). A transcript of these remarks can be found at Exhibit OOO 11 – Transcript of Exhibit CC22.
21   Exhibit KKKK 18 –Thabiso Johannes Thelejane.
22   Exhibit A – Post-Mortems, pp. 41–65; ZZZ 5 – Naidoo/Steyl Report, pp. 14–15.

came to a stop in the muscles of his leg. It struck him with such force that his legs would have immediately collapsed beneath him. He would not have been able to stand again, or even to sit up. He would have been rendered immobile. He was not close to the police officer who shot him: the nearest rifle cartridge was found more than forty metres away from him. The rocks around him – like the rocks around Johannes Thelejane's body – were peppered with bullet scars, suggesting a rapid burst of uncontrolled fire on the part of the police officers. He, too, did not die at once. He couldn't move himself, and he lay still on the ground while the police approached. Someone realized that he was still alive – and instead of treating his injuries, they dragged him across the ground and bound his hands behind his back, using tight plastic cable-ties. He was shoved into a sitting position, but his injuries meant that he could not hold himself upright. He slumped forward, unable to shift himself. He was bleeding, gasping for breath, and in pain. The police did nothing to help. They restrained him, and abandoned him – and, in doing so, ensured that his death would soon follow.[23]

Nkosiyabo Xalabile was a little further away, at the southern end of the outcropping. A month earlier, he had been in Elliotdale, in the Eastern Cape, back at his family's home to marry his bride. A few days earlier, his greatest worries were how to pay off their wedding debts, how to build a family while moving between Marikana and the Eastern Cape, and perhaps how to balance the habits of his single life – coaching his casual soccer team, for example – with his new responsibilities.[24] In these moments, though, he pushed himself into a small gap between a tree trunk and rock, most likely hoping that the shrubs would hide and protect him. He crouched down, but could not make himself invisible. He was shot in the back of his neck, by a police officer standing above his body: either perched on top of the rocks, shooting down into the crevasse at a half-seen figure, or standing in front of Xalabile as he crouched down, his neck bent to the ground. Xalabile died from this bullet wound. After his death, his body was moved by the police: his hands were found positioned behind his back, as if they had been bound and then released.[25]

'The killing zone'

At the centre of the area is large conglomeration of boulders, marking out the highest part of Scene Two. In the report prepared after the massacre by two independent forensic experts, it is suggested that the some police officers most likely climbed these boulders and – standing above the bushes and earth – aimed their

---

23   Exhibit A – Post-Mortems, pp. 66–90, and Exhibit ZZZ 5 – Naidoo/Steyl Report, p 14.
24   Exhibit KKKK 41 – Nkosiyabo Xalabile.
25   Exhibit A – Post-Mortems, pp. 646–661. Also Exhibit ZZZ 5 – Naidoo/Steyl Report, p. 23.

rifles and handguns down through the branches and at the crouched figures of the hiding miners.[26] Ten men were shot and killed by the police in the network of crevasses between the rocks and beneath the dry bushes, in the area around the high boulders. In the years afterwards, this area at the heart of Scene Two became known as the 'killing zone'.

The independent forensic experts suggest that the majority of the wounds sustained by the victims in this area can be explained by one of two possible alternate scenarios: either the police opened fire from all sides of the area, and bullets bounced off of the rocks and the dirt, hitting the workers from all directions; or, in the second, some of the police officers climbed the central boulders and, standing above the workers, aimed their weapons downwards and fired recklessly at the workers.[27]

For these experts, the second scenario was the more likely of the two. It explained more of the wounds found on the ten men who were shot and killed in this 'killing zone' than the other explanation. Although some of the injuries that these men bore could have come from bullets ricocheting off of the rocks, and others might have been caused by accident and cross-fire, there were too many injuries that could not be plausibly explained this way. Nor could stray bullets explain how these men all died so close to each other, their bodies clustered on the ground.[28]

Tokoti Mangcotywa was one of the men killed in this zone. In August 2012, he was sixty-one years, and when he had come to work in Marikana had left eight children and large extended family in Sterkspruit, on the Lesotho border. He was hiding on the ground, between two rocks. He was shot from the front in his chest, and from behind in his buttocks. He may have turned as he was first struck, and scrambled on the ground as he was shot at again. As he bled, he stopped moving on the ground. He rested his head against a rock, propping it up. As he died, another man fell beside him – probably at the same time – and rested his weight on Tokoti's legs.[29]

Janeveke Raphael Liau was the man who had fallen across Tokoti's body. He was forty-seven years old, and left a wife, four children, and an extended family. He died from a single wound in his chest, caused by a single handgun bullet.

---

26   ZZZ 5 – Naidoo/Steyl Report, p. 25.
27   In the conclusion to ZZZ 5 – Naidoo/Steyl report, the experts assert that at least three rifles were fired from 'upon the large central Koppie boulder', and that the 'general impression' was that the 'koppie was encircled by SAPS personnel and vehicles'. Although these have sometimes been presented as alternate scenarios, they are not mutually exclusive – although one may be preferred as more likely.
28   For the overall disposition of the bodies, see Exhibit JJJ 162 – Scene 2 Bodies, read with 7.7.7.7. 48 – Post-Mortem Analysis, which sets out the code used to identify the individual bodies.
29   Exhibit A – Post-Mortems, pp. 103–125; ZZZ 5 – Naidoo/Steyl Report, pp. 16–17.

A cartridge matching this bullet was found on top of the large central boulder. Both Tokoti Mangcotywa and Janeveke Liau were shot from above: discarded cartridges were found on top of the central boulders, but no similar cartridges were found at any of the other possible places from which the police could have stood to have hit their bodies at these angles. They could not have posed any threat at the moment of their deaths.[30]

Mafolisi Mabiya had found his way into the crevasses between the rocks. He huddled alongside another worker, Thabiso Mosebetsane, in the shadow of the rocks and beneath a thin shelter of branches and leaves. Mafolisi was struck by a bullet in the back of his head. The angle of this wound suggests that he was shot from above, and that he was facing away from the police officer who shot him. This is the only wound on his body. He fell, his arms spreading wide, and died immediately. At the moment of his death, his wife was still at the hospital, watching over their sick child. She had not yet heard anything about the day's events – and would only suspect anything about her husband's death later, when she took their child home, and found him missing.[31]

Thabiso Mosebetsane was a religious man. He had met his wife a year earlier, when had been travelling a circuit across the Eastern Cape as part of his church group. She did not know that he was crouched alongside Mafolisi Mabiya. She did not know that he was shot twice in the head, the two shots following each other in rapid succession. There were no other wounds to his body. The trajectory of the bullets suggests that he was most likely shot from the central boulders – or, possibly, from an open patch of land to one side of the killing zone. He certainly posed no threat to the police officer who killed him. Instead, he was effectively executed by a distant police officer.[32]

Ntandazo Nokhamba loved soccer, and used to coach a youth team at his family's home in Libode, in the Eastern Cape. His wife remembered that he would still bring them soccer boots and other equipment, even though he was living in Marikana for most of the year. 'He would come home three times a year', she said, 'and would phone three times a day'. She spoke to him during the strike: 'Ntandazo used to phone me at 06:00 in the morning to tell me he was going to participate in the strike. He would phone again after 22:00 in the evening, when he came back from the strike. Ntandazo did not feel good [about it] because people were getting killed'. On Thursday morning, he had called as usual. She remembered that he had 'asked about the children. He said that he would call again after returning from the

---

30   Exhibit A – Post-Mortems, pp. 126–147; ZZZ 5 – Naidoo/Steyl Report, pp. 16–17.
31   Exhibit A – Post-Mortems, pp. 166–190; ZZZ 5 – Naidoo/Steyl Report, p. 18. See also: KKKK 29 – Mafolisi Mabiya.
32   Exhibit A – Post-Mortems, pp. 148–165; ZZZ 5 – Naidoo/Steyl Report, p. 18. There is a concern that the State Pathologist misinterpreted the trajectory of some of his injuries: FFF 20 – Medico-Legal Report, Annexure C, p. 2. See also: KKKK 14 – Thabiso Mosebetsane.

koppie. I expected his call, but it did not come'.[33] Ntandazo was killed by a single bullet wound to the chest. He died quickly.[34]

Fezile Saphendu was crouched next to him, and was almost certainly killed by the same bullet. The bullet had hit Fezile first, tearing through his body, before coming to a final stop in Ntandazo's chest. They fell together. Unlike Ntandazo, Fezile was not a fan of soccer. He was more likely to be found at home, in his time off. According to his brother, 'Fezile liked to sing and to joke. He also loved to cook … He was a caring and respectful person. He got along with elderly people'. He was twenty-four years old, and had lived in Marikana for the past three years, having replaced his elder brother at Lonmin. He was not married, and had no children. After being shot, he fell backwards, his face turned towards the sky. He bled to death, resting against Ntandazo.[35]

Mphumzeni Ngxande had left the mountain at midday to eat lunch at home in Nkaneng. His wife remembered that he ate in rush, gulping his food down: 'He didn't even take five minutes, and he said he had to go back because he wants to hear what Mr Mathunjwa had to say'. He went back to the mountain shortly after 13:00. His wife remained at home. 'Later', she said, 'I heard the gun shots. I tried to go and get closer to the incident, but I couldn't. I heard that the police were shooting the strikers, so I waited there by the road, looking for my husband. Then most workers passed, but he was not among them'.[36] She did not see him because he had joined the group running away from the police and the informal settlement, and had found himself among the rocks of Scene Two. He crawled through the shrubs and over stones to the centre of the area. He waited there as the police approached. He must have heard the sound of gunfire, first at the edges of the site and then, coming closer. He must have looked up and seen a police officer mounting the rocks above him – and then he was shot, and killed. He was struck in the front of his chest. The bullet pierced his heart, and remained in his body. He was shot again, scratched across the thigh. He was almost certainly shot from above, and he would have died within seconds.[37]

Sitelega Meric Gadlela was also killed by a bullet wound to the chest. He was bending down, facing away from the shooter. He fell forward and to the side, striking the dusty earth between the shrubs and bushes. He died quickly. He had lived and worked in Marikana, for Lonmin, for twenty-three years, ever since he had left his family home in Swaziland. For half of his life, he had split his life between his two homes. Now, he died in the sight of one – and far too far away from the other.[38]

33 Exhibit KKKK 8 –Ntandazo Nokhamba.
34 Exhibit A – Post-Mortems, pp. 191–215; ZZZ 5 – Naidoo/Steyl Report, p. 18.
35 Exhibit A – Post-Mortems, pp. 216–239; ZZZ 5 – Naidoo/Steyl Report, p. 19. See also: KKKK 15 –Fezile David Saphendu.
36 Exhibit KKKK 16 – Mphumzeni Ngxande.
37 Exhibit A – Post-Mortems, pp. 240–262(b); ZZZ 5 – Naidoo/Steyl Report, p. 20.
38 Exhibit A – Post-Mortems, pp. 263–294; ZZZ 5 – Naidoo/Steyl Report, p. 20.

Henry Mvuyisi Pato had only arrived in Marikana just over a year earlier. He had left his parents, his sibling, his two children, and their mother in Mbizana, in the Eastern Cape. He had only been able to visit them once in the last year, but tried to phone them regularly. During the strike, he had avoided the subject of the strike – his father remembered that he had said nothing about the police, or the violence that was unfolding in Marikana. He lived alone in Marikana, and was alone when he was shot in the back of his neck and killed by the police. He was facing away from the man who shot him. He may have stood still for a moment, and felt the wet back of his neck with his hand. He fell, his body twisted unnaturally. He bled to death, alone at the end.[39]

Telang Mohai was in the killing zone when he was struck by rubber bullets.[40] He must have been staggered by the force, and would have lost his balance. He stumbled, bending towards the ground. He was then shot in the back with live ammunition. The post-mortem notes suggest that he was either bending low at the time, or lying flat on the ground. He was shot at chest height, by a man standing behind him. He did not die immediately. A photograph of the scene, taken in the moments after the shooting stopped, shows him lying alive on the ground. He survived for about an hour, breathing heavily among the bodies of the dead. He was eventually moved from the site, and taken away in an ambulance – but it was too late, and he died on the way to the hospital.[41]

All ten of these men were likely to have been killed in the five minutes after 16:12 – the moment in which the police first reported the sound of live fire in the area. The radio records suggest that noise, confusion, and chaos erupted in and around the killing zone of Scene Two for these minutes. Police officers at one edge of the area seem to have heard shots fired by other police officers, hidden from them by the screen of boulders and winter-dry trees. They assumed that they were hearing shots fired by the protestors. They opened fire, indiscriminately, aiming at the rocks: the air grew thick with smoke, shimmered with heat, and rocked with the harsh noise of barking dogs, the explosive pop of gunfire, the yells of the miners, and the shouts of the police.

No defence has ever been offered for these murders – because there is no defence that can be.[42] There can be no doubt that the police action in this Kill-

---

39 Exhibit A – Post-Mortems, pp. 295–322; ZZZ 5 – Naidoo/Steyl Report, p. 21–22.
40 Mr Mohai died after being removed from the site. The independent experts could not identify the exact location of his shooting, but photographs taken in the immediate aftermath show him next to Mr Ngxande in the 'Killing Zone'. For this reason, I have included him in this section, as one of the victims of the killing zone.
41 FFF 20 – Medico-Legal Report, Annexure C, p. 8; KKK 10 – SAPS Summary of Forensic Experts Reports, p. 32.
42 The Heads of Argument filed on behalf of the SAPS suggested: 'There is no direct evidence indicating which member [of the police] was responsible for which fatality ... the nine deceased persons may have died not as a consequence of

ing Zone at Scene Two was nothing short of murderous. They acted without oversight, self-control, or imagination. They acted brutally, with unconsidered, overwhelming violence. They gave no quarter: they shot men in the head, in the back of the neck, in their backs. They shot men who were standing, who were crouched down, who were lying prostrate on the ground. The police did not act in self-defence, but rather in callousness and cruelty.

'Let us surrender, gentlemen'

On the edges of the scene, Shadrack Mtshamba was still hiding with a group of other workers among the rocks and the bushes on the outskirts of the killing zone. He had seen water cannons shooting streams of coloured water at the boulders, intended to flush the workers out of their hiding places. He had heard the police officers gathering:

> We could not see the policemen. We heard bullets, shots being fired, and the bullets hitting the rocks. We were kneeling below these rocks ... The sound of gunfire ... at that time had become more from all sides. Some of the bullets sounded as though the people were shooting from sites near, and some were shooting from the other side.

One of the workers was driven to panic by the sounds. He suggested that the group should come out of hiding, hands raised, and surrender to the police. Mtshamba told the story of this one attempt:

> I think he said it twice, shouting, shouting above the noise that was there. He was the first one to raise up his arms. He was in front of the group that was with me. He raised his hands. As he was raising his hands, he was shot at ... After the shot was fired, he then bent down again, again he raised his hands, kept on saying, 'Let us surrender, gentlemen, let's surrender'.
>
> [...]
>
> Again a shot was fired at him, he was shot in the region of the stomach. He bent down. The third bullet hit him in the leg. He then fell and went on his knees. Another one who was standing next to the one who was shot also raised up his hands, and when he came up with his hands raised, he was shot in the region of the head ... He fell on his face. We all then became scared because we saw the people [who were] surrendering being shot.

They didn't move, hoping to be missed.[43]

---

shots aimed directly at them but rather as a consequence of them being struck by rounds fired for other reasons, travelling through the area' (paras 217–218). The police have offered no explanation – other than accident – for the deaths that occurred here.

43 Mtshamba, Day 275, pp. 35,138–35,140.

Thobile Mpumza may have been one of the men that Mtshamba saw. He was the last worker to be killed at Scene Two.[44] The police have told several different stories to explain his death – but their own stories contradict each other. There is no way to be certain how he died, or even to be certain that he was one of the men that Mtshamba saw. But one account of Mpumza's death, told by a police constable, comes close to confirming Mtshamba's account. Constable Sebatjane described Mpumza emerging from the bushes, alongside at least one other man. Mpumza tried to surrender. When the police officers approached him, he rose up again and the officers – according to Constable Sebatjane – feared for their lives, shot in his direction, and killed him.[45] A second version, however, suggested that Mpumza had ran out of the bushes alone, and had charged blindly towards an officer – who then shot at him in self-defence.[46]

The two stories told by the police officers are incompatible with each other. They cannot both be true. And neither can explain the fact that Mpumza was shot thirteen times with high-velocity bullets. Neither can explain why he was struck both from the front and from the sides. He may have been turning as he was struck, spun by the force of the bullets, or he may have been shot by policemen ranged all around him. He was certainly shot by many different men – not just the one. His body was moved after his death, and the exact site could not be analysed.[47]

The response of the police officers in the immediate aftermath of his death was captured on shaky, blurred cell-phone camera footage. It gives a sense of the callousness of the officers in these moments: 'That motherfucker', a police officer says, in English, 'I shot him at least one time. He keeps coming, coming'. He then speaks in Afrikaans: 'I had him then. I emptied it. He still came'. Then, switching back to English, he notices items on the ground that might suggest traditional medicine: 'There's Muti there. There's Muti ... Leave it. Leave it. Ja, that's a Muti shit. Ja'. And then – gleefully addressing the body: 'Doesn't work, hey, Baba'.[48]

When he stepped out from among the rocks and bushes, Thobile Mpumza was only twenty-six years old. His sisters remembered him as a child, and as an

---

44 The death of Mr Mpumza is dealt with at pp. 15–16 of the Naidoo/Steyl Report (ZZZ 5), which suggests that his body may have been moved after his death to its recorded location. There is therefore no certainty that Mr Mpumza was the individual seen by Mr Mtshamba – but the circumstances of his death are too similar to be coincidence.
45 Exhibit TTT 7.1 and 7.2 – Const. Sebetyane's / Sebatjane typed and manuscript statements contain Sebatjane's account of the event.
46 Exhibit 6.1 and Exhibit 6.2 – Statement (and Additional Statement) of Const. Buthelezi contain the second account described here.
47 Exhibit A – Post-Mortems, pp. 19–40; ZZZ 5 – Naidoo/Steyl Report, pp. 15–16.
48 Exhibit OOO 11 – Transcript of CC 22 contains a transcript of Capt. Rylands' cell phone calls, which include these statements.

adult who had kept up many of the enthusiasms of his younger days. Much of his energy had been directed towards his soccer club at home:

> He used to do stuff for the players he played with. If he was coming home, he would bring them some balls and some other things to give to them. An example of how he cared for people, he would bring balls for some and socks for others. And for the rest, he'd have gym shorts.

They insisted that he was not a violent man. He had been drawn into the strike, even though he had been fired for participating in an earlier labour dispute. And even though they had tried to persuade him to leave the strike, he had refused. He told them that it was fine, and that, really, 'there's no problem with doing so because no one is fighting'.[49]

In the face of the brutality of the police at Marikana, gentleness did not prevail. His sisters weep when they remember his words, and his faith in others. They blame the police: 'He gave himself up', they say, 'but that didn't save him, and he was killed'.

In the aftermath

By 16:22, the shooting had stopped. An eerie quiet fell over the scene: smoke drifted across the boulders, coloured water dripped from the bushes, and the late afternoon light gilded the bare branches. Men lay on the ground: some dead, some crouched in hiding, and others badly injured.

Motiso Otsile van Wyk Sagalala was one of these injured men. He had been shot several times: the back of his shoulder was scarred by a bullet wound, as were the sides of his arms. Two other bullets had struck him in the chest, causing serious trauma. We do not know where exactly he was shot: there are no photographs of his body, and no police officer has owned up to shooting him. All we know is that he was eventually placed in a police vehicle – still alive – and taken to the nearby hospital. He did not survive the night. The Commission of Inquiry that followed was told that he died in hospital, but it turned out that this was a lie. Motiso Otsile van Wyk Sagalala died in the back of the police vehicle, ignored by the officers who were driving him away from the site.[50]

---

49 Interview with Xolelwa and Phelokazi Mpmuza, Matatiele, 4 December 2015.
50 Exhibit A – Post-Mortems, pp. 702–721. As Mr Sagalala did not die on site, but rather after removal from Scene 2, his death is not discussed in the Naidoo/Steyl report, or other forensic reports. In this report – and in the evidence given to the Commission – he is said to have died in hospital, alongside Mr Ntsoele and Mr Mohai. However, in later reports, it has become clear that the Commission was misled. Mr Sagalala died in police custody, after his removal from Scene 2. This was revealed during a later IPID investigation, and reported in the media in 2017. See, Greg Nicolson, 'Marikana Massacre: "He is fine, let him die"', *Daily Maverick*, 20 March 2017. See also the notes in Bruce, 'The Sound of Gunfire'.

Molefi Osiel Ntsoele had been shot in the back. He was forty years old, and had worked for Lonmin for the past five years. His family was waiting for him in Lesotho. They were building a new house, making decisions, and planning for the future. Those plans were now about to collapse. Molefi was taken to the hospital, alive and bleeding, and died that evening. His wife, long after the news of his death, could only say: 'There has been a hole that has been left in my life'.[51]

These men – along with Telang Mohai, who had been shot in the killing zone, and many others who were seriously but not fatally injured – lay on the ground for about an hour, injured and dying, while the police secured the site. The police largely ignored them. They photographed some bodies, and bound the hands of others. They left the injured to bleed, unaided and untreated. No medical care was given – not one officer made an attempt to staunch the workers' open wounds.

It was only at 16:48 that the police permitted paramedics to approach the workers at Scene One, and then at Scene Two.[52] They arrived on the site a few minutes later, and began to treat the injured. They arrived about an hour after the first shooting had begun, and about half an hour after the last shots had been fired at Scene Two. By the time they arrived, it was too late for several men who would otherwise have lived – such as Bongani Mdze, who had only been shot through the upper arm at Scene One. Their injuries were now too severe to be treated, and they too would join the lists of the dead. Others, though, were luckier: the paramedics reached them in time to treat their immediate wounds, stop their bleeding, and stabilize them where they lay.

Later, ambulances would arrive and take the injured from the site. They would be admitted to hospitals in the region – and kept there, until they were arrested.

* * *

Meanwhile, the police had been busy. They rounded up the surviving workers, finally allowing them to surrender. They questioned the workers, shouted at them, and then arrested them. According to Shadrack Mtshamba's account:

> It was after some time that the shooting became quiet. They then took us out, they told us all to come out then. They made us lie down on the ground ... They kept telling us to turn around as we were lying there, searching us and loosening the clothing that we had on to see if we did not have any weapons that we were hiding.[53]

---

51 Exhibit A – Post-Mortems, pp. 722–739. Because Mr Ntsoele died in the hospital, and not on the site, he is not discussed in the forensic reports compiled on the killings that took place at Scene 2.

52 This time comes from the Evidence Leaders' timeline (ZZZ 10), drawing on images in C 38 – Flir Clip. (This is a set of videos recorded by the SAPS). See the comments in the previous chapter on the delaying of the paramedics.

53 Mtshamba, Day 275, pp. 35, 140.

Mtshamba's account chimes with those given by men at Scene One. He saw people forced to the ground, threatened and intimidated, beaten by the police and quizzed about a traditional healer.

> We were instructed to crawl on all fours towards … the armoured vehicles which were there. I saw some people being hit, the kierie [clubs] being taken from them, they were hit, and asked, they were asking where is the *sangoma*, and such questions. We were told that we are useless, we're killing police who have done nothing wrong, that we are killing government people. They said that if it was in some other country they would pour petrol on us and set us alight.[54]

Mtshamba and his fellow workers were terrified: at Scene One, they had seen the police shoot at workers as they rounded the kraal, and at Scene Two they had just again seen the police shoot at workers crouched between rocks, at workers who were on the ground, at workers who were surrendering. Now, they heard police officers threaten them – and could only believe that the police were capable of fulfilling even the most violent and the most outlandish of these threats.

The workers were made to crawl across the ground and into the police vehicles. Once inside, the heavy doors were closed, and they were forced to spend three hours lying on the hard floors of the vehicles, shut off from the light and the world outside. They heard the police moving around outside. They heard them celebrating the deaths of the other workers, and releasing steam. They could see nothing, know nothing for sure. All they could do was imagine what was happening.

After a long wait, the engines roared back into life and Mtshamba and the others were driven from the site of the killings to the neighbouring Patani police station. They were all arrested and processed. It took hours for them to be processed: Mtshamba was later listed as accused number 241 out of about 270 men on a lengthy charge-sheet drawn up by the police against the surviving miners. The charges themselves were left blank, at first.[55] It was only after the better part of a week that Mtshamba and others learned what they had been arrested for – the murder of their thirty-four colleagues, the men killed by police bullets at both Scene One and Scene Two on 16 August.

The cover-up begins

These charges seem to have formed part of a concerted effort by the police to evade responsibility for the deaths at Marikana. From the first moments after silence fell across the two scenes, police officers and commanders met and spoke

---

54 Mtshamba, Day 275, p. 35,141.
55 Mtshamba, Day 275, pp. 35,142–35,145. In this exchange 272 people are said to have been arrested. The official police figure was 259 – Exhibit JJJ 118.8 – SAPS Lonmin Mine Unrest: Marikana, Thursday 16th August 2012. The discrepancy may be explained by a number of arrests that took place in hospital.

to each other for the purpose of manufacturing an explanation that would justify their actions, absolve them of blame for the deaths of thirty-four men, and protect themselves.

The substance of these discussions has never been disclosed, but the actions of the police in the hours after the shooting provide a strong sense of what was being planned. In the minutes after the shooting, a few police officers began photographing the bodies of the dead and the faces of the injured and arrested miners – at least in part to provide evidence of the identities of these men at trial. These photographs showed the initial position of many of the bodies of the deceased, and showed that some of the men who would later die were still alive in these early moments. There is good reason to believe that these photographs were not licensed by the commanding officers – and that, in fact, they were simply taken out of habit by ordinary police officers.[56] And although these officers were following procedure, they soon stopped photographing the scene: as the paramedics arrived late to the scene, and as the sun set, they put the caps back on their cameras. These photographs would be given over to the police commanders, and then hidden away on computer hard drives – filed away, and kept secret for many months after the massacre itself.

The day continued. At about 18:00, an hour after paramedics were permitted on the scene, and as they were leaving with the injured, the police began their cover-up.

They gathered up weapons from across the site, taking knives, knobkerries, a small firearm, and spears from where they had fallen, or been abandoned, or thrown down when the workers had surrendered. They gathered armfuls of weapons, and then walked around the two sites – and began to plant these weapons on or beside the bodies of the men that they had only just killed. They then photographed the bodies again, intending to create a record that suggested that the dead had been armed.[57]

Only a comparison between the earlier photographs and the ones taken later – after the weapons had been put in the hands of the mute dead – revealed this deception.[58] Henry Mvuyisi Pato had been shot in the back of his neck in the Killing Zone at Scene Two. He died quickly. At the time of his death, his hands were empty and he was unarmed. After his death, though, police officers approached his body with a large yellow-handled panga – a long bush knife. They lifted the

---

56 Exhibit JJJ 29 – Ramalana's photos of the 16 August.
57 See Exhibit K – Slides contrasting photos of Capt. Mohlaki and W/O Ramanala. Ramanala's photographs (Exhibit JJJ 29) were taken earlier, and show the bodies in their original position. Mohlaki's were taken later, and show several bodies having been moved – and having had weapons planted near or underneath their bodies.
58 This is the indisputable conclusion of the Evidence Leaders at the Commission after an examination of Exhibit K. An analysis of these photographs is found at paras 1,116–1,121 to the Evidence Leaders' Heads of Argument. I have drawn upon their conclusions in this account of the planted weapons.

dead weight of his arm, and slipped the panga underneath his body, positioning it so that it seemed as if he had been carrying it before he had collapsed over it.[59] They photographed this carefully constructed scene, and said nothing about the fakery that went into making it. The same was done at the site of Makhosandile Mkhonjwa's death. He had been shot at Scene Two by police officers who claimed that he had been charging towards them. His wounds contradicted this story: he was shot and killed from the side, and not from the front. More than this: in the photographs taken shortly after his death, there are no weapons around his body. But in those taken more than an hour later, four weapons – two sticks, a spear, and an iron rod – can be seen scattered on either side of him. These were planted by the police after his death. There can be no doubt that this was meant to support the story told by the police of his death – a story in which the police were absolved of any responsibility for Mkhonjwa's unjustified death.

There is similarly clear evidence that the police planted weapons on at least four other bodies at Scene Two. The bodies of Ntandazo Nokhamba, Fezile Saphendu, Mphumzeni Ngxande, and Nkosiyabo Xalabile were moved. The police gathered up weapons that had fallen in the area around them, and then moved them nearer to the bodies of the deceased. The police slid knives under their arms, dropped spears beside them, and dressed up the sites of their deaths to make it seem as though they had been armed when they died – as though they had been about to attack.

These photographs could only have been intended to provide a justification for the police killings at Scene Two, and to obscure the responsibility of the police for the deaths. They aimed to provide evidence – manufactured evidence, although that was not immediately obvious – for the police's official story: that the workers had posed an immediate threat to the police, to journalists, and to any other bystanders and that any action taken – including the use of deadly force – was justified in self-defence. This was a lie. But the lie was made to seem, for a while, to be plausible.

In the media

At 18:00, the evening news carried the first stories about the shooting at Scene One. The newsreader on the national broadcaster – the SABC – read out his script: 'Paramedics have arrived at the Lonmin Platinum Mine in Marikana in the North West where several people are feared dead and many other wounded after violence erupted again between police and striking workers'. The smooth

---

59 A detailed example of the analysis can be found in Appendix 1 of the Evidence Leaders' Heads of Argument, which shows how the weapon planted on Mr Pato's body can be seen in earlier photos at a different site on the ground; it also demonstrates that the earliest photos do not show it in Mr Pato's hand, but that Mohlaki's later photos show that it has been placed beneath his lifeless hand.

voice continued, moving seamlessly from a description of the event to an apparent explanation for the violence: 'It's alleged that some mine workers started shooting at the police, who retaliated. Police had been trying to negotiate with workers to disperse'.[60]

The newsreader then handed over to a recording provided by a journalist embedded behind the police lines. Her voice was rushed, breathless:

> They gave them a final warning, dropped some grenades, tear gas, and then started shooting at these striking mineworkers. We are currently seeing twelve people that we believe is either heavily injured, or might be dead. We are also seeing paramedics rushed to the scene. Currently the police are not giving out any information as to the status of these people but we believe that they might be dead.

The newsreader continued: 'Police first fired tear gas to try and disperse the striking miners, then the shooting erupted'. He then played a recording of 'the moment the police opened fire'. The airwaves cracked with the sound of popping guns – disturbingly banal, like the sound of popcorn bursting inside a closed pot – before closing the report: 'Moving on to other news now…'

As this report went out over the airwaves, we now know that the police were busy on site – moving the bodies of the dead, planting weapons on and around them, and constructing a narrative that exonerated them. Although the journalists could not have known this at the time, their stories would feed into and foster the narrative that the police wanted to tell – a narrative that scapegoated the workers.

This was the first story that most of the country would have heard about the events 16 August 2012. Almost all of this story has since been proven to be incorrect. There is no evidence that the police had attempted to negotiate on 16 August 2012 – and, instead, much evidence that they acted to frustrate the negotiations that were already taking place. Nor is there any evidence that the police fired tear gas to disperse the miners, nor any evidence that warnings – whether shouted out, or in the form of a warning shot – were ever given to the striking workers. And although one mineworker does seem to have fired a homemade gun at Scene One,[61] this took place after the police had already opened fire with

---

60   SA FM 'News at 6', 16 August 2012, www.youtube.com/watch?v=DKL6TxrvQX8 (Acc. March 2021).

61   Video footage of the moments around and before the massacre capture what appears to be the sound of a single shot coming from a group of mineworkers: Exhibit RRR 17 – Join of Reuters footage. According to police witnesses, they heard at least one and perhaps two shots in this scramble. See Exhibit QQQ 9 – Consolidated Statement of Lt-Col Thupe, para. 26. A makeshift handgun was found near Scene One, after the massacre. However, there has never been any indication that this weapon could be linked to any individual striker; there has never been any indication that anyone was injured in any way by this weapon; and there is a great deal of uncertainty around the timing of its firing. In all, there is little weight to be

tear gas, rubber-bullets, and water cannon – and at almost the same seconds that the police fired live ammunition, killing seventeen workers.

But despite these inaccuracies and falsehoods, the story that went out that Thursday evening provided the first attempt to give an explanation of the killings. Over the next several days, this rapidly came to be the dominant version of the shooting. It was a version that tracked closely onto the interpretation favoured by the police: it cast the workers as aggressors, and painted the best possible picture of the police – imagining that that they provided immediate warnings, that they only fired their guns in self-defence, and that paramedics were 'rushed' to the scene to treat the injured miners, instead of being held back and delayed for almost an hour.

As with the police's official narrative, this story had no place for the events at Scene Two. The journalists reported on what they had seen – the confusion and the killings at Scene One – and did not question what had happened in the hours after they had been ushered from the site. On the evening of 16 August 2012, there was as yet no certainty about how many people had died, how many people had been injured, and what would happen next. Instead of emphasizing that uncertainty, though, the police and compliant journalists offered a false certainty – one that pretended that the causes of the clash were clear, and the victims were in fact the aggressors.

The story that emerged on the evening of the massacre was one that misled the public, hid the truth from the victims' families, and would take years of investigation and challenge to contradict.

---

placed on these allegations – except to note that they might well be true, and yet change nothing about the massacre itself.

Part III

After the Massacre

9

Burying the Dead

ON THE evening of Thursday, 16 August 2012, Zameka Nungu sat down to dinner with her children at her home in Mount Fletcher, in the Eastern Cape. The radio was playing in the background. She heard the news open with a report on Marikana.

Zameka listened, and was gripped by fear:

> Before then, I was worried but I did not fear for his life. After hearing about the killings … I became frantic with worry. I tried calling him, and his phone was off. I did not know what to do. I could not eat. I walked out of the house, and just kept walking, not knowing where I was going.[1]

She received no reassurance. The news that evening only said that there had been a deadly clash, and that miners had been killed. The exact number of the dead was still uncertain, and the names of those killed – or even of those injured – was still unknown to journalists. Overall, the story was reported in vague and broad terms.

That night Zameka went to sleep not knowing whether her husband was alive or dead. The next day brought no more news, and as each day passed and she heard nothing, her hopes receded. Her fears grew. She tried to find out what had happened to him, and why she could no longer reach him on his phone. On 19 August – three days after the shooting – one of her husband's colleagues told her that they had been to the hospital, and to the nearby Phokeng mortuary, but they could not find any sign of him. On 21 August – two days later, and five days after the shooting – she received a call from a family member 'who told me that Jackson had been killed as a result of the strike'. That family member had been contacted by Teba, a labour brokering company appointed by Lonmin to communicate with the family. She had been told that 'Jackson was among the people who had been killed, but they did not furnish any details'.

On Monday 27 August – almost a week after the news of her husband's death reached Zameka Nungu – a group of Jackson's friends and colleagues were finally able to see his body at the mortuary in Rustenberg. It had been difficult for them

---

1   Exhibit KKKK 32 – Jackson Lehupa. Interview with Zameka Nungu, Matatiele, 4 December 2015.

to do so. 'They wanted to see Jackson's body, but the people at the mortuary would not allow them to do so'. At first, the mortuary staff sent Jackson's friends away: first, 'they told them to choose a coffin for his body'. It was only after they had done so, and only after they had returned on the next day, that they were permitted to identify Jackson's body – and even then 'they were only shown the body from the neck up'.

Jackson's body was released on 31 August. He was buried with his family in the Eastern Cape on 1 September, but the funeral did not ease Zameka's mind: 'They could not tell me anything in much detail because I was in distress. I just couldn't understand much of what anyone was saying to me because I was in shock.'

Afterwards, she was left with suspicions about Jackson's death, about the long wait to simply hear that he was dead, even about the conduct of the mortuary staff: '[His friends] were not shown the rest of his body, nor were they provided with a post-mortem report', she said in a statement. 'No one from the mortuary or the mine told me the cause of his death. To this day, I have not received an official explanation.'

'They only let me look at the head'

There was nothing unusual about Zameka Nungu's experience in the days and weeks after the massacre. The families of the men killed on 16 August 2012 all shared these experiences – they struggled to find out whether their loved ones were alive or dead, they struggled to find the bodies of the deceased, and they had to learn to mourn.

This was true, even if the families were in Marikana. Ntombizile Mosebetsane was living in Nkaneng at the time of strike and the massacre. Over the past week, she had gone about her own life while her husband, Thabiso, had gone to the koppie. She had accepted his comings and goings during the strike, but when he did not come home of the evening of 16 August, she began to worry. The next morning she took action: 'On the 17th, his friend's wife and I, we headed straight to the koppie, and we go there and found it swarming with police'. There was no sign of Thabiso at the site, though, and no information about him. 'We tried to get answers about what had happened, [but] the police told us to go to Number One [station]. When we got there, no one paid us any attention. So we left, and headed for the police station in Marikana. They told us that they knew nothing.' The police gave her 'a long list of telephone numbers to call' but these numbers did not help. They led to a scattered set of police stations in the region, each of which Ntombizile visited, searching for news about her husband.[2]

She had no luck at any of the local police stations. Next, she went to the hospital. 'We got there and found they had compiled a list. It was on a trailer, or what looked like a trailer, and this trailer had a list of names of people who had either

---

2 Interview with Ntombizile Mosebetsane, Matatiele, 4 December 2015.

been arrested or killed or hospitalized, but he wasn't on any of these lists'. Without any clear indication of whether he was alive or dead, hospitalized or arrested, Ntombizile continued to search across the area for news about her husband.

The weekend passed. On Monday, 20 August, Ntombizile and her friend visited the police stations in the area again. Meanwhile, a group of their friends travelled to the Phokeng mortuary, about sixty kilometres away from Marikana, to follow up on a rumour that the bodies of some of those killed in the massacre were being kept there. They learned that the rumour was true. But not even that was straightforward: 'They returned with the message that they'd been asked to return the next day. It was late, so then they went back on the 21st, and they were given photographs'.

Five days after he was killed at Scene Two, Thabiso Mosebetsane was identified from these photographs, and Ntombizile finally knew that her husband was dead.

Both Zameka Nungu and Ntombilize Mosebetsane learned that their husbands had been killed after five days of wrenching uncertainty. Not everyone, though, was able to begin the work of mourning on this day – and, indeed, for some of the families, that work was postponed and made harder by mistakes in the identification of the dead.

Nosihle Ngweyi spent the long days after the massacre waiting for news about her husband, Michael. She was in Umtata, in the Eastern Cape, and relied on family and friends in Marikana to pass on anything that they knew. On Tuesday 21 August, a representative of the Teba labour brokerage contacted Nosihle's brother, and informed him that Michael had been killed. He told his sister, and she was shattered by the news: 'I felt traumatized. I never thought that my husband had died in the strike. I kept believing that he was arrested and would be released soon. I felt severe pain and heartache, and I did not want to believe that he had died. I could not believe.'[3]

But what should have been the end of the period of uncertainty and the beginning of mourning was complicated that same day when other family members in Marikana went to the Phokeng police station and were told by a police officer that 'when he shouted Michael's name, someone answered ... The police said that since he answered when his name was called, Michael was alive and detained at Phokeng'. They would not allow any of the family members to see him, however, and told them that they should come back on Thursday. The police would not bend, even when they were told that his wife thought that Michael was dead. They insisted on the delay.

Nosihle was told about what had happened at the Phokeng police station, and that there was a chance that her husband was actually alive – and that the news from the labour brokers had been wrong. She clung to this possibility. 'This was a great relief to me, and I was very happy that my husband had survived'.

---

[3] Exhibit KKKK 42 –Michael Ngweyi.

When social workers came to visit her, to attempt to discuss Michael's death, she wanted to dismiss them: 'They were shocked when I told them that my husband was not dead'. They did not leave, though. 'The social workers asked me how I would feel if I heard my husband was dead ... They talked to me as if my husband was dead, as if they were preparing me to accept [his] death.' Nosihle did not know what to believe – should she believe that her husband was being held in Phokeng station, or should she believe him dead?

It was only on Thursday 23 August that her doubts were finally resolved. Her family members returned to the Phokeng station, where they were told that there had been a mistake. Michael had not been in the cells. He was indeed dead, but his body had not been formally identified – and the family had been asked back to the station to arrange to formally identify his body. They were taken to a memorial service held in Marikana, and confirmed that it was indeed Michael's body. They then had to call Nosihle, and tell her that the labour brokerage and the social workers had been correct. She listened the news: 'I felt pain ... I had truly believed that he had survived ... I had been told that my husband had died, was alive, and had died. I felt severe pain'.

There is no good way to learn that your husband has died, but Nosihle Ngweyi's experience stands out as particularly awful. The uncertainty, the failures of communication, the spurned hopes, and the inescapable pain all amplified the horror of the period. It is almost impossible to imagine the swirling rush of emotions, the mix of hope and despair that she had to have felt. But the fact of her pain is inescapable.

All the widows, the mothers who outlived their sons, the children and the sisters and the brothers and the cousins and the friends of those who died, shared in this grief.

For them, every day in this period brought a new horror. All the bodies had to be identified by a family member or a close friend – and, often, it had been days or even weeks before someone could be traced, contacted, and brought to the North West Province to look at the body. The physical effects of these delays were awful. When Matsepang Ntsoele had to identify the body of her husband, she could barely recognize him: 'When I was brought to view his body, they would not allow me to see the rest of his body. They only let me look at his head. He looked terrible, his skin was pitch black and he had a wound on his head.'[4] Betty Gadlela had the same experience when she saw her husband's body: 'I was confused. My husband was light in complexion, but when we saw him he was pitch black. No one in my family could recognize him. He had burn-like symptoms and a very bad odour, like he was rotten. This was only a week after his death.'[5]

---

4   Exhibit KKKK 20 – Molefi Osiel Ntsoele.
5   Exhibit KKKK 24 – Sitelega Meric Gadlela.

'It felt like a dream'

In the days and weeks that followed, the families struggled to come to terms with the deaths of their loved ones. Their lives were dogged by tragedy. Mzukisi Sompeta's father outlived his son by a few weeks, dying early in October.[6] Makhosandile Mkhonjwa's family were already mourning his father's death, shortly before August, and now had to bury their son. His sister miscarried 'as a result of the shock and the stress'. The family struggled, 'devastated' by their losses.[7]

Others were also shaken. Betty Gadlela could not believe that her husband was dead. She could not believe that the face she had seen – distorted, swollen, blackened by decay – was her husband. Nothing was real. Without him, her life seemed to have no meaning, or worth. 'When I received the news that my husband was killed in the strike by the police it felt like a dream. When days went by and I realized my husband was really dead, I tried to end my life with poison'.[8]

Betty Gadlela survived, after her sister saved her. But her life continued to be shaped by the necessity of mourning – by the need to come to terms with the absence of her husband. She said, later, at the Commission of Inquiry: 'I can't get his death out of my mind. His death changed my life. With him alive, I had the comfort to know I could always rely on him for everything. But he is no more.'

* * *

The families now had to bury their dead. Almost all wished to bring the dead back to their family homes, to be buried alongside their loved ones in the Eastern Cape, in Lesotho, and elsewhere. They incurred significant financial costs to do so: they had to transport the bodies across the country, bury them in freshly dug graves, and embark upon a long process of formal mourning.

Babalo Mtshazi's mother travelled with her sister and an older relative from their home in Libode, in the Eastern Cape, to Marikana. They went to the mortuary to identify and collect her son's body. They were speechless with grief. 'We all wanted to ask how he died, but my uncle could not even ask the questions because he was hurting and unable to deal with things at that time.' This was only the beginning of what they had to do. Once they had collected Babalo's body, they had to prepare to bring it back to his family's home.

> We performed a ritual in terms of our customs whilst at Marikana, before taking Babalo's body back to the Eastern Cape Province. We took the coffin to the koppie, where we spoke to his spirit in terms of our customs, we uttered the words, 'Babalo, you died here, we are taking you home for your burial'.

---

6 Interview with Nomawabo Sompeta, Lusikisiki, 2 December 2015.
7 Exhibit KKKK 7 – Makhosandile Mkhonjwa.
8 Exhibit KKKK 24 – Sitelega Meric Gadlela.

From there, they transported his body across the country, where they buried him with full ceremony, slaughtering a cow and six sheep to mark the formal rituals. Even still, the family's mourning continued long after the burial.[9]

The Gadlela family's mourning process could stand as an example of what many of the other families were enduring. Betty Gadlela, as Sitelega Gadlela's widow, wore a head-covering to the funeral, to hide her face. She was not able to speak to her husband's colleagues as they mourned him. She was then expected to remain at home for a full month. She was expected to wear mourning clothes for a year from the time of her husband's death and burial. Her mother was also expected to mourn alongside her, and to wear mourning for six months. Sitelega's mother would ordinarily have done so too, but as a *sangoma* she was exempted from the ordinary rules. This was important, because as each woman put aside the mourning dress – at six months for the mothers, and a year for the widows – the family would also be expected to slaughter a goat or a cow. This would be an almost impossible expense for the family. In his community, in Lesotho, Gadlela had been a pastor – a figure who did not own livestock. The family did not have enough money to purchase the animals to slaughter, and so had to face difficult decisions about which family members would officially enter mourning – and who would have to refrain from it.[10]

Few of the families knew each other in these first weeks and months, but they were all undergoing experiences that few people should ever have to endure. All had to endure days of uncertainty, waiting to find out if their loved ones had been killed; all had to put up with the indignities of approaching police stations and hospitals and morgues to trace the bodies of their loved ones; all had to face the inability of the police, hospital assistants, or even company representatives to explain where, how, and why their husbands, brothers, and sons had died. In these weeks, their lived were reshaped by shock, by doubt, by disbelief, by horror, and by abiding grief.

One after another asked the same questions, and complained about the same silences. Nonesile Xalabile tried to find out why his son, Nkosiyabo, had been killed.

> At Lonmin, a white manager told us our family members were killed by police officials. He said some people were killed, so the police ended up shooting the workers ... The manager seemed afraid to say more because people were asking a lot of questions about the tragedy, in particular people were asking as to why the workers were killed instead of Lonmin talking to them. He was just evasive and did not give answers.

---

9 Exhibit KKK 39 – Babalo Mtshazi
10 Exhibit KKKK 24 – Sitelega Meric Gadlela.

Nonesile did not know exactly where his son had been killed, other than at the second koppie. He did not know who had pulled the trigger, or even why they had killed him.[11]

The other surviving family members shared these questions. Betty Gadlela said: 'I want to hear why my husband was killed. What wrong did he do to the government or Lonmin?' Nosihle Ngweyi complained that, 'No one has told us who killed Michael. From what we know he was shot by the police during the strike.'[12] Khanare Monesa's brother, Motlalepula, summed up his questions from Lesotho: 'I want to know what happened to my brother, and I want to know exactly what events led to his death. I want to know what will happen to those who killed him.'[13]

The first official responses

From the time of the massacre to the weeks in which the dead were buried, these answers were impossible to find. The official responses that came from the government, the mine, and the police all avoided providing any detail or any explanation that would not seem to justify the police's actions.

These official responses began immediately after the massacre. On the morning of Friday 17 August 2012, South Africa's President at the time, Jacob Zuma, visited Rustenburg and made a speech about what he called the 'Marikana Lonmin mine workers' tragedy'. The speech answered none of the questions that the families were beginning to ask. The President began by saying that he was in the region 'to be with the people of the North West, the workers in our mines, the families of those who have lost their lives or been injured, and with the Police Service in this hour of mourning'. He chose his words carefully. He used the same phrase over and again: 'the events of the past few days … the events of the past few days and hours … these events'. He avoided describing what had actually happened at Marikana, and kept his comments as vague and as apolitical as possible. His approach to the massacre was summed up in one line: 'today is not an occasion for blame, finger-pointing, or recrimination'.[14]

Despite this, there were some signs in his speech that indicated where his sympathies lay. He suggested that while this day was not one for blame, it was nonetheless one for 'reminding ourselves of our responsibilities as citizens'. He reminded his audience that the right to protest was linked to the need for that

---

11   Exhibit KKKK 41 – Nkosiyabo Xalabile.
12   Exhibit KKKK 42 – Michael Ngweyi.
13   Exhibit KKKK 21 – Khanare Monesa.
14   'Statement from President Jacob Zuma on the Marikana Lonmin Workers Tragedy Media Briefing Rustenburg', 17 August 2012, www.gov.za/statement-president-jacob-zuma-marikana-lonmin-mine-workers-tragedy-media-briefing-rustenburg (Acc. March 2021).

protest to be peaceful: 'It is one of the cornerstones of our hard won democracy.' 'However', he said immediately, 'as I said, this is not a day to apportion blame.' It is hard to read these words as anything other than suggesting that the cause of 'the events of the past few days' lay in the violence of the strike, and not in the actions of the police.

Still, this was not explicitly said – and the President chose to use this occasion to announce that he had 'decided to institute a Commission of Inquiry' which would 'uncover the truth about what happened here'. 'The inquiry', he added, 'will enable us to get to the real cause of the incident, and to derive the necessary lessons.' He said no more about the proposed Commission in this speech, and said nothing about when the Commission might begin, or what it might investigate.

At least, though, the President's speech acknowledged the need to 'uncover the truth' about what had happened at Marikana. Lonmin's official statement barely acknowledged what had just happened, and chose instead to focus on the need to 'rebuild ... relationships, starting today, building back trust and trying to move forwards'. In the interest of doing so, the company announced that it would provide 'funding for the education of all the children of employees who lost their lives'. It also announced that it was establishing a 'Help Desk' at its hospital 'which will help families with the identification of bodies, assist with all the burial arrangements and offer bereavement counselling'. The massacre – in this light – was something that was now in the past. To dwell on it would be harmful. It was better to look ahead.[15]

And this is what the company sought to do, suggesting – like the President – that the original problem lay in the strike, and that the resumption of business was now urgent:

> a stable mining sector is vital to the economic future of this country. If the industry continues to be damaged by illegal actions, it is not just the economy which suffers, but all our employees, their families and dependents. We need our employees to come back to work and we need to get mining again.

* * *

The National Commissioner of Police, Riah Phiyega, also issued a statement that Friday morning. She echoed the President in her avoidance of detail, and her unwillingness to say what had happened. She too began by describing it in vague and neutral terms as 'the event that unfolded yesterday which resulted in the loss of lives'. But Phiyega did not share the President's desire to avoid 'blame, finger-pointing, or recrimination'.

---

15 Simon Scott (Chief Financial Officer) 'Lonmin Statement on Marikana Situation', 17 August 2012. Republished on *Politicsweb*. www.politicsweb.co.za/news-and-analysis/lonmin-will-cover-education-costs-of-dead-employee (Acc. March 2021).

Instead, she told a story that cast the workers as villains. She described a week of 'faction fights' and violence leading up to Thursday afternoon. She suggested – inaccurately – that 'three more employees [had been] shot in the hostels in separate incidents' by the strikers on Saturday. She said that Sunday had seen 'reports of five employees shot and taken to hospital' as well as 'two security officers ... hacked to death by protestors' while 'striking workers infiltrated production areas, assaulting three on duty employees, fatally wounding one and torching six motor vehicles'. On Monday, she added, 'three bodies of mine employees were found dead. SAPS members were attacked while escorting the protestors. Two SAPS members [were] hacked to death, one critically wounded currently in hospital. Three protestors [were] fatally wounded and five wounded in the Police response to the attack'.

She claimed that in the face of the violence of the striking workers, the police took action 'to seek a non-violent and peaceful solution' to restore 'order'. This failed, however. On Thursday 16 August, she said, 'we had received information from various sources that the protestors would not end their strike peacefully'. The police therefore decided to employ 'a defensive action to disperse the protesters from their stronghold'. According to her story,

> when the police started deploying the barbed-wire fencing, the group of protestors armed with dangerous weapons and firearms, hastily flanked the vehicles deploying the wire. They were met by members from the police who tried to repost the advance with water-cannon, teargas as well as stun-grenades. The attempt was unsuccessful and the police members had to employ force to protect themselves from the charging group.

Meanwhile, the police had driven 'armed protestors' to a 'high bushy ground in the close vicinity', where the police surrounded them 'and attempted to force the protestors out by means of water cannons, rubber bullets and stun grenades'. At this point, 'the militant group stormed towards the police firing shots and wielding dangerous weapons. Police retreated systematically and were forced to utilize maximum force to defend themselves'.[16]

The National Commissioner's account of the events of the strike and of the massacre was a mixture of half-truths, lies, and exaggerations designed to demonize the striking workers and justify the police's actions. Her account of the sequence of events on Thursday 16 August was deliberately flawed: she conflated the initial laying down of barbed wire, and the discussion between workers and the police, with the later movement of workers off the koppie; she suggested that the workers had charged the police before the tear-gas, water cannon, and stun grenades had been fired – which was false; and she suggested that the massacre

---

16   South African Government, 'General Phiyega Pronounces on Mine Unrest', 17 August 2012. www.gov.za/general-phiyega-pronounces-mine-unrest (Acc. March 2021).

at Scene Two had happened at about the same time as the initial shooting, captured by the media, and that the deaths that had happened there had all happened after workers had 'stormed' the police – which was patently false. Throughout she described the violence associated with the workers as barbaric – people were 'hacked to death' – and that of the police as self-defence. She concealed the role of the police in initiating the violence of Monday 13 August, once again describing the police killed by workers as 'hacked to death' and the protestors killed by police as 'fatally wounded'. The story as she told it was not true.

Nonetheless, it served its purpose – which was to cast the workers as the aggressors of the strike, and to indemnify the police from any responsibility for having caused the workers' deaths. It also served to justify the actions that the police were taking after the massacre. They arrested 259 people associated with the strike – participants, workers, activists.[17] Some of these men were arrested as they lay on the dirt at Scene One and Scene Two. Others were arrested in the nearby hospitals, wounded. And yet others were simply rounded up, captured by the police as they fled the site of the massacre. The National Commissioner announced that these men were facing 'various charges ranging from public violence, murder and attempted murder, malicious damage to property, armed robbery, illegal gathering and possession [of] dangerous weapons'.

If the families were looking for answers in the statements made by the President or Lonmin, they would have found nothing – nothing to illuminate, and nothing to offend. But if they had heard the statement made by the National Commissioner that the dead were to blame for their own deaths and that the police were guilty of no more than self-defence, they would have been profoundly hurt.

'The best of responsible policing'

What was said in public, though, was only a taste of what the police were saying to themselves – and only the first draft of the story that they were planning to tell the country about the massacre. If the families had heard what the police were saying to each other – out of the hearing of journalists – they would not only have been hurt. They would have been horrified at the callousness and inhumanity of these speeches.

On the afternoon of Friday 17 August – the same day as she released her public statement – the National Commissioner addressed a gathering of police officers who had been active at Marikana, 'arranged by Employee Health and Wellness personnel for prayer and counselling'. Phiyega told her officers that their behaviour over the past several days represented 'the best of responsible

---

17   This is the figure given in Exhibit JJJ 118.8 – SAPS Lonmin Mine Unrest: Marikana, Thursday 16th August 2012. Other sources (discussed in the previous chapter) suggest that 272 men were arrested.

policing'. She added: 'You did what you did because you are being responsible, you were making sure that you continue to live your oath of ensuring South Africans are safe, and that you equally are a citizen of this country, and that safety starts with you.' She told them to remember that 'all we did was to do our job'. Their leaders would always be on their side.[18]

She also told them not to worry about the President's announcement of the Commission of Inquiry to investigate the strike and the massacre. The officers should remember that 'the commission of inquiry is not about us as police' but rather about 'violence in the mines ... the mobilisation that we have experienced ... the facts that we have presented [and] the mining industry as such ... So do not think you are being persecuted as police, and do not fear anything'.

As she praised the assembled police officers for their conduct at Marikana, told them not to concern themselves with the Commission, and finally asked them to applaud themselves, the National Commissioner was accompanied by the national Minister of Police, Nathi Mthethwa. The Minister listened to everything that his Commissioner had said, and made no effort to disagree. Instead, he took up the microphone after her speech and told the officers that as a representative of 'the Government, the Executive as a whole [and] the President of the Republic, Commander in Chief of all the armed forces in this country' he could say that 'we are all behind you'.

He praised them, again, and said that

> we are confident that what you have done you did it in trying to ensure that the rule of law reigns in South Africa. We are not going to allow anyone to run amok in the country, to want to turn South Africa into a banana republic ... We must ensure that at all times we do everything in our power so that anarchists do not think SA is their stage.

* * *

It was against this background of support and encouragement that the police convened a nine-day long meeting at the Roots Conference Centre in Potchefstroom to prepare an official version of the events of the strike and the massacre to present to the coming Commission of Inquiry. From 27 August 2012 onwards, senior police officers worked to get their stories straight: they compiled timelines out of scattered records, scribbled pieces of paper, and rough notes; they ironed out inconsistencies and contradictions in their records; they rehearsed

---

18 The recording of this speech was submitted to the Commission as Exhibit WW 6 – Speech by National Commissioner Phiyega. A partial transcript of this recording, focusing on the Police Commissioner's words, was submitted into evidence as Exhibit FF 12 – Transcript of WW6. The Minister's remarks are taken from the transcription of the recording offered by the Evidence Leaders in their Heads of Argument, at para. 898.

their lines, and ensured that each would use the same words to tell the same story before the Commission.[19]

If this was all that they had done, the meeting would have been uncontroversial. But their planning went beyond simply clarifying their stories, and ironing out inconsistencies. Instead, they appear to have attempted to manufacture evidence to support an inaccurate story about the massacre, and to have attempted to destroy evidence that contradicted their preferred story.[20]

The initial part of this process involved manipulating the stories that the police witnesses were to tell the Commission. This was more than ensuring that the stories were consistent with each other. Instead, the police developed the story originally given by the National Commissioner. They suggested that the killings on Monday 13 August had been sparked by an action taken by the miners themselves – and not by police officers' panicked reactions to their presence. They suggested that on Thursday 16 August the police had only acted after the strikers had attacked them on several different occasions, and after all ordinary crowd control measures had been taken.[21] They hid the chaos and confusion of the day, and constructed a misleading timeline.

The second part of the process involved manipulating the evidence produced at the site of the massacre, to conceal the fact that police officers had planted weapons on and around the corpses of the dead after the massacre – as described in the previous chapter. The first set of photographs taken in the immediate aftermath of the shooting were deleted from the computer drives that were to be shared with the Commission, and replaced with the images taken over an hour later. The first set of images showed the miners as they had actually died. The second showed them after they had been moved by the police, and with weapons placed in their stiffened hands.

In addition, the police set out to either alter or make up records of their discussions during the strike. They altered the notes that senior police officials took during the strike. They altered the minutes of the JOCOM meetings to match these notes, and the story that they intended to tell.[22] They deleted inconvenient

---

19   The Evidence Leaders have compiled lists of the different draft documents produced at Roots (Exhibits JJJ 189 and JJJ 190) to demonstrate the development of this narrative. See the Evidence Leader's Heads of Argument, paras 913–929.
20   The conclusions here are those reached by the Commission's Evidence Leaders, who dedicate ten pages of their Heads of Argument to showing how the SAPS used the meeting at the Roots Conference Centre to plan testimony, hide evidence, and manufacture false stories so as to mislead the Commission.
21   In addition to the statement of the National Commissioner, see Exhibit HHH 28 – SAPS Report: Mine Unrest at Lonmin Marikana, and the transcript of General Mpembe's comments on 17 August 2012 quoted in the Evidence Leaders' Heads of Argument, at para. 390.
22   The Evidence Leaders derived this conclusion from a comparison between Exhibit

references, and tried to hide their lack of preparation by pretending that the plan drawn up on the morning of 16 August had in fact been developed earlier in the week.[23] They tried to hide the meeting of the National Management Forum on the Wednesday evening, and they succeeding in either losing or destroying the records of what the National Commissioner said at that meeting.[24] They cut off any dangling threads.

All of this effort was in support of the story that the National Commissioner was still telling the country – a story that concealed the truth of what happened at Marikana.

The first challenges

In the first weeks after the massacre, it seemed as though the police story might prevail. The initial news reports depended heavily on information provided by the police, and drew extensively on the narratives given by the police spokesmen: not only for facts and figures about the numbers of the dead, but also for analyses and explanations of the strike and the violence that had followed.[25] Some journalists registered their concerns about the police version, but did not develop these into full critiques – instead, they noted that 'conflicting versions' of the events 'abounded'.[26]

But a serious challenge to the police's account did come, late in August and early in September. On 23 August 2012, the South African online newspaper *Daily Maverick* published a report by Mandy de Waal on the investigations of a group of academics led by Professor Kate Alexander, who ran the Centre for Social Change at the University of Johannesburg. The team pointed out the police's

---

JJJ 168 – JOC Hand Written Notes: 16 August 2012 and Exhibit TT 4 – Minute of JOCCOM (JOC) meeting of 16 August. It was put to General Annandale in cross-examination that there were significant discrepancies between these versions of the JOCOM minutes. He was unable to explain them. (Testimony of General Annandale, Day 156 (27 November 2013), pp. 17,613–17,615.)

23 The Evidence Leaders examined the 'plans' put forward by the police as Exhibits JJJ 150–152 and JJJ 163.1–4 and demonstrated that they were produced during the week of the Roots Conference. Evidence Leaders' Heads of Argument, para. 922–924.

24 See the discussion in Chapter 6 of this meeting, and the missing records.

25 It is instructive to consider the early reporting collected in Thanduxolo Jika, Lucas Ledwaba, Sebabatso Mosamo, and Athandiwe Saba, *We Are Going to Kill Each Other Today: The Marikana Story* (Johannesburg, NB Publishers: 2013). While some of these stories are more sceptical than others, the majority are heavily reliant on the statements of police spokesmen to explain the strike and massacre.

26 SAPA, 'Conflicting Accounts of Lonmin Shooting', *IOL Business Report*, 17 August 2012, www.iol.co.za/business-report/companies/conflicting-accounts-of-lonmin-shooting-1365104 (Acc. March 2021).

efforts to clean up the site of the massacre. Alexander described how the police had gathered up 'rubber bullets, canisters, live ammunition shells and that sort of thing' as well as burning the grass to remove bloodstains. The effect seemed to be to remove as much forensic evidence as possible from the site. Alexander's team also highlighted evidence that pointed to the existence of a second site of the massacre – which Alexander called the 'killing koppie' – about which no news article had yet appeared to describe to the public.[27]

On 8 September, a second story appeared on the *Daily Maverick*. Greg Marinovich – an award-winning photojournalist and writer – had spent the previous fortnight testing the limits of the police's story. His article – titled 'The murder fields of Marikana. The cold murder fields of Marikana' – examined the shreds of physical evidence that the police had left on the site, particularly at Scene Two. He visited the sites, and photographed the crevasses between the rocks. He found the markings that represented the locations of the bodies and tried to square these locations with the story that the Police Commissioner had told on 17 August – that the police had killed a 'militant group' that was charging towards them. He immediately realized that there was no way to reconcile the physical evidence at Scene Two with the stories the police were telling.[28]

Their interventions also came at the right time: on the same day that de Waal published her article, 23 August 2012, the President officially announced the inauguration of the new Commission of Inquiry into the events at Marikana. On 12 September 2012, just four days after Marinovich's explosive article, the formal Terms of Reference for this Commission were published. Everything that the Commission was to do, it would do in the shadow of this new public debate. The interventions of these academics and journalists had now begin to pick at the seams of the official story – pulling at its loose threads, and exposing its flaws. Their work made it impossible for the police's cover-up operation to succeed, and started a serious public debate about the role of the police – one that might eventually answer the families' many questions.

---

27 Mandy de Waal, 'Marikana: What Really Happened? We May Never Know', *Daily Maverick*, 23 August 2012, www.dailymaverick.co.za/article/2012-08-23-marikana-what-really-happened-we-may-never-know (Acc. March 2021).

28 Greg Marinovich, 'The Murder Fields of Marikana. The Cold Murder Fields of Marikana', *Daily Maverick*, 8 September 2012, www.dailymaverick.co.za/article/2012-09-08-the-murder-fields-of-marikana-the-cold-murder-fields-of-marikana (Acc. March 2021). In addition to further follow-up articles at the time, Marinovich has gone on to write an important journalistic account of the massacre and of the role of investigative journalism in uncovering the police's misconduct. Greg Marinovich, *Murder at Small Koppie: The Real Story of the Marikana Massacre* (Capetown, Penguin SA: 2016).

10

The Farlam Commission

A WEEK after the massacre, the families of the deceased were still in shock. Most of them had only just learned that their loved ones had been killed. Only a few had been able to see the bodies, and only this few had been able to identify the dead with their own eyes. Almost none of them had been able to bury their husbands, their sons, their brothers, and their friends. Their grief was still raw, and they had only begun to mourn.

Meanwhile, the government was moving ahead with its own plans. On Thursday 23 August 2012, South Africa's President, Jacob Zuma, issued a further statement in which he announced new details about the planned Commission of Inquiry into the events that had taken place at Marikana. He said that he had appointed a recently retired judge of the Supreme Court of Appeal, Ian Farlam, to Chair the Commission. Farlam would be assisted by two other Commissioners, both of whom were senior members of the legal profession, Bantubonke Tokota and Pingla Hemraj. These three Commissioners would be responsible for investigating 'matters of national and international concern arising out of the events in Marikana'.[1]

The President was not speaking to the families of the dead when he made his announcement. Only a few of them were aware of the government's plans to institute the Commission of Inquiry. Some would not hear about it until months had passed, and the Commission's work had already started. Ntombizile Motsebetsane, for example, left her home in Marikana after her husband's death and after her search for his body. She returned to her family in the Eastern Cape, where she did not hear any news about the launch of the Commission. She only learned about the Commission after the end of the year, several months after the announcement, and it was only in 2013 that she began to attend it. Neither she nor many of the other families were told of the government's plans.[2]

Instead, the President was speaking to a very different audience – one that was primarily comprised of the media, both national and international, and one

[1] The Presidency, Republic of South Africa, 'Appointment of Judicial Commission of Inquiry on the Marikana Massacre', 12 August 2012. www.thepresidency.gov.za/speeches/appointment-judicial-commission-inquiry-marikana-tragedy (Acc. November 2020).
[2] Interview with Ntombizile Motsebetsane, Matatiele, 4 December 2014.

that was primarily concerned with an idea about national political and economic stability in the wake of the strike. It was to this audience that Zuma directed his statement, and the press conference that preceded it. He emphasized the independence and the powers of the Commissioners, as well as their accomplishments. He spoke of the need for the Commission to 'uncover the truth' – and let it be known that he would not prejudge any matters until its work was done.[3] The conference and the later statement were immediately praised. In an article published on 23 August, Ranjeni Munusamy said that Zuma had shown 'compassion, attentiveness, assertiveness' while demonstrating that he was 'presidential'. Indeed, she concluded that – in speaking – 'he became the Jacob Zuma he had once promised to be: The People's President'.[4]

This response was very much in line with what scholars suggest may be the principal purpose of many Commissions of Inquiry: to divert attention away from an immediate political crisis, to move the resolution of that crisis into an unknowable future, and to protect the government of the moment from the effects of that crisis. In this cynical view, the work done by any commission and its commissioners – their efforts to gather evidence, uncover truth, and make judgments – is only important to a government insofar as this work delays a political reckoning.[5] As Munusamy's striking response shows, the announcement of the Commission's establishment was already enough to begin to divert parts of the media away from any criticism of the government's failure to respond to the strike, or to control the violence of its own police force.

But Munusamy's fawning article was not the only article to appear on 23 August 2012. The same publication – the online *Daily Maverick* – published

3 The Presidency, 'Appointment of Judicial Commission of Inquiry'.
4 Ranjeni Munusamy, 'Marikana: Zuma Reclaims His Soul, and His Presidency', *Daily Maverick*, 23 August 2012, www.dailymaverick.co.za/article/2012-08-23-Marikana-zuma-reclaims-his-soul-and-his-presidency (Acc. March 2021).
5 The classic study of the political and intellectual use of Commissions of Inquiry in South Africa is Adam Ashforth, *The Politics of Official Discourse in Twentieth-Century South Africa* (Oxford, Clarendon Press: 1990). See also – for a comparative analysis – Adam Ashforth, 'Reckoning Schemes of Legitimation: On Commissions of Inquiry as Power/Knowledge Forms', *Journal of Historical Sociology*, 3.1 (1990), pp. 1–22. The most prominent post-Apartheid commission (among a plethora of commissions) was the Truth and Reconciliation Commission of the 1990s. The political significance of this was captured by Richard A. Wilson, *The Politics of Truth and Reconciliation in South Africa: Legitimizing the Post-Apartheid State* (Cambridge, CUP: 2001). These – and other – works emphasize the political role of Commissions in addition to their information-gathering and narrative-establishing roles. This might be read alongside Peter Alexander, 'Marikana Commission of Inquiry: From Narratives Towards History', *Journal of Southern African Studies*, 42.5 (2016), pp. 815–839, which suggests some of the tactics used in the Commission to divert attention from questions of responsibility or culpability.

Mandy de Waal's report on the work of those researchers at the University of Johannesburg who doubted the police's story.⁶ This report highlighted the physical evidence that was either missing or destroyed, and pointed out inconsistencies in the police's story. At the same time as one journalist was accepting the government's attempts to change the narrative around the massacre, others were thus refusing to be diverted. They did not stop asking inconvenient questions – or pushing the government to give the Commission real authority to conduct proper investigations into the police's actions.⁷

Over the coming years, the Commission under Ian Farlam's leadership would struggle to position itself within these tensions. It had to answer a series of questions about its purpose: did it exist only to give the government the time and space to control national and international perceptions about its role in the massacre, or did it exist to uncover a hidden truth? What kinds of questions could the Commission ask, and who could answer them? What kinds of findings, recommendations, and judgments could it reach? And what could it say and do – and what, more importantly, not say, or do?

'I want to know'

Although not all the families of the deceased knew about the Commission when it was first announced, over the next several months – leading up to and after its first hearing – they all came to learn about it and to hold opinions on what it should be doing.

One thing that all the families of the deceased agreed on was that they wanted to know exactly what had happened to their loved ones. David Sagalala, the son of Motisa Sagalala, said to his lawyers: 'I want to see where my father died and how he died.'⁸ Phumeza Mabiya, the wife of Mafolisi Mabiya, said: 'I want to know the truth about why my husband was killed.'⁹ Nombulelo Ntonga, the wife of Bongani Nqongophele, said on her own behalf and on behalf of her family: 'I expect the Commission of Inquiry to investigate how and why my husband was killed. Bongani's mother wants to know why Bongani had to be killed in such a cruel manner.'¹⁰ Again and again, whenever they were asked, they said the same words – 'I want to know'.

---

6   Mandy de Waal, 'Marikana: What Really Happened?' as discussed in the previous chapter.
7   The Commission's work lasted several years. It would be impossible to list all the articles and editorial pieces that challenged and developed its work. However, it would be remiss not to note the work of Greg Marinovich, Niren Tolsi, Paul Botes, and Greg Nicolson, in particular. These journalists repeatedly published in the South African media, and provided important critical voices throughout the process.
8   Exhibit KKKK 22 – Motiso Osiel Sagalala.
9   Exhibit KKKK 29 –Mafolisi Mabiya.
10 Exhibit KKKK 12 – Bongani Nqongophele.

They wanted to know how their loved ones had died: where they had been killed, how, and who had killed them. They wanted to know why this person had been shot, and not that one? Had they been singled out, for some reason, or were they killed by accident? Nomawabo Sompeta, the mother of Mzukisi Sompeta, was clear: 'I want to hear for myself what my son did and to whom, since he was only requesting a salary increase'.[11] Andile Yawa, the father of Cebisile Yawa, said: 'I want to find out from the Commission, how did our children die?'[12] Or, as Nokwanele Phakati, wife of Makhosandile Mkhonjwa, put it: 'I want the Commission to find out what happened on the day. The police are people that are respected and trusted in society to protect us. Why did they shoot people who had a wage dispute with their employer?'[13]

In the eyes of the families, the task of the Commission was to answer these questions: to explain how their loved ones had died, and why they had been killed.

Once these questions had been answered, they also hoped that the Commission would restore some order to their worlds. 'I want the wrongdoers to be brought to justice', said Joyce Jokanisi, Semi Jokanisi's mother, 'in particular the police'.[14] David Sagalala agreed: 'I want those responsible for [my father's] death to be arrested and brought to justice because everyone who breaks the law must be held accountable.'[15] The underlying logic of their demands was given voice by Zameka Nungu, Jackson Lehupa's widow, who clarified what was at stake in the Commission's work:

> According to the law, when someone kills another they must be arrested. I want to know what the police's job is. Is it not to arrest people? Why did they kill people like my husband? Is it the law in this country that when policemen kill people they shouldn't be brought before the courts of law? Because if these people had killed any other people, or the police themselves, they would have been arrested? Or is the law partial?[16]

Finally, they wanted some security. The men who had been killed at Marikana had often been the sole breadwinners in their families, the ones who put food on their families' tables, who sent their children to school, who assured their parents' years of retirement. The families' losses were not only emotional but also material. In the months that followed the massacre, the families struggled to make ends meet – and had no idea how they would continue to survive in the years to come.

---

11 Exhibit KKKK 9 – Mzukisi Sompeta.
12 Exhibit KKKK 25 – Cebisile Yawa.
13 Exhibit KKKK 7 – Makhosandile Mkhonjwa.
14 Exhibit KKKK 4 – Semi Jokanisi.
15 Exhibit KKKK 22 – Motiso Osiel Sagalala.
16 Exhibit KKKK 32 – Jackson Lehupa.

Andile Yawa summed up the families' concerns, saying: 'And now that our children have died, we want to know what is going to happen to our families now'.[17] Thembinkosi Saphendu, the brother of Fezile Saphendu, concurred: 'My family would like the Commission to get to the truth about who is to blame for my brother's death. We need answers so that we can know who to claim from. We are not working, we need jobs in order to survive.'[18] One of Thobile Mpumza's sisters put her dilemma crisply: 'I want to know how we will get help. Who is going to take responsibility for his death because he was the one who used to take care of us.'[19]

The vision that the families held for the Commission was centred around the deaths of their loved ones. They wanted the Commission to uncover the details of these deaths, to discover why they had happened, and to hold someone responsible for having caused them to happen. They wanted the Commission to re-establish the order of their lives – to bring justice, and to end their suffering. They wanted the Commission to set their private and public worlds to rights. They wanted it to recognize their lives and their losses.

The Terms of Reference

But this was not the official vision for the Commission.

On 12 September 2012, the government published the formal Terms of Reference for the Commission, setting out the Commission's powers to investigate and the framework within which it was expected to conduct its investigations. These Terms of Reference identified which parties the Commission could investigate, what kinds of questions it could ask of them, how long it would have to conduct its investigations, and what kinds of conclusions it could draw.[20]

A close reading of this document shows that the Commission was expected to investigate the development of the strike, the failures of the unions and the mine to control it, the failures of the police to prevent the deaths that took place during it – and only then to examine the events of the massacre. It was granted the ability to examine these events, but only from certain perspectives. These perspectives were those that emphasized the agency of organizations, rather

---

17 Exhibit KKKK 25 – Cebisile Yawa.
18 Exhibit KKKK 15 – Fezile David Saphendu.
19 Exhibit KKKK 13 – Thobile Mpumza.
20 The official terms of reference were published in the South African *Government Gazette* in September 2012: South African Government, 'Proclamation by the President of the Republic of South Africa No. 50, 2012', *Government Gazette*, No. 35680 (12 September 2012). As noted below, these Terms of Reference were amended at various times – principally to extend the Commission's sitting. The original version and the various amendments can all be found on the Department of Justice's website, on a page dedicated to documents produced by the Commission: www.justice.gov.za/comm-mrk/documents.html (Acc. March 2021).

than individuals, and that sought to explain the killings by reference to the failure or success of policies – rather than by reference to individual actions. The massacre was seen as a matter to be addressed through policy changes, and not through holding specific actors liable for their actions.

Six potential parties were identified: Lonmin, the South African Police Services, AMCU, the NUM, the Department of Mineral Affairs ('or any other government department or agency') and, finally, any other 'individuals and loose groupings' who may have played a role in 'fomenting and/or promoting a situation of conflict or confrontation'.[21]

The Commission's main focus was to be on the strike. It was to investigate Lonmin, the police, and the two unions to see whether 'by act or omission' any of them had 'directly or indirectly caused loss of life or harm to persons or property'. It was to ask whether Lonmin and the two unions had 'exercised [their] best endeavours to resolve any dispute that may have arisen (industrial or otherwise)' between them. It was to examine the mining company's 'policy, procedure, practices and conduct relating to its employees and organized labour', to consider whether it had 'employed sufficient safeguards and measures to ensure the safety of its employees [and] property', and to ask whether these could have led to the 'prevention of the outbreak of violence between any parties'. The Commission was also tasked with finding out whether the two unions – AMCU and the NUM – had 'exercised effective control over [their] membership and those persons allied to [them] in ensuring that their conduct was lawful and did not endanger the lives and property of other persons'. In this context, the Commission was also to look at whether the actions of the relevant government departments had been 'appropriate in the circumstances and consistent with their duties and obligations according to law'.[22]

The massacre was not primarily the focus of the Commission's Terms of Reference. The questions the Commission were to ask of the police showed this. It was only empowered to consider

> the nature, extent and application of any standing orders, policy considerations, legislation or other instructions in dealing with the situation which gave rise to this incident; the precise facts and circumstances which gave rise to the use of all and any force and whether this was reasonable and justifiable in the circumstances.

It was also required 'to examine the role played by SAPS through its respective units, individually and collectively in dealing with this incident; and whether by any act or omission it directly or indirectly caused loss of life or harm to persons'.[23]

21   Section 1.1–1.6.
22   Section 1.5.
23   Section 1.2.

The powers of the Commission to make meaningful recommendations after the close of its investigations were also limited. The Terms of Reference empowered the Commission 'where appropriate' to 'refer any matter for prosecution, further investigation or the convening of a separate enquiry' but did not empower the Commission to make criminal or other findings about the guilt or innocence of individual actors. It could not make any final findings. It had only the power to recommend that others – 'the appropriate law enforcement agency, government department or regulator' – take its findings further.[24]

Finally, the Terms of Reference also assumed that the Commission's work would – given these limits – be concluded very quickly. They stated that 'the Commission shall complete its work within a period of four (4) months from the date hereof' and that it 'must submit its final report to the President within a period of one (1) month after the date on which the Commission completes its work'. This meant that the Commission was expected to complete its investigations by mid-January 2013, and submit its final Report by about 12 February 2013.[25]

There was an clear tension between the official framework established by these Terms of Reference and the vision articulated by the families of the deceased: where they sought specific clarity about individual deaths, these terms presumed that the Commission would instead be examining failures of departmental policy; where the families sought prosecutions, justice, and restitution for their losses, these terms presumed that the Commission could recommend only new enquiries or further investigations, and would quickly bring its work to an end. The only hope for the fulfilment of the families' expectations would be the decision of an ambitious Commissioner to exploit the ambiguities of the Terms of Reference – and to push for a more aggressive investigation. But it would soon be clear that this would not happen.

The first days of the Commission

The Commission sat for the first time on Monday 1 October 2012. Judge Farlam opened this first sitting with an apology for having begun the morning half an hour later than scheduled, following an initial media briefing. He then moved on to some 'general remarks' that, he said, were

> addressed particularly to the families of those who, and the next of kin of those who died in the incidents that form the subject of our inquiry ... out of respect to all those present here whose family members died as a result of the incidents which we are called upon to investigate.[26]

---

24 Section 5.
25 Section 4.
26 Transcript of Day 1 of the Marikana Commission of Inquiry (1 October 2012), pp. 1–8 in particular.

He wanted to 'convey our deepest heartfelt sympathy and condolences' to the families of the dead, and to 'acknowledge and thank [them] for having made time to attend these proceedings'. He told these families – who, he said, he had been 'advised' were 'in our midst' – that

> we cannot measure your grief or loss, but we believe that as we relive the events that culminated in the 16th of August, that we will do so in the firm belief that getting to the truth of what, how, and why it happened will be part of the healing and restoration process.

This speech was meant to be followed by a piece of theatre: the names of the dead would be read out, one after the other, by a member of the Commission. As the names were read out, the relevant family members were asked to stand. A minute's silence would follow, and then the legal parts of the proceedings – lawyers introducing themselves, and so on – would begin.

As the roll-call of the dead began, however, it became clear to people in the auditorium that things were not proceeding as planned. The names were read out, a pause after each one: 'Thobile Mpumza. Thabiso Thelejane. Anele Mdizeni. Makhosandile Mkhonjwa…' No one stood. 'Julius Mangcotywa. Janeveke Liau…' Still nothing. 'Thabiso Mosebetsane…' Nothing, no one, no movement. The names kept coming, but not one family member appeared.

At the end of the roll-call, the Commission continued as if nothing unexpected had happened – as if the families had indeed stood in the auditorium, as if the gesture of respect had been effective. The Chairperson asked the Evidence Leaders – a team of lawyers employed by the Commission to organize and present evidence – to introduce themselves, and to spell their names for the transcribers. He turned to the lawyers of each of the parties, and asked them to introduce themselves and their clients. This takes up nineteen pages of the official transcript of the hearing. It is only on the twenty-sixth page that one of the lawyers – Dumisa Ntsebeza, representing at the time twenty families of the dead – is able to point out the obvious: that many of the families had only just been informed of the Commission's sitting, and others did not know about it. No one had been supported to travel across the country to attend it, and no family member was present in the room. This was a matter to be urgently resolved, he said.

All of this was observed by those in the audience – lawyers, journalists, and others. At least some of it was captured by the television cameras, or at least those that were not focused entirely on the stage and the flood-lit tables of Commissioners.[27] The attempt to frame the Commission as a 'healing and restoration

---

27 The SABC broadcast many of the Commission's hearings live. These are archived on YouTube – sometimes at length, and sometimes in shorter clips. The clip for the first part of the first day can be found at www.youtube.com/watch?v=RhZcZT6Bz18 (Acc. March 2021). Further visual versions of these scenes can be seen in Rehad Desai's documentary, *Miners Shot Down* (2014).

process' directed in part at the families of the deceased failed miserably. The theatrical event of the day was not the acknowledgement of the survivors' grief – but instead the revelation of their glaring absence, casting doubt on the sincerity of the Commission's work.

* * *

Things did not improve at the start of a second set of sittings, when the families were finally present – their transport and accommodation now having been arranged. On this morning, the Commission's Evidence Leaders began a presentation of the video material that had been made available to the Commission. Although the families were now present, the introduction and moments of silent mourning offered on the first day of the hearings – when they were not there – were not repeated.

After lunch, Geoff Budlender, representing the Evidence Leaders, began by explaining that this presentation represented footage of 'the events only of the 16th August'. It was footage provided by news organizations, and not by the police. He was interrupted almost immediately. First, the Chair asked to have the lights turned down to 'make it easier for the people concerned to see'. As soon as Judge Farlam had finished speaking, Dumisa Ntsebeza, once again interrupted:

> Mr Chairman, can I just make a request before we show, are shown any footage. As I indicated I would like to make sure that there are people who will counsel the members of the family in the event that anything they might see, might traumatize them to an extent where such service is necessary. I would like to be sure that they are here.[28]

These concerns were dismissed. Farlam acknowledged the point, but suggested that it didn't apply to the 'preliminary footage' that was to be shown, and noted that a member of his staff had 'gone off, I think in search of the people responsible for counselling should it be required. But I suggest', he added, 'we start in the meanwhile anyway with the preliminary footage'.

The first clip was shown, and then the second – at which point the quiet of the auditorium was shattered. Screams and cries burst out in the room. Some women collapsed, and had to be carried out of the room. Others wept, loudly, their hands pressed to their faces, eyes screwed shut. Others were shaking, the blood draining from their skin, men and women alike. They sat silent, in the midst of commotion.

On the screen in front of them, raw footage from the scene of the massacre was being shown. This was the first time that the families had seen this footage – and the first time that they had seen their loved ones at the site of the massacre: running, falling. Dying.

---

28   Transcript of Day 4 of the Marikana Commission of Inquiry (23 October 2012), pp. 251–256.

At this point, Budlender spoke up, asking to be allowed 'to pause to make sure that everyone is assisted who needs to be assisted. There are people here. I must apologise', he added, his voice uneven, clearly shaken, 'I hadn't realized that footage was on the clip. I hadn't thought that we had reached the shooting yet.'

Farlam responded:

> I would actually like to see that final clip again more slowly, but I think we must wait until the grieving parties have had an opportunity to leave the auditorium … May I ask the interpreter to ask those present who are vitally, personally involved if they would not wish to have an opportunity to leave because it is obviously very distressing for them?

He then adjourned the hearings for a few moments.

During this adjournment, the families were ushered out of the auditorium, and settled in another room. This room had been intended to provide a separate translation service for the few non-isiXhosa speaking family members, but was now converted into a makeshift counselling venue. Meanwhile, the video continued to be shown in the other room – uninterrupted by their grief, or disturbed by the fact of their presence.

It was hard to have any faith in the Commission after these displays of thoughtlessness.

'I felt completely lost'

Overall – including these events – the first days of the Commission were deeply disorienting for the families. Few knew what to expect from the hearings themselves. Some of them were confused by the proceedings, not knowing when or how often the Commission would sit. Almost everyone was confused by the technical language, the complexities of the translation process, and the seeming friendliness between the lawyers for the police, for the NUM, the Evidence Leaders, and the Commissioners.

As Zameka Nungu put it, after the end of the Commission: 'My first time at the Commission was very confusing … if I think back to that first time, I felt completely lost'.[29] Xolelwa Mpumza, who lost her brother, said: 'It was not an easy time. It was very painful [The first day] was not pleasant.'[30] Lanford Gcotyelwa, who attended the Commission for the Mati family, agreed. He remembered the Commission as 'a source of confusion for us. We were really in the dark … It was tough. The initial stages of the Commission were tough. Tough! We didn't know what the dates were. We would go to sleep not knowing what the next date would be.'[31]

---

29 Interview with Zameka Nungu, Matatiele, 4 December 2015.
30 Interview with Xolelwa and Phelokazi Mpumza, Matatiele, 4 December 2015.
31 Interview with Lanford Gcotyelwa, KuNdile, 3 December 2015.

Meanwhile, they were meeting each other for the first time. These men and women were forced into an uneasy intimacy, sharing a shattering grief – but no memories, no family, no network of relations. In some cases, not even a language. Still, they spoke to each other. They took their tea breaks in a room separate from most of the other participants in the Commission, and spoke there. They tried to understand what was happening, and to learn the vocabulary of the hearings. Lanford Gcotyelwa remembered this period, explaining that:

> We would talk about nothing else but about the Commission and the way that it was being handled. In the beginning it was not handled in the right way. That is mostly what we discussed all the time … and about how rough the judge seemed to be towards the lawyers that were representing the miners. As far as I could tell, the only people that cared about the families were the lawyers that were representing us, and not the crew that had Judge Farlam.

For these families, the hearings that followed these first disastrous days did little to answer their questions, or ease their minds.

In November 2012, they heard the testimony of Joseph Mathunjwa, the President of AMCU – who argued strongly that the framing of the Commission's questions to him and about his union were misleading and dangerous. The strike was not driven by a rivalry between AMCU and the NUM, and neither union had any control over it. The strikers were dissatisfied with their existing union representation – and while he did encourage them to join AMCU in response, the truth was that they were striking outside of the union system. It was in his personal capacity that he had appealed to the striking miners on 15 and 16 August – not as a head of a rival union.[32] Two months later, in January 2013, they heard Erick Gcilitshana and Senzeni Zokwana, who represented the NUM, explain that their union had been active on behalf of the miners – and that, in the NUM's eyes, the strike had not been necessary. They disagreed with Mathunjwa: they thought that it was due to AMCU's efforts to expand its presence on the mine that disruption and dissatisfaction had taken root. The NUM had faced threats and violence from workers, culminating in the confrontation outside the NUM offices on 11 August 2012 – and that, in the face of that, the union had done everything that it could to de-escalate the situation, including calling the police to manage it.[33] The families heard that neither union would accept responsibility for the strike.

Throughout these months, too, the families heard the testimony of several police officers, including Lt-Col Botha, who filmed the massacre from a helicopter in the sky above, and Captain Mohlaki, who observed the aftermath of the

---

32   Joseph Mathunjwa's testimony begins on Day 21 of the Commission (27 November 2012).

33   Erick Gcilitshana's testimony begins on Day 35 (23 January 2013) and Senzeni Zokwana's begins on Day 41 (31 January 2013).

massacre and photographed the scene for the police.[34] These men described the events of the strike and the massacre from the perspective of officers who had been at a distance from the action – in the air, or at the back of the police forces. They were sometimes caught out in contradictions – Mohlaki, for example, could not explain the inconsistencies between early and later photographs that showed weapons arranged around the dead bodies. But they stuck to the story that the police had concocted earlier: that the mineworkers were violent, were rushing at the police, and the police acted in self-defence.

In this, they were merely laying the ground for the Commission's lengthy examination of the National Commissioner of Police, Riah Phiyega, who occupied the stand for more than a month. She was heard from the middle of March until late in April.[35] She was examined and cross-examined by each of the legal teams present at the Commission: she was pushed to explain the police's actions, to justify the police's conduct, to apologize for the police's violence, to acknowledge the miners' struggles, to respect the families' grief. But for week after week after week, Phiyega refused to apologize, refused to admit to any fault on the part of the police, refused to explain. Instead, she insisted that – in all circumstances – the police had always acted correctly. Her officers had always followed the correct procedures, had only ever taken justifiable decisions, had only ever done what was necessary. She refused to acknowledge that any of them could even have been mistaken in that decisions that had led to the deaths of thirty-four men on 16 August 2012.

Phiyega's testimony was so repetitive and so monotonous, so aggressive and impatient in tone, and so clearly uninterested in responding to any criticisms of the police – even clearly justified criticisms – that it forced many commentators to question the value of the Commission. Neither the Evidence Leaders nor any of the other legal teams were able to crack her stubborn demeanour, extract any concessions from her, or learn anything new about the police's actions. Instead, Phiyega seemed to demonstrate the police's imperviousness to interrogation – and thus to demonstrate the relative powerlessness and futility of the Commission's investigations.

Over the next months, other high ranking police officers testified in front of the Commission – repeating, again and again, the same story – with occasional minor variations. These officers were sometimes caught out in contradictions, but largely blustered their way through hostile cross-examinations. The approach taken by the Commission to these cross-examinations – of treating the Evidence Leaders as merely one set of interested lawyers, often hostile to

---

34   Lt-Col Botha was examined from Day 5 (29 October 2012) and Capt. Mohlaki from Day 6 (30 October 2012).

35   General Phiyega first testified on Day 64 (14 March 2013). She testified over the course of several weeks. She then returned to testify again from Day 288 (10 September 2014).

the witnesses, and of allowing each of the different legal parties to cross-examine each witness at length – assisted them in this, by allowing questions to be repeated and letting contradictions to be forgotten in the endless back-and-forth of the hearings. These witnesses often took refuge in technical responses, focusing on police policy, on the particularities of training, and on the attributes of particular types of weapons. They sought to avoid speaking of the massacre in anything like human terms.

* * *

'I had hoped the Commission would capture the important bits, that the truth would be revealed', Lunga Jokanisi said, remembering the hearings into his son's death. 'From where I was sitting, I realized there was no truth to it. There was a lot of beating around the bush ... I am still left wondering. If it was up to me, there'd be another commission'. The police had been allowed to say whatever they wanted, without contradiction. No one would take responsibility. He suggested that the Commission was too closely aligned to the state to be honest: 'It's like me electing someone I get along with, I say to them, go and investigate for me there'.[36]

His distrust was echoed by others, such as the Mangcotywa family, whose representative said: 'I also feel that they were not fully transparent or truthful, I mean the Commission. I can see that there, Farlam was not very strong in his convictions, or perhaps the whole thing was being controlled by the government, I don't know. It wasn't satisfactory to us'.[37] They attended the hearings, listened to the testimonies of police and politicians, and wondered why the Commission was protecting the police witnesses from questioning, and giving them the dignity that they had denied to the murdered miners.

For Zameka Nungu, though, there was no need to speculate as to why the Commission was failing them. Her conclusion was simple: 'we thought that the truth would come out of it. But then the truth just kept slipping further and further away, until today'.[38]

36 Interview with Lunga Jokanisi, Lusikisiki, 2 December 2015.
37 Group interview with the Mangcotywa family, Sterkspruit, 6 December 2015.
38 Interview with Zameka Nungu, Matatiele, 4 December 2015.

11

Communities of Resistance

IN THE early days of the Commission, the families often felt alone. They had been told that someone had to attend the hearings, and they had been told that this was where they would learn the truth about what had happened to the dead. But when they arrived, they found a hall filled with lawyers, police officers, and journalists, all speaking a specialized language, and dealing with a specialized set of questions.

At first, the families relied on their own lawyers and their support teams to navigate the complexities of the Commission. They asked questions about the processes of the hearings, about the language of the lawyers, and about meaning of the debates that were taking place around them. They sought to clarify points of order, and to ensure that their particular needs – not just for care at the Commission, but for contact with and support from their families at home – were acknowledged.[1]

After a while, the families began to find their feet at the Commission. They shared translators, and a team of lawyers. They also shared accommodation – first in Rustenburg, when the Commission sat there, and then in Centurion. They ate their meals together, they spent the Commission's tea breaks together, and they mourned together: not only in private, but in public ceremonies at Marikana and elsewhere. Throughout all of this, they spoke to each other – about other experiences they shared, about the migrant lives they held in common, and about their own thoughts.

These conversations helped them to orient themselves. They shared opinions on the lawyers, and their approaches to cross-examination. They complained about the lack of respect that they felt the Commission was paying to their legal team. And they thought about the consequences of the Commissioners' attempts to appear to be neutral: in particular, they noticed that the Commissioners would not refer to the events of 16 August 2012 as a massacre. 'They were very hard on the lawyers that represented the families and the mineworkers', Lanford Gcotyelwa said. 'So much so that they would even get censored. I

---

1 Interview with Khuselwa Dyantyi, Lusikisiki, 1 December 2015. Ms Dyantyi was the Families' Liason at the Commission, employed by SERI to support the families that they represented at the Commission.

remember clearly when Advocate Mpofu referred to the incident as a massacre, how he would get shut down and told not to use the word because it had not been proven to be one'. He had no sympathy for this attempt to be neutral. 'But it was ... Why do you need to prove it when it was right there in front of you?'[2]

These shared experiences stretched beyond the walls of the Rustenberg Civic Centre. As representatives of the families travelled between the Commission and their homes in the Eastern Cape, in Lesotho, and elsewhere, they sometimes travelled together. The families that lived in the same rural regions came to know each other. The Matis and the Jijases lived several hours apart from each other, but were close enough to be in regular communication when they were in the Eastern Cape.[3] The Sompeta family, the Jokanisi family, the Gwelane family, and the Zibambele family all lived near to each other and travelled together – sometimes to the Commission, sometimes to closer meetings in Kokstad, a secondary town in the region where they were occasionally given food parcels by Lonmin's representatives.[4] They attended ceremonies together – and for those who became involved in politics, attended rallies together.

Others began to forge new lives for themselves in and around Marikana. Several months after the massacre, the families asked their lawyers to approach Lonmin to request that they be allowed to take on work for the mining company. Lonmin had long had an informal practice of employing a family member of a retiring worker, often allowing sons to replace fathers on the mines. Now, some of the widows wanted the same consideration – to be allowed to work in their husbands' places and to earn the living that their families had now lost. Zameka Nungu and Betty Gadlela were among these women, and soon came to know each other. They were both employed by Lonmin as cleaners, and 'became especially close' through the additional shared experience. Neither enjoyed the work of cleaning offices and toilets – as Zameka said, 'I'm not thrilled about it, because before this I never used to work. My husband used to work, and now I have to … I work because I have no other way out' – but nonetheless, the work helped keep their families afloat. Their companionship supported them as they rearranged their lives after the massacre.[5]

The connections forged between families and between individuals were not the only sources of support, however. In the Commission itself, the arrested and injured miners came to be close allies of the families, as did the representatives of AMCU. Outside, in the broader world, the families and the miners were

2   Interview with Lanford Gcotyelwa, KuNdile, 3 December 2015.
3   Group Interview with the Mati Family, KuNdile, 3 December 2015.
4   Interview with Nomawabo Sompeta, Lusikisiki, 2 December 2015, and interview with Lunga Jokanisi, Lusikisiki, 2 December 2015.
5   Interview with Zameka Nungu, Matatiele, 4 December 2015. See also the interviews with both women in the film Dara Kell (dir.), *Imbokodo: The Widows of Marikana* (Brava/SERI, 2016).

supported by several organized groups – including Sikhala Sonke, a group that represented the women of Marikana, AMCU itself, political activists, and other communities scattered across the country that sought to demonstrate their solidarity with the victims and the survivors of the massacre. Each of these groups represented forms of solidarity and support, and together formed communities of resistance in the name of the dead of Marikana.

The women of Marikana

Since the adoption of a national Mining Charter in 2002, women have been legally able to work in all parts of the mining industry, including as labourers below ground.[6] Indeed, by law at least ten per cent of jobs in the industry are meant to be occupied by women. This meant that, by 2012, approximately 43,000 women were working in the mining industry, although only a very small number of these worked underground. Many of these women were working as winch operators and equipment helpers. This was in part because some types of work are still largely reserved for men – even though there is no official basis for this job reservation. Asanda Benya, who has conducted the most detailed research on the women mineworkers of Marikana, has highlighted the exclusion of women from employment as rock drill operators. She has shown how women face informal discrimination in the sector – from training programmes that actively discourage them from certain types of work, to harassment from male peers, to the imposition of wider social expectations about their self-presentation, deportment, and speech on their daily working lives on the mines.[7]

As very few women were working at the underground rock face in Marikana, they did not form a significant portion of the first group of workers to begin to protest or to embark upon the strike. As they strike proceeded – and, in part, as the dangers of participation increased and the striking workers sought to build closer ties with each other through shared practices and experiences – their initial absence became a matter of principle and policy. Women were not invited to the koppie, and the site became a place of male bonding – what Benya has called

---

6   This Charter has most recently been revised in 2018: 'Broad-Based Socio-Economic Empowerment Charter for the Mining and Minerals Industry, 2018', *Government Gazette*, 27 September 2018. The Charter derives from the Mineral and Petroleum Resources Development Act (28 of 2002). Although the focus of the Charter is on Broad-Based Black Economic Empowerment, it requires mines to list all beneficiaries – linking national and regional demographics to local employment figures.

7   See, among other articles, Asanda Benya, 'Absent From the Frontline, But Not Absent From the Struggle: Women in Mining', *Femina Politica-Zeitschrift für feministische Politikwissenschaft*, 22.1 (2013), pp. 44–47; 'The Invisible Hands: Women in Marikana', *Review of African Political Economy*, 42.146 (2015), pp. 545–560; and 'Going Underground in South African Platinum Mines to Explore Women Miners' Experiences', *Gender & Development*, 25.3 (2017), pp. 509–522.

'a symbolic gendered ... space'. But even so, women – miners and others – were never far from the protest.

Some women lived with their husbands in Nkaneng and the other areas in and around Marikana. They shared their daily lives during the strike: Mphumzeni Ngxande would go home for lunch with his wife. Mafolisi Mabiya's wife was visiting him with their child. John Ledingoane would drive his girlfriend to work, before joining the strike.[8] These women sent their husbands out to work or to participate in the strike each morning; they met them in the evenings; they ate together, when they could; they talked about the day's events, when they could; they shared hopes and fears. For these women – wives, girlfriends, sisters, colleagues – the strike was as much a part of their fabric of their lives as their loved one's work would ordinarily have been. They provided material and moral support, worried about the consequences of the strike, and did their best to hold their households and their lives together in the face of the heavy storm-clouds.

Others sought to play a more obviously active and more public role in supporting the strike. Several women in the area began to organize during the strike, ensuring that food was being distributed among the households of the striking workers. They also arranged for food to be taken to the koppie. Some went further. As 'Nokwakhe Precious Caweni' (a pseudonym used by Bridget Ndibongo, a researcher at the University of Johannesburg, to name a local activist) said, in an interview:

> On the morning of 16th of August we saw police gathered around. Some were riding horses, while others came in police vans and hippos. The police started fencing the area. This scared me, and I decided to mobilise women in the community. I blew a whistle going around the community calling all women to unite behind the miners' struggle ... We marched to Number One [mine] to speak to management.[9]

She continued: 'unfortunately we never reached the office. We had just passed Wonderkop Stadium [when] we started hearing gun shots. There was smoke everywhere, then we all started crouching, we were choking from the tear gas. I was not sure what was going on, all I saw was smoke and people running around'. The women ran towards the clash – but were stopped by a group of fleeing miners. 'They told us to go back, because people were being killed like flies in the mountain ... [But] we refused to sit around while innocent people were slaughtered like chickens. If it was our turn to die then so be it, we were prepared to die with our loved ones.'

---

8   Exhibit KKKK 16 – Mphumzeni Ngxande; KKKK 29 – Mafolisi Mabiya; KKKK 5 – John Ledingoane.
9   The thesis is Bridget Ndibongo, 'Women of Marikana: Survival and Struggles', MA thesis, University of Johannesburg (May 2015). The interview with is presented in full at pp. 98–109.

The police, though, kept them away from the killing sites – 'they told us that they would shoot if we came any closer'. They could only watch from a distance, and try to guess at what had happened while they sought to bear some kind of witness.[10]

This impromptu march was a sign of the willingness of many of the women of Marikana – some direct family members of the striking workers, others their colleagues at the mines, others simply their neighbours in the settlement – to make their support for the miners' strike public and visible.

In the immediate aftermath of the strike, it was these women who resumed the struggle in Marikana. That night, Nokwakhe Caweni and others began to recognize the scale of the massacre.

> People's husbands did not come back home, none of my tenants came back home. I started calling all the miners I knew to find out if they were okay, but none of them were answering their phones. I was scared that they had all been killed by the police. It felt like there was a cloud of darkness that day hanging over our heads.

The next morning, she and many others went to the site of the massacre to confront the police. 'We asked them why they were killing innocent people. They did not give us a response. They were angry and threatened to shoot us if we did not disperse. But we did not care, we refused to be intimidated.'[11]

Afterwards, they went to the police station to try to see the arrested miners. When they were stopped, they moved to the hospital to see those who had been injured – 'but even when we got there we were prevented from seeing the miners'. They dispersed, but continued to support the families of those who had disappeared. They went to police stations, hospitals, and mortuaries. 'There was no time to be scared or even think about what we were doing ... No one deserved to be killed for fighting for their rights. We left our houses and mixed with them. We were prepared to die with them.'

* * *

Their activism continued in the weeks and months that followed. In September, a local councillor, Paulina Masuhlo, was attempting to engage with the communities in Marikana to hold the police to account when she was shot and killed during a police raid in the settlement.[12] In the wake of this killing – on top of and beyond all of the killings in the preceding months, and on top of the continu-

---

10 This was captured by the SAPS records in Exhibit FFF 25 – SAPS JOC OB, entry 986.
11 Ndibongo, 'Women of Marikana', pp. 104–105.
12 Mandy de Waal, 'Marikana's Theatre of the Absurd Claims Another Life', *Daily Maverick*, 20 September 2012, www.dailymaverick.co.za/article/2012-09-20-marikanas-theatre-of-the-absurd-claims-another-life (Acc. March 2021), and Poloko Tau, 'Mouthpiece for Strikers Dies', *The Star*, 21 September 2012, www.iol.co.za/the-star/mouthpiece-for-strikers-dies-1387962 (Acc. March 2021).

ing imprisonment of many of the arrested and injured workers – the women of Marikana embarked on protests to keep the crises in their communities in the country's consciousness.

Some of them also came together to form a local social movement, Sikhala Sonke – which means, in seSotho, 'We Cry Together'.[13] Under the initial leadership of Nokhulunga Primrose Sonti, this group first came together on 22 August 2012 and was formally registered in January 2013. Sikhala Sonke's mission, as stated in its constitution, was to 'empower women and children in the community through skills training, such as farming, teaching, sewing and starting a vegetable garden, and job creation'. The intention behind this was to help women in Marikana to become self-sufficient, and to support those whose lives and livelihoods had been devastated by the strike and the massacre. Sikhala Sonke also took the lead in addressing the management of Lonmin in the months and years after the massacre. They partnered with other groups, such as the Marikana Support Campaign and shareholder activists based outside of the country, to force the mining company to answer – year after year – not only for its failure to negotiate with the strikers and resolve the strike peacefully in 2012, but also for its longstanding failures to implement the promises included in its various Social and Labour Plans – including the promises to develop Marikana, protect the area against environmental degradation, and to build many new houses.[14]

Women in Marikana, at least partially represented by Sikhala Sonke, played an active role, too, in the memorialization of the massacre. They were key figures in the practical organization of the first annual commemoration of the massacre, held in Marikana on 16 August 2013.[15] Although much of this labour took place out of the public gaze, some of the women were visible on the main stage of the event. In particular, Primrose Sonti – as the principal face of Sikhala Sonke –

13   Ndibongo, in her thesis, 'Women of Marikana', discusses Sikhala Sonke and its activism, pp. 138–140. See also Camalita Naicker, 'Worker Struggles as Community Struggles: The Politics of Protest in Nkaneng, Marikana', *Journal of Asian and African Studies*, 51.2 (2016), pp. 157–170, Benya, 'The Invisible Hands', and Nyonde Ntswana, 'Striking Together: Women Workers in the 2012 Platinum Dispute', *Review of African Political Economy*, 42.146 (2015), pp. 625–632.
14   For more on the engagement with the Support Campaign, see: www.marikanajustice.co.za (Acc. March 2021).
15   Ndibongo, 'Women of Marikana', discusses this Commemoration at pp. 127–128. It was also widely reported on at the time. See Greg Nicolson, 'Images of Marikana: August 16, 2013', *Daily Maverick*, 16 August 2013, www.dailymaverick.co.za/article/2013-08-16-images-of-marikana-august-16-2013 (Acc. March 2021) for a visual overview of the event. Primrose Sonti's involvement was also highlighted shortly before, in a SAPA article, 'Marikana Women Want a Bright Future', *News24*, 14 August 2013, www.news24.com/fin24/womens-wealth/news/marikana-women-want-a-bright-future-20130813 (Acc. March 2021).

spoke at the commemoration, while a group of women staged a play dramatizing the strike and the massacre.

The activism of these women helped forge connections across and within a community of men and women, mineworkers, and local residents – both during the strike itself, and in its immediate aftermath. The work of Sikhala Sonke had helped to keep that community's activism – for respect, for a decent environment and a decent life – alive in the wake of the devastation left by the massacre. These women supported each other, the injured and the arrested survivors of the massacre, and the families of those who did not survive. They provided, and continue to provide, a source of solidarity and sympathy, as well as amplifying the voices of the residents of Marikana.

AMCU and the miners' strike of 2014

In the immediate aftermath of the massacre, the police arrested over two hundred and fifty miners, including those who had been injured, and thus already in police custody, and those who were unlucky enough to have been captured while they were fleeing the scene. These arrested and injured miners were held for several weeks, and charged with a range of offences – including, most notoriously, murder and bearing joint responsibility for the deaths of their colleagues at the hands of the police.[16] The women of Marikana pressured the police and the government to release these workers – or, if not, to charge them properly and permit them to apply for their bail.

Joseph Mathunjwa's union, AMCU, also took the part of these workers. The union helped organize legal representation for the arrested miners, and – although not all of this group were its members – extended their interest to cover the whole of the group. The union was clearly motivated in part by its longstanding desire to build support among the workers on Lonmin's mines, but it was also responding to the horrors of the massacre. The workers remembered both Mathunjwa's attempts to intercede during the day before the massacre, and his appeal to the workers on 16 August 2012. To them, he seemed sincere in his concern, in his regret for his inability to have saved lives, and in his anger with the police. To them, Mathunjwa was the first person willing to fight on their behalf, against the police and the tide of public opinion.

The effect of this on the politics of labour at Marikana was significant. By the end of the first year after the massacre, AMCU had ceased to be the minority union in Lonmin's Marikana mines. On 13 August 2013 – three days before the first anniversary of the massacre – Lonmin recognized AMCU as the majority union on its mines. It was now the leading union in the platinum sector. At the core of its message was a statement of solidarity with the workers who had been killed at Marikana, and a reiteration of their demand for a living wage – pinned to R12,500.

---

16 See the discussion of these arrests in Chapters 7 and 8.

The test of the relationship between AMCU and the miners came shortly afterwards, when negotiations between the union and the mining company came to standstill. The union demanded that the R12,500 per month wage demand be met for underground workers and rock drill operators. It also demanded increases for other workers. The company refused, and offered a range of smaller adjustments: AMCU was unable to accept these offers – and so declared that its workers would embark upon a mass strike across the platinum sector until its demands were met.[17]

In the middle of January 2014, AMCU held mass meetings with its members at each of the major mining companies in the Rustenburg region. After receiving instructions to go ahead with a strike, the union applied for a 'strike certificate' from the Commission for Conciliation, Mediation, and Arbitration (CCMA), the statutory body established to regulate and resolve labour disputes – which meant that the ensuing protests would be recognized and protected in ways that the miners' strike of 2012 had not been. On 23 January 2014, the strike began – and approximately 70,000 workers associated with AMCU downed tools. Negotiations continued behind the scenes – but to little avail. In February, the negotiations broke down. Early in March, AMCU organized further public marches and protests. The union drafted memoranda and press releases, confronting the mining companies and insisting on their demands. Nothing, though, seemed to shift the positions of either the companies or the union.

In April, the mining companies decided to bypass the official processes of negotiations – and instead of communicating with the formal majority union sought to communicate directly with their employees. The ironies of this situation were not lost on anyone: in 2012, Lonmin had refused to communicate directly with its miners and had insisted on only speaking through the official union. Now that this union was less overtly sympathetic to it, Lonmin and the other companies were attempting to subvert the system that they had once so fiercely defended. If they had been as flexible in August 2012, perhaps the massacre itself would have never happened.

The ironies continued: AMCU found itself in the position of seeking to prevent the mining companies from communicating directly with their workers, and asked the country's labour courts to interdict them from sending out text messages to the striking workers. They failed, and the messages were sent – but the workers remained unconvinced of the sincerity of the companies' offer, and

---

17   In this account of the Miners' Strike of 2014, I've drawn extensively on Luke Sinwell with Siphiwe Mbatha, *The Spirit of Marikana: The Rise of Insurgent Trade Unionism in South Africa* (London, Pluto: 2016); and Naadirah Munshi, 'Platinum Politics: The Rise, and Rise, of the Association of Mineworkers and Construction Union (AMCU)', MA thesis (University of the Witwatersrand, March 2017). See also Andrew Bowman and Gilad Isaacs, 'The 2014 Platinum Strike: Narratives and Numbers', *Review of African Political Economy*, 42.146 (2015), pp. 643–656.

preferred to continue their now four-month long strike.[18] This strengthened AMCU's hand in the negotiations, and – over the next month – discussions of the wage offer resumed.

* * *

Meanwhile, the strike continued. Over 70,000 households were dependent on the wages of these platinum miners – and, for the five months of the strike running from February through June, none of these miners were able to draw a wage from the mines.[19] In the first phase of this strike, no one realized how long it might last – or made clear plans to ensure the survival of these households. The existence of a strike fund for members was only announced by AMCU in April 2014, and even then these funds were earmarked for social responsibilities, such as emergency care and funeral costs.[20]

In the meantime, many of the workers were struggling to put food on the table, or to purchase the basic necessities of life. Their children's school fees, their transport costs, even their purchasing of toiletries were all endangered – and, in some cases, had to be dropped entirely. Hunger became an everyday part of their lives. Anything that they might have saved in advance of the strike – whether a small pot of money, or material goods, or even canned food – was soon finished. The longer the strike continued, the more desperate the situation became.

For some of the mineworkers, the agony of this deepening crisis could only be justified by the thought of those who had come before, and those who would follow. As one worker told a student researcher at the University of the Witwatersrand, Naadirah Munshi:

---

18   See the media coverage, including: Govan Whittles, 'AMCU takes Lonmin to Court', *Eye Witness News*, 20 May 2014, https://ewn.co.za/2014/05/20/Platinum-strike-Lonmin-reaches-out-to-Amcu (Acc. March 2021); Martin Creamer, 'Lonmin to Oppose AMCU Labour Court Interdict', *Engineering News*, 19 May 2014, www.engineering-news.co.za/article/lonmin-to-oppose-amcu-labour-court-interdict-2014-05-19 (Acc. March 2021); Chantelle Benjamin, 'Labour Court Returns to Negotiation Table with AMCU, Miners', *Mail and Guardian*, 21 May 2014, https://mg.co.za/article/2014-05-21-labour-court-judge-returns-to-negotiation-table-with-amcu-miners (Acc. March 2021). As Benjamin's article makes clear, the court's behaviour was unusual – with the judge attempting to intervene in the negotiations as well as ruling on the question of the interdict. See Munshi, p. 91. The final judgment of the Labour Court, refusing the interdict, is *Association Of Mineworkers And Construction Union v Lonmin Platinum (Comprising Eastern Platinum Ltd And Western Platinum Ltd) and Others* (J1134/14) [2014] ZALCJHB 196; (2014) 35 ILJ 3097 (LC) (2 June 2014).

19   Bowman and Isaacs estimate that 70,000 platinum miners were on strike during 2014.

20   Natalie Greve, 'AMCU Opens "Strike Fund" for Members, Calls for Donations', *Mining Weekly*, 15 April 2014, www.miningweekly.com/article/amcu-opens-strike-fund-for-members-calls-for-donations-2014-04-15 (Acc. March 2021).

The things that we are striking for, we are not doing it for us. We are doing it for the other employees who have been shot and killed two years ago ... The next generation, they will find everything in good manner; like everything is going to be in a good place.'[21]

They held the sacrifices of the miners killed at Marikana in their minds, and trusted that their own struggles would make a new, better world.

The support that AMCU and the miners had shown for the community in and around Marikana after the massacre now formed the basis of an extension of solidarity to the striking miners. Sikhala Sonke and the women of Marikana attempted to help the striking miners, through distributing the products of their vegetable gardens, supporting their families, and by helping to ensure that their stories of struggle, sacrifice, and commitment were being spread beyond the region. Others, too, offered their support. Gift of the Givers – a national charitable organization – partnered with AMCU to distribute food parcels and toiletries to miners and their families.[22] These parcels could not cover all miners and all areas, but were vital to the survival strategies of many families. So too were informal and unstructured forms of support from local businesses – such as small extensions of credit and unsecured loans. These, however, were largely unsustainable – and soon, many local businesses were going under.

Although AMCU's negotiating position had been strengthened by the commitment of its members to the strike, this situation could not continue indefinitely. Hunger and deprivation in the miners' households were worsening. The union needed to end the strike as much as the mining companies did – and so, over the last few weeks of May and the first weeks of June, an acceptable compromise offer was hammered out.

In essence, the mining companies agreed to the substance of the union's demand for a full wage packet of R12,500 per month for underground workers, including RDOs – but required that the implementation of this increase be spaced out over several years, as a series of incremental step-changes to existing wage agreements. Each year, the underground workers would receive an increase of about R1,000 on their monthly salaries – which would take their basic wage to about R9,000 in 2016. A package of benefits would then raise this to the symbolic figure of R12,500. Surface-level workers received similar wage increases, although their final figure was lower. Despite the care with which they were to be implemented, these raises were, of course, far above inflationary pressures and represented a significant concession by the mining companies.

They also represented a significant victory for AMCU. Although the immedi-

---

21 See Munshi, 'Platinum Politics', p. 109.
22 Rebecca Davis, 'Marikana: Gift of the Givers Brings Food to Striking Miners', *Daily Maverick*, 10 September 2014, www.dailymaverick.co.za/article/2012-09-10-marikana-gift-of-the-givers-brings-food-to-striking-miners (Acc. March 2020).

ate wage increase would not fulfil all of its promises to its members, the willingness of the mining companies to pin their offer to the symbol of R12,500 – to the symbol of the struggle that had ended in the deaths of so many men at Marikana – was remarkable. It enabled Joseph Mathunjwa and AMCU to claim to have inherited the mantle of the struggle of the miners of Marikana, and to have completed it.

But it also demonstrated to the surviving miners, their families, and to the communities that included them, that the deaths at Marikana had not been for nothing. The struggles of the dead had not been forgotten. Their dreams were shaping the politics of the moment, and laying the ground for a new generation of workers and activists – a generation that would be shaped by the memory of the miners' sacrifices first during the strike of 2012 and then the strike of 2014.

Solidarity beyond Marikana

It was not only those directly connected to the communities in Marikana, though, who recognized the link between the struggles and sacrifices of the miners in August 2012 and their own place in the world. Shortly after the massacre, Julius Malema – the recently expelled leader of the African National Congress's Youth League – began to visit Marikana and to engage with the miners. Malema, according to at least one interview, decided to form a new political party in the wake of the government's willingness to use violence to suppress the strike. This party – the Economic Freedom Fighters (EFF) – was founded by a group of men who had all previously been members of the governing ANC, and who were seeking to distinguish their new movement from their old political home.[23] They found their first cause in the miners of Marikana. The party has held rallies in Marikana; it has invited miners to participate in these rallies, and to tell their stories about the strike and the massacre; it has supported the arrested and injured miners in their legal struggles with the state; and it has even offered places on its electoral lists to men and women closely associated with Marikana. Primrose Sonti – the founder of Sikhala Sonke – has been a Member of Parliament for the EFF since 2014, and Dali Mpofu – the lead legal representative for the arrested and injured miners at the Commission of Inquiry – held a

23 For early reports of Malema's engagement at Marikana, see: Sipho Hlongwane and Greg Marinovich, 'Lonmin: Malema Fans the Flames, but the Victims are Still Out in the Cold', *Daily Maverick*, 18 August 2012, www.dailymaverick.co.za/article/2012-08-18-lonmin-malema-fans-the-flames-but-the-victims-are-still-out-in-the-cold (Acc. March 2021); Faranaaz Parker and Nickolaus Bauer, 'Marikana: Malema Sparks Chaos at Memorial Service', *Mail and Guardian*, 23 August 2012, https://mg.co.za/article/2012-08-23-malema-sparks-chaos-at-marikana-memorial-service (Acc. March 2021). For the story that links the massacre to the birth of the EFF, see: Vhahangwele Nemakonde, 'How the Marikana Massacre Gave Birth to the EFF', *The Citizen*, 16 August 2017, https://citizen.co.za/news/south-africa/1614452/how-the-marikana-massacre-gave-birth-to-eff (Acc. March 2021).

senior office in the party. As its electoral fortunes have improved, the EFF has continued to remember the workers of Marikana.

It was not just in the arena of elite politics, though, that solidarity has been shown. Other communities of resistance have emerged organically, out of the soil of people's identification with the struggles of the men and women of Marikana. Activists in informal settlements across the country, for example, have seen in these struggles their own fights, and saw in the faces of the dead, their own faces. For them, the miners' struggle was part of the wider struggle for a true democracy in South Africa – for the truly equal and just society that had not yet been fully born.

The residents of informal settlements across the country have often faced repression by the police, and their struggles have often been mischaracterized or ignored by the state and the media. They have been demonized as 'land invaders', and their shacks have been described as public nuisances or as health threats, and they have regularly faced harassment by the police and the state. Informal settlements often fall outside the protections of the law, and so the structures within these settlements – the residents' homes – are often destroyed: sometimes by private security guards employed by the official land owners, and sometimes by the police themselves.[24]

These demolitions are often confrontational. Armed security guards, municipal officers, and policemen pull down the makeshift homes of the residents of these settlements. They rip apart sheets of corrugated iron and wooden planks; they rummage through the residents' belonging, and toss them into the dirt; they push people aside, and leave them without a home. Unsurprisingly, the residents of these settlements often try to resist these demolitions – seeking to persuade the security guards and police to leave the site, sometimes even through threats of violence. Equally unsurprisingly, the police and security guards have responded to the possibility of resistance with increased violence and force – even sometimes violently assaulting residents.

In the wake of the massacre, many of the residents of these informal settlements recognized a similarity between the casual violence of the police in Marikana and the casual violence of official security guards and police in their own lives. The number of deaths at Marikana was no doubt greater than what would be expected in the course of a clash in an informal settlement – but deaths do happen in these clashes, as well as injuries, and of course the destruction of their homes. The effect of a clash between residents and police was to devastate the residents' lives.

---

24 See Julian Brown, *South Africa's Insurgent Citizens: On Dissent and the Possibility of Politics* (London, Zed: 2015) for an overview of these practices of repression – and of the many forms of resistance taken by the residents of these settlement. See also: Marie Huchzermeyer, *Unlawful Occupation: Informal Settlements and Urban Policy in South Africa and Brazil* (Trenton, NJ, Africa World Press: 2004).

In the months and years after the massacre, the residents of many informal settlements across the country adopted the name 'Marikana' as their own. In Durban, a new land occupation in the Cato Crest section of Cato Manor was named 'Marikana' during a period of often-violent confrontation between the residents, representatives of the municipality's 'Land Invasion Control Unit', and the police. A second land occupation in the same city was also given the name 'Marikana' by its residents.[25] Meanwhile in Cape Town, at the other side of the country, yet another informal settlement adopted the name. In about February 2013, a small collection of a few dozen shacks on private land attracted the attention of the land owner and the local police forces. After a series of demolitions carried out by the police brought public attention to the occupation, and alerted others to the availability of land in the area. Before long, the settlement began to grow – and confrontations between the police and the new residents escalated. Over the course of several months, more than a dozen demolition actions took place – mostly conducted by the City of Cape Town's 'Anti-Land Invasion Unit', sometimes supported by the police services. In these conditions, the residents saw themselves as subject to the unjust and unrelenting violence of the state – an experience that they believed that they shared with the murdered miners of Marikana.[26]

The naming of informal settlements has always been a political action. Often, informal settlements have been named after prominent political figures – Joe Slovo, Winnie Mandela, Thabo Mbeki, Nelson Mandela. These indicated both political preferences on the part of the residents of these settlements, and – of course – the political trajectories of the moment. If a political figure was seen to be sympathetic, the naming of a settlement after her was a signifier of respect, and connection. If a political figure was seen to be particularly influential, then the naming of a settlement after her might be intended to provide symbolic shelter against assault.

In this context, the choices of so many embattled residents of informal settlements to adopt the name 'Marikana' as their own is significant. It links their struggles to those of the miners. It links the injustice of their own treatment to

---

25 Richard Pithouse, 'Subaltern Politics & the Elite Public Sphere: The Marikana Land Occupation in Cato Manor, Durban, in 2013 and 2014', in Daniel Plaatjies et al. (eds), *State of the Nation: South Africa 2016* (Pretoria, HSRC Press: 2016), 241–256; Shauna Mottiar, 'Protest and Participation in Durban: A Focus on Cato Manor, Merebank, and Wentworth', *Politikon*, 41.3 (2014), pp. 371–385.
26 Socio-Economic Rights Institute (SERI), *Our Place to Belong: Marikana Informal Settlement*, Informal Settlements Research Report (SERI, 2019); Rayner Teo, 'The Organisation of a Land Occupation: A Case Study of Marikana, Cape Town', MA thesis, University of Cape Town (2015); Heike Becker, 'Remembering Marikana: Public Art Interventions and the Right to the City in Cape Town', *Social Dynamics*, 44.3 (2018), pp 455–471.

that of the massacre. And it links the memory of the miners' strike and their lives to the lives of tens of thousands of men and women across the country.

These choices help to keep the story of Marikana alive, and to spread it among people who have no personal connection to the miners – people who never met them and never loved them, people who never worked alongside them, people who have not directly benefitted from their sacrifices. These men and women may never meet any of the families of those who died at Marikana, may never work on the mines, may never even step foot in Marikana – and yet, for them, too, the symbolism of the massacre seeped into and defined their shared daily lives.[27]

* * *

The adoption of the name of 'Marikana' for informal settlements across the country was one way in which people could mark and commemorate the massacre. Another was for them to share the story of what had happened during the massacre – to make sure that the memory of Marikana was not only something held by the families of the dead, but something shared by all South Africans.

At the forefront of these commemorative efforts have been a small number of activist film makers, academics, and journalists. The first significant publication to come out after the massacre – and the first to try to tell the story of the strike from a position of sympathy with the miners – was written by the team of academics at the University of Johannesburg that had begun to interrogate the police's story immediately after the massacre. This book included several long interviews with miners about the strike, and gave the broader public the first real sense of the miners' own stories. This has been followed by other books, dealing with other aspects of labour politics on the mines.[28]

Journalists, too, have written about the massacre. Very few of these books attempt to move beyond the police's official story, though.[29] Only one of them – Greg Marinovich's *Murder at Small Koppie* – seeks to understand the miners' positions, and the rationality of their decisions to strike. This book tells the story

---

27 These interventions have also moved into more traditionally urban spaces, echoing their own local struggles. See: Becker, 'Remembering Marikana'.

28 Peter Alexander et al., *Marikana: A View from the Mountain and a Case to Answer* (Johannesburg, Jacana: 2012). Other early academic commentators, including Philip Frankel, *Between the Rainbows and the Rain: Marikana, Migration, Mining, and the Crisis of Modern South Africa* (Johannesburg, Agency for Social Reconstruction: 2013) focused more on structural questions, and not on the workers themselves.

29 These include: Thanduxolo Jika et al., *'We Are Going to Kill Each Other Today': The Marikana Story* (Cape Town, Tafelberg: 2013); and Gia Nicolaides, *Reporting from the Frontline: Untold Stories from Marikana* (Johannesburg, Jacana: 2014). Neither of these books reveals any new details about the strike, or the massacre.

of how the police sought to cover up their actions in the course of the massacre, and of how their duplicity was uncovered by his own investigations and others.[30] These stories have been important to the creation of a broad public understanding of the events.

But the most influential attempts to influence the public story about the Marikana massacre have come from film makers. Rehad Desai – an activist and film maker – began to compile coverage of the events at Marikana almost as soon as the strike began. Over the year that followed the massacre, he and his team conducted interviews, attended the Commission's hearing, and attempted to get access to as many different sources of video footage of the massacre as possible. In May 2014, he released *Miners Shot Down* – the most comprehensive effort to describe the key events of the strike and to explain what had happened in the massacre itself.[31]

Miners Shot Down has provided the most public counter to the official story told by the police, the presidency, and much of the media in the aftermath of the massacre. In the years following its release, Desai and his colleagues have fought to have the film broadly distributed and shown, first in cinemas across the country, and then on public television channels. These attempts have often been fraught with potential conflict, and the SABC, the state-backed national broadcaster, has occasionally been accused of attempting to censor the film – either by scheduling the film at inconvenient times, or by changing the schedule at the last minute, or by refusing to show it.

Other film makers have followed in the wake of *Miners Shot Down*, and have sought in particular to draw attention to the experiences of the women of Marikana – both those who are members of Sikhala Sonke and those who have survived the deaths of their loved ones in the massacre. Aliki Saragas's *Mama Marikana* focuses on the women of Sikhala Sonke and tells their story.[32] *Imbokodo: The Widows of Marikana*, a short film by Dara Kell, produced by the Socio-Economic Rights Institute of South Africa, which provided legal representation and support to the families of the dead, tells the stories of Zameka Nungu and Betty Gadlela, among others, as they began to work in Lonmin's Marikana mines several years after their husbands had died.[33]

All of these efforts – by academics, journalists, and film makers – have contributed to a continuing public challenge to the official story of the strike and the massacre. The stories they tell resonate with the ideas about Marikana held by the residents of informal settlements across the country, a story of courage and resistance in the face of public indifference and horrifying police violence. For

---

30 Greg Marinovich, *Murder at Small Koppie: The Real Story of the Marikana Massacre* (Cape Town, Penguin SA: 2016).
31 Rehad Desai (dir.), *Miners Shot Down* (Uhuru Productions, 2014).
32 Aliki Saragas (dir.), *Mama Marikana* (UCT Film, 2015).
33 Dara Kell (dir.), *Imbokodo: The Widows of Marikana* (Brava/SERI, 2016).

these story-tellers, the events at Marikana represent an ongoing critique of the current political order in South Africa – the order that permitted the massacre to take place in August 2012, and that order that continues to permit other injustices to occur across the country.

12

'Let us Not Lose Hope'

AT THE end of the Farlam Commission's first year, on Day 133 of the hearings – 19 September 2013 – there was a moment in which it might have reinvigorated itself.

On this day, the Evidence Leaders announced that they had reason to believe that the police had been actively seeking to mislead the Commission by manipulating the evidence given to the parties. Geoff Budlender, speaking for the Evidence Leaders, explained that they had finally been given access to the police's hard drives, after several attempts to force the police to hand over these records. They had found significant discrepancies in the police's evidence.

> First, we have obtained certain documents which the SAPS previously said were not in existence. Second, we have obtained documents which in our opinion ought to have been previously disclosed by the SAPS, but which were not. Third, we have been given documents which give the impression that they are contemporaneous documents, contemporaneous with the events which they describe, but which appear to have been constructed after those events to which they refer ... Fourth, we have obtained documents which in our opinion demonstrate that the SAPS version of the events at Marikana as described in the SAPS presentation to this Commission, and in the evidence of SAPS witnesses to this Commission, is in material respects not the truth.[1]

In other words: they had caught the police lying. The police had hidden documents. They had manufactured false evidence. Officers had been lying while under oath.

After this statement, the Commission took a week-long break. When the hearings resumed, though, the police fought back and both the Evidence Leaders and the Commission crumbled. The police's legal representatives, led by Senior Counsel Ishmael Semenya, complained vigorously about the Evidence Leaders' statement and the way in which it had been reported. The Evidence Leaders – rather than pressing their point – accepted that the reporting of their

---

[1] Transcript of Day 133 of the Marikana Commission of Inquiry (19 September 2013), especially pp. 14,106–14,111.

statement had been overheated, and offered an apology to the police's legal team for the ways in which their words might have been misinterpreted. They emphasized that they held no decision-making role in the Commission, and that their suggestions should not be understood to bind the Commission. It was up to the Commissioners to decide if their claims were true.[2]

The Commissioners agreed. Pingla Hemraj asked that it be put on the record that, 'as Commissioners, we are not arriving at any conclusions, provisional or otherwise, until we've heard all the evidence and seen all the documentation in this process. I think we want to place that on record'. Ian Farlam concurred – and then suggested that, now that 'some of the confusion that previously existed because of what happened last week' had been dispersed by the Evidence Leaders' apology, the hearing could resume as if all was as normal. 'We can now continue with our eyes on the ball', he said, to the whole room, '[and] consider the evidence that the witness is going to give, and the questions are going to be put to him'.[3] And so the Commission resumed – as did its polite, restrained, and credulous examination of the next police witnesses.

The families of the dead struggled with this. They saw that there had been an opportunity for the Commission to take an active role in challenging obvious lies and holding the police, and the mine, and everyone else to account. But that opportunity had been missed. The resumption of the Commission's collegial routines seemed a betrayal of its mission – and seemed to demonstrate that the Commissioners were more concerned with the reputations of their colleagues and the police than they were with finding out the truth. The speed with which the Evidence Leaders' allegations were dismissed, the ease with which the Commission returned to its existing routines, even the Commissioners' insistence on the suspension of their judgment – all of these things worked to reinforce this impression. Nothing, it seemed, could ever change.

As Semi Jokanisi's father put it: 'I had hoped that the Commission would capture the important bits, and that the truth would be revealed. [But] from where I was sitting, I realized that there was no truth to it. There was a lot of beating around the bush'.[4]

The Police case continues

And so, in the eyes of the families, the miners, and their supporters, the exchange between the Commissioners, the Evidence Leaders, and the police's legal representatives demonstrated that the Commission was more concerned with maintaining an atmosphere of collegiality than it was with investigating the police's misconduct. This led them to treat the remaining months of hearings with even

---

2   Transcript of Day 134 of the Marikana Commission of Inquiry (25 September 2013.
3   Day 134 (25 September 2013), p. 14,129.
4   Interview with Lunga Jokanisi, Lusikisiki, 2 December 2015.

greater scepticism. A series of police commanders and officers testified under oath. The Provincial Commissioner and Deputy Commissioner of the Police in the North West, Lieutenant-General Mbombo and Major-General Mpembe, told their stories, as did the commanding officers on the ground, including Major-General Naidoo and Major-General Annandale.[5] Their accounts were unsurprising. Despite the evidence that the police had trumped up much of their story – and that their claims were based on falsified documents – the story they told merely repeated the earlier police story.

The Commissioners listened impassively to these stories. Although they occasionally asked some pointed questions – and although they continued to allow the Evidence Leaders and others to conduct more aggressive cross-examinations – they chose to emphasize their independence by keeping their opinions quiet. They allowed the police to continue to tell their story, without indicating what they thought.

For the families, the Commissioners' display of impassivity in the face of these statements was yet another demonstration of the Commission's weakness in the face of power – a weakness first displayed during the testimonies of political figures:

> The other thing that we didn't like at the Commission is the way the case was handled. When it came to questioning the ministers, the procedure changed ... I've just forgotten what that rule was that they made up ... they resisted questioning a minister, they would put a thirty-minute limit [on cross-examination]. What can you possibly ascertain in thirty minutes? They were trying to protect them. We didn't like that.[6]

Only one police witness departed from the official line. Lieutenant-Colonel Salmon Vermaak, who had filmed part of the strike from a police helicopter, and who had been involved in the police operations that had led to the massacre, broke ranks. This was not a disinterested choice: he told the Commission that the police's lawyers were planning to blame him for the massacre. This, he felt, was unfair – and so he had decided to tell the Commission the full truth, and to reveal how the police had really acted.[7]

---

5   Mbombo's testimony began on Day 177 (29 January 2014); Mpembe's on Day 145 (8 November 2013); Naidoo's on Day 188 (20 February 2014); and Annandale's had begun earlier on Day 77 (22 April 2013).
6   Interview with Lanford Gcotyelwa, KuNdile, 3 December 2015.
7   Vermaak's testimony to the Commission shifted significantly over the years. His early statements hewed more closely to the official police line. However, as his relationship with the police hierarchy altered, so too did his statements. The early statements – drawn up late in 2012 and early in 2013 – are conventional. The later – drawn up in 2014 – are significantly more critical of his commanders. Compare, for example, Exhibit HHH 4 – Statement of Vermaak dated 30 August 2012 with Exhibit LLL 8 – Lt-Col Vermaak Statement dated 21 January 2014. By the time of his oral testimony, his position had settled.

Vermaak said that on Monday 13 August 2012 he had seen Maj.-Gen. Mpembe order tear gas to be fired at the workers. This was a direct contradiction of Mpembe's testimony, in which he had denied giving this order. Vermaak insisted that Mpembe had lied. He also insisted that this clash had been caused by the police's mismanagement of the protest.[8] He suggested that he thought that the commanders had been out of their depth throughout the strike, that they were unprepared, and that their so-called plans had been useless – indeed, the plans had barely existed at all.

But even though he criticized his fellow police commanders, Vermaak was not sympathetic to the mineworkers. He believed that the police had been unprepared because they did not understand how bloodthirsty and how irrational the miners were. He said that mining strikes were always more violent than other kinds of protests, and that the invocation of traditional religion by some of the miners had signalled an atavistic faith in their own invulnerability.[9] In this context, the police should have been prepared to protect themselves against the workers – and that this might have allowed them to avoid the massacre. In other words: more managed police violence would have been necessary to avoid the unmanaged violence of the massacre on 16 August.

Vermaak was not the only one to describe the miners as violent, irrational, and bloodthirsty. His account resonated with the story told by the police's final star witness – an anonymous man known in the Commission as 'Mr X'. Mr X claimed to have been involved in the strike, and to have seen the private behaviour both of the presumed leaders of the strike and of ordinary mineworkers. Both, he claimed, had committed atrocities – and so, in fear of retribution, he insisted on anonymity.[10]

Mr X told the Commission that there was a committee leading the strike, and that the members of this committee had all taken part in a gory ritual using the flesh of Hassan Fundi, one of the security guards who had been killed on the Sunday evening. This ritual had been overseen by the tradi-

---

8   Vermaak's oral testimony to the Commission began on Day 205 (24 March 2014).
9   For example: Vermaak, Day 205 (24 March 2014), pp. 25,207–25,211.
10 Mr X's statement to the Commission is Exhibit LLL 26 – Statement of Mr X. The Evidence Leaders' conclusions about Mr X's evidence and testimony seem to me to be incontrovertible: 'the evidence of Mr X is so plainly contrived, and so plainly false in a number of the most material respects, that it is unsafe to place any reliance on it'. They note that at least some of the episodes described by Mr X are 'plainly fabricated', that his evidence was 'contrived and false', 'incomprehensible' and 'inconsistent', 'invented' and 'contrived in order to justify the conduct of the SAPS'. They recommended that the Commission place no weight on it at all. Their critiques are unanswerable, and no party other than SAPS attempted to defend Mr X's testimony. (See the Evidence Leaders' Heads of Argument, pp. 77–89, for their analysis of Mr X's false testimony.)

tional healers, and was intended to provide them with some sort of mystic protection during the strike. He suggested that these traditional healers had held some sort of authority over the strike, and had helped cloud the minds of the striking workers. He also suggested that Joseph Mathunjwa and AMCU had played a role in organizing the strike. He claimed that the miners were intending to attack the police – that they believed that they would be protected from harm through the rituals conducted by the traditional healers, and that they were so bloodthirsty that they planned to murder all the police officers at Marikana. In his eyes, he told the Commission, it was clear that the police had been acting in self-defence.

Mr X accused specific miners of atrocities – of violence and of murder, of despoiling the bodies of the dead, of intending to commit further acts of violence. He spoke for hours before any critical questions were asked, and painted a horrific picture.[11]

But, of course, the entirety of Mr X's testimony collapsed under cross-examination.

He was rapidly shown to have contradicted himself. He was shown to have misidentified figures in photographs – including, notoriously, misidentifying himself as being in a photograph when he was not. He was shown to have lied about his whereabouts at various points in the strike, about his role in the strike, about his ability to recognize individuals, and about his ability to have seen the events that he claimed that he had seen. His entire testimony was shown to be a tissue of lies – falsehoods made up to show the miners in the worst possible light, and the police in the best.

And yet, nonetheless, throughout his testimony and the questioning – a process which lasted for eleven days, spread out over two months of hearings – the families watched as the three Commissioners listened to his falsehoods. The Commissioners held their opinions to themselves, and said nothing that would suggest that they disapproved of the statements being made in front of them – nor did they say anything that suggested that they were shocked by the exposure of Mr X's many lies. They continued to withhold judgment – to emphasize that they 'were not arriving at any conclusions, whether preliminary or otherwise' before the very end of the hearings. In the face of the clear dishonesty of the police commanders and its star witnesses, in the face of the evidence of the attempts of the police to manufacture a story and to coerce testimony, and in the face of the implausible viciousness of Mr X's wild claims this performance of neutrality served only to convince the families of the Commission's failure.

---

11   Mr X's testimony began on Day 252 (30 June 2014) and occupied eleven days of the hearings.

'The truth is bitter'

Nonetheless – and despite the erosion of their faith in the Commission's processes – the families were still determined to ensure that the stories of their loved ones would be told. They had to be heard, by the country if not by the Commissioners themselves.

The families' team of lawyers had been negotiating with the Commission about the status of the families' presentations for almost two years. There had been several disputes: would they be presented by sworn witnesses, as ordinary testimony, or would they be presented in some other way? Their lawyers insisted that the family members should be spared the trauma of cross-examination by the lawyers for the police, for the NUM, for the government. They also insisted that the Commission should take into account the personal stories of the victims of the massacre and the families that survived them.[12] This was unexpectedly controversial, and the police's lawyers – in particular – pushed back against the idea that the families should be allowed to testify without being cross-examined. Any evidence put to the Commission, they argued, would have to be tested by a critical voice – and so, if the Commission wanted to take the families' stories into account, it would have to allow them to be tested.[13]

This was an irreconcilable difference.

The presentations were postponed over and over again. Finally – in the last days of the Commission's hearings – the dispute was resolved, and the presentations were scheduled. The words of the family members would be read out by their legal representatives, while a PowerPoint presentation with photographs and information accompanied them. The family member concerned would be in the main hall, following their lawyer's words. At the end of the presentation, the family would be given an opportunity to add any further words to the presentation – to speak directly to the Commission, and the Commissioners. They would not face cross-examination, or any form of questioning from the police's legal team. The status of their evidence was, however, still unclear – but they would, nonetheless, be permitted to speak.

On Day 273 of the Commission's hearings, 13 August 2014, almost exactly two years since the strike had begun, the families were finally able to present their stories to the Commission and the public. Their presentations focused on telling the stories of their loved ones – on highlighting their childhoods, their dreams, their everyday lives, and their hopes. The presentations also told the Commission about the effect of the massacre on their own lives – how they learned about the deaths, how they mourned in the immediate aftermath, how they were still trying to put their lives back together, to hold their families together, and to put

---

12   This is from discussions with the lawyers representing the majority of the families of the deceased.

13   See the SAPS position read into the record on Day 273, pp. 34,870–34,871.

food on their tables. The presentations told the stories of their lives as they now were, after the massacre.[14]

The first phase of presentations came from the families of those who had been killed during the strike, whether by miners or in the clash that had taken place on Monday.

The presentations then continued with the stories of the striking mineworkers. These stories emphasized the lives of those who had died, their relationships, their hopes, their dreams, and the tangled connections between their migrant lives and their hard work and their decisions to participate in the strike. In her statement, read out on her behalf, Nomawabo Sompeta described her family's shattered routine: 'My son visited home twice a year. He phoned us every week. He was supposed to come home for his annual leave only a week after the day on which he died'. She told the Commission that he 'loved gospel songs, especially Dikokele Jehovah', that he was 'building us a house', and that his salary had supported his whole family. She said very little about the strike, remembering only that

> Even during the strike my son found time to phone us. He told us that there was a strike at Lonmin. I told him to come back, but he said he could not leave his fellow workers. He did not talk much about the strike itself, but said they were sitting on a koppie ... He also did not mention or talk about the police. He told me that he would switch his phone off during the day.[15]

After the family had heard about his death, his brother went to Marikana. 'They observed a bullet wound in the chest of my son. We were told that he was shot by the police at the koppie. When we washed his clothes we saw bloodstains on the T-shirt and the fabric was also damaged. His jersey had holes from the back and a hole which looked like a bullet hole in the chest'. She remembered that, 'His colleagues from Marikana attended his funeral ... None of them were able to tell us how he died. We are deeply hurt by Mzukisi's death. We do not know where to turn'.

Similar notes were struck by the other presentations. Noktula Zibambele remembered that her husband

> liked football. He was not a violent man. He liked phoning us when there was a big soccer match. I enjoyed talking to him. He had a reputation for being a spiritual person, and for his love for the church ... He phoned us every day, and would send a call-back message if he could not call.

---

14 Transcript of Day 273 (13 August 2014) and Day 274 (14 August 2014) at the Marikana Commission of Inquiry. See also: Exhibits KKKK 1–44 (Families Presentation) which bundles the presentations made by the families and their representatives over these two days.

15 Exhibit KKKK 9 – Mzukisi Sompeta.

He had managed to call them during the strike, and she had begged him to come home.[16]

Noluvese Noki remembered her brother Mgcineni, known as Mambush, as 'a happy man [who] did not like fights and never fought. He was always laughing and smiling. He was very forgiving and he liked soccer'. She told the Commission how,

> on the 19th August 2012 in the morning family members gathered to talk about my brother's death and how they were going to tell me. Little did they know that whilst they were gathering I had just called Mbulelo who had just told me that my brother died. I started crying, and the elders and family members came to where I was ... I was hurting and still am. I cried throughout ... The pain was unbearable.[17]

Where these presentations sought to tell the stories of the dead, and of their families, the comments and interventions made by some of the family members after spoke to the present – to their ongoing pain, and to their frustrated hopes for the Commission.

Matsepang Ntsoele chose to speak after the end of her family's presentation. She stood up in the hall and told the Commission that

> I am in terrible pain [because] of what happened to my husband due to Lonmin because up till now we do not know what happened that ended up with our husbands being killed. When our husbands left home it was because of hunger ... the Bible says everyone should reap what he sows.

She said, 'to all the families who lost their loved ones at Marikana, God be with you, and all the people involved in this Commission, God should give them the wisdom, all of them, to be able to resolve this matter peacefully'.[18]

At the end of his family's presentation, Snobuyo Noki – cousin to Noluvese and Mambush – asked to speak on his own behalf. He said that he wanted to address the three Commissioners directly. He wanted to sum up what he thought, what he knew, what bothered him in the Commission. He said to them: 'Mr Chair, what bothers me most is that my brother should be seen as a killer ... What Mambush wanted on the koppie was the truth ... The truth is bitter here in South Africa'.[19]

Zameka Nungu, too, spoke.

> I am hurting, Mr Chair and the Commission. My heart is bleeding, crying, complaining about Lonmin. If Lonmin could not have afforded to pay them they could have simply dismissed them and sent them back home. They

---

16   Exhibit KKKK 10 – Thobisile Zibambele.
17   Exhibit KKKK 11 – Mgcieni Noki.
18   Matsapang Ntsoele, Day 273 (12 August 2014), pp. 3,941–3,942.
19   Snobuyo Noki, Day 273 (12 August 2014), pp. 34,909–34,910.

should not have called the police to kill our husbands. The police are now sitting with their wives and their children, their life goes on, our life does not go on. Instead of seeing light, we're seeing darkness. You wake up in the middle of the night and cry, not knowing who is going to stop you from crying because you're sleeping alone.[20]

She added, 'The truth is bitter, people don't want the truth'.

And then, she ended with a prayer: 'Let us have hope that one day God will answer. Even if the Commission goes on, but it is not above God, God is everything.'

The Commission's final Report

The Commission officially ended its hearings on 14 November 2014 – the three-hundredth day of the hearings. On the first day of the Commission's hearings, Judge Farlam had addressed the families of the deceased, even though they were not in the room at the time, and sought to frame its work as 'part of the healing and restoration process'. Three hundred days later, he now made a brief speech thanking key figures: the municipalities that had hosted the Commission, the government officials and administrators who had enabled it to operate, the Commission's researchers and Evidence Leaders, 'the legal practitioners who represented the various parties', and the media who had covered its work.[21]

In the Commission's last moments, he concluded his list of thanks without mentioning the families of the deceased, their loved ones, or the promised process of healing.

These promises had long been forgotten.

'As I've said', Farlam concluded, heartily,

> I want to thank all the people that I've mentioned, and to say that it's ultimately been a much more harmonious Commission than I thought it would be in the beginning. I was very pleased to see the – issues I won't go into, but by and large the Commission has proceeded and all the people have taken part in a very harmonious way.

After the end of the hearings, it was time to write the Report. The last amendment to the Commission's Terms of Reference gave the Commissioners until the end of March 2015 to complete and deliver their report to the President. Once it was in the President's hands, he would decide whether and when to publish the Report.[22]

---

20 Zameka Nungu, Day 274 (13 August 2014), pp. 35,003–35,006.
21 Transcript of Day 300 of the Marikana Commission of Inquiry (14 November 2014), particularly pp. 39,715–39,717.
22 Proclamation 66 of 2014, 'Amendment to the Terms of Reference of the Commission of Inquiry into the Tragic Events at or near the area commonly known as the

After the end of the hearings, the families returned to their homes – some to the Eastern Cape, some to Lesotho and other places, and others to Marikana itself. Some women, like Zameka Nungu and Betty Gadlela, took up their jobs in Lonmin's offices. Others tried to resume their everyday lives, as best as they could, without the routines of the Commission – to return to making sure that their children were going to school, that their families were fed, that their families and their communities were still there, still mourning. These were not easy months. Many of the families were struggling with their finances, and were dependent on charitable support from Lonmin as well as on donations from public groups and organizations.[23] None of them spared much thought for the 'harmonious' note on which the Commission had chosen to end its hearings.

Instead, they waited – with little remaining hope – for the release of the Report.

The wait stretched out. There was no news at the end of March – no announcement that the Commission had submitted its report, as required, to the President, at the end of that month, or that he had received it. It seemed as though either the Commissioners had missed their deadline, or the President was choosing to withhold the Report. The lawyers for the families wrote to the President's office, asking for information on the status of the Report – but received no response.[24] Another month passed, and April ended without any further news. By now, the families, the arrested and injured miners, and their legal representatives were increasingly concerned.

And still, nothing. At the end of May, seven weeks after the Report was due to have been submitted, lawyers for the arrested and injured miners and for the families took further action. They wrote to the President, asking for the Report to be made public – and when these letters went unanswered, they went to court to demand its release.[25]

This case was heard at the beginning of June. However, in the course of the highly public litigation, the President's legal team and spokespeople committed to releasing the Report at the end of the month – voluntarily, without requiring the order of a court. The judge declined to grant the relief requested by the families and miners. The President would be permitted to release the Report on his

---

Marikana Mine, in Rustenberg, North West Province, South Africa', in *Government Gazette*, No. 38030 (26 September 2014).

23 For a summary of Lonmin's support to the families, see Exhibit XXXX – presentation of Lonmin support to the families.

24 The letters discussed are disclosed in the affidavits filed in the course of this litigation. They are available at http://seri-sa.org/index.php/advocacy/expanding-political-space/marikana (Acc. March 2021).

25 A copy is at: http://seri-sa.org/images/Correspondence_to_H.E_J_Zuma_26_May_2015.pdf (Acc. March 2021).

own schedule – and any complaints about it would only be considered in the wake of its official release.[26]

* * *

When the Report was finally released on 15 June 2015 – thirty-four months after the massacre – it was accompanied by a summary read out over the national radio by President Jacob Zuma.[27] Despite their doubts, the families listened to his broadcast, and hoped that the Report would identify the causes of their loved one's deaths, explain the circumstances that had led to them, and assign some responsibility. They hoped that the Commission had held the mining company and the state to account, and that it would require them to pay the families some kind of compensation.

Their hopes were dashed, again.

Where the families sought the certainty of knowing how their loved ones had died, the Report dealt unevenly and inconsistently with the deaths of the forty-four men killed during the strike and in the massacre. Instead of examining each individual's death, the Report dealt with the deaths in groups – those killed during the strike, and those killed at Scene One and Scene Two. It also dealt with the deaths differently.

When it summarized the events that led to the deaths of ten men during the strike, the Report avoided drawing any conclusions. Its statement on the death of Mr Sokanyile, during the clash between police and protestors on Monday 13 August was typical: after surveying the events of the clash, the Report then stated that 'there are three potential explanations as to who shot Mr Sokanyile. They are (a) he was shot by the group of Colonel Vermaak, (b) he was shot by the group of Constable Yende, and (c) he was shot by the group of Captain Thupe'. It concluded that, therefore: 'It is not possible for the Commission to decide on the evidence before it which explanation is correct. Consequently the question as to by whose group and in what circumstances Mr Sokanyile was shot must be referred for further investigation.'[28]

This statement left his family in no better place than they had been before: they already knew he had been shot by the police, but not how, why, or by whom. The

---

26 The judgment is: *Magidiwana and Another v President of the Republic of SA and Others* (40805/15) [2015] ZAGPPHC 637 (12 June 2015).

27 An archive of the livestream of President Zuma's statement can be found at www.sabcnews.com/sabcnews/president-zuma-releases-marikana-report (Acc. March 2021). The full report was formally published in the *Government Gazette* of 10 July 2015 (No. 38978). It can be accessed at www.justice.gov.za/comm-mrk/docs/20150710-gg38978_gen699_3_MarikanaReport.pdf (Acc. March 2021). In the following notes, I refer to paragraph numbers in the Report for specific claims/quotes.

28 Report, Chapter 8, Section B, para. 50.

Commission's recommendation only underlined its abject failure of imagination. Instead of exercising its powers to investigate the circumstances of Mr Sokanyile's death, it chose to rely on what it had been told by the police. Because the police had not given the Commission a full story, and the Commission had not demanded one, it could not explain Mr Sokanyile's death. This was an absurd conclusion.

This approach reached a climax in the Report's description of the deaths at Scene One and Scene Two. The section of the Report that describes the killings at Scene One opens with a list of the names of the men who died at this site. It then spends more than fifty pages summarizing the submissions on the events leading up to the shooting, and on the legal liability of the police officers. It accepted that: 'A number of the shooters may have exceeded the bounds of what can be regarded as reasonable self- or private defence' and that many of the bodies were marked by wounds in the chest and head. It then describes the deaths:

> When the shootings stopped at scene twelve bodies were lying on the ground near the kraal. Eleven grouped together in the middle of the kraal and the fenced road to Nkaneng ... The second group, described earlier as the 'kraal edge group', were piled up together near the entrance to the kraal.

The Report notes that some of this group were injured by shotgun pellets and – rather than detailing how each of these men were shot, where they were injured, and how they died – moves immediately into a discussion of the legality of using shotgun pellets in a crowd management situation. This scene is then left, the Report moves on, and these men remain 'piled up' as a mass of the dead.[29]

This need not have been the case. The causes of deaths of each the four men who were shot at the edges of Scene One – John Ledingoane, Babalo Mtshazi, Bongani Nqongophele, and Thembinkosi Gwelani – were individually specified in the Report. The Commission was able to state that 'Mr Nqongophele was killed by a single R5 bullet that ricocheted and hit him close to his right eye and injured his brain. He appears to have survived for at least an hour.'[30] The Commission was able to explain what had killed each of these men, and how they had died. At least their families could know how and where their own loved ones had left the world.

But the families of the other men killed here – the families of Michael Ngweyi, Patrick Akhona Jijase, Bonginkosi Yona, Andries Motlalepula Ntsenyeho, Mzukisi Sompeta, Jackson Lehupa, Mongezeleli Ntenetya, Mphangeli Tukuza, Thobisile Zibambele, Cebesile Yawa, Mgcineni Noki, and Khanare Monesa – would learn nothing from the Commission's Report about how their loved ones had

---

29 Report, Chapter 11. Sections A to D deal with the lead up to the shooting. Sections E to H cover the shooting and its aftermath. The comments on private defence are made at para. 39 of Section G of Chapter 11. The comments on the bodies and their wounds follows from para. 50 of this same section.

30 Report, Chapter 11, Section G – para. 51.

been killed. They would not learn who had been shot in the head by the police, or who had been injured and died because they were prevented from receiving the treatment that could have saved them. They would not learn anything that might help them explain their loved ones' deaths – not because the Commission did not have the information, but because it did not seem to understand that these details could possibly be important to the families.

A different set of problems bedevilled the Commission's attempt to deal with the deaths at deaths at Scene Two.[31] Here, the stories that the Report tells are confusing and hard to pin down. It summarizes the testimony of the police witnesses, then summarizes their admissions and contradictions under cross-examination. It presents the events of this part of the massacre from the police's view, repeating the police witnesses' claims to have been attacked by unidentified 'strikers' – and only then, after this, does it identify these faceless strikers as individual men – as Sitelega Gadlela (referred to in the description of his death as 'Mr Gadava') and Makhosandile Mkhonjwa, for example.[32] The descriptions of the ways in which these men died are provided, in the Report, only in the words of the men who killed them.

Still, the Report does also quote the conclusions of the independent forensic experts to describe the injuries that brought about the deaths of nine of the seventeen men killed at Scene Two. But not everyone was captured by this process. The deaths of Anele Mdizeni, Thabiso Thelejane, Nkosiyabo Xalabile were noted, but the causes of their deaths were not mentioned. The deaths of Telang Mohai, Motiso Sagalala, and Molefi Ntsoele – all of whom died from injuries caused by the shooting at Scene Two – were likewise noted, but their injuries were not described and the causes of their deaths were not specified. The police's story about Sagalala's death – that he had died in hospital, and not in police care – was simply accepted, unquestioned.[33] Only a later investigation would reveal the truth, and expose the Commission's shameful credulity.

Overall, the Report is inconsistent in how it engages with these deaths – so inconsistent, in fact, that it regularly mis-spells the names of the dead: Mosebetsane's name is spelled 'Mosepetsane' when his death is described, Ngxande is spelled 'Nxande' in the list of the dead, and Gadlela is – as mentioned above – spelled 'Gadava' when the time came to address his death. This casual sloppiness was not merely disrespectful – it was typical of the Report's approach, in which the details of the lives and deaths of the men who were killed at Marikana were largely disregarded in the interests of summarizing the police's testimonies.[34]

31 This is covered in Report, Chapter 12.
32 For comments on Mr Gadlela, see Chapter 12, Section A, paras 34 and 47.
33 The sole comment on Mr Sagalala is at the start of this chapter, in the introduction preceding Section A, where he is listed as 'died in hospital'.
34 These mis-spellings occur at multiple points. See the list of the names of the dead at the start of Chapter 12, in which Mr Ngxande's name is mis-spelled; Chapter 11,

The families had wanted the Commission to specify the causes and the manners of their loved one's deaths – to strip away the confusion and mystery that had plagued them for almost three years. At the end of the six hundred and forty-five pages of the Commission's Report, this task remained incomplete. Only a few of the families could say that the Commission had determined how their loved ones had died. The rest had to be satisfied with the Report's broad-brush approach to the deaths – describing and dismissing them all in summary form.

'It cannot be said'

The families had also wanted the Commission to identify the police officers and commanders who would bear responsibility for the deaths of their loved ones – to identify the officers had pulled the triggers that killed their family members, and the commanders who had ordered those triggers to be pulled. In this, too, the Commission's Report disappointed them.

The Commission found that it could not say which police officers fired which bullets which hit which strikers – and that since that exact chain could not be recreated, no individual officer could be held liable for any actual death. 'The evidence indicates', the Report reads,

> that R5 bullets tend to disintegrate when entering the body of a victim. This is what happened at Marikana. As a result it is not possible on the ballistic evidence to connect any member who shot at Marikana with any person who died ... it cannot be said that any shooter is guilty of murder because it cannot be shown which of the shooters actually killed anyone.

The most that could be considered, the Report concedes, is that those who fired their weapons while exceeding the grounds of justifiable self-defence might at most face convictions for 'attempted murder'.[35]

In its conclusion, the Commission found that most of the police officers at Scene One were probably acting in reasonable self-defence, as they believed themselves – however erroneously – to be under attack. A minority might not be covered by this justification, however. 'There are indications that some may have may

---

Section E, para. 7 (c), in which Mr Mosebetsane's name is mis-spelled, and Chapter 12, Section A, paras 24 and 37 in which Mr Gadlela's name is mis-spelled. Although there is no question that proofing and spelling errors will creep into any long document – and I have no doubt that there are indeed errors in this long book – the persistence of these errors through the multiple releases of the Report (first, after the President's announcement on 25 June 2015, and then in the *Government Gazette* of 19 July 2015) as well as their prevalence throughout the text speak of a carelessness with the identities of the dead, and a shameful disregard for those who have survived them.

35 See Chapter 11, Section G, para. 42, and Chapter 23, Section D – Recommendation regarding the shooters at Scene 1.

well have exceeded the bounds of self- or private defence, in which case there is at least a prima facie case that they are guilty of attempted murder'.[36] The Commission only concluded that this question should be subject to further investigation.

In regard to the deaths at Scene Two, the Commission's Report took an even more cautious approach. It listed the evidence that suggested that the miners had been killed intentionally, as well as the evidence that suggested that the site had been tampered with by the police after the shooting, but concluded that this was not sufficient on its own to ground any charge. 'These issues cannot be determined simply by plotting the position of the cartridge cases in relation to the bodies of the deceased and the positions of the injured persons and without full explanations from the shooters of their actions.' Although the Commission unquestionably had held the power to undertake such an exercise or to demand such explanations, it had not done so – and so, once again, the reluctance of the police witnesses to testify saved them. The question of liability for the deaths at Scene Two was thus also passed off – and yet another investigation recommended.[37]

As may be expected, the Commission was also unable – and, sometimes, unwilling – to determine whether or not any of the commanding officers had explicitly ordered their subordinates to open fire on the miners. In regard to Maj.-Gen. Mpembe's actions on Monday 13 August, it accepted his word that he had not ordered his officers to fire tear gas at the strikers – but in doing so, it did not offer any alternative explanation for the police's undisputed use of tear gas. It simply dismissed all testimony to the contrary, as well as any other possible evidence.[38] When the Commission considered the question of whether or not police officers at Scene One had been ordered to open fire, it decided that although there was evidence that at least some officers on the ground had given commands that could have been interpreted as orders to shoot, this 'does not, in the Commission's view, take the matter any further because it is clear on the evidence of Lieutenant Colonel Classen and Captains Loest and Thupe they they perceived the members to be under threat so they would on the probabilities have fired in any event'.[39] Or, in other words: it did not matter whether or not an order was given, because the police would have fired anyway.

Although the Commission did criticize senior members of the police for embarking upon the action without an appropriate plan, and for adopting a plan that was not consistent with the police's standing order or best practice guidelines, it did not find that any individual police officer or police commander could be linked to any individual death – and so it chose to do no more than to recommend yet further investigations.

---

36   Chapter 23, Section D, para. 5.
37   Chapter 12, Section J – Referral and Recommendations.
38   Chapter 8, Section B, para. 40–44.
39   See Chapter 11, Section G, para. 32.

* * *

In the last pages of its report, the Commission dealt with the suggestions made by its own Evidence Leaders, as well as by the legal teams of the families, the arrested and injured miners, and others, that the state be required to pay compensation for the deaths of all those killed by the police – and possibly even those killed by the miners in the course of the week-long strike.

The Commission raised several points in response to these suggestions. It mentioned that many of the dependents of the dead had already begun the process of instituting actions against the state and against Lonmin – and that 'for all the Commission knows, those person who were injured or suffered damages as a result of the actions of some of the strikers may also be contemplating instituting claims against Lonmin'. Although it did not explicitly say so, it seems clear that the Commissioners were concerned that any finding they made in the context of the Commission's investigations might have an unplanned effect on other, future claims.

And so they decided that – although 'it is clearly desirable that the legal issues raised by the events at Marikana should be resolved without further lengthy and expensive legal proceedings' – they could do nothing. 'The Commission is not satisfied that its terms of reference are wide enough to cover the question'.[40]

The Report would make no recommendations on compensation.

'Whatever is covered, God will reveal'

The Report ended with a chapter of 'concluding remarks' – more than half of which were concerned with criticizing the striking miners and their allies during and after the strike. It referred to a 'fear factor' that surrounded the Commission and that had prevented some witnesses from testifying. It did not specify any particular threats that these witnesses had faced – nor did it suggest that any attempts to mitigate them had been taken – but did suggest that fears of reprisal were 'understandable'.[41]

It also chose to add that

> this report would not be complete without a condemnation in the strongest possible terms of the violent manner in which the strike was sought to be enforced, and the brutality of the attacks upon those persons who suffered injuries and who died prior to 16 August 2012. Whilst the strikers aver that they first took up arms to protect themselves against the attack by NUM, a version which the Commission had found to be untrue, as set out above,

---

40 See Chapter 23 – Capita Selecta. Unlisted subsection titled 'Proposed recommendations with regard to Compensation'.
41 Chapter 27 – 'Concluding Remarks'. See in particular Section B – 'Violence on the part of the strikers'.

they have not placed any evidence before the Commission to explain why they found it necessary to resort to violence to achieve any of their aims.

It highlighted the 'gratuitous violence of the attacks' on the security guards, and suggested that the presence of weapons in the hands of the strikers 'must point to an intention on their part to use violence at every instance to promote their cause'. This meant that the strikers were at least 'partly responsible' for Lonmin's unwillingness to negotiate, and for increased 'police presence' at Marikana itself.

> Whilst there exist adequate mediation and negotiation channels to enable issues to be resolved in matters of protests, strikes and stand offs, it might be a salutary lesson, for the citizens of the country, to take away from Marikana, that the taking up of arms and the resorting to violence is neither constructive nor appropriate in protecting and enforcing one's rights.

The tone and substance of this final condemnation of the striking workers stands out because no such similar condemnation is given in this report to the actions of the police officers and commanders – actions that led to the death of thirty-seven men. Individual police officers are defended in the Report, their actions excused and justified, and their liability for their actions minimized. The violent actions of some striking workers are – by comparison – taken to stand for the actions of all those who participated in the strike, and all are thus condemned vehemently by association.

* * *

The families of the deceased were disappointed by the final Report. In their eyes, and in the eyes of those who supported them, it was a travesty. It avoided drawing conclusions – almost always because it had failed to exercise its powers to conduct effective investigations. It had chosen instead to relinquish responsibility to one or another different investigative body. It had ignored the stories told to it by the families of the dead, and treated their loved ones as interchangeable victims – victims whose names it could not even be bothered to spell correctly or consistently.

Their own stories had gone unheard, their own questions unanswered.

The clear implication of the final chapter of the Report – that the 'lesson' of Marikana was not that the police and the mine and the government should have been more concerned to protect the lives of both striking and non-striking workers but that workers exercising their rights should do so unarmed and in a supplicatory manner – was merely an insult added on to their ongoing injury.

In the face of three wasted years, and hundreds of wasted pages, the only comfort that the families of the deceased could take was in the knowledge that the Commission would not have the last word.[42] The stories of their loved ones' lives and deaths were known across the country. Their stories were told and retold by men and women working in Marikana, by men and women living in informal settlements, by the strangers who had watched documentaries and read books, who now knew the names of Mgcineni Noki, of Jackson Lehupa, of Thembelakhe Mati, and of all the others. Nothing in the Commission's Report could change that.

The families no longer had faith in the official processes of the Commission and the state, but they would not lose hope. As Zameka Nungu had said in her prayer months earlier, nothing – not the Commission, not the state, not Lonmin, not the police – can stand above the truth, or stand beyond the final judgment. 'One day God will respond ... Whatever is covered, God will reveal ... Even on that day, God was present. God is still there, let us not lose hope. Let us not lose hope.'

And so, let us not lose hope.

---

42 At present, most of the documents submitted in evidence, all of the transcripts, and all of the Heads of Argument – as well as a number of different miscellaneous documents – are archived on the South African Department of Justice's website: www.justice.gov.za/comm-mrk/index.html (Acc. March 2021) A back-up copy (hosted by SERI and the Wits History Workshop) of most of these files – including the documents submitted in evidence and the transcripts – can be found on: http://marikana-conference.com (Acc. March 2021).

Conclusion: The Work of Mourning

Mzukisi Sompeta was thirty-seven years old when he was killed by the police at Scene One of the massacre. He was survived by his parents, his siblings, their children, and his own daughter. The family had not told his mother, Nomawabo, about the strike, because they had been worried about her blood pressure. Then – out of the blue – visitors began to arrive at her home in Lusikisiki, and told her that her son had been killed. 'I was never sane after that', she said, 'I can't lie'.[1]

The next days were lost in the chaos of events. Mzukisi's younger brother travelled to Marikana to identify his body. People tried to talk to Nomawabo, but she could not follow what they were telling her. Her husband was deeply shaken. Nomawabo remembered that: 'He lamented that all his sons were dying, because prior to that one had been shot dead ... and then another one who was sick. Finally, there was this one, shot dead in Marikana. He couldn't bear it.'

On 22 October 2012, barely two months after Mzukisi's death, his father followed him. From the date of the massacre, he had been ill. 'By the time we got to the funeral he was shaking ... Yes, and then he died too'. Nomawabo was lost. She went to Marikana and to the initial sittings of the Commission, but found no comfort there. 'I was unable to handle it', she said. 'Oh, it was sad. I only went because they called for someone to go. As a result, when I came back I started limping ... This was caused by my heartache. I was in a lot of pain.' Her family intervened, and told her stop – 'because I would cry too much'. Her daughter began to go instead.

Meanwhile, years passed, and Nomawabo remained at home, aching in grief. 'It's bad', she said, at the end of 2015. 'It's really bad. You see, this leg, I have to hobble along because when this happened everything started to go haywire until I didn't know anymore. When mysterious things happen to you, when your husband dies, and your son dies ... You just don't know what to do.'

* * *

For the families, the work of mourning took place both in private and in public.

In private, Nomawabo Sompeta and the others in her position grieved for the loss of their loved ones – whether these loved ones had been their sons, their husbands, their brothers, or their fathers. They grieved in their own personal

---

1 Interview with Nomawabo Sompeta, Lusikisiki, 2 December 2015.

ways: alone, silent, weeping, enduring. In private, they were able to remember and mourn.

In public, though, the families had to put themselves and their grief on display. They had to attend the funerals of their loved ones. Many of them had to wear mourning for a year, and to seclude themselves from parts of the world. They participated in cleansing ceremonies in Marikana and at home. They raised tombstones to mark the graves of their loved ones. They sat in the halls of the Farlam Commission, their faces sombre, sometimes angry. They attended commemorations in Marikana and Rustenberg, where they sat on stages beside union leaders and politicians. They were filmed for documentaries. They spoke to journalists and even academics.

In the years after the massacre, the private and the public grief of these families were intertwined with their material circumstances. It was not enough that they had to live with their grief, and not enough that this grief was put on display. The world is too hard. Nomawabo Sompeta lost both her son and her husband, and with them her family's only steady income. She had to rely on her pension, on the piecemeal wages her other children could scrape together, on the charity of strangers, and even handouts from the mining company. Out of this, she had to hold her household together, cover the costs of two funerals and two periods of mourning, and make sure that her fatherless granddaughter was able to attend school.

A similar story could be told for each of the families. In Ntabankulu. Florence Mati mourned her husband – and struggled to raise and support their six children, the youngest of whom was barely eight when his father was killed. She had to keep him school, and help his oldest siblings set out on their lives. She had to live with her husband's mother and sister, his cousins, nieces and nephews – all of whom had depended on the regular income that his job had provided.[2] In Lusikisiki, Lunga Jokanisi mourned the death of his son, and found himself – now in retirement – having to return to work to support his children and grandchildren.[3]

For two and a half years the families had linked their private and public mourning to the proceedings of the Farlam Commission of Inquiry. They had lived in a state of suspension – grieving privately, mourning publicly, and waiting for their ongoing struggles to cease, for the weight of their burdens to be lifted from their shoulders, or at least lightened. But the eventual release of the Farlam Commission's Report on 25 June 2015 did nothing to lighten these burdens, or to make the work of mourning their dead – whether in private or in public – any easier.

The Report did not tell each and every one of the families' how their loved ones had died, or why. It did not settle public debates about the nature of the strike, or the responsibility of the police for the deaths on 16 August 2012. It did not provide any compensation to the families for the loss of material support, or for the trauma of their loved ones' deaths. It did not hold anyone to account. It

---

2   Interview with Florence Mati, KuNdile, 4 December 2015.
3   Interview with Lunga Jokanisi, Lusikisiki, 3 December 2015.

left many of the families in the same position as they had been at the start of the Commission – uncertain, uncompensated, and frustrated by the impossibility of seeing justice.

At the end of 2015, three years after the massacre, months after the release of the Report, with their expectations of the Commission frustrated and their hopes for a secure future foundering, the families had to find new ways to continue on through the days – to continue the work of mourning, of remembering, and of living.

New legal challenges

They did not have to do so alone.

In the weeks after the Commission's Report was released, the families' lawyers instituted a series of damages claims against the Minister of Police.[4] They sought to claim compensation for the loss of material 'support' suffered by the families on the deaths of their principal breadwinners, and they sought also to claim compensation for 'grief and suffering' caused to the families by the state's complicity in the killing of their loved ones. The claims relied upon the recognition that the police actions at Marikana were unlawful – that the actions of the commanders and their subordinates had been unreasonable, disproportionate, and not authorized by any proper legal authority. In this context, it was a widely accepted principle that the organ of state responsible for the unlawful killings could be required to pay damages for loss of 'support' incurred because of these deaths.

The second part of the claim – for compensation for damages caused by 'grief and emotional suffering' – was novel. South African law does not readily recognize claims for intangible losses, and the idea that families could demand some form of material compensation for the emotional and mental pain, grief, and suffering that they had undergone was one that went beyond the ordinary terms of the law.[5] Nonetheless, it was important to include it – even if only to force the government and the public to recognize that this immaterial suffering was central to the experiences of the families in the wake of the massacre. If the government chose to hide behind the technicalities of the law, it would have to choose to reject these claims. It would have to state explicitly that it was only the loss of material support – of money, of a wage – that really mattered.

4   The Particulars of Claim were launched on 10 August 2015. The document is online at: http://seri-sa.org/images/MARIKANA_-_PARTICULARS_OF_CLAIM_-10_August_2015_FINAL_FOR_FILING.pdf. The many annexures – listing the economic and personal details of the claimants – are not accessible. A press release summarizes the claim: http://seri-sa.org/images/Marikana_PressStatement.pdf (Acc. March 2021).

5   A. Mukheibir and G. Michell, 'The Price of Sadness: Comparison between the Netherlands and South Africa', *PER: Potchefstroomse Elektroniese Regsblad*, 22.1 (2019), pp. 1–36.

In addition to the claims for payment of damages, the families also asked – in the neutral language of the law – for 'an apology from the defendant to the plaintiffs'.

This last claim was of central importance to the families. They needed material and financial support to make their way through the world. But they also needed the police, and the government, and general public to recognize and acknowledge what had happened. For this to happen, they needed the police to apologize, because an apology would make it clear to everyone that their loved ones had been killed without reason and without cause. It would make it clear that the lies and allegations peddled by the police at the Farlam Commission and in the press – that the miners were in the process of attacking, and that the police acted in self-defence; that there was a conspiracy to murder the police; that the miners were real threats to the country's order – were false, and that the police had accepted responsibility for their actions during the massacre.

These were very complex legal documents. These demands were made in the names of more than three hundred people, each of whom had to provide detailed information about the losses they had suffered as a result of the deaths at Marikana. The deadline for filing the initial particulars of claim came before the Commission's Report was released. After months of careful planning, spent gathering the personal circumstances of several hundred family members, the lawyers found themselves forced to guess at what the Commission's findings would be – and then later, after the Report was released, consider again how to reconcile its findings with the factual and legal claims that they had advanced. This meant that the process of drawing up the documents had begun during 2013 and 2014; that they were filed with the court early in 2015; and that – after the release of the Report in June that year – the circumstances of the litigation were still developing as the third anniversary of the massacre came and went.[6] The complexity of the case, and the resistance of the Ministry of Police, meant that it would take years for it to be decided.

* * *

And so, at the end of 2015, a group of lawyers and researchers from the Socio-Economic Rights Institute (SERI) – the legal representatives of the families and AMCU at the Commission, and now the team pushing the damages claims – came to consult with the families in their home communities across the country.[7] They brought with them an entourage of volunteers, activists, and

---

6   This information comes from discussions with the lawyers for the families of the deceased.

7   I participated in this outreach programme. The descriptions of the events, as given below, come from my own research notes and observations. During these events, I conducted formal interviews with several members of the families of the deceased – as noted in the references throughout – as well as taking part in more informal conversations with them, their families, and their neighbours.

documentary film makers. There was another aim to these visits, beyond simply consulting with the families – the intention was both to hold both a series of private consultations with the families, and to hold series of public events that would help inform their communities about the events of the massacre, the processes of the Commission, and the current situation of the families.

The public side of these events was at least as important as the private meetings. It seemed as though everyone had an opinion on what had happened at Marikana – who was at fault, how the miners should have acted, how the police could have acted, how the families should have responded. These opinions were based on rumours, half-truths, and lies. But even so, they were an unending drain on the energies of the families. As Zameka Nungu put it, she had to keep on challenging 'the people who were not there', the people who relied on 'hearsay', the 'naysayers' – all of whom felt able to comment on her husband's life and death.[8]

Zameka, as well as the members of the other families, hoped that the public part of these events would help them to speak to their neighbours about the massacre. They hoped that their lawyers would be able to dispel the worst of the rumours, and help establish a shared understanding of what had happened in the strike and the massacre. If this succeeded, then – while they waited for compensation, and for justice – at least they would not be so alone in their home communities.

One day in Ntabankulu

At the start of November, SERI visited families in Lesotho, in the Free State, and in the area around Marikana. At the end of the month, they began a two-week-long trip through the Eastern Cape. They visited Dutywa, where the Ntenetya and Mabiya families lived, before moving on to Xorha, where they met with the Nqongophele, Xabalile, and Mdizeni families. In Mqanduli, they were hosted by the Noki and Saphendu families, and in Lusikisiki, by the Sompeta, Jokanisi, Zimbambele, and Gwelani families. In the first week of December, they would go to Matatiele, and Sterkspruit to meet the Mdze, Lehupa, Thelejane, Mosebetsane, Mpumza, and Mangoctywa families. At the mid-point of this trip, they stopped at Ntabankulu to meet the Matis and Jijases.

This mid-point visit took place on 3 December 2015. Anyone watching would have seen a convoy of rented cars drove down the roads that wound along valleys and up hills to the Mati family homestead in Ntabankulu. The cars inched up the slope. Their drivers were clearly uncomfortable with the sheer drops alongside the roads, and unfamiliar with the steep gradient of the hillsides. They drove cautiously, taking corners slowly and keeping a steady distance from each other.[9]

---

8   Interview with Zameka Nungu, Matatiele, 4 December 2015.
9   The notes on the conversations held between the families and their representatives come from my notes on these meetings. I am grateful to the participants for permitting me to listen in to their conversations, and to use some of these comments in

The cars arrived at the homestead at about 08:00. The visitors immediately set to work, alongside local assistants. A marquee was unfurled on the school's field: a metal frame was stretched into place, thick ropes were wrapped around spikes hammered into the earth. A portable generator was placed outside the marquee, and trestle tables were set up inside. The caterers were scheduled to arrive later, with large tubs of food. A small group of film makers would help the volunteers set up a portable projector and screen, speakers and microphones. The programme was scheduled to being at 09:00 – but with all this work, and with the time that it would take people to walk to the school, no one was hurrying to meet the time.

The Mati family gathered in a large single-roomed building. The walls were whitewashed, and the floor polished smooth. Chairs, couches, cushions, and boxes were spread through the space. The whole family – old men and women, children and infants alike – found their places. The lawyers and researchers filed in, and sat in the empty spaces between the family members. After a series of greetings, everyone settled down to the work that had brought them together: discussing the progress of the damages claims, and working out together how best to proceed in the future.

They spoke for an hour. Nomzamo Zondo, SERI's Director of Litigation, explained the steps that had been taken to date, and where the case currently stood in the courts. She asked for the family's opinions on what should be done next: should they permit the government's lawyers to continue to take their time, and hope to be able to pressure them into entering into an agreement, or should they take a more aggressive approach and try to force them into court?

The Matis deliberated. 'We do want compensation', one family member said, 'because this is a member of our family. He had a very big role to play. No amount of money will ever amount to that. Do you understand what I'm saying? No amount of money can be worth more than a person's life, but it will make a difference.' But it was important to trust in the processes. 'I don't think that anybody is above the law. We will wait until then.' Others agreed, although cautiously:

> We see how things are going. We are paying attention. The lack of clarity is designed to put us off track, but our lawyers are on the right side of the law … In our hearts we were starting to believe that our lawyers were losing. Too many years have gone by. On the other hand, we do understand that the legal process is quite a lengthy process. It has many ins and outs. So I

---

this narrative. I have removed all financial and personal details, and not named any individual family members in this context. Likewise, I have only named those who chose to speak on their own behalf as part of the formal events in my descriptions of the speeches at the outreach. I have chosen to allow the men and women who asked public questions to remain anonymous in the context of this narrative.

am standing up to say I know how hard you fight. Carry on. You will work with us right up to the end. That is my hope. We have not been ousted because the commission of inquiry is done.[10]

* * *

At the end of the hour, the family filed out of the room and made their way across the yard to the white marquee set up outside the school. While the family had been talking, the volunteers had unstacked the plastic chairs and set them up in rows; a projection screen had been unfurled at one end of the space; speakers had been mounted on three-legged stands; and the microphones had been connected. The neighbouring community had arrived and had found seats. Older women sat at the front, their grandchildren sprawled at their feet, slipping in and out, playing.

It took a while for the crowd to settle down. The Matis took their seats in the front row. Eventually, the programme began – with introductions, a shared prayer, and some words from the school's headmaster. After this, Mzoxolo Magidiwana was supposed to speak about his experiences during the strike and the massacre – but he had been called away to an urgent court hearing that day, and could not give his presentation. Instead, the programme moved forward to a screening of *Miners Shot Down* – a documentary built from news footage of the strike and the massacre.

It is a hard film to watch. The miners can be seen alive at its start, and can be recognized. They are seen dead at the end – and no matter how carefully the film makers worked to obscure the faces of the dead there can be no doubt, when watching, that these are the corpses of men who were once friends, neighbours, and family. At every screening, the audience would respond to the scenes – sometimes in anger, sometimes in shock, but always with overwhelming sadness.

After the screening, Yolokazi Mati, Tembelahke's daughter, came forward to speak on behalf of the family. The crowd quietened down, and listened. 'Greetings to everyone', she said. 'I am Thembelakhe's child. He died fighting for money in Marikana. He was very much loved by us. We adored him … We are who we were because of him.' She spoke about his death at the hands of the police, and the lingering effects of that knowledge on her life.

> We are very disgusted by the police. It does not matter that some of them had nothing to do with it. As long as it's a policeman, I am disgusted by him because the reason my father is lying where he is, is because of them … Our father put us through school. Our home depended on him for everything. As it is now, we have nothing to eat because of the police.

She spoke quietly, but her voice remained firm.[11]

---

10 Notes on Mati family discussion, KuNdile, 3 December 2015.
11 Notes on Public Discussion, KuNdile, 3 December 2015.

An elder member of the family then stood up to speak. He addressed the political context of the meeting, condemning the state and – especially – the National Commissioner of the Police for their callousness:

> A poor Black person in this world is nothing but a dog, and it's clear that he will continue to be treated like a dog. Today we are being killed by the ANC. In 1960 … the Prime Minister … spoke exactly like Phiyega after the Sharpeville massacre. When he addressed the police force he commended them on a job well done. He said, it's clear that you know your work. Even as Phiyega speaks, history is written down.

His history was incorrect – there is no evidence that the Apartheid state's President made such a statement in 1960 – but his fury was evident, and justified. The audience listened with respect, but – with some few exceptions – they did not join in his anger.

Instead, they continued to listen as the lawyers and researchers explained the Commission's findings and recommendations. They heard about the Commission's recommendations for further investigations – and that some of these investigations should be conducted by the National Prosecuting Authority with the aim of determining who should be charged with criminal offences arising out of the conduct of both the police and the miners at Marikana. They heard about the absence of any actual prosecutions at the time, and the continuing careers of the political figures most closely associated with the events at Marikana. And they heard more about the ongoing struggles of the miners – of the continuing struggle of miners to organize and insist on increases.

Then, it was time for the audience to speak. The first person to stand up and reach for the microphone was a local man, a worker in Marikana, who had been in the town – but not, it seems, on the koppie or in the crowd – at the time of the strike. 'I have a question that I want to pose', he said. 'Why has Riah Phiyega not been fired and jailed for the death of the miners in Marikana? I want her to be imprisoned like any other murderer.' The second person to speak was a stranger, a visitor from Kokstad who was in the area working with the school. 'As a citizen of South Africa', she said,

> I was touched when I saw the DVD … No one in my family was implicated there, but because of the blood we share as a Black nation and as God's people, I am deeply affected … I had questions that have nagged me for a very long time, and today I got the answer.

She explained what she meant by this: 'I see what went down. I was under the impression that our brothers were under a spell. That was my belief. But today my eyes have been opened.'

Over the next hour, several more people spoke. They asked questions about responsibility, accountability, and punishment: would the police officers who fired on the workers be identified? Would their commanding officers be held responsible for ordering them to fire – or, at least, for failing to exercise proper control over these officers? Who bore the greater responsibility – the officers who fired the weapons, or the commanders who encouraged or allowed them to do so? And, of course, what would be the right punishment for those responsible for the massacre?

They asked questions about compensation, and survival: what would happen to the families of those who were killed? What would happen to those who were injured by the police, arrested and charged with the murder of their fellows, and only belatedly exonerated? Would they be able to return to work, or would they be compensated in another way? Would anyone consider the effect on the miners' broader communities – which had depended on them in many ways, some material and others not? Would there be any attempt to use this opportunity to consider how the migrant labour system was still tearing the fabric of their communities apart, or would there be any attempt to compensate them for these injustices?

In addition to these questions, they also expressed their anger and disappointment at the country's political elite. 'It's clear that justice is a scarce commodity', one said. 'I had invited the local councillor, but he didn't show up. That can only mean that there's a sector of people who believe that they are doing the right thing and yet, are still doing the wrong thing. Misleading the people is not right.'

Others spoke about the failure of government officials to listen to the complaints of the miners – both during the strike, and in the present moment. The invulnerability of the political leaders associated with the massacre – Cyril Ramaphosa, in his capacity as the messenger between Lonmin and the government, Nathi Mthethwa as the Minister of Police, and Susan Shabangu as the Minister of Mineral Affairs – was also raised, as the audience asked if they would face any consequences for their actions.

And, finally, they offered their condolences to the families of the dead. They, too, mourned the men killed at Marikana – they mourned for the lives lost, for the potential wasted, and for the country. They shared in the families' grief, and asked them – what should happen now?

Some answers

Only some of these questions could be answered on that day in Ntabankulu. At the end of 2015, none of the Commission's recommendations had been meaningfully implemented. It was impossible to know whether or not anyone would be recommended for prosecution, or if these prosecutions would eventually succeed. The families' damages claims were still open – and the government's response still uncertain. No one could yet say whether they would ever be compensated. And the political situation was still largely unchanged – the same high officials occupied the same positions; the same bureaucrats were still in place; the government continued.

Another five years have now passed, and some of these questions can be answered.

Has anyone been held responsible for the deaths at Marikana?

In the years since 2015, both the Independent Police Investigative Directorate (IPID) and the National Prosecuting Authority (NPA) have held investigations and made initial recommendations. However, this has been a complicated process. In April 2017, IPID completed its round of investigations and identified over seventy police officers and commanders who – it said – bore responsibility for the deaths caused by the police at Marikana. It handed this list of names over to the NPA, with the expectation that this would trigger the NPA's authority to institute prosecutions. This did not happen. Instead, four months passed without action. In August 2017, the media reported that the NPA had received this list, but had taken no action. In response, the NPA issued a rapid series of contradictory statements. It suggested, first, that it had not received the list from IPID; then, that the list was missing information; and then, finally, that the list was still being examined by the relevant prosecutors – in whose power the final action would lie.[12]

Six months later, in March 2018, nine senior police commanders were finally arrested and charged by the NPA with a series of crimes arising out of their actions during the strike at Marikana.[13] The most senior figure was Maj.-Gen. Mpembe, the operational commander on the ground at Marikana during the strike and on the day of the massacre. Mpembe was charged with murder in relation to five of the deaths that took place on Monday 13 August 2012 – that is, the deaths of three miners, Semi Jokanisi, Thembelakhe Mati, and Phumzile Sokhanuile, as well as the deaths of two police officers, Hendrik Tsietsi Monene and Sello Ronnie Lepaaku. In addition, the death of Motiso Otsile van Wyk Sagalala in police custody on 16 August 2012 was laid at the feet of Mpembe, and three other police officers. These men were charged not with his murder, but with attempting to conceal the fact of

---

12 See media reports: 'No Police Officer Prosecuted Yet for Involvement in Marikana', *Power 987*, 17 August 2017, www.power987.co.za/featured/no-police-officer-prosecuted-yet-for-involvement-in-marikana (Acc. March 2021); 'Ipid Submits Last Docket in Marikana Probe', eNCA, 23 August 2017, www.enca.com/south-africa/ipid-submits-last-docket-in-marikana-probe (Acc. March 2021); Sifiso Jimta, 'Marikana Cops to Face the Law!' *Daily Sun*, 23 August 2017, www.dailysun.co.za/News/National/marikana-cops-to-face-the-law-20170823 (Acc. March 2021).

13 Jeanette Chabalala, 'Officers in Court for Marikana Tragedy', *News24*, 15 March 2018, www.news24.com/news24/southafrica/news/officers-in-court-for-marikana-tragedy-20180315 (Acc. March 2021); Molaole Montsho, 'Former North West Top Cop to Appear in Court Over Marikana Shooting', *IOL*, 17 December 2018, www.iol.co.za/news/south-africa/north-west/former-north-west-top-cop-to-appear-in-court-over-marikana-shooting-18625904 (Acc. March 2021).

his death in police custody – which is a separate offence. On top of this, Mpembe was also charged with lying under oath at the Commission.

Their first court hearing took place in the North West High Court over a year later, in June 2019.[14] After a few days, it was postponed and next heard in October 2020.[15]

On 29 March 2021, after further delays and hearings, the North West High Court acquitted those accused of the charges related to the death of Motiso Otsile van Wyk Sagalala. The Court held that the NPA had not succeeded in making out its case that Mpembe and the other accused had intentionally concealed the facts around Mr Sagalala's death in police custody. Nor had the NPA succeeded in making out a case that Mpembe had intentionally lied about the circumstances of Mr Sagalala's death in his later testimony under oath at the Commission of Inquiry. The Court therefore found that Mpembe and his co-accused were not guilty of concealing Mr Sagalala's death, and acquitted them on all the related charges.[16]

This judgment, however, did not deal with the charges linked to the deaths of the five men who were killed on Monday 13 August 2012. The trial of Mpembe, and other officers, is still to continue – and it is, at the time of writing, uncertain when the North West High Court will come to a conclusion about these serious charges.

In the meantime, however, it is important to note that this trial is only concerned with the events of the first significant clash between the striking miners and the police. As I write, no one has yet been identified, arrested, or charged for their roles in the massacre itself. It is possible that many of the officers and commanders on the list of seventy-two names sent by IPID to the NPA may have acted to cause the deaths on 16 August 2012. But as of 2021, the NPA has not recommended that anyone be prosecuted for their roles in the deaths of thirty-four men at Scene One and at Scene Two. Not one commander. Not one officer. The deaths still cry out.

---

14   ANA Reporter, 'Police Accountability Demanded for Marikana Massacre', *IOL*, 10 June 2019, www.iol.co.za/news/south-africa/police-accountability-demanded-for-marikana-massacre-25836517 (Acc. March 2021); ANA Reporter, 'Court Hears Cops Were in the Same Building When Marikana Miner Was Declared Dead', *IOL*, 15 August 2019, www.iol.co.za/news/south-africa/north-west/court-hears-cops-were-in-the-same-building-when-marikana-miner-was-declared-dead-30835782 (Acc. March 2021).

15   Sarah Smit, 'Marikana Murder Trial Resumes', *Mail and Guardian*, 16 October 2020, https://mg.co.za/news/2020-10-16-marikana-murder-trial-resumes (Acc. March 2021).

16   *SABC News*, 'Mpembe, Three Others Acquitted of 2012 Marikana Unrest Charges', 29 March 2021, www.sabcnews.com/sabcnews/mpembe-three-others-acquitted-of-2012-marikana-unrest-charges (Acc. March 2021).

In a brief comment given in October 2020, the NPA's North West spokesperson said:

> Look, it has been a long process. It has been a long process. But at the end of the day investigations have to be thorough ... We were not going to come to court without things being thoroughly checked ... To put a tight case forward to ensure prosecution, it takes time. It takes time.[17]

At this moment, that time is almost ten years.

And – in the light of the comments made by the North West High Court about the quality of the case brought by the NPA against Mpembe and others for their alleged failure to report the circumstances of Mr Sagalala's death – it seems sadly unlikely that any of the promised prosecutions will proceed in the near future.

And so: has anyone been held responsible for the deaths?

The answer is still: 'No'. No one has been held responsible for the vast majority of the deaths that occurred in Marikana in 2012 – and it is possible that no one will be.

Have the families been compensated for their losses?

The mining company, Lonmin, has made some efforts to provide support to the families of the deceased. The day after the massacre, before the Commission was even being contemplated, Lonmin announced that it would pay for the children of the dead miners to attend school. In its statement of 17 August 2012, Lonmin stated that it would 'provide funding for the education of all the children of employees who lost their lives. This funding will cover education costs from primary school to university'.[18] It provided no explanation of how it would identify the recipients of its charity, nor how it would manage these costs – whether it would pay the costs of the children's existing education, or whether it would control the place and nature of their future schooling.

It took some time for these questions to be resolved, but by the time the Commission ended most of the children of the miners killed at Marikana were being educated at the expense of the mining company.[19] By late 2015, Nomawabo Sompeta's granddaughter, fifteen years old at the time, was attending a boarding school in Port Edward, about two and a half hours' drive away from her family's home. Several others were making their way through school, on Lonmin's charity.[20]

This was important to the families, but it was not enough to compensate them for their losses. The education of their children might help them in the

---

17 Smit, 'Marikana murder trial resumes'.
18 This promise was made in the statement issued by Lonmin in the immediate wake of the massacre: 'Lonmin Statement on Marikana Situation'.
19 See Exhibit XXXX – Lonmin Support to the Families' presentation.
20 Interview with Nomawabo Sompeta, Lusikisiki, 2 December 2015.

future – but in the present moment, the families still needed to eat, to keep their roofs over their heads, and to support themselves. And so, while they therefore accepted Lonmin's support for their children's education, they did not regard it as sufficient restitution for their losses. They continued to argue that both the company and the state should compensate them, and ensure that they could survive the coming years.

The damages claims filed against the police services were key to their efforts. The government and its legal advisors strongly resisted the arguments of the claim filed by the families and their lawyers, and for several years alternated between obstructive litigation and ambiguous negotiations. By the end of 2018, however – and after the application of a great deal of public pressure by the Marikana Support Campaign, and other civil society actors – the government agreed to a partial settlement. It accepted liability for the loss of income incurred by the families as a result of the deaths of their loved ones, and agreed to pay out a large sum, divided among the families, and calculated according to the nominal earning potential of each of the deceased. In the first half of 2019, these sums were finally paid out.[21]

However, this did not bring the claim to an end. The second part was still unresolved – and the government continues to dispute that it was liable for the emotional and intangible damages caused by the deaths in Marikana. At present, there remains no agreement on this point.

In the meantime, the communities within which the families live continue to struggle for recognition. Although the mining company and the government could accept – under certain, often limited, circumstances – that they might owe some compensation to the immediate families of the men killed in the massacre, the broader argument made by members of these communities at the public meetings in 2015 went beyond this. These men and women argued that the damage to their communities went beyond the personal grieving of the families, and that the deaths of the miners at Marikana had robbed all of their friends, their neighbours, and their extended networks. Neither the company nor the government has engaged with their arguments, and neither accepts any responsibility for the frayed social fabric caused both by slow strains of the migrant labour system and by the horrific shock of the massacre. For these communities – unlike those of the families who live with them – there is little chance that their claims will ever be recognized as being real.

Almost ten years after the massacre, it is still only possible to give a partial answer to the question posed in 2015. The families have been given some compensation for their losses in the massacre. But their claims are not yet fully resolved, and there remain many issues outstanding – not the least of which is the demand, in the families' claims, for a formal apology from the government.

21 The details come from a discussion with the legal team at SERI, representing the families of the majority of the miners in this compensation claim.

Have there been any political consequences?

The most prominent political figures associated with the massacre remain in positions of authority and power. Only a few have suffered public consequences.

Cyril Ramaphosa was a director of Lonmin at the time of the massacre – and formally outside of politics. In the years since, however, he has returned to the political arena. In December 2012 – just four months after the massacre – he was elected Deputy President of the African National Congress. In 2014, he was appointed Deputy President of the country. He held this office at the time of the Commission's Report – which found that he bore no special responsibility for the deaths at Marikana. This was not widely accepted, as activists argued that there was a significant difference between the legalistic definition of responsibility used by the Commission and the moral definition that should ground questions of political responsibility.[22] Nonetheless, the Commission's finding helped insulate Ramaphosa from the political consequences of his involvement in mediating between Lonmin and the government. Two years later, he was narrowly elected the leader of his political party and – early in 2018 – rose to become President of South Africa. At the time of writing, he continues to occupy the highest political office in the country.

Nathi Mthethwa was the Minister of Police at the time of the massacre. He held this office until May 2014, when he was moved to become Minister of Arts and Culture. He was in this position when the Commission's Report was released. In its report, the Commission declined to make any concrete findings for or against Mthethwa – arguing that the absence of direct evidence of the substance of his conversations with the National Commissioner of Police meant that it could not make any positive findings of any sort. Mthethwa remained in the cabinet after the release of the Commission's Report – even though he was not cleared of direct involvement in the chain of events that led to the police's actions. After the most recent elections, he remains in cabinet as the Minister for Sports, Arts and Culture. At no moment since the massacre has he been out of the national cabinet – and he remains one of the most powerful political figures in the country.

Susan Shabangu was Minister of Mineral Resources at the time of the massacre. She held this office until May 2014, when – like Nathi Mthethwa – she was moved to a different ministry, becoming Minister of Women in the Presidency. The Commission's Report – released a year later – found that she bore no particular responsibility for the events of the massacre. It also found that she had not perjured herself on the stand – as the representatives of the Injured and

---

22   Peter Alexander, 'Cyril Ramaphosa's Marikana Massacre "Apology" is Disingenuous and Dishonest', *The Conversation*, 11 May 2017, https://theconversation.com/cyril-ramaphosas-marikana-massacre-apology-is-disingenuous-and-dishonest-77485 (Acc. March 2021).

Arrested miners had suggested. She had not lied, the Commission found. Any discrepancies in her statements were merely due to 'faulty recollection'. After the Report's release, she remained in her position until February 2018, when she was moved again, becoming Minister of Social Development. She held this position until May 2019, when – after not being reappointed the cabinet for the first time since 1996 – she resigned as a Member of Parliament, and left politics.

These three figures were the most prominent politicians involved in the events that lead to the massacre. None of them have suffered any political or public consequences for their involvement. They were largely – if not entirely – absolved of responsibility by the Commission. Their careers have not merely survived the scandal – they have flourished in the years since the massacre.

There is one further political figure to consider: Riah Phiyega, the National Commissioner of the Police. Phiyega was appointed to her position by the country's president in 2012. Despite attracting a great deal of criticism from civil society, the media, and the Commission itself Phiyega held her office throughout the three years of the Inquiry, and until the release of its final Report. That Report found that she had been improperly influenced by political considerations in her response to the strike, and that she had failed to act as impartially and as neutrally as she should have. It also criticized her demeanour under examination, and cast doubts on the truthfulness of her submissions to the Commission. Three months after the release of the Report – which should have been damning – then-President Zuma finally suspended Phiyega, pending the conclusion of a further investigation into her conduct as National Commissioner. This investigation would find her unfit to hold office. But this did not lead to any action. Instead of being fired, Phiyega remained on suspension for twenty months – almost two years – during which she was always paid her full salary. Her five-year term as National Commissioner ended when her contract ran out.

And so even Phiyega was able to survive the public recognition of her unfitness for office and complicity in the events that lead to the massacre. She was not fired when she left the office of the National Commissioner in June 2017. In November of that same year, she was appointed as the Chief Executive Officer of the Safer South Africa Foundation – a charitable foundation established by the country's leading police union, POPCRU. The foundation's purpose is 'to mobilise under-resourced communities to build awareness and ability to work together in crime prevention.'[23] Phiyega's qualifications to lead community-policing outreach programmes must be in some doubt, after the massacre and the recommendations of the investigations into her own behaviour, but the Chairperson of the Foundation's board did not seem to have any difficulties with this. He told the media, on her appointment, that: 'We are aware of the challenges, but when we scrutinized them, we found nothing that would prevent her from

---

23 www.safersouthafrica.org/about (Acc. March 2021).

contributing to Safer South Africa'. He added, going further: 'I love Riah Phiyega. She is a good woman. I think she will do a great job.'[24]

No charges have been laid against Phiyega for her role in the massacre at Marikana.

A community of memory

Zameka Nungu wanted her husband, Jackson Lehupa, to be remembered as she remembered him: 'My husband was not a violent person; he was a good person. He could never pick a fight with anyone.'[25] Florence Mati wanted Thembelakhe to be remembered for his humour, and his honour: 'He was a jolly person. Locally, he was cherished. He always had good advice, and the community will remember him as an advisor. He was a stand-up guy, both in the community and at home. He had a strong backbone, he never faltered.'[26] Nomawabo Sompeta wanted her son, Mzukisi, to be remembered as a generous boy:

> Every time he arrived, he would give me about R1000 and say, Mama go and offer it to the church … He was a funny guy, a storyteller, and he was generous to me. If anything had to be done around the house, he would ask me, Mama, what would you like?[27]

For Xolelwa Mpumza, her brother would always be a child in her memory: 'a good child, he was quiet and didn't talk much. He never got into fights… He loved people.'[28]

These women – and all the widows, parents, children and surviving family members – strove to remember their loved ones as they had been when they were alive. They told and retold the same stories, fixing them in their memories. They passed these stories on to young children, to neighbours, to strangers – all in the hope that they could keep some part of their loved ones alive.

This is a key part of the work of mourning – the work of grieving, and of remembering. The dead cannot be forgotten, cannot be allowed to fall back into the abyss of impersonal anonymity. Ordinarily, the families of the dead would work to keep their memories fresh. Sometimes, in a close community, their neighbours, their friends, and their daily acquaintances would share in this work by telling stories of their encounters with the dead, sharing their own memories, and reminding each other of their losses. In some communities, churches and other religious bodies – with funeral masses, memorials, and gravesites – help to support this draining work.

24 The quotes on Riah Phiyega's appointment come from Loyiso Sidimba, 'Phiyega Bounces Back', *IOL*, 9 November 2017, www.iol.co.za/news/south-africa/gauteng/phiyega-bounces-back-11926676 (Acc. March 2021).
25 Interview with Zameka Nungu, Matatiele, 4 December 2015.
26 Interview with Florence Mati, KuNdile, 3 December 2015.
27 Interview with Nomawabo Sompeta, Lusiksiki, 2 December 2015.
28 Interview with Xolelwa and Phumzile Mpumza, Matatiele, 4 December 2015.

Conclusion: The Work of Mourning

The deaths at Marikana were not ordinary deaths, though. They came too soon. They came too violently. And they came at the hands of the police – the men and women who have been empowered by society and the state to protect us against cruel violence and arbitrary murder.

And so, the work of mourning the dead of Marikana – of remembering them, of commemorating them – cannot be ordinary. It cannot be left only to the families of the dead, or their neighbours. The deaths at Marikana affect all of us. We live in its shadows. If we live in South Africa, we live with the state that used its police force to control the strike – and that, in part through incompetence and in part through malice, shot and killed thirty-seven mineworkers in Marikana. If we live outside the country, we participate in the economy that drives platinum mining in the area – the economy that relies on the labour of the men and women who travel across the country to work in the mines at Marikana, the economy that profits from keeping the wages of these men and women low, the economy that underpins every part of our modern, global, technologically advanced world. There is no place on this earth that is untouched by the platinum industry – and no place where we can live without being affected by the murder of the miners at Marikana.

And so, we share the responsibility of mourning the dead. We must not forget what happened at Marikana – why the miners were in this part of the world, why they chose to go on strike, what they fought for. We must not forget the cost of their struggles – not only the men killed by the police, but the men killed in clashes with some miners and in moments of horrific violence. We must not forget the faceless men and women who sat around ordinary conference tables in anonymous rooms and took decisions that led to the deaths of thirty-four men. We must not forget that they either kept no record of their discussions, or destroyed them to escape accountability. We must not forget that the police commanders anticipated bloodshed, and made their plans on that basis. We must not forget that there were many opportunities to avoid to violence – and that these opportunities were spurned by the mining company and by the police. We must remember that the deaths at Scene One were avoidable; we must remember that the deaths at Scene Two were inexcusable. We must remember that the police tried to hide the truth of their actions. We must remember how many different people were happy to let them do so – happy to believe whatever they were told, without questioning, happy to join in with the police's lies. We must remember all of this – and we must never permit any of these things to slip out of our memories.

And so, in remembering, we join in solidarity with those who mourn their husbands, their fathers, their sons. Not every community is made in one place, or is made up of people who have met each other. Some communities are made differently – by acts of word and deed, acts of imagination. These are the communities of people who share a struggle in different times and places – the communities of workers across the world, the communities of those who struggle for freedom from autocracies, of those who struggle for recognition in our fallen world; the communities of those who share beliefs and interests – religions, languages, cultures, practices; and the communities of those who choose to associate themselves with each other despite all their differences – despite differences in experiences, in languages, in lives. These communities come together because they believe in the power of people to be more than subjects – they believe that the people, together, can be the agents that drive the histories of our time.

One such community might be the community of those who work to remember – to mourn, to grieve, to commemorate – the deaths at Marikana. These are the people that remember the history of the events that led to the massacre, a history that is, in Zinn's words, 'disrespectful of governments and respectful of people's movements of resistance'. These are the people who see in the struggles of the miners for a better wage, in the work of their wives and their children and their families, a struggle for justice – a struggle 'to resist, to join together, occasionally to win'.

It is a community founded on the need to remember, a community of memory. It is a community that, today, includes the families of the deceased and their supporters; that includes members of the Marikana Support Campaign, and Sikhlele Sonke, and unionists, and the residents of informal settlements across South Africa; that includes lawyers, and researchers, and film makers, and writers; that includes shareholder activists, and those who challenge the practices of the mining industry across the world; that includes all those that remember the names of the dead –

Hassan Fundi	Thobile Mpumza
Sitelega Meric Gadlela	Babalo Mtshazi
Thembinkosi Gwelani	Mphumzeni Ngxande
Patrick Akhona Jijase	Michael Ngweyi
Semi Jokanisi	Mgcineni Noki
Julius Langa	Ntandazo Nokhamba
John Ledingoane	Bongani Nqongophele
Jackson Lehupa	Mongezeleli Ntenetya
Ronnie Lepaaku	Andries Motlalepula Ntsenyeho
Javaneke Raphael Liau	Molefi Osiel Ntsoele
Frans Mabelane	Henry Mvuyisi Pato
Mafolisi Mabiya	Fezile David Saphendu
Tokoti Mangcotywa	Phumzile Sokanyile
Thembelake Mati	Mzukisi Sompeta
Eric Thapelo Mabebe	Thabiso Johannes Thelejane
Anele Mdizeni	Mphangeli Tukuza

Conclusion: The Work of Mourning

Bongani Mdze
Makhosandile Mkhonjwa
Telang Mohai
Tsietsi Hendrik Monene
Khanare Elias Monesa
Thabiso Mosebetsane
Isaiah Twala
Motiso Otsiele van Wyk Sagalala
Nkosiyabo Xalabile
Cebisile Yawa
Bonginkosi Yona
Thobisile Zibambele

Sources and Interpretation

Note on sources

This book has drawn on a number of primary and secondary sources to construct a coherent narrative of the events of the strike and the massacre at Marikana. I hope that this brief note will help guide other scholars to these sources, and help them navigate the large body of evidence that can either ground challenges to my interpretative claims, or develop them to focus on other aspects of Marikana.

It is important to state at the outset that I have worked closely with the legal representatives of the families of the deceased, the Socio-Economic Rights Institute of South Africa (SERI) on this project, since its early phases at the end of 2012. Through this relationship, I have had privileged access to the process of constructing legal arguments on behalf of the families, and to the families themselves. This has undoubtedly influenced the work I have done on the book – and the ways in which I have read the evidence. However, it is also important to note that SERI has no editorial control over my work – and that the responsibility for the claims made and conclusions drawn in this book is mine alone.

Primary sources

The largest set of primary sources for this book – and for any other attempt to tell the story of what happened at Marikana – is the archive of evidence and testimony created by the Commission of Inquiry between late 2012 and late 2014. The majority of the documents are available online, officially at a dedicated website hosted by the Department of Justice: https://justice.gov.za/comm-mrk/index.html.

My work with SERI has also led us to create a separate public record of the archive of evidence created for the Commission. My experience with previous government Commissions – including, most notably, the Truth and Reconciliation Commission (TRC) – is that website archives are often unreliable, and sometimes fall into disrepair. Certainly, the TRC's dedicated website has not always been reliably accessible.

In recognition of this, we have created a mirror of the documentary archive of the Commission, at: www.marikana-conference.com/index.php/marikana-exhibits. This website contains copies of the documents hosted by the Department of Justice – while following a principle of caution in redacting sensitive documents.

As this implies, there are limitations on what can be publicly accessed on these sites. The most important limitations are on the Post-Mortem Reports (Exhibit A) and on some of the photographic and visual evidence put forward by the SAPS – including images of the dead. Anything which might permit the visual identification of the individual deceased has been held back – for reasons which are obvious, and powerful. There is one unfortunate consequence, however: because the SAPS embedded many of these images in their initial presentation to the Commission, the whole of the presentation – which includes the most egregiously misleading statements made by the police early in the Commission – has been redacted.

There are some secondary limits on this information to consider. The majority of the video and audio sources are not locally hosted on the Department's website. Where available, they have been hyper-linked to YouTube versions – which themselves are not necessarily maintained by the Department. This means that several of these links are currently dead, and point nowhere. This is likely to be a problem in future.

At present, however, the majority of these documents entered in the Commission's record remain publicly available on the Department's website. These are listed by the Exhibit number – which can be cross-referenced to the notes in my main text.

* * *

In this work, I have also been able to access records that are not available on the website – and some of the recordings that are no longer easily accessible – with the consent of the legal representatives of the families of the deceased. I have worked with SERI since late 2012 on this project, and have had access to their archive of the material put into evidence. This has required some careful negotiation and consideration. I have only made use of this material when it relates directly to the families that SERI represents, and have not relied on it when I have not obtained permission from other actors – including the family of John Ledingoane, who was represented by the Legal Resources Centre (LRC) at the Commission of Inquiry.

I have also refrained from using any material which might identify specific police officers, or others who might be linked to specific acts of violence or shooting. These are still questions for the courts to resolve. They are also unnecessary to address in the context of this book – which is concerned with different questions.

The archive of transcripts

The Commission sat for 300 days, and a transcript of every one of those days is available – also on both websites. These are verbatim transcripts, and of course suffer from all the potential problems of such records. They are sometimes inconsistent in how they spell or sound out names. There are occasional homophones, and other minor errors. And – most obviously – they do not always manage to capture the nuances of a speaker's tone, voice, and presentation.

In a few cases this can be corrected. Some of these transcripts can be read alongside video recordings of the testimony – which were broadcast daily on YouTube during the run of the Commission. This is an imperfect fix, however. While a number of these recordings remain accessible on the website, there is no central record or list of links. It is necessary to search the website for specific days and times, and to hopefully find the appropriate recording. I have to accept, though, that this is a chancy process – and it is currently unlikely that the whole archive of video recordings is likely to be made available by the Department of Justice.

For now, the transcripts will simply have to be read as texts.

But this raises another important issue to consider with regards to the use of these transcripts. Although they are almost all presented in English – which was the principal language of the Commission – this presentation often obscures the role of translation. Witnesses testified in many different languages – and verbatim transcripts in their language of choice are only available for those police witnesses who chose to testify in Afrikaans. (These can be read alongside English translations.)

The witnesses who testified in isiXhosa, or seSotho, or isiZulu all did so with the aid of live translators. These translators worked on site, and provided near-simultaneous translation for the Commissioners, the various legal teams, and the media. The transcripts of these testimonies record the translations – and not the original language. This can be seen in the moments in which one or another lawyer interrupts the discussion to query or challenge a particular translation in the moment. It is otherwise invisible, however. The transcripts do not record the language of the speaker (except, again, when the police testify in Afrikaans).

Until the audio and video recordings of the Commission are more widely available, there is little that can be done about this. It is important, however, to recognize that the words quoted are not always exact – and that the inevitable distortions of translation are sometimes at work. These transcripts need to be read very carefully – and their use needs to take place within this matrix of interpretative difficulties.

Questions of interpretation

It is necessary to say a few words on the need for caution in the interpretation of this archive. It was produced for the Commission of Inquiry, which is itself a quasi-judicial body. This particular Commission chose to organize its hearing as if in a courtroom: encouraging adversarial encounters between different parties and their legal representatives. Most notably, the Commissioners appear to have treated their own Evidence Leaders – theoretically, the inquisitorial arm of the Commission – as one among many of the adversarial parties, and placed little reliance on their work.

The consequence of this is that the documents themselves rarely provide an unmediated glimpse into the thoughts of witnesses, or the events that they record. The witness statements have been drafted by legal counsel, and although they often hew close to the voice of the witnesses, as heard in their verbatim testimony, they are nonetheless constructed texts. Likewise, the documents placed in evidence may have been reviewed by legal teams beforehand – and, in at least some cases, will have been altered to fit a particular narrative, or a particular version of events.

These documents must be read and used with caution. Again, this should not be taken to mean that these documents are tainted and unusable. This is not the case. But no one document is sufficient on its own to establish events or ground an interpretation. They must read alongside each other, and they must be reconciled, wherever possible. The work of the Evidence Leaders at the Commission – far more so than the work of the Commissioners, as recorded in the final Report – provides a very useful starting point for evaluating the plausibility of many of the documents.

At the end of the day, however, the documents, the testimonies, and the evidence that they contain are not all of equal plausibility, or authenticity. I have endeavoured throughout to weigh up the different sources, and to provide a balanced and defensible interpretation of each. But this is a process that others might undertake differently – and if further information becomes available in the future (whether through the ongoing prosecutions of police commanders, or through other avenues) another scholar may find themselves weighting this material differently.

Interviews, etc.

In addition to these documentary sources, and archived transcripts of testimony, I have also conducted interviews with members of some of the families of the deceased. The majority of the formal interviews took place during my visit to the Eastern Cape at the end of 2015. I accompanied SERI's representatives on this visit, and was assisted by their fieldworkers and researchers during these interviews.

As indicated in the text, I was also given access to private discussions between the families and their legal representatives, and to public conversations between the families and their neighbours. Although I have been careful not to include any identifying details that might have emerged from these engagements, they have shaped my analysis of the evidence, the trajectory of my narrative, and the emphasis of my book.

Secondary sources

In writing this book, I have also been able to draw upon the body of secondary literature that has emerged since 2012. Some of these works deal directly with the events of the strike and the massacre, but more of them deal with the history of mining, the direction of labour politics, and the economic effects of the strike.

Sources and Interpretation

These works are extensively cited throughout the book, and I will not rehearse those citations here. Instead, I intend to make a few brief comments to help readers and other scholars to contextualize both these sources and my interpretations of them.

Articles and books

The first scholarly work was brought out in an early attempt to reframe the police's narrative. The collaborative project led by Kate Alexander at the University of Johannesburg's Centre for Social Change published a book within four months of the massacre – *Marikana: A View from the Mountain and a Case to Answer*. This book placed interviews with miners and unionists alongside attempts to provide preliminary interpretations of the events, based on the information then available.

Their book made no claim to be a final or definitive account of the strike and massacre, but rather set out the broad outlines of a counter-history of Marikana. It also made alternative accounts and key evidentiary contradictions available. It intended to challenge the growing hegemony of the police's narrative – and while it did not succeed in fully doing so, it certainly helped destabilize its plausibility. Overall, this book's suggestions have proven to be more correct than not – although its factual claims are sometimes disputable, and there is now far more information available to thicken and complicate its story of the strike and massacre.

I hope that my debt to Alexander et al.'s pioneering work is clear – even as I hope that this book moves beyond its earlier claims. As I have suggested elsewhere, there is more information now available – and it is possible for this book to build a more detailed account of the events that constituted the strike and massacre.

But, insofar as the scholarship has developed since the publication of Alexander et al.'s work, it has tended to focus on the broader contextual questions raised by the strike. That book and mine are, at present, the only two to link a scholarly approach to evidence with the project of telling a full story of the events on the ground.

At times, this has led to the strange sight of scholars debating the strike and the massacre at Marikana not on the basis of an alternate investigation of the events of the strike and the massacre, but instead on the basis of other studies of other strikes, in other times. In these comments, attempts to describe the experiences of the workers are dismissed as naïve or romantic on the basis of the behaviour of workers in other strikes, and an idea of the pervasive violence of mineworkers' activism. This is notable in the articles published by Botiveau and Breckenridge in 2014, in which they use a study of a violent mining strike in 1994 to criticize Alexander et al.'s account of the strike at Marikana. Their characterization of the 1994 strike may well be accurate – but it cannot then be used to dismiss the only account of the workers' strike at Marikana that was available at the time.

Other scholars have been more generous, and attempted to place the dispute at Marikana in context: Philip Frankel's work, for example, places it in the longer history of mining activism and labour exploitation in the region. Chinguno's work focuses on the Implats strike, and its links to the later Lonmin strike; Sinwell's focuses on the later strike of 2014 – and how they developed out of the forms of struggle and solidarity developed in Marikana. Asanda Benya's work on the women of Marikana, for example, takes the story of the massacre as set out by Alexander et al. for granted, and focuses instead on women's activism alongside and after the strike. Others – such as Munshi's work, cited earlier – focus on the development of AMCU, and its consequences for the NUM. Few of these works, however, contain an attempt to develop or build on the narrative first set out in December 2012.

The secondary literature demonstrates the potential range of scholarly work on Marikana – moving out from the events of the strike and the massacre to consider the different social groups affected in the region, the implications of the dispute for the mining economy, and the potential political implications for union organization. The literature is by no means complete, and I expect to see it continue to grow.

News reports and other media

But scholarly literature is not the only source of intellectual debate about Marikana. The first cracks in the police's account of the massacre were exposed by investigative journalists, and the published articles of Greg Marinovich, in particular, have been central to political efforts to reframe the story of Marikana. It is important, therefore, to give proper acknowledgement to some media reports.

The many news reports and journalistic publications about Marikana occupy a grey zone between primary and secondary sources. Several of these include novel evidentiary claims, and quotes from official spokespeople, bystanders, and commentators. These claims are not found elsewhere, and so must be drawn from these published articles. As will be clear from the citations throughout the book, I have often done this – and these sources have enriched the narrative I have told.

Some of these articles have also included critical analyses of the events at Marikana, and could be said to sit alongside the more formal academic literature in providing interpretations of the events of the strike and the massacre. The work of journalists such as Marinovich, Greg Nicolson, Niren Tolsi, and Rebecca Davis in South Africa (all cited in the book) has been central to presenting this kind of analysis.

Special mention must be made of Marinovich's book, *Murder at Small Koppie*, which sets out the investigations that he undertook to reveal the truth about the second phase of the massacre, and to challenge the police's self-serving narrative. This book describes many of the events of the strike and the massacre in ways that resonate with the version that I have given in the book – and, as with Alexander et al.'s work, its overall account is convincing. However, it is a journalist's book and not a scholar's: it does not provide detailed sourcing for its claims, rendering it difficult to engage with in an academic manner. It is a major work on the massacre, however – and more convincing in its depiction of the strike than most formally academic texts. It is also a powerful account of how investigative journalism works.

In this context, it is worth noting that the most important original reporting on Marikana has tended to come from sources outside of the largest print media. The *Daily Maverick*, in particular, provided a home for the earliest critical reports on the massacre. It has continued to publish important journalism in the years afterwards. Most of the journalists that I have cited with respect have published on this website.

Similarly, some international journalists have published significant pieces of long-form reporting on the events at Marikana. Work by Nick Davies and Jack Shenker, both in the United Kingdom, is particularly notable in this context. Both have provided closely reported and careful accounts of aspects of the strike at Marikana.

But other venues – and other writers – have often acted more to simply repeat and amplify the press releases and official statements of the police and government. These articles may sometimes include useful nuggets of information – quotes, statistics, and descriptions – but they do not provide any useful critical or analytical insight into the events they discuss. Although there are exceptions, much of the daily journalism published in and around the massacre should be treated with caution. The evidentiary claims made in these sources must always be checked against other claims, and the statements reported should not be taken for granted.

Nonetheless, no account of the events at Marikana would be complete without including the extensive work of investigative journalists and reporters on the strike, the massacre, and the unfolding events that have followed on the Commission.

It is after all due to them that we know enough to challenge the police's story.

Bibliography

Abel, Richard L. 1995. *Politics by Other Means: Law in the Struggle against Apartheid, 1980–1994*. London, Routledge.
Abraham, Vicky. 2018 'Marikana Massacre: Witnesses to Slaughter at Scene 2', *City Press*, 11 February. www.news24.com/news24/SouthAfrica/News/marikana-massacre-witnesses-to-slaughter-at-scene-2-20180211-2 (Acc. March 2021).
Alexander, Peter. 2016. 'Marikana Commission of Inquiry: From Narratives Towards History', *Journal of Southern African Studies*, 42.5.
Alexander, Peter. 2017. 'Cyril Ramaphosa's Marikana Massacre "Apology" is Disingenuous and Dishonest', *The Conversation*, 11 May. https://theconversation.com/cyril-ramaphosas-marikana-massacre-apology-is-disingenuous-and-dishonest-77485 (Acc. March 2021).
Alexander, Peter, Thapelo Lekgowa, Botsang Mmope, Luke Sinwell, and Bongani Xezwi. 2012. *Marikana: A View from the Mountain and a Case to Answer*. Johannesburg: Jacana.
Ally, Shireen and Arianna Lissoni (eds). 2017. *New Histories of South Africa's Apartheid-Era Bantustans*. Abingdon, Routledge.
Amnesty International. 2016. *Smoke and Mirrors: Lonmin's Failure to Address Housing Conditions at Marikana South Africa*. Amnesty International.
ANA Reporter. 2019. 'Court Hears Cops Were in the Same Building When Marikana Miner Was Declared Dead', IOL, 15 August. www.iol.co.za/news/south-africa/north-west/court-hears-cops-were-in-the-same-building-when-marikana-miner-was-declared-dead-30835782 (Acc. March 2021).
ANA Reporter. 2019. 'Police Accountability Demanded for Marikana Massacre', IOL, 10 June. www.iol.co.za/news/south-africa/police-accountability-demanded-for-marikana-massacre-25836517 (Acc. March 2021).
Ashforth, Adam. 1990. 'Reckoning Schemes of Legitimation: On Commissions of Inquiry as Power/Knowledge Forms', *Journal of Historical Sociology*, 3.1.
Ashforth, Adam. 1990. *The Politics of Official Discourse in Twentieth-Century South Africa*.
Baskin, Jeremy. 1991. *Striking Back, a History of COSATU*. London, Verso.
Bauer, Nickolaus. 2012. '"Because He Cares": Malema Sticks His Oar in at Implats', *Mail and Guardian*, 29 February. https://mg.co.za/article/2012-02-29-because-he-cares-malema-sticks-his-ore-in/ (Acc. March 2021).
Becker, Heike. 2018. 'Remembering Marikana: Public Art Interventions and the Right to the City in Cape Town', *Social Dynamics*, 44.3.
Beinart, William. 2001. *Twentieth Century South Africa* (2nd Edition). Oxford, OUP.
Benchmarks Foundation. 2011. 'Rustenburg Community Report: 2011'. Benchmarks Foundation.

Benjamin, Chantelle. 2014. 'Labour Court Returns to Negotiation Table with AMCU, Miners', *Mail and Guardian*, 21 May. https://mg.co.za/article/2014-05-21-labour-court-judge-returns-to-negotiation-table-with-amcu-miners (Acc. March 2021).

Benya, Asanda. 2013. 'Absent From the Frontline, But Not Absent From the Struggle: Women in Mining', *Femina Politica-Zeitschrift für feministische Politikwissenschaft*, 22.1.

Benya, Asanda. 2015. 'The Invisible Hands: Women in Marikana', *Review of African Political Economy*, 42.146.

Benya, Asanda. 2017. 'Going Underground in South African Platinum Mines to Explore Women Miners' Experiences', *Gender & Development*, 25.3.

Beresford, Alexander. 2012. 'Organised Labour and the Politics of Class Formation in Post-Apartheid South Africa', *Review of African Political Economy*, 39.134.

Bezuidenhout, Andries and Sakhela Buhlungu. 2007. 'Old Victories, New Struggles: The State of the National Union of Mineworkers', in Sakhela Buhlungu, John Daniel, Roger Southall, and Jessica Lutchman (eds), *State of the Nation: South Africa 2007*. Cape Town, HSRC.

Bond, Patrick. 2014. *Elite Transition: From Apartheid to Neoliberalism in South Africa* (2nd edition). London, Pluto.

Bonner, Philip. 1994. 'New Nation, New History: The History Workshop in South Africa, 1977–1994', *The Journal of American History*, 81:3.

Botiveau, Raphaël. 2014. 'The Politics of Marikana and South Africa's Changing Labour Relations', *African Affairs*, 113.450.

Bower, Tom. 1993. *Tiny Rowland: A Rebel Tycoon*. London, Vintage.

Bowman, Andrew and Gilad Isaacs. 2015. 'The 2014 Platinum Strike: Narratives and Numbers', *Review of African Political Economy*, 42.146.

Bratton, Michael. 2013. 'Briefing: Citizens and Cell Phones in Africa', *African Affairs*, 11.447.

Breckenridge, Keith. 2014. 'Marikana and the Limits of Biopolitics: Themes in the Recent Scholarship of South African Mining', *Africa: Journal of the International African Institute*, 84.1.

Brewer, John D. 1994. *Black and Blue: Policing in South Africa*. Oxford, Clarendon Press.

Brown, Julian. 2015. *South Africa's Insurgent Citizens: On Dissent and the Possibility of Politics*. London: Zed.

Brown, Julian. 2016. *The Road to Soweto: Resistance and the Uprising of 16 June 1976*. Woodbridge, James Currey.

Bruce, David. 2017. *Commissioners and Commanders: Police Leadership and Marikana massacre*. Pretoria, ISS Monograph 194.

Bruce, David. 2018. 'The Sound of Gunfire: The Police Shootings at Marikana Scene 2, 16 August 2012'. Pretoria, ISS Research Report.

Bundy, Colin. 1979. *The Rise and Fall of the South African Peasantry*. Cape Town, David Philip.

Butler, Anthony. 2019. *Cyril Ramaphosa* (revised edition). Johannesburg, Jacana.

Capps, Gavin. 2012. 'Victim of its Own Success? The Platinum Mining Industry and the Apartheid Mineral Property System in South Africa's Political Transition', *Review of African Political Economy*, 39.131.

Capps, Gavin and Stanley Malindi. 2017. 'Dealing with the Tribe: The Politics of the Bapo/Lonmin Royalty-to-Equity Conversion', *SWOP/MARTISA Working Paper*, 8.

Cawthorn, R. Grant. 1999. 'Seventy-fifth Anniversary of the Discovery of the Plantiniferous Merensky Reef: The Largest Platinum Deposits in the World', *Platinum Metals Review*, 43.4.

Chabalala, Jeanette. 'Officers in Court for Marikana Tragedy', *News24*, 15 March. www.news24.com/news24/southafrica/news/officers-in-court-for-marikana-tragedy-20180315 (Acc. March 2021).

Chinguno, Crispen. 2015. 'The Shifting Dynamics of the Relations between Institutionalisation and Strike Violence: A Case Study of Impala Platinum, Rustenburg (1982–2012)', PhD Thesis (Sociology), University of the Witwatersrand.

Cohen, Andrew. 2011. 'Lonrho and Oil Sanctions against Rhodesia in the 1960s', *Journal of Southern African Studies*, 37.4.

Cohen, Andrew. 2016. 'Lonrho and the Limits of Corporate Power in Africa, c. 1961–1973', *South African Historical Journal*, 68.1.

Cole, Peter. 2018. *Dockworker Power: Race and Activism in Durban and the San Francisco Bay Area*. Urbana, University of Illinois Press.

Cousins, C.A. 1959. 'The Bushveld Igneous Complex: The Geology of South Africa's Platinum Resources', *Platinum Metals Review*, 3.3.

Cramer, L.A. 2000. 'Presidential Address: Platinum Perspectives', *Journal of the South African Institute of Mining and Metallurgy*, 100.5.

Creamer, Martin. 2014. 'Lonmin to Oppose AMCU Labour Court Interdict', *Engineering News*, 19 May. www.engineeringnews.co.za/article/lonmin-to-oppose-amcu-labour-court-interdict-2014-05-19 (Acc. March 2021)

Crush, Jonathan. 1989. 'Migrancy and Militance: The Case of the National Union of Mineworkers of South Africa', *African Affairs*, 88.350.

Crush, Jonathan. 1994. 'Scripting the Compound: Power and Space in the South African Mining Industry', *Environment and Planning D: Society and Space*, 12.

Davan, Anna. 2000. 'The Only Problem was Time', *History Workshop Journal*, 50.1.

Davies, Nick. 2015. 'Marikana Massacre: The Untold Story of the Strike Leader Who Died For Workers' Rights', The Guardian (UK), 19 May. www.theguardian.com/world/2015/may/19/marikana-massacre-untold-story-strike-leader-died-workers-rights (Acc. November 2020).

Davis, Rebecca. 2014. 'Marikana: Gift of the Givers Brings Food to Striking Miners', *Daily Maverick*, 10 September. www.dailymaverick.co.za/article/2012-09-10-marikana-gift-of-the-givers-brings-food-to-striking-miners (Acc. March 2020).

de Waal, Mandy. 2012. 'Marikana: What Really Happened? We May Never Know', *Daily Maverick*, 23 August. www.dailymaverick.co.za/article/2012-08-23-marikana-what-really-happened-we-may-never-know (Acc. March 2021).

de Waal, Mandy. 2012. 'Marikana's Theatre of the Absurd Claims Another Life', *Daily Maverick*, 20 September. www.dailymaverick.co.za/article/2012-09-20-marikanas-theatre-of-the-absurd-claims-another-life (Acc. March 2021).

Ellis, Stephen. 1998. 'The Historical Significance of South Africa's Third Force', *Journal of Southern African Studies*, 24.2.

eNCA. 2017. 'Ipid Submits Last Docket in Marikana Probe', 23 August. www.enca.com/south-africa/ipid-submits-last-docket-in-marikana-probe (Acc. March 2021).

Esitang, Temogo Geoffrey and Stefan van Eck. 2016. 'Minority Trade Unions and the Amendments to the LRA: Reflections on Thresholds, Democracy, and ILO Conventions', *Industrial Law Journal*, 37.

Frankel, Philip. 1979. 'The Politics of Passes: Control and Change in South Africa', *The Journal of Modern African Studies*, 17.2.

Frankel, Philip. 2001. *An Ordinary Atrocity: Sharpeville and its Massacre*. Johannesburg, Wits University Press.

Frankel, Philip. 2013. *Between the Rainbows and the Rain: Marikana, migration, mining, and the crisis of modern South Africa*. Johannesburg, Agency for Social Reconstruction.

Friedman, Steven. 1987. *Building Tomorrow Today: African Workers in Trade Unions, 1970–1984*. Johannesburg, Ravan.

Ginzburg, Carlo. 1999. *The Judge and the Historian: Marginal Notes on a Late-Twentieth Century Miscarriage of Justice*, trans. Anthony Shugaar. London, Verso.

Greve, Natalie. 2014. 'AMCU Opens "Strike Fund" for Members, Calls for Donations', *Mining Weekly*, 15 April. www.miningweekly.com/article/amcu-opens-strike-fund-for-members-calls-for-donations-2014-04-15 (Acc. March 2021).

Hartford, Gavin. 2012. 'The Mining Industry Strike Wave: What Are the Causes and What Are the Solutions?' *GroundUp*, 10 September. www.groundup.org.za/article/mining-industry-strike-wave-what-are-causes-and-what-are-solutions (Acc. March 2021).

Hirson, Baruch. 1984. *Year of Fire, Year of Ash: The Soweto Revolt – Roots of a Revolution?* London, Zed.

Hlabangane, Nokuthula. 2018. 'Of Witch Doctors, Traditional Weapons, and Traditional Medicine: Decolonial Meditations on the Role of the Media after the Marikana Massacre, South Africa', *African Identities*, 16.3.

Hlongwane, Sipho. 2012. 'Lonmin Strike: Why the R4,000 Figure is No Trivial Matter', Daily Maverick (27 August). www.dailymaverick.co.za/opinionista/2012-08-27-lonmin-strike-why-the-r4000-figure-is-no-trivial-matter (Acc: November 2020).

Hlongwane, Sipho and Greg Marinovich. 2012. 'Lonmin: Malema Fans the Flames, but the Victims are Still Out in the Cold', Daily Maverick (18 August). www.dailymaverick.co.za/article/2012-08-18-lonmin-malema-fans-the-flames-but-the-victims-are-still-out-in-the-cold (Acc. November 2020).

Hornberger, Julia. 2011. *Policing and Human Rights: The Meaning of Violence and Justice in the Everyday Policing of Johannesburg*. Abingdon, Routledge.

Horrell, Muriel. 1963. *A Survey of Race Relations in South Africa: 1962*. Johannesburg, SAIRR.

Horrell, Muriel. 1971. *Legislation and Race Relations: A Summary of the Main South African Laws which affect Race Relations*. Johannesburg, SAIRR.

Huchzermeyer, Marie. 2004. *Unlawful Occupation: Informal Settlements and Urban Policy in South Africa and Brazil*. Trenton, NJ, Africa World Press.

Independent Complaints Directorate. 2011. *Annual Report 2010/2011* (Republic of South Africa). www.ipid.gov.za/sites/default/files/documents/ICD%20

Annual%20Report%202010-11.pdf (Acc. March 2021).
James, Deborah. 2014. 'Deeper Into a Hole? Borrowing and Lending in South Africa', *Current Anthropology*, 55.S9.
James, Deborah and Dinah Rajak. 2014. 'Credit Apartheid, Migrants, Mines and Money', *African Studies*, 73.3.
Jeeves, Alan. 1985. *Migrant Labour in South Africa's Mining Economy: The Struggle for the Gold Mines' Labour Supply, 1890–1920*. Kingston, McGill-Queens University Press.
Jika, Thanduxolo, Lucas Ledwaba, Sebabatso Mosamo, and Athandiwe Saba. 2013. *We Are Going to Kill Each Other Today: The Marikana Story*. Johannesburg, NB Publishers.
Jimta, Sifiso. 2017. 'Marikana Cops to Face the Law!' *Daily Sun*, 23 August. www.dailysun.co.za/News/National/marikana-cops-to-face-the-law-20170823 (Acc. March 2021).
Khulumani Support Group. 2016. 'We Have to Talk, We Need Changes': Voices from Platinum Belt Mine Workers and Worker Communities. Khulumani Support Group.
Lamb, Guy. 2018. 'Police Militarization and the "War on Crime" in South Africa', *Journal of Southern African Studies*, 44.5.
Lemon, Anthony (ed.). 1991. *Homes Apart: South Africa's Segregated Cities*. Cape Town, David Philip.
Lodge, Tom. 1983. *Black Politics in South Africa*. Johannesburg, Ravan.
Lodge, Tom. 2003. *Politics in South Africa: From Mandela to Mbeki*. Oxford, James Currey.
Lodge, Tom. 2011. *Sharpeville: An Apartheid Massacre and its Consequences*. Oxford, OUP.
Lonmin plc. 2012. 'Annual Report and Accounts for the Year Ended 30 September 2012'. www.lonmin.com.
'Lonmin Statement on Marikana Situation', 17 August 2012. Republished on *Politicsweb*. www.politicsweb.co.za/news-and-analysis/lonmin-will-cover-education-costs-of-dead-employee (Acc. March 2021).
Mabin, Alan. 1992. 'Comprehensive Segregation: The Origins of the Group Areas Act and its Planning Apparatuses', *Journal of Southern African Studies*, 18.2.
Malindi, Stanley. 2016. 'Continuity or Rupture? The Shaping of the Rural Political Order through Contestations of Land, Community, and Mining in the Bapo ba Mogale Traditional Authority Area', MA Thesis, University of the Witwatersrand.
Marais, Hein. 2011. *South Africa Pushed to the Limit: The Political Economy of Change*. London, Zed.
Marais, Lochner. 2018. 'Housing Policy in Mining Towns: Issues of Race and Risk in South Africa', *International Journal of Housing Policy*, 18.2.
Marinovich, Greg. 2012. 'The Murder Fields of Marikana. The Cold Murder Fields of Marikana', *Daily Maverick*, 8 September. www.dailymaverick.co.za/article/2012-09-08-the-murder-fields-of-marikana-the-cold-murder-fields-of-marikana (Acc. March 2021).
Marinovich, Greg. 2016. *Murder at Small Koppie: The Real Story of the Marikana Massacre*. Cape Town, Penguin SA.

Marks, Monique. 2005. *Transforming the Robocops: Changing Police in South Africa*. Pietermaritzburg, UKZN Press.

McDonald, Donald and Leslie B. Hunt. 1982. *A History of Platinum and its Applied Metals*. London, Johnson Matthey.

Macfarlane, Richard. 2007. 'Historiography of Selected Works on Cecil John Rhodes (1953–1902)', *History in Africa*, 34.

Magubane, Bernard. 1975. 'The "Native Reserves" (Bantustans) and the Role of the Migrant Labour System in the Political Economy of South Africa', in Helen I. Safa (ed.), *Migration and Development*. The Hague, Mouton.

Marks, Shula. 1970. *Reluctant Rebellion: The 1906–8 Disturbances in Natal*. Oxford, OUP.

Montsho, Molaole. 2018. 'Former North West Top Cop to Appear in Court Over Marikana Shooting', *IOL*, 17 December. www.iol.co.za/news/south-africa/north-west/former-north-west-top-cop-to-appear-in-court-over-marikana-shooting-18625904 (Acc. March 2021).

Moodie, T. Dunbar. 2015. 'Becoming a Social Movement Union: Cyril Ramaphosa and the National Union of Mineworkers', *Transformation*, 72/73.

Moodie, T. Dunbar. 2015. '"Igneous" Means Fire from Below: The Tumultuous History of the National Union of Mineworkers on the South African Platinum Mines', *Review of African Political Economy*, 42.1.

Moodie, T. Dunbar. 2016. 'Making Mincemeat out of Mutton: Social Origins of the NUM Decline on Platinum', *Journal of Southern African Studies*, 42.5.

Mottiar, Shauna. 2014. 'Protest and Participation in Durban: A Focus on Cato Manor, Merebank, and Wentworth', *Politikon*, 41.3.

Mukheibir, A. and G. Michell. 2019. 'The Price of Sadness: Comparison between the Netherlands and South Africa', *PER: Potchefstroomse Elektroniese Regsblad*, 22.1.

Munshi, Naadirah. 2017. 'Platinum Politics: The Rise, and Rise, of the Association of Mineworkers and Construction Union (AMCU)', MA Thesis (Sociology), University of the Witwatersrand.

Munusamy, Ranjeni. 2012. 'Marikana: Zuma Reclaims His Soul, and His Presidency', *Daily Maverick*, 23 August. www.dailymaverick.co.za/article/2012-08-23-Marikana-zuma-reclaims-his-soul-and-his-presidency (Acc. March 2021).

Murray, Colin. 1992. *Black Mountain: Land, Class, and Power in the Eastern Orange Free State, 1880s to 1980s*. Edinburgh, Edinburgh UP.

Naicker, Camalita. 2016. 'Worker Struggles as Community Struggles: The Politics of Protest in Nkaneng, Marikana', *Journal of Asian and African Studies*, 51.2.

National Union of Mineworkers. 2012. '30 Years of Unbroken Revolutionary Trade Unionism Struggle: Secretariat Report to the 14th National Congress' (Johannesburg, NUM).

Nemakonde, Vhahangwele. 2017 'How the Marikana Massacre Gave Birth to the EFF', *The Citizen*, 16 August. https://citizen.co.za/news/south-africa/1614452/how-the-marikana-massacre-gave-birth-to-eff (Acc. March 2021).

Ndibongo, Bridget. 2015. 'Women of Marikana: Survival and Struggles', MA thesis, University of Johannesburg.

Nicolaides, Gia. 2014. *Reporting from the Frontline: Untold Stories from Marikana*. Johannesburg, Jacana.

Nicolson, Greg. 2012. 'Impala Strike: Welcome to the Age of Retail Unionism', *Daily Maverick*, 22 February. www.dailymaverick.co.za/article/2012-02-22-impala-strike-welcome-to-the-age-of-retail-unionism (Acc. March 2021).

Nicolson, Greg. 2013. 'Images of Marikana: August 16, 2013', *Daily Maverick*, 16 August. www.dailymaverick.co.za/article/2013-08-16-images-of-marikana-august-16-2013 (Acc. March 2021).

Nicolson, Greg. 2017. 'Marikana Massacre: "He is fine, let him die"', *Daily Maverick*, 20 March.

Nieftagodien, Noor. 2017. 'Life in South Africa's Hostels: Carceral Spaces and Places of Refuge', *Comparative Studies of South Asia, Africa, and the Middle East*, 37.3.

Ntswana, Nyonde. 2015. 'Striking Together: Women Workers in the 2012 Platinum Dispute', *Review of African Political Economy*, 42.146.

Parker, Faranaaz and Nickolaus Bauer. 2012. 'Marikana: Malema Sparks Chaos at Memorial Service', *Mail and Guardian*, 23 August. https://mg.co.za/article/2012-08-23-malema-sparks-chaos-at-marikana-memorial-service (Acc. March 2021).

Parnell, Susan, Edgar Pieterse, Mark Swilling, and Dominique Wooldridge (eds). 2002. *Democraticising Local Government: the South African Experiment*. Cape Town, UCT Press.

Pithouse, Richard. 2016. 'Subaltern Politics & the Elite Public Sphere: The Marikana Land Occupation in Cato Manor, Durban, in 2013 and 2014', in Daniel Plaatjies, Charles Hongoro, Margaret Chitiga-Mabugu, Thenjiwe Meyiwa, Muxe Nkondo (eds), *State of the Nation: South Africa 2016*. Pretoria, HSRC Press.

Posel, Dorrit. 2004. 'Have Migration Patterns in Post-Apartheid South Africa Changed?' *Journal of Interdisciplinary Economics*, 15.3–4.

Power 987. 2017. 'No Police Officer Prosecuted Yet for Involvement in Marikana', 17 August. www.power987.co.za/featured/no-police-officer-prosecuted-yet-for-involvement-in-marikana (Acc. March 2021).

Pycroft, Christopher. 2000. 'Integrated Development Planning and Rural Local Government in South Africa', *Third World Planning Review*, 22.1.

Ramdhani, Narissa. 1986, 'Taxation without Representation: The Hut Tax System in Colonial Natal, 1849–1898', *Journal of Natal and Zulu History*, 11.

Rotberg, Richard and Miles F. Shore. 1988. *The Founder: Cecil Rhodes and the Pursuit of Power*. Oxford, OUP.

Rueedi, Franziska. 2020. 'The Hostel Wars in Apartheid South Africa: Rumour, Violence and the Discourse of Victimhood', *Social Identities*, 26.6.

SABC News. 2021. 'Mpembe, Three Others Acquitted of 2012 Marikana Unrest Charges', 29 March. www.sabcnews.com/sabcnews/mpembe-three-others-acquitted-of-2012-marikana-unrest-charges (Acc. March 2021).

Samuel, Raphael (ed.). 2016[1981]. *People's History and Socialist Theory*. Abingdon, Routledge.

SAPA. 2012. 'Conflicting Accounts of Lonmin Shooting', *IOL Business Report*, 17 August. www.iol.co.za/business-report/companies/conflicting-accounts-of-lonmin-shooting-1365104 (Acc. March 2021).

SAPA. 2012. Reuters, 'Lonmin Mine's Union Crisis Calms', *Mail and Guardian*, 15 August, https://mg.co.za/article/2012-08-15-lonmin-mines-union-crisis-calms.

SAPA. 2014. 'Marikana Women Want a Bright Future', *News24*, 14 August. www.news24.com/fin24/womens-wealth/news/marikana-women-want-a-bright-future-20130813 (Acc. March 2021).

Savage, Michael. 1986. 'The Imposition of Pass Laws on the African Population in South Africa, 1916–1984', *African Affairs*, 85.339.

Segal, Lauren and Sharon Court. 2011. *One Law, One Nation: The Making of the South African Constitution*. Johannesburg, Jacana.

Shenker, Jack. 2015. *Marikana: A Report from South Africa* (London, Zed Books).

Sidimba, Loyiso. 2017. 'Phiyega Bounces Back', *IOL*, 9 November. www.iol.co.za/news/south-africa/gauteng/phiyega-bounces-back-11926676 (Acc. March 2021).

Simons, H.J. and R.E. Simons. 1969. *Class and Colour in South Africa, 1850–1950*. Harmondsworth, Penguin.

Sinwell, Luke with Siphiwe Mbatha. 2016. *The Spirit of Marikana: The Rise of Insurgent Trade Unionism in South Africa*. London, Pluto.

Smit, Sarah. 2020. 'Marikana Murder Trial Resumes', *Mail and Guardian*, 16 October. https://mg.co.za/news/2020-10-16-marikana-murder-trial-resumes (Acc. March 2021).

Smith, David M. (ed.). 1992. *The Apartheid City and Beyond: Urbanization and Social Change in South Africa*. Abingdon, Routledge.

Snyman, Louis, and Robert Krause. 2013. 'Qualitative and Quantitative Assessment of Lonmin's Social and Labour Plan'. Johannesburg, Centre for Applied Legal Studies.

Socio-Economic Rights Institute (SERI). 2019. *Our Place to Belong: Marikana Informal Settlement*, Informal Settlements Research Report.

South African Government. 2004. Mineral and Petroleum Resources Development Act (28 of 2002); Department of Minerals Rources 'Broad-Based Socio-Economic Empowerment Charter for the South African Mining and Minerals Industry'.

South African Government. 2010. 'Speech by the Minister of Police, EN Mthethwa, MP on the Occasion of the Budget Vote no 24 and 22', 6 May. www.gov.za/speech-minister-police-en-mthethwa-mp-occasion-budget-vote-no-24-and-22-parliament-cape-town (Acc. March 2021).

South African Government. 2010. 'Speech Delivered by the Deputy Minister of Police, Honourable Fikile Mbalula, on the Occasion of the 2010/11 Safety and Security Budget Vote', 6 May. www.gov.za/speech-delivered-deputy-minister-police-honourable-fikile-mbalula-occasion-201011-safety-and (Acc. March 2021).

South African Government. 2012. 'General Phiyega Pronounces on Mine Unrest', 17 August. www.gov.za/general-phiyega-pronounces-mine-unrest (Acc. March 2021).

South African Government. 2012. 'Proclamation by the President of the Republic of South Africa No. 50, 2012', *Government Gazette*, No. 35680, 12 September; original version and amendments at www.justice.gov.za/comm-mrk/documents.html (Acc. March 2021).

South African Government. 2012. 'Statement from President Jacob Zuma on the Marikana Lonmin Workers Tragedy Media Briefing Rustenburg', 17 August.

www.gov.za/statement-president-jacob-zuma-marikana-lonmin-mine-workers-tragedy-media-briefing-rustenburg (Acc. March 2021).

South African Government. 2012. 'Tribute Delivered by the Premier of Gauteng Ms Nomvula Mokonyane at the Memorial Service for the Marikana Disaster held at the Johannesburg City Hall', 23 August. www.gov.za/tribute-delivered-premier-gauteng-ms-nomvula-mokonyane-memorial-service-marikana-disaster-held (Acc. March 2021).

South African Government. 2015. 'Marikana Commission of Inquiry: Report on Matters of Public, National and International Concern Arising Out of the Tragic Incidents at the Lonmin Mine in Marikana, in the North West Province'. www.justice.gov.za/comm-mrk/docs/20150710-gg38978_gen699_3_MarikanaReport.pdf (Acc. March 2021).

Stewart, Paul. 2013. '"Kings of the Mine": Rock Drill Operators and the 2012 Strike Wave on South African Mines', *South African Review of Sociology*, 44.3.

Tait, Sean and Monique Marks. 2011. 'You Strike a Gathering, You Strike A Rock', *SA Crime Quarterly*, 38.

Tau, Poloko. 2012. 'Mouthpiece for Strikers Dies', The Star, 21 September. www.iol.co.za/the-star/mouthpiece-for-strikers-dies-1387962 (Acc. March 2021).

Teo, Rayner. 2015. 'The Organisation of a Land Occupation: A Case Study of Marikana, Cape Town', MA thesis, University of Cape Town.

The Presidency, Republic of South Africa. 2012. 'Appointment of Judicial Commission of Inquiry on the Marikana Massacre', 12 August. www.thepresidency.gov.za/speeches/appointment-judicial-commission-inquiry-marikana-tragedy (Acc. November 2020).

Theron, J., S. Godfrey, and E. Fergus. 2015, 'Organizational and Collective Bargaining Rights through the Lens of Marikana', *Industrial Law Journal*, 36.

Thompson, E.P. 1991[1963]. *The Making of the English Working Class*. Harmondsworth, Penguin.

Tolsi, Niren and Paul Botes. 2015. 'Marikana – the Blame Game: A Special Report', originally published in the *Mail and Guardian*, currently accessible at www.sahistory.org.za/archive/marikana-blame-game-special-report-niren-tolsi-and-paul-botes (Acc. August 2021).

Turrell, Rob. 1987. *Capital and Labour on the Kimberley Diamond Fields, 1917–1890*. Cambridge, CUP.

van Onselen, Charles. 2001[1982]. *New Babylon, New Ninevah: Everyday Life on the Witwatersrand, 1886–1914*. Cape Town, Jonathan Ball.

Walker, Cherryl. 1991. *Women and Resistance in South Africa* (2nd edition). Cape Town, David Phillips.

Wells, Julia C. 1993. *We Now Demand! The History of Women's Resistance to Pass Laws in South Africa*. Johannesburg, Wits University Press.

Whittles, Govan. 2014. 'AMCU takes Lonmin to Court', *Eye Witness News*, 20 May. https://ewn.co.za/2014/05/20/Platinum-strike-Lonmin-reaches-out-to-Amcu (Acc. March 2021).

Wilson, Francis. 1972. *Migrant Labour in South Africa*. Johannesburg, South African Council of Churches.

Wilson, Richard A. 2001. *The Politics of Truth and Reconciliation in South Africa: Legitimizing the Post-Apartheid State*. Cambridge: CUP.
Wolpe, Harold. 1972. 'Capitalism and Cheap Labour-Power in South Africa: From Segregation to Apartheid', *Economy and Society*, 1.4.
Worger, William. 1987. *South Africa's City of Diamonds: Mine Workers and Monopoly Capitalism in Kimberley, 1867–1895*. New Haven, CT, Yale University Press.
Zinn, Howard. 2010[1980]. *A People's History of the United States* (expanded edition). New York, Harper Perennial.

Films

Desai, Rehad (dir.). 2014. *Miners Shot Down* (Uhuru Productions).
Kell, Dara (dir.). 2016. *Imbokodo: The Widows of Marikana* (SERI/Brava Media).
Saragas, Aliki (dir.). 2015. *Mama Marikana* (UCT Film).

Index

Adriao, Dennis   124–125, 126
Anglo Platinum (Amplats)   48–52, 55
Annandale, *Major-General*   209
Apartheid   22–23
Association of Mineworkers and
  Construction Union (AMCU)
  and Commission of Inquiry into the
    Marikana Massacre   108, 182, 187,
    192, 193
  at Lonmin   53–54, 56, 62, 84, 119
  and Lonmin strike (2012)   80, 94, 95,
    100, 106–107, 198–199, 200–201, 211
  after Marikana massacre   197–198
  origins and growth   52–53, 55–56

Bapo ba Mogale   31–32, 33, 34, 36
Blou, Henry   63, 64, 65
Bophuthatswana   31, 49
Botha, *Lt-Col.*   187, 188
Broad-Based Socio-Economic
  Empowerment Charter for the South
  African Mining and Minerals Industry
  (2002) 38, 193
Budlender, Geoff   185, 186, 207
Building Motor Engineering Allied
  Workers Union   52

Cape Town   203
Caweni, Nokwakhe Precious
  (pseudonym)   194, 195
Cele, Bheki   103
cell phones   115
Claasens, *Lt-Col.*   118
Commercial Workers Union of South
  Africa   52
Commission for Conciliation, Mediation
  and Arbitration (CCMA)   53–54, 198
Commission of Inquiry into the Marikana
  Massacre (Farlam Commisssion)
  announcement, powers and terms
    of reference   3, 170, 177, 178, 179,
    181–183, 215
  archive and evidence   3–4, 6–7, 9–11,
    156, 245–248
  and compensation   222
  and families of the dead and
    strikers   177, 179–181, 183–187, 189,
    191–192, 208, 209, 211–213, 215, 216,
    217, 220, 223–224, 226–227
  and police   173, 182, 187–189, 207–210,
    212, 228
  report   5–6, 7, 8, 215, 216–224,
    226–227, 238–239
commissions of inquiry   178
communities   241–242
Congress of South African Trade Unions
  (COSATU)   45, 46
Council of Unions of South Africa
  (CUSA)   44

De Beers Consolidated Mines   21, 22
Desai, Rehad   205
Durban   203

Economic Freedom Fighters (EFF) 201
Farlam, Ian   177, 183–184, 185, 186, 187,
  189, 208, 215
Farlam Commission of Inquiry *see*
  Commission of Inquiry into the
  Marikana Massacre
Federation of Unions of South Africa
  (FEDUSA)   52
Five Madoda   49, 50, 55, 56
Fundi, Hassan   70–71, 83, 242

Gadlela, Betty   166, 167, 168, 169, 192,
  205, 216

Gadlela, Sitelega Meric   149, 166, 167, 168, 169, 219, 242
Gcilitshana, Erick   187
Gcotyelwa, Lanford   18, 19, 34, 36, 45, 50–51, 74, 90, 92, 186, 187, 191–192
Gegeleza, Saziso   67–68
Gift of the Givers   200
Group Areas Act (1950)   23
Gwala, Xolani   106, 107
Gwelani, Thembinkosi   137–138, 218, 242

Hemraj, Pingla   177, 208
history from below *see* people's history
homelands   23–24, 26, 27, 34
hostels   18–19, 24, 27, 33, 34, 38, 39, 45; *see also* mine compounds

Imbokodo: The Widows of Marikana (film, Dara Kell)   205
Impala Platinum (Implats)   54, 55, 56, 104
Independent Police Investigative Directorate (IPID)   234
influx control   24–27; *see also* pass laws
informal settlements   202–204

Jamieson, Albert   95, 96, 97–98
Janse van Vuuren, Hermanus Andries   72, 73
Jijase, Patrick Akhona   7, 134, 218, 242
Joint Operational Command (JOCOM) *see* Lonmin strike (August 2012), Joint Operational Command
Jokanisi, Joyce   180
Jokanisi, Lunga   73, 89, 91–92, 189, 208, 226
Jokanisi, Semi   73–74, 89–90, 91–92, 226, 234, 242

Kgladi, Tsepo   107
Kgotle, Abram   64, 127
Kwadi, Jomo   127

Labour Relations Act (1995)   47 n.12
Langa, Julius   77–78, 79, 83, 84, 242
Langa, Mary Segwegwe (née Funzama)   77, 78
Ledingoane, John   137, 138, 194, 218, 242, 246

Lehupa, Jackson   8, 36, 39, 73, 74, 114, 132–133, 163–164, 180, 218, 224, 240, 242
Lehupa, Zameka *see* Nungu, Zameka
Lepaaku, Sello Ronnie   83, 89, 91, 234, 242
Lepaaku, Shuna   91
Liau, Janeveke Raphael   147–148, 184, 242
local government   34
Lonmin (formerly Lonrho)
    and AMCU   53–54, 56, 62, 84, 119
    board of   47–48
    and Commission of Inquiry into the Marikana Massacre   182
    K3 and K4 shafts   72–73, 77, 84–85
    Karee shaft   53–54, 56, 62
    Marikana platinum mine   32, 33
    and NUM   47, 64, 65, 95, 119, 127
    response to Marikana massacre   170, 172
    and strike *see* Lonmin strike, management role
    support for strikers' families   192, 216, 226, 236–237
    and workers' living conditions   37, 38–41
Lonmin strike (August 2012)
    Chronology
        background   60–63, 73–74, 115–116
        Women's Day meeting (Thursday 9 August)   59–60
        march to Lonmin office (Friday 10 August)   63–65, 74–75, 79, 82
        march to NUM office (Saturday 11 August)   67–69, 75, 77, 79, 80–81, 82–83
        march to Nkaneng hostel and aftermath (Sunday 12 August)   69–71, 75, 77, 83
        prelude to Marikana massacre (Monday 13 August to Thursday 16 August)   77–92, 93–111, 113–119, 210
    General
        deaths   71–72, 73, 75, 78, 79, 89, 90–92, 105, 217–218

Joint Operational Command
(JOCOM)   83, 84, 85, 116, 117, 118, 125, 175
koppie meeting place
(Wonderkop)   72, 74, 81–82, 84–85, 99, 120
leadership of   64–65, 80, 108
management role   64, 65, 83, 84, 93, 94–98, 99, 100, 101, 104, 106, 107, 116, 119–120, 122, 123, 124, 127, 168, 196, 198, 241
and the media   106–107, 118–119, 204, 205–206, 250–251
izinyanga role   5, 81–82, 210–211
and police   63, 72, 77, 78–79, 82–84, 85–86, 87–88, 89, 90, 95–97, 98–101, 104, 108–109, 110–111, 116–119, 120–121, 217–218, 235
security officers   59–60, 63, 64, 66–67, 70–72, 85, 86, 96
and violence   5, 65, 66, 68–69, 70, 71–73, 75, 77–78, 95, 106–107, 210, 222–223
weapons   67, 69–70, 85, 86–87, 100
women's role   120, 193–195, 205
Lonrho (later Lonmin)   30–32

Mabebe, Eric Thapelo   72–73, 83
Mabelane, Frans   70, 71, 83, 242
Mabiya, Buhle   115, 148
Mabiya, Mafolisi   115, 148, 179, 242
Mabiya, Phumeza   115, 148, 179, 194
Mabuyakhulu, Vusi   59, 60, 64–65, 66, 68–69, 75
Magidiwana, Mzoxolo   128, 129, 135–136, 141, 231
Malema, Julius   104, 201
Mama Marikana (film, Aliki Saragas)   205
man in the green blanket *see* Noki, Mgcineni
Mangcotywa, Julius Tokoti   24, 28, 147, 148, 184, 242
Mantashe, Gwede   97

Marikana
adoption of name   203–204
employment   34, 37
informal settlements   27–28, 34–35, 36–37, 39–41
origin and description   32, 35
pollution   37, 40
socio-economic conditions and crime   35–37, 38–39, 40
Marikana massacre (Thursday 16 August 2012)
charges   154, 172, 197, 233
compensation and prosecutions for unlawful killing   227–228, 230–231, 232–233, 234–236, 237
consultations with victim's families and communities   228–233
deaths and injuries   1–2, 4, 7–8, 131–138, 141, 163–169, 177
deployment of police Nyalas   120–121, 126, 128, 129, 141, 142
evidence *see* Commission of Inquiry into the Marikana Massacre, archive and evidence
inquiry *see* Commission of Inquiry into the Marikana Massacre
Mathunjwa's intervention and responses   122–124, 127–128, 187, 197
and the media   122, 125, 126, 157–158, 159, 163, 175–176, 178–179, 204–206, 250–251
mourning and memories of victims   225–226, 240–241, 242
official responses   169–173
paramedics   135, 136, 154, 156, 157, 159
police falsification of evidence   1–2, 4–5, 6, 7, 10 n.18, 125 n.37, 156–157, 174–176, 179, 188, 204–205, 207–208, 241
police operational plan   125–126, 129, 175, 221, 241
police version of events   170–175, 176, 179
prelude to   93–100

scene one (kraal)   1, 2, 4, 128–138,
    139–140, 141–142, 157–159, 171–172,
    218–219, 220–221, 235, 241
scene two (third or small koppie)   1,
    2, 3, 5, 140–141, 142–155, 171–172,
    176, 219, 221, 235, 241
Seoka's intervention   124, 127, 128
Marikana Support Campaign   196, 237
Masibi, Mogomotsi   71
Masuhlo, Paulina   195
Mathunjwa, Joseph   52, 106–107,
    108–109, 110, 119, 122–123, 127–128, 187,
    197, 211
Mati, Florence   17, 27, 36, 74, 90, 92, 226,
    240
Mati, Thembelakhe   17–18, 19, 27, 28, 34,
    36, 45, 74, 90–91, 92, 224, 226, 234, 240,
    242
Mati, Yolokazi   231
Mati family   230–232
Mbalula, Fikile   103
Mbombo, Mirriam   83, 84, 85, 99,
    100–101, 103, 104, 110, 111, 118–119, 127,
    209
Mdizeni, Anele   113–114, 145–146, 184,
    219, 242
Mdze, Bongani   134–135, 154, 243
media *see* Lonmin strike and the media;
    Marikana massacre and the media
Merafe, *Lt-Col.*   126
Merensky Reef   29, 30
migrant labour   18, 19–21, 22, 23, 24, 26,
    27, 28, 233
mine compounds   21–22, 33; *see also*
    hostels
Mineral and Petroleum Resources
    Development Act (2002)   38
Miners Shot Down (film, Rehad
    Desai)   205, 231
mineworkers
    female   193
    living out allowance   39–40, 41, 61
    occupational health and safety   43, 45
    union recognition   43–44, 47
    see also rock drill operators
Mining Charter (2002) *see* Broad-Based
    Socio-Economic Empowerment
    Charter for the South African Mining
    and Minerals Industry
mining industry   4, 19–20, 21–22, 30,
    37–38; *see also* specific companies
Mkhonjwa, Makhosandile   114, 144–145,
    157, 167, 180, 184, 219, 243
Mkhonjwa, Nokwanele *see* Phakati,
    Nokwanele
Mohai, Telang   150, 154, 219, 243
Mohlaki, *Captain*   187–188
Mokwena, Barnard   96, 100, 101, 104, 106,
    107, 127
Monene, Hendrik Tsietsi   83–84, 88–89,
    91, 234, 243
Monesa, Khanare Elias   7, 131, 138, 169,
    218, 243
Monesa, Motlalepula   169
Mosebetsane, Ntombizile   164–165, 177
Mosebetsane, Thabiso   148, 164–165, 184,
    219, 243
Mouthpiece Workers Union
    (MPWU)   51–52, 53
Mpembe, William   83, 84, 85, 86–87, 88, 89,
    108, 109, 110, 209, 210, 221, 234–235, 236
Mpofu, Dali   192, 201–202
Mpumza, Phelakazi   36
Mpumza, Thobile   36, 152–153, 181, 184,
    240, 242
Mpumza, Xolelwa   186, 240
Mr X (witness at commission of
    inquiry)   210–211
Mthethwa, Nathi   97, 98, 103, 104, 173,
    233, 238
Mtshamba, Shadrack   141, 151, 154–155
Mtshazi, Babalo   136, 167–168, 218, 242

Naidoo, *Major-General*   209
National Prosecuting Authority
    (NPA)   234, 235–236
National Union of Mineworkers (NUM)
    and Commission of Inquiry into the
        Marikana Massacre   182, 187
    history   45, 46–47, 48–52, 53
    and Implats strike (2012)   54, 55, 56
    and Lonmin   47, 64, 65, 95, 119, 127

and Lonmin strike (2012)   62, 66, 67–69, 75, 77, 79, 80–81, 82–83, 106–107, 108
Natives Laws Amendment Act (1952)   23
Ncube, Thandeka   94, 95
Ngema, Bongani   69 n.29
Ngweyi, Michael   133, 165–166, 169, 218, 242
Ngweyi, Nosihle   165–166, 169
Ngxande, Mphumzi   149, 157, 194, 219, 242
Nkaneng (Marikana)   26, 39, 70, 129, 141, 194
Nokhamba, Ntandazo   148–149, 157, 242
Noki, Mgcineni (Mambush, the man in the green blanket)   8, 80–81, 82, 84, 85, 86, 93, 109, 113, 121, 124, 126, 128, 129, 131, 214, 218, 224, 242
Noki, Noluvese   214
Noki, Noluvuyo   113
Noki, Snobuyo   214
Nqongophele, Bongani   136, 179, 218, 242
Nqongophele, Nombulelo *see* Ntonga, Nombulelo
Ntabankulu (Eastern Cape)   17–18, 229–233
Ntenetya, Mongezeleli   128, 131, 218, 242
Ntonga, Nombulelo   179
Ntsebeza, Dumisa   184, 185
Ntsenyeho, Andries Motlalepula   113, 123, 128, 134, 218, 242
Ntsileng, Itumeleng   143 n.11
Ntsoele, Matsepang   166, 214, 242
Ntsoele, Michael Molefi Osiel   114–115, 154, 166, 219
Nungu, Zameka   36, 39, 73, 114, 132–133, 163, 164, 165, 180, 186, 189, 192, 205, 214–215, 216, 224, 229, 240
Nzuza, Xolani   80–81, 82, 84–85, 93, 105

pass laws   20–21, 23, 24, 25–27
Pato, Henry Mvuyisi   150, 156–157, 242
pensions   48–50
people's history   11–13, 242
Phakati, Nokwanele   180

Phatsha, Siphethe   43, 45, 69–70, 128, 139–140
Phiyega, Riah   2, 99, 103, 104, 110, 111, 116, 170–173, 188, 232, 239–240
platinum   29–30, 32, 241

Ramaphosa, Cyril   44–46, 47–48, 94, 95, 96, 97, 98, 104, 110, 111, 233, 238
Rhodes, Cecil John   21
rock drill operators (RDOs)   43, 53, 54, 59–63, 65, 80, 95, 193
Rowland, Roland (Tiny)   31, 32

Safer South Africa Foundation   239–240
Sagalala, David   179, 180
Sagalala, Motiso Otsile van Wyk   153, 180, 219, 234, 235, 236, 242
Saphendu, Fezile David   7, 149, 157, 181, 242
Saphendu, Thembinkosi   181
Scott, *Lt-Col.*   99, 118, 125
Sebatjane, Constable   152
Seedat, Mahomed   127
Segwaelane (Marikana)   33, 34, 37, 40
Semenya, Ishmael   207
Seoka, Johannes   124, 127, 128
Setelele, Malesela William   67
Shabangu, Susan   97, 98, 233, 238–239
Sikhala Sonke   193, 196–197, 200, 205
Sinclair, Graham   63, 64, 65
Socio-Economic Rights Institute (SERI)   228, 229–230, 246, 248
Sokanyile, Phumzile   82, 90, 91, 92, 217–218, 234, 242
Sompeta, Mzukisi   8, 114, 133, 167, 180, 213, 218, 225, 240, 242
Sompeta, Nomawabo   180, 213, 225, 226, 236, 240
Sonti, Nokhulunga Primrose   196–197, 201
South African Broadcasting Corporation (SABC)   106–107, 205
South African Communist Party (SACP)   46
South African Police Service (SAPS, formerly South African Police, SAP) and Commission of Inquiry into the

Marikana Massacre 173, 182, 187–189, 207–210, 212, 228
falsification of evidence at Marikana Massacre *see* Marikana Massacre, police falsification of evidence
and Implats strike 55
and the Lonmin strike *see* Lonmin strike, police structure 102–103
and use of violence 101–102, 103, 202
strike committees 56
strikes
  Amplats (1996) 49, 50–51, 52, 55, 56
  Douglas Colliery (Mpumulanga, 1999) 52
  Five Madoda (1996) *see* strikes, Amplats
  Implats (2012) 54–55, 56, 104
  Lonmin (2012) *see* Lonmin strike (August 2012)
  Lonmin (2014) 198–201
  on the mines (1980s) 44, 45, 46
  wildcat 56

Tatane, Andries 101–102, 103
Temeke, Mike 97
Thelejane, Johannes Thabiso 145, 146, 184, 219, 242
Tokota, Bantubonke 177
trade unions 26, 43, 44, 47; *see also* names of specific unions and federations

Tukuza, Mphangeli 132, 218, 243
Twala, Isaiah 104–105, 243

Vermaak, Salmon 209–210
violence *see* Lonmin strike and violence; mineworkers, violence of; South African Police Service and use of violence

women
  and Lonmin strike (2012) 120, 193–195, 205
  and Lonmin strike (2014) 200
  post-massacre role 195–197

Xalabile, Nkosiyabo 146, 157, 168–169, 219, 243
Xalabile, Nonesile 168–169

Yawa, Andile 180, 181
Yawa, Cebisile 132, 180, 218, 243
Yona, Bonginkosi 133–134, 138, 218, 243

Zibambele, Noktula 213–214
Zibambele, Thobisile 131–132, 213–214, 218, 243
Zokwana, Senzeni 97, 106–107, 108, 109, 110, 187
Zondo, Nomzamo 230
Zuma, Jacob 3, 169–170, 172, 177–178, 217

www.ingramcontent.com/pod-product-compliance
Lightning Source LLC
Chambersburg PA
CBHW051606230426
43668CB00013B/1997